THE JEWISH PEOPLE

HISTORY • RELIGION • LITERATURE

THE JEWISH PEOPLE

HISTORY • RELIGION • LITERATURE

Advisory Editor
Jacob B. Agus

Editorial Board
Louis Jacob
Jacob Petuchowski
Seymour Siegel

JUDAISM AND CHRISTIANITY

Selected Accounts, 1892-1962

Preface and Introduction

by

JACOB B. AGUS

ARNO PRESS

A New York Times Company

NEW YORK • 1973

Reprint Edition 1973 by Arno Press Inc.

Preface and Introduction Copyright © 1973
  by Arno Press Inc.

THE JEWISH PEOPLE: History, Religion, Literature
ISBN for complete set: 0-405-05250-2
See last pages of this volume for titles.

Manufactured in the United States of America

————◆————

Library of Congress Cataloging in Publication Data
Main entry under title:

Judaism and Christianity.

   (The Jewish people: history, religion, literature)
   Collection of reprinted journal articles.
   Includes bibliographical references.
   CONTENTS: Abrahams, I. Professor Schürer on life
under the Jewish law.--Cohen, S. S. The place of Jesus
in the religious life of his day.--Friedländer, M. The
Pauline emancipation from the law.--[etc.]
   1. Judaism--Relations--Christianity--Addresses,
essays, lectures.   2. Christianity and other religions
--Judaism--Addresses, essays, lectures.   3. Judaism--
Apologetic works--Addresses, essays, lectures.   I. Arno
Press.   II. Series.
BM535.J824   296.3'87'2   73-2212
ISBN 0-405-05276-6

CONTENTS

Moore, George Foot
CHRISTIAN WRITERS ON JUDAISM (Reprinted from *Harvard Theological Review*, Vol. XIV, No. 3, Cambridge, Mass., 1921)

Schechter, S[olomon]
THE LAW AND RECENT CRITICISM—A Discourse on C. H. Toy's *Judaism and Christianity*, London 1890. (Reprinted from *The Jewish Quarterly Review*, Vol. III, London, 1891)

Schechter, S[olomon]
SOME RABBINIC PARALLELS TO THE NEW TESTAMENT (Reprinted from *The Jewish Quarterly Review*, Vol. XII, London, 1900)

Wolfson, Harry A.
HOW THE JEWS WILL RECLAIM JESUS (Reprinted from *The Menorah Journal*, New York, 1962)

PREFACE

The essays included in this volume illustrate several aspects of one basic question — how did Jewish scholars in the past century regard the emergence of Christianity out of the Jewish faith?

Max Güdemann, a Rabbi in Vienna at the turn of the century, deals with the contrast between letter and spirit in the Jewish and Christian traditions. S. Krauss shows how the stereotype of a mythical Jew was built up in the early centuries. Montefiore was a pioneer in interpreting the New Testament from the standpoint of Judaism. M. Friedländer calls attention to the viewpoint and role of Diaspora Jewry in the rapid growth of the Christian Church. Samuel S. Cohon summarizes the results of Jewish scholarship in respect of the historical Jesus. Louis Ginzberg, the preeminent scholar, casts light on the ambivalent status of Apocalyptic literature in the Jewish world. Harry A. Wolfson's essay is an incomparable gem-poetic, insightful and unforgettable.

Several essays challenge directly the prevailing and traditional Christian view of the Jewish religion. Solomon Schechter points out that reverence for law need not be construed as "unspiritual." Israel Abrahams criticizes the chapter on Jewish Law in Emil Schürer's famous *A History of the Jewish People in the Time of Christ*. The long essay of George Foot Moore on "Christian Writers on Judaism" marked a crucial turning point in Christian appreciation of the inner life of rabbinic Judaism.

INTRODUCTION

Ours is the age of the Dialogue. We have seen the Abyss and we have drawn back in horror. If hate can achieve such fantastic power over the minds of men, there is no time to lose. All men of good-will must search their collective consciences and pool their efforts to eliminate the foul ghosts of the past that haunted and bedeviled our western heritage.

Ghosts flee from daylight and the open air. The Jewish-Christian Dialogue, in all its varying facets, is an attempt to blend the love of faith with the truth of historical insight, on the one hand, and the pragmatic needs of our time, on the other hand.

This book is dedicated to the elucidation of the basic theme of the Dialogue — Judaism and the New Testament.

Judaism and Christianity meet theologically on the following common ground — the Hebrew Bible, reverence for Wisdom as a bond with the Divine Being, and the genius of prophetic inspiration. Beginning with the last element, we note that rabbinic Judaism maintained that biblical prophecy had come to an end. Yet, it also asserted that the Holy Spirit guided the deliberations of the Sages. Hillel attributed this blessing to all pious Israelites — "You may rely upon the Israelites, the Holy Spirit is upon them. If they are not prophets, they are sons of prophets."[1] The deliberations of the Sages were aided by a Divine Echo.[2] The medieval philosopher, Judah Halevi, expressed the general belief when he asserted that the *Mishnah* and *Talmud* were composed with Divine assistance (The Kuzari 3,73).

Faith in prophetic inspiration consisted in the belief that God aids our endeavors to penetrate the *deeper meaning* of His Torah and the concomitant belief that God works through history, generating ever greater understanding of His Revelation. The Will of God is generally known and fixed, like the laws of nature, but when grave decisions have to be made, a new surge of His Power might be available. So, in the rabbinic tradition, a prophet could not set aside a *halachah*, or establish a new *Halachah*, but he could decide which *halachot* were to be applied in his day.[3] Divine inspiration in the interpretation of a biblical book was claimed by the writers of the Dead Sea Scrolls.[4] (The ideal of the Prophet was continued in Judaism, down to our own day. See my essay, "The Prophet in Modern Hebrew Literature" in *Dialogue and Tradition*, p. 385.)

A parallel development of the operation of the Holy Spirit lies at the very heart of Christianity. Whether the view prevailed that the Holy Spirit worked through the community as a whole, or through the bishops, or through the Papacy, or through the mystics, the obligation of penetrating to the deeper meaning of the Bible was incumbent upon every generation. And Jesus illustrated this obligation by his comment on divorce, sifting the divine intent from "the hardness of the heart," which conditioned an earlier saying.[5]

We dare say that in every faith derived from the Bible, a renaissance took place whenever theologians returned to a fresh study of Holy Writ. The reinterpretation of Scripture, in the light of the prophetic emphasis on justice, compassion and love, is the common task of Jews and Christians.

In our day, we bring to the study of the Scriptures in particular, and the past generally, certain tools and insights that were scarcely available in previous generations — which brings us to the second component of theological common ground, the element of Wisdom.

The obligation to pursue the quest of wisdom in order to understand the implications of faith is of the essence of biblical religion, since the books of Wisdom formed part of Holy Writ. The Sages formulated the matter succinctly: "If there is no wisdom, there is no piety; if there is no piety, there is no wisdom" (Abot 3,14). Similarly, in Christianity, Wisdom was extolled, and Greek philosophy preoccupied the attention of the Patristic Fathers, since Clement of Alexandria.

Wisdom today has the added dimension of history-mindedness in all its facets — a recogniton of the context in which every event must be viewed, a critical and comparative approach to all documents, an understanding of the fluidity of meaning and its determination by psychological and sociological factors.

The duty to study history in order to understand the meaning of Providence is already stated in Deuteronomy 32.7. But while history was in the past one of the handmaidens of theology, it now asserts its own independent validity, compelling theology to take account of its data. History-mindedness need not degenerate into an all-questioning historicism; on the contrary, by deepening our awareness of our human limitations, as individuals and as heirs of a specific tradition, it heightens our appreciation of the third part of the prophet Micah's admonition — "to do justice, to love mercy, and to walk humbly with the Lord, thy God" (Micah 6,8).

We cannot enter into a full analysis either of the viewpoints presented by the historians in this anthology or of the perspectives which have emerged in our generation, particularly in the last decade. A unitary consensus among Jewish scholars concerning the personality of Jesus, or in relation to the emergence of Christianity, did not exist in the past, nor can we speak of one today. However, we appear to be moving toward certain general affirmations, which might prove most helpful in establishing a sound basis for the Jewish-Christian Dialogue.

The central theses that emerge from the study of the New Testament in the context of Jewish-rabbinic literature are as follows:

First, that the teaching of Jesus did not imply the repudiation either of Judaism or of the Jewish people.

Second, that the closer we come to the Apostolic community, centered in Jerusalem, the less we encounter any suggestion of the "rejection" of Israel.

Third, that the New Testament passages implying the "rejection" of the Jewish people, as a reversal of its having been previously chosen, were superimposed upon the earlier traditions of the Church after the Fall of Jerusalem; that the essence of Christian teaching, according to medieval interpreters, consisted in the repudiation of Judaism.

Fourth, that all such anti-Judaism and anti-Jewish passages resulted in part from the gradual transference of the Gospel-tradition, from the Jewish to the Hellenistic culture-sphere, during the seventy year period, (65-135 A.D.); in part, from the impassioned bitterness of the second and third centuries, when the New Testament canon attained its present form; in part, from a persistent, unhistorical and unreflective reading of the New Testament.

Fifth, that it is incumbent upon Christian scholars, as seekers of truth in love and love in truth, to eliminate anti-Jewish and anti-Judaism inferences from their interpretation of the New Testament.

Sixth, that it is incumbent upon Jewish scholars to reclaim the New Testament as an integral part of their domain of study and to develop the implications of the teaching that Christianity is an "ecclesia for the sake of heaven," employed by God as an instrument whereby humanity is being prepared for "the kingdom of heaven," *malchut shomayim.*

It is hoped that the essays included in this anthology will contribute greatly toward the emergence of a new sense of spiritual fraternity between Jews and Christians.

NOTES

(1) Tosefta, Pesahim 4,13. Jer. Talmud 6,1. The version of the Babylonian Talmud, Pesahim 66b. does not mention the Holy Spirit.

(2) The reference to Hillel in Tosefta Sota 13,3. Pesikta Rabbati, Ch. 35. The relation of Halachah to prophecy is examined in detail by A. Urbach in *Tarbitz,* 1947.

(3) B. T. Shabbat 104a. He could revive a law, that was forgotten. The term used here is "Tsofim," which means mystical visionaries. In this sense, the Sages were considered the heirs of the prophets. (B.T. Baba Bathra 12a. where the strange comment is given — "A Sage is better than a prophet." A prophet's authority did not extend to concessions to idolatry, even as a temporary expedient. Sanhedrin 90a.)

(4) "The Habakkuk Commentary," *Pesher Habakkuk* is a case in point. Note particularly this sentence — "And as for what it says, *that he may run who reads it,* this means the teacher of righteousness, to whom God made known all the mysteries of the words of his servants, the prophets." "The Dead Sea Scrolls," ed. Millar Burrows, N.Y. 1955, p. 368

(5) Matt. 19,8. A similar view is stated in the Talmud, Kiddushin 21b. in reference to the law described in Deuteronomy 21, 10-14)

JACOB B. AGUS
Baltimore, Maryland

PROFESSOR SCHÜRER ON LIFE UNDER THE JEWISH LAW

by
I[SRAEL] ABRAHAMS

PROFESSOR SCHÜRER ON LIFE UNDER THE JEWISH LAW [1].

I MUCH appreciate the generous welcome with which this Society greeted the proposal of a Jewish member to read a paper on Life under the Pharisaic Law. I have nothing very fresh to tell you; indeed my purpose is rather to protest that what has already been said by Jewish apologists should have been wholly overlooked by Prof. Schürer in the new edition of his great book. I may claim one accidental qualification for my present task. I have lived, and in a sense still live, under the Pharisaic Law myself. I have felt its limitations, I have groaned under its lack of sensibility to all that we call aesthetic. I have resented its narrowness, its nationalism, on the one hand, and its claim to the Jew's undivided allegiance on the other. It does not apply to all men, yet it asks the whole man when it does apply to him. But I have also known the Law's manifold joys, its power of hallowing life, its sturdy inculcation of right, its sobriety of discipline, its laudable attempt to associate ritual with heart service, its admission that the spirit giveth life, its refusal to accept that the letter killeth. I have known men devoted to the minutest ritual details, yet simple, spiritual, saintly. Thus I have enough sympathy with the Law to do it justice, not enough sympathy to do it the injustice of unqualified flattery. The scorn and indignation of Jesus rouse answering echoes in my own consciousness, as in the

---

[1] A paper read before the Society of Historical Theology at Oxford on Feb. 2, 1899.

consciousness of all honest Jews. But many modern
theologians go far beyond Jesus in their onslaught upon
Pharisaic legalism. They accept the letter of his attack,
but reject its spirit. He criticized the defects of the Law,
they attribute a double dose of original sin to the very
Law itself, under which Jesus was nurtured and from
which he derived so much inspiration. A Jew has a ready
heart for the reproof of Jesus, he cannot tolerate the
Pauline doctrine that the Law is the strength of sin.
There were many failures among the observers of the
law, but the cause of the failure was not always the Law
itself. As Prof. Wallace writes: "This we may be sure of,
that Judaism would not have lasted through the fearful
ordeal of mediaevalism, had it not been something nobler
than a mere system of rules, codified into endless multiplicity of detail. Do not let us abuse the Law because of
the lawyers (some of whom must be bad); or charge the
righteous with the petty conceits of Pharisaism." To
this I add, that the life which I have lived under the
Law convinces me that Prof. Cheyne is right in asserting
that amidst the thorns of legalism there are delightful
blooms, the efflorescence of the religious spirit of Judaism.
Against Prof. Schürer's judgment based on books, I can
protest an experience based on life. Literature may be
a criticism of life, but in cases such as this, life is also a
criticism of literature.

Of course I do not maintain that a theologian is dis-
qualified from criticizing the Law unless he be born and
bred in the Synagogue. But there is no other branch of
research in which the evidence of facts is so disregarded as
in the science of theology. Here we deal with principles
which affect men's lives, and we rarely turn to those lives
as the touchstone by which to judge our principles.
Rabbinic theology is concerned not with an extinct race
or a primitive and obsolete theory of being. The race
now numbers more individuals than when Jesus moved
on earth, the devotion to the theory is greater now than

ever. Hence, the theologian who would understand the
Pharisees must cast an occasional glance into the life of
Judaism to-day. And it is not as though Schürer's
criticism assumes merely the function of a criticism of
books or even of actions. It is a criticism of motives
and feelings, of the heart and mind as well as of the social
organism. Surely the outsider ought to attach some
importance to the evidence of insiders on questions which
strike to the inmost root of being. The only reason for
refusing to listen to Jews about Judaism, as it actually
affects their consciousness and their conscience, would be
a conviction that Jews cannot be trusted as witnesses, that
they are sure to perjure themselves in order to win
a dialectical victory. But this is a charge which Schürer—
who has few scruples of charity where the Pharisees are
concerned—evidently hesitates to bring. The evidence
tendered by Jews must indeed be severely cross-examined,
but it should be heard. An even more serious charge
against Schürer and the scholars who blindly follow him
is this. Granted that they are justified in founding their
criticism of the Law on books, they ought at least to read
the books. I think that this Oxford Society will go with
me in holding that the critics of the Law should qualify
themselves to read the originals of the documents on which
they rely. Now Prof. Schürer seems to confess that he
has no first-hand knowledge of the Rabbinical writings.
This confession I infer externally from his citing the
Mishnah from translations and from his omission of the
original texts of Mishnah and Talmud from his splendid
lists of authorities, and internally from his limited knowledge and actual mistakes. This fact, that Schürer relies
on second-hand sources, accounts for the remarkable coin-
cidence that the whole of the section which deals with
"Das Leben unter dem Gesetz" is exactly and verbally
reproduced from his former edition. A stray reference or
two have been added, and a phrase has been modified in
a foot-note. But in all these years he has not felt impelled

to revise a single syllable of this, the most dogmatic chapter of his great work. " Littera scripta manet." This would have been simply impossible were Schürer a real student of Rabbinical literature. That literature is so vast, so difficult, so ill-arranged, so beset with contrary currents, that no real student of it but would find himself constantly compelled to re-examine his material, to recast his conclusions, to amend, to modify, to reconsider, to add, to retract. Besides, an opinion about the Rabbinical theology sometimes depends on an impression derived from extensive reading of the Talmud as a whole, not from particular passages cited by controversialists. And what is the second-hand material to which Schürer so often trusts? Prof. Dalman in his new work, *Die Worte Jesu,* severely censures the mechanical reliance placed by modern theologians on the very class of writers references to whom form the staple of Schürer's notes. Jewish students have been crying this out in the wilderness for many a long year. Perhaps a hearing will be given now to Dalman's vigorous plea against dilettantism—I use Dalman's own word—in the ranks of Christian critics of Rabbinism. Lightfoot, Schöttgen, Eisenmenger, Wettstein, and even the canonical Weber, are all pronounced obsolete or inadequate by Dalman. Yet if you take these sources away, what is left to most theologians who write on the religion of the Pharisees?

It is, I can assure you, not a pleasant duty to speak adversely of Schürer's great work. There is a Rabbinic proverb, "Into a well from which thou hast drunk water, cast no stones." I am deeply indebted to Schürer, as every student of his period must be. His new edition converts a great book into an even greater. My admiration for it is not measured or conditioned by my opinion of the one particular section to which I am devoting myself this evening. Schürer is a prince of bibliographers, an ideal critic and historian. He is learned, he is judicious, and only occasionally dogmatic enough to refuse to modify

a literary opinion such as e.g. on the authenticity of the
Vita Contemplativa. But when he deals with the Pharisaic
Law his learning becomes antiquated, and his judgment
biassed. His mind is closed against new impressions.
Even where his statements have been directly challenged he
does not so much as refer to his challengers. He has been
taken to task for mistranslations; these remain unaltered.
The facts of actual life under the Law have been brought
to his notice; he has refused to listen. The heading
" Irrwege " still figures as the title of one of Schürer's
subdivisions on the Law. Wrong ways indeed the Rabbis
trod, but they never strayed into the " Irrwege " which
Prof. Schürer attributes to them.

Let me first point to some specific mistakes in which
Prof. Schürer has persisted. He had a whole chapter on
the " Reinheitsgesetze," in which he enumerates the baleful
effects of these laws of ritual cleanness on the daily life of
the Jews. But Mr. Montefiore in his criticism of Schürer
adduced strong evidence to show that these laws applied
only to priests and to laymen visiting the temple; that
under normal circumstances laymen might contract uncleanness without scruple. He further argues, and I quite
agree with him, that all " those distinctions respecting the
various capacities of different utensils to contract uncleanness, over which Prof. Schürer makes merry . . . are merely
the precipitate of the discussions of the schools, and were
probably unknown to nine-tenths of the pious and observant
Israelites in the age of Christ." Of this serious criticism
Schürer takes no note, yet it is obvious that if true, as
I hold it is, it vitiates much of Schürer's argument.
Maimonides even contends that the laws of uncleanness
were designed to " keep people away from the Sanctuary,
and to prevent them from entering it whenever they
liked." In other words these ritual minutiae were a safe-
guard against the danger of making a mechanical ritual
use of the Temple.

Even worse is it with Schürer's treatment of the Rabbinic

legislation regarding vows and oaths. He not only ignores the patent facts that Jesus' famous "Yea, yea; Nay, nay" is exactly paralleled in the Talmud, that the Rabbis held the breach of one's spoken word as grievous a sin as idolatry, that such an offence estranged the offender from the Divine presence; not only does Schürer refuse to notice this side of the oath question at all, but on the basis of assured mistranslations he founds the charge that the Pharisees departed from morality and ignored the "Höchste Pietätspflicht" in the matter of vows and oaths (pp. 493-4). To prove the former charge Schürer cites the Mishnah Shebuoth iv. 13, but he confounds *patur*, i.e. free from legal penalty, with *mutar*, i.e. morally lawful. To prove the second charge he adduces Mishnah Nedarim ix. 1, which he both mistranslates and misinterprets. These errors have been long ago brought to Schürer's notice by Prof. Schechter, but the passage remains unaltered in Schürer's new edition.

This is the method not of the historian but of one determined to formulate an indictment. Schürer does not criticize the Law, he condemns it. He passes the severest sentence without any recommendation to mercy. Why should he be merciful when he can see no extenuating circumstances? He does not analyse the good and evil of the Rabbinic system, for to him it is wholly evil. Toy and Wendt agree that Jesus was directing his anger at exceptional villains, but Schürer, when he condescends for a moment to admit that there were a few good Pharisees, proceeds at once to qualify his admission by a vigorous repetition of his general condemnation. And what a condemnation it is! The Jew obeyed the Law from the meanest motives of reward, his religious and moral life was completely externalized, his conscience was silenced, he could not distinguish between the highest moral truth and the trivialities of a ceremonial ritual. Formal accuracy in carrying out the law, not the doing of the good as such, was the end aimed at. The Jew was crushed under a burden of duties; the Sabbath and everything else was subjected to the minutest and most wearisome regulations. Even prayers were only uttered to fulfil a duty, and thus all living piety was destroyed. Fasting was an external-ized means of putting pressure on God. A composition with the letter of the Law was sought at the sacrifice of honesty. At every step, at every hour, throughout his life, the Jew was tortured by dead and deadening formulas. Life was a torment to the earnest man, while those who attained to mastership in the Law almost inevitably sank into the vice of pride and self-righteousness. And this is Prof. Schürer's whole account of Life under the Law! In his *Apologetics*, if I remember aright, Dr. Bruce discusses Jewish legalism as one of God's experimental failures in the evolution of a perfect religion. If Prof. Schürer has given a true account of that legalism, the experiment must have been devised not by God but by the devil.

Underlying Prof. Schürer's whole case against the Pharisaic religion is the assumption that a life of the spirit is incompatible with a very fully developed ritual. He makes little effort to prove that this incompatibility actually manifested itself; he rather assumes it as a logical necessity. Because the letter often casts out the spirit, he concludes that letter and spirit can never nest together. But there is no church without ritual, letter and spirit always coexist. That ritual meets a real need of the spirit, follows from its universality in all forms of religion. The question as to the result of the combination of spirit and letter can therefore never be solved *a priori*, but must in each case be submitted to the test of experience and of fact.

Schürer, assuming *a priori* that spirit and letter are mutually exclusive, is incapable of putting Rabbinism to this test. He cannot find anything spiritual in Rabbinism, because he has decided that nothing spiritual can be there. And when anything that betokens inwardness forces itself upon his notice, he feels justified, nay bound, to explain it

away. Christian theologians give to every saying of Jesus
the widest and most generous extension that the sayings
can possibly bear. And it is right to do so. No Jew
should seek to belittle any of the great and inspiring
utterances of the Prince of Peace. The world must make
the most and not the least of its spiritual treasures. But
when a Rabbi says a good thing, theologians will only
allow to it the minimum of meaning that the words extort
from them. On the one side generosity, on the other
grudging. It would need, however, the whole evening
to illustrate this double dealing as between the Law and
the Gospel. We are told that the Jewish God was a King
exacting homage, but when the Gospel uses the Jewish
expression "the Kingdom of Heaven," Dr. Fairbairn rightly
points out that the Divine paternity and the Divine
sovereignty are complementary ideas. The Jewish God
is far off because he is located in heaven, but when the
Lord's prayer addresses "our father in heaven," Canon
Gore comments, "not in heaven because he is far off, but
because he is raised above all the ignorance and pollution
of man." The Jew, we are told, had a communal not
a personal soul, but when the Lord's prayer opens "*our*
father," Mr. Gore remarks, "I must begin with losing my
selfishness, with recollecting that I am only one of the
great body of God's children." But not only are Rabbinic
expressions pressed against Rabbinism with an uncritical
rigour, but its good things are treated with the sneer of the
special pleader. When in the *Pirke Aboth* Antigonos of
Socho said, "Be not as slaves that minister to the master
with a view to receive recompense," Schürer declares that
this "is by no means a correct expression of the ground
principle of Pharisaic Judaism." Marti, by the way, calls
the same saying "*abnorm.*" This is like the Bible critics
who pronounce Jonah a freak, but Esther typically Jewish.
Yet Jonah is read in every Synagogue on the day of
Atonement, and Antigonos' saying is more often on
a Jewish preacher's lips than any other Rabbinic maxim.

Again, when R. Eleazer inveighs against those who make
of prayer an appointed duty, a denunciation repeated over
and over again in the Rabbinic literature, Schürer brushes
it aside as an inconsistency.   It is an inconsistency with
Pharisaic Judaism as it is conceived by Schürer, not with
Pharisaic Judaism as it really is.   Just as the writers of
some of the most spiritual Psalms in the Psalter loved the
Temple and its ritual with an intense affection, just as
Hillel could present at once the ideal of spirituality and
the ideal of devotion to the technicalities of legalism, just
as in mediaeval times Ibn Gebirol could write that purest,
most spiritual of meditations, " the Royal Crown " and then
proceed to draw up a metrical survey of the 613 commandments of the Pentateuch, so have I known a modern Jew,
who refused to knock at his own door on the Sabbath, yet
died in early manhood a martyr to his spiritual aspirations.
This is the essential fact about the Jewish legalism.
Together with the trivial, the legal, the ritual, which
Schürer treats as the whole of Pharisaism, there were the
spiritual, the ennobling, the joyous elements which Schürer
discards as abnormal or inconsistent.

Many Pharisees undoubtedly held an external view of
the Law as something imposed from without, and they
regarded themselves as bound to obey it because it was
the Law.   This unfortunately applies to all revealed
religions, for the ideal " Not my will but thine " is to many
Christians an ideal, I fear, only because it is written in
a text.   But the external view of the Law was not the
final statement of the belief of the higher Jewish mind.
The Pharisees attempted to reduce the Law to general
principles.   One expounded it as the outcome of such
fundamental morals as " Love thy neighbour as thyself."
Another held that the Law was summed up in the great
saying of Micah, " What does the Lord require of thee but
to do justly, to love mercy, and to walk humbly with thy
God."   This betokened a sense that the Law itself required
a sanction.   In his new treatise *Die Ethik des Judenthums*,

Prof. Lazarus offers ample proof that some Rabbis held the Law not moral because it was commanded, but commanded because it was moral. The commandments were not commandments because they were written, but they were written because they were commandments. So when pre-existent, creative wisdom is in Ben Sira identified with the Law, the Law is law because it flows from the fount of wisdom, not wise because it is Law. Hence, again, the doctrine found in early Rabbinical writings that the Law was revealed because it was necessary, not necessary because it was revealed. There were laws indeed which were only known from revelation—these were the ceremonies, but there were laws which, without revelation, man must have discovered for himself. These included the fundamentals of social morals, the prohibition of murder, robbery, adultery. Schürer seems to be quite oblivious of this distinction, but it became an established principle in Jewish theology. Maimonides explains it in the sixth of his eight chapters on Ethics, while Ibn Ezra in his *Foundation of Morals* distinguishes as primary those laws of morality which are ingrained in the human heart and not derived from revelation. Though one usually thinks of the Decalogue as the expression of revelation *par excellence*, Ibn Ezra actually includes among the primary, self-discoverable laws the whole of the Decalogue with the exception of the ordinance of the Sabbath. To Ibn Ezra there were three revelations, of God in nature, of God in the conscience, of God in the Law.

There was another idea which helped to save the Law from becoming a merely mechanical system, and this idea was already to the fore in Pharisaic Judaism. Prof. Schürer says nothing of the spiritualizing effect of the idea of the *Imitatio Dei*, which pervades the Rabbinical theology. God is holy, be thou holy; God is merciful, be thou merciful. It has, perhaps truly, been said, that only a Christian can understand a Christian's passion for Christ. I think that only a Jew knows the Jew's passion for God,

the depth of his love, the joy of his service.   To God the
Pharisee ascribed all the virtues ; stern justice, the tenderest
mercy ; God was the object of reverence, the object of love ;
king, saviour, father ; the monarch on high, the familiar
friend on earth.   Man's ideal was to attain to something of
the Godly nature, and the Law was the means to that end.
The Pharisee's love for it led him to childish absurdities,
to the most trivial excesses.   But so conceived, on the one
hand as the expression of the divine will, on the other as
the expression of man's moral nature, the Law brought the
human soul into relation with God, and it could never
become the mere code of external observances which it
seems to Schürer.   "An unchaste thought is a sin;" "the
thought of sin is even worse than sin itself." "The All-
Merciful desires man's heart" ran another familiar phrase.
The inwardness of the religious ideal is brought out in the
comments of the Sifre on the text, "And thou shalt love
the Lord thy God with all thy heart.   With all thy heart,
with thy good and evil inclinations, let not thy heart be
divided but whole towards God. . . . With all thy soul.
Love him even to the surrender of thy soul. . . . With all
thy might.   Whatever measure God metes out to thee, be
it the measure of happiness, be it the measure of sorrow,
love him with all thy might."   But perhaps this religious
inwardness comes out best in such a passage as the following Pesikta: "Good and upright is the Lord, therefore will
he instruct sinners in the way.   They asked wisdom what
is the punishment of the sinner ?   Wisdom answered, Evil
shall pursue him.   They asked prophecy and were told,
The soul that sinneth shall die.   They asked the Law.
The Law said, Let him bring a trespass offering and be
absolved.   They asked God himself.   God answered, What
is the punishment of the sinner ?   Let him repent of his sin
and receive my pardon."

All this did not save average Judaism from the pitfall of
mechanical obedience, but it was a constant corrective to
the danger and was by no means without effect.   The

Archbishop of Canterbury, in his Charge, argues that the Pharisee did good but was not good, that he always applied a rule, and thus experienced none of that moral struggle which accompanies the application of the conscience to questions of morality. But this is no argument against Pharisaism, it simply is the *reductio ad absurdum* of the theory of the nature of Rabbinism which the Archbishop shares with Schürer. The Pharisee had his moral conflicts, like every other human being; duties sometimes pulled him two ways, and for all such cases he had no guide but his own sense of right or wrong, his own moral nature built up by obedience to the Law. Detailed as the Jewish Law was, it did not, it could not, prescribe in advance for a tithe of the moral decisions that he must daily make. "But," Prof. Schürer would reply, "I am not so sure of that. Even the prayers were minutely controlled, and if the prayers why not the conscience?" Certainly there were many prescriptions as to the hour at which the Shema might be said, and the liturgical ordinances were sufficiently comprehensive. But again this is not the whole truth. There was some fluidity in the *contents* of the liturgy. In the Talmud there are numerous private prayers which were composed and used by individual Rabbis. Just as at an earlier date new Psalms easily found their way into the Canon, so, right up to the age of printing, new hymns found their way into the Synagogue. The Midrash on Psalm 4 says, "Pray in the synagogue, or in the field, or in thy house, or on thy bed, or if thou canst not pray on thy bed, let thy heart meditate a prayer and be thou silent. Be silent from the sin thou wast about, and if thou dost this, what says the text in the next verse: Offer sacrifices of righteousness. I shall esteem it as though thou hadst built an altar and offered thereon a multitude of sacrifices." In a score of places the Pharisaic Rabbis insist that prayer must be heart, not lip worship. All this did not save many Jews from praying mechanically, from using words without thought. Worse still was this when

Hebrew, though not familiarly known, remained the language of the liturgy. But the Synagogue has hardly done worse in this respect than the Roman Catholic Church. The fault must not be entirely assigned to the Law. It is a fault incident to all liturgies. You bid man pray when his heart dictates, but you fix an hour for public worship. You put the words into the mouth of him who prays, yet you ask him to pray as though the words were his own. You wish him to use his heart, yet you are bound to give him a prayer-book. Even in churches where there is no fixed liturgy, I am told that after a few weeks experience of the pastor, a watchful member can perfectly well anticipate the exact formulae which the pastor's extemporized outpourings will use. Happily for Church and Synagogue alike, we can always fall back on the Psalter which use cannot stale nor blunt. One would almost suppose from Schürer that the Pharisees had forgotten the Psalms.

Externalism, according to Schürer, attached even to the motives and the results of obedience to the Law. The Pharisee obeyed because he expected rewards, but he felt obedience to be a grievous burden. And the expectation was of the most arithmetical and mechanical character. Forcing against him a metaphor which is echoed also in the Gospels, the critic tells the Pharisee that he was a chafferer who basely demanded God's tat for his own tit. Like Robinson Crusoe he cast up accounts of profit and loss ; so many good works, so much rewards. It is not easy to reconcile this picture with the theory usually raised on the authority of James ii. 10, that the Pharisees considered a single failure in obedience sufficient to undo all their piety, sufficient to rob all their piled-up works of their saving value. The Pharisees indeed held that righteousness would be rewarded, they held act and consequence to be causally connected. They could not conceive God as just and yet indifferent to the justice of man's conduct. Moreover they believed in the Covenant, and steadfastly trusted in God's fidelity to it. But their theory of Retribution did not begin and end with the principle of measure for measure. God's fidelity to the Covenant was an act of divine grace, calling for Israel's responsive obedience but not signed or sealed by Israel's merits. They held that God rewarded, but that man must not serve him because of the reward. The saying of Antigonos which Schürer thinks abnormal underlies the whole Rabbinic theology. "He who fulfils a commandment and expects a reward is a sinner." "None shall do the commandments to win reward, but all that ye do must be done from love." "Blessed is the man who delighteth in his commandments. R. Joshua ben Levi says the meaning is that man only desires to do the commandments but does not want the rewards connected with them." Add to this the remarkable Rabbinical doctrine of the Chastisements of Love, and the evidence is complete that though the Pharisees believed that in a just world God must proportion happiness to merit, must indeed pay measure for measure, yet they were not slaves who served God for reward. This conclusion is fully confirmed by the Jewish liturgy. If the Covenant is appealed to it is not on the ground of present righteousness, but on the ground of the idealized righteousness of the fathers. Man is always described in the Jewish liturgy as utterly empty of works, as altogether destitute of righteousness, and as dependent for salvation solely and only on the infinite mercies of God. I will spend fewer words still over Schürer's other count. He thinks that the Law was a burdensome yoke. The controversy is again between logic and fact. Logic is with Schürer, fact is with the Law. *A priori*, obedience to the Rabbinic Law should have been unspeakably wearisome, actually it was an ineffable joy. Against Schürer's logic there is the evidence of twenty-five centuries of Jewish literature, liturgy, and life. The most wondrous feature of life under the Law—its irrepressible joyousness—is obliterated by Schürer by a stroke of the pen.

In my criticism of Prof. Schürer I have more or less
followed Mr. Montefiore's and Prof. Schechter's lines. The
gravamen of my charge is that Schürer's third edition is in
this section identical with the second, that the criticism
levelled against it has been entirely unnoticed. It is true
that any revision would have been very inconvenient.
These chapters of Schürer have been so extensively used
and relied on, that were Schürer to admit himself wrong
in any point, he would upset the structures of many
a disciple and copyist.

Is this to go on? Is the Law to be searched for no
other purpose than to find justifications for Paul? Are
the Rabbinical sayings to be examined simply as foils to
the Gospel? Or is the Law to be studied as a whole, with
no other aim than to get at the truth, to understand its
excellences *on its own lines* as well as its notorious faults
when absolute tests are applied? The only book in which
I have read a real attempt to get at the truth about the
effects of the Law on Jewish life and character is Anatole
Leroy Beaulieu's *Israel among the Nations.* He castigates
the Jews, but he discriminates. Jews do not expect
a wholly favourable verdict, they do not expect that the
Law will be pronounced an altogether good thing. They
know themselves that it is not an altogether good thing,
they do not believe at all in religious finality. But Jews
have the right to demand that there shall be what
Prof. Cheyne calls a fresh investigation of essential
Judaism. This investigation must be made by Christians
if it is to win due authority; most Jews indeed who are
thoroughly conversant with the Talmud know nothing of
current theology. But the investigation must be made by
men who will study faithfully the original sources, who
will immerse themselves in the Rabbinic world and know
its highways and byways as they know their own city,
who will at every turn test their theories by comparison
with actual results in the Jewish life of the past and of
to-day. These investigators, if they refuse the evidence

of Jewish lovers of the Law, must also refuse the evidence
of those who hate the Law, whether these adversaries be
canonical Apostles or German Professors. Why is it that
a man like Mr. Montefiore has been moved to such unwonted
heat when dealing with Schürer's charges against the Law?
It was because the Law is criticized with a harshness,
a one-sidedness, an ignorance, an injustice seldom paralleled
in the history of theology. What would you think were
a Jew to tell you that the war of ritual now raging in the
English Church is a war of external ceremonies, and that
this is the only subject that really interests Anglican
Christians? Yet this is how the Pharisees are treated.
That my complaint is just you may see from this. I and
many Jews with me have no resentment whatever
against the general spirit of the criticism to which the
Law was subjected by Jesus, against his healthy onslaught against externalism. When Jesus overturned
the money-changers and ejected the sellers of doves from
the Temple he did a service to Judaism for which
Judaism may one day be adequately grateful. But
were the money-changers and the dove-sellers the only
people who visited the Temple? And was every one who
bought or sold a dove a mere formalist? Last Easter I was
in Jerusalem, and along the façade of the Church of the
Holy Sepulchre I saw the stalls of the vendors of sacred
relics, of painted beads and inscribed ribbons, of coloured
candles, gilded crucifixes, and bottles of Jordan water.
There these Christians babbled and swayed and bargained,
a crowd of buyers and sellers in front of the Church sacred
to the memory of Jesus. Would, I thought, that Jesus
were come again to overthrow these false servants of his,
even as he overthrew his false brothers in Israel long ago.
But I will also tell you what I did not think. I did not
think that the buying and selling of sacred relics was the
sole motive which had brought thousands of pilgrims to
Jerusalem, I did not say, Here is the whole of the Gospel,
this is its inevitable end, its sure outcome. I knew that

there is more in Christianity than this, that there are other
Christians than these. Nay, as I turned away I thought
that perhaps if I had the insight to track a dealer in relics
to his inmost soul, I might after all find there a heart warm
with the love of Christ.

I. ABRAHAMS.

THE PLACE OF JESUS
IN THE
RELIGIOUS LIFE OF HIS DAY

by
Samuel S. Cohon

E

THE PLACE OF JESUS IN THE RELIGIOUS LIFE
OF HIS DAY*

SAMUEL S. COHON
HEBREW UNION COLLEGE

UNLESS the ghost of non-historicity be raised, the conclusion
is unavoidable that Jesus spent his brief life-span as a Jew
among fellow Jews. Neither his words nor his acts suggest that
he personally seceded from the faith of his fathers or that he consciously organized a separate body that would take its followers
outside of the Synagogue. Whatever his views of his personal
mission, he lived, labored and died a Jew.

Our uncertainties begin when we seek more detailed light on
his relation to his fellow-Jews and on the place which he occupied
in the religious life of his day. Here we are baffled by the familiar
difficulties of the legendary and confused character as well as of
the paucity of the sources. A few clear-cut statements in the Talmud might have dispensed with many guesses. But history was not
the province of Rabbinical literature. Where we look in vain for
information on the Maccabees, on the schools of Hillel and Shammai,
or on a Bar Cochba, we can hardly expect to find a clear account
of the central figure of an antagonistic religion. The few scraps
bearing on Jesus are more valuable psychologically as evidence
of the reaction of the leaders of the Synagogue toward the early

---

* New Testament quotations in this paper are taken from James Moffatt's
translation.

Church than as historical testimony of the life and character of Jesus.[1] Where the Talmud is invaluable for the student of Christian origins is in the evidence which it furnishes concerning the social and religious conditions and tendencies of the age of Jesus and his disciples, evidence which is indispensable to correct and to supplement one-sided impressions produced by Josephus and the New Testament.

Neither are we on terra firma when we turn to the Synoptic Gospels. Here, too, we deal not with objective history but with Tendenz-Schriften, which more frequently reflect the faith of the early Church and its antagonism toward the Synagogue than the actual facts about Jesus. Judging by the earnest discussions of moot questions relative to Gospel sources, no royal road has thus far been laid through these mazes that might lead us directly to the historical Jesus. Whatever conclusions are drawn on the basis of the Synoptics are consequently not wholly free from subjective judgment and must be considered provisional.

I. THE MESSIANIC PORTRAITURE OF JESUS

The cumulative testimony of the Apostolic age is that the appearance of Jesus was in the first instance a phenomenon in the evolution of Judaism. It presented a striking manifestation of, or, as the Church claims, the revelation of Messianism, which historical circumstances rendered fruitless for Judaism and all important as the fons et origo of Christianity. To establish the Messiahship of their hero is the chief preoccupation of the Gospels. While they record many things about him, their information is manifestly cast in a Messianic mould of a type familiar to us from Jewish literature[2]. Accordingly it is well nigh impossible to say where *Midrash* ends and where history begins.

[1] This testimony has been gathered and discussed by J. Klausner in the opening chapter of his work on *Jesus of Nazareth*.

[2] Not only the Apocalyptic writings but even so philosophical a work as the Wisdom of Solomon contains a picture of the righteous man who suffers for the sins of his generation, which has much in common with the ideal of the Messiah. It is interesting to note that he is called God's son. See Ch. 2 12–20.

The Messianic pattern employed by the Synoptists in the portraiture of Jesus is a composite one. The Davidic, Prophetic and Priestly Messianic characters are here blended into a unity. His birth at Bethlehem, his consciousness of special authority, his selection of the Twelve, corresponding to the twelve tribes of Israel, his mysterious deeds, his dramatic pilgrimage to Jerusalem, his crucifixion as King of the Jews, and his resurrection, are presented as incidents in the progress of Jesus from the earthly to heavenly Messiahship.

How indelibly Messianism is impressed upon the Gospel narratives may be judged from their reports of the conceptions which the people formed of Jesus. Mark and Luke inform us that he was taken for John the Baptist, for Elijah, and for "one of the prophets". Matthew adds that he was identified also with Jeremiah.[3]

The "one of the prophets" is evidently an allusion to Deut. 18 8 which predicts the rise of a prophet like unto Moses.[4] Matthew conceives the role of Jesus as that of a prophetic lawgiver transcending Moses. At first sight we are tempted to regard these identifications as having been suggested by the prophetic character of Jesus. More careful inspection yields different results. The identification with Moses can be understood in the light of the apocalyptic "Assumption of Moses."[5] Here not a Davidic Messiah but Moses plays the central role in the Divine Kingdom, which is to be ushered in by God Himself after a day of repentance. Moses was created before the foundation of the world to serve as the mediator of His covenant. He fed the people, and in great compassion guided them on their way, and daily interceded in their behalf. He was "God's chief prophet throughout the earth, the most perfect teacher in the world." His relation to the people of Israel did not terminate at his death. He was appointed by God to continue as their intercessor in the spiritual world. Seventeen

---

[3] Mark. 8 27–30; Matt. 16 13–20; Luke 9 18–21.

[4] Cf. Mark. 9 3 and parallels. Cf. also Acts 3 22 and 7 37.

[5] Written, according to Charles, between the years 7 and 70 C.E. See *Apocrypha and Pseudepigrapha* II, p. 411.

hundred fifty years after his death (c. 75 to 107 C. E.) God Himself will intervene in their behalf.[6]

In the Midrash, Jeremiah figures as a second Moses. Supposed parallels of every important event in the career of one are traced in the other.[7] Quite naturally the Messianic character of the one was transferred by some people to the other. As to Elijah,[8] before coming to figure as precursor of the Davidic Messiah, he was presented in Malachi as the direct herald of the Kingdom of God. As such he also appears in Sirach.[9] John theBaptist's proclamation of the dawning Kingdom of God seems Messianic.[10] Luke states expressly that under the influence of Messianic expectations "Everybody thought to himself about John, 'can he be the Christ'?"

Many of the dramatic words and acts of Jesus' ministry, while appearing prophetic, therefore seem to have been intended to demonstrate his qualifications as the Messiah.[11] His prediction

[6] Assumption of Moses 1 14, 17; 9 9ff.; 11 16; 12 6; 10 11ff.

[7] *Pesikta of Rab Kahana*, ed. Buber, XIII: 36 and *Yalkut Shimoni* on the Torah 919, on Jer. 256 and on Lament. 999. In 2 Macc. 15 12–16 Jeremiah appears to Judas in a dream and delivers to him a golden sword wherewith to crush the foe.

[8] See Ryle and James, *Psalms of Solomon*, Intr. LIV (b) on Elijah and Jeremiah as Messianic types.

[9] Sirach 48 10–11. Possibly also in 1 Macc. 4 46; 14 41 Elijah is meant, though not expressly named. Here he figures in the role in which the Haggadah often presents him.

[10] See C. R. Bowen, "John the Baptist in the N. T.", *Am. J. Th.* XVI (1912), pp. 90–106; "Prolegomena to a New Study of John the Baptist" in *Studies in Early Christianity*, ed. by S. J. Case; also E. W. Parsons on "John the Baptist and Jesus" in the same volume, pp. 129–171.

11 Thus the miracle of the drying up of the fig tree (Mark 11 12–14; Matt. 21 18–19), which astounded the disciples and has perplexed the commentators, becomes intelligible when viewed as a Messianic sign. It is based on Song of Songs 2 13, התאנה חנטה פגיה, literally 'the fig-tree spiceth her figs.' The word חנטה was evidently understood by the Evangelists as meaning 'embalmeth.' As the entire Song of Songs was considered an allegory in which the Messianic drama is the main theme, the drying up or 'embalming' of the fig-tree was naturally taken as one of the portents that had to be fulfilled. Cf. Song of Songs *Rabba ad loc., Pesikta Rabb.* XVII.

of the destruction of the Temple and his cleansing of the Temple are direct imitations of Jeremiah's Temple Sermon (Ch. 7). The latter is also a fulfillment of the purification of the Levites, predicted in Malachi 3 1—5. Jesus often repeats the words of the prophets and reinforces their message. However, his claim is not that he be recognized as a prophet in the sense of being a spokesman of God and a herald of righteousness. He announces no new principle about either God or man that would rank him with the literary prophets, such as Amos, Hosea, Micah, Isaiah, Jeremiah, Ezekiel or Deutero-Isaiah. He moves on a wholly different plane. Instead of dealing with the problems of Israel in this world, he concerns himself with questions of the world to come. His religious spirit expresses itself in forms familiar to us not from literary prophecy but from apocalyptic writings. Not even his disciples claimed that he was primarily a prophet, nor did the Jewish people refuse him a hearing or Pilate crucify him as a prophet. We are thus compelled to consider the Gospel designation of him as Prophet, like the other designations of King and High Priest, as an attribute of Messianism.

The special authority that his followers noted in his preaching, which was so unlike that of the scribes, consisted according to Mark in his power of casting out demons. He went about preaching in the synagogues and exorcising evil spirits.[12] Selecting the Twelve he likewise dispatched them "to preach with the power of casting out demons."[13]

F. C. Grant rightly concludes that Mark's "portrait of Christ is distinctly not that of a social prophet or leader ... Instead, he represents Jesus as primarily a religious teacher who is at the same time the Christ, the beloved son of God, the Messiah—but Messiah in a higher sense than the contemporary Jewish leaders understood, the Messiah who came to 'minister' and 'to give his life a ransom for many.' "[14]

Shall we dismiss these Messianic elements in the portraiture of

[12] Mark. 1 22–27; Matt. 4 23ff.; 12 15ff.; Luke 6 17–19.
[13] Mark. 3 15; 6 7; Matt. 10 1; Luke 6 12ff.
[14] F. C. Grant in *Studies in Early Christianity*, p. 259.

Jesus as the pure invention of his disciples and as the mere expression of the faith of the early Church without the least warrant on his own part? Such a claim is not far removed from the negation of the historicity of the Gospels altogether. In view of the persistence of the testimony, it is difficult to escape the conclusion that sometime during his ministry, Jesus grew conscious not only of a unique personal relationship to God but that in addition he came to think of himself as the long expected Messiah. From this consciousness of himself sprang his entire mode of conduct, his sense of special authority in healing and teaching, his peculiar attitude toward sinners and his apocalyptic teachings. The Prophetic lesson, which, in accordance with Jewish practice, he read on the Sabbath in the synagogue at Nazareth, from the sixty-first chapter of Isaiah, he thought fulfilled in himself. It is the ideal which he sought to translate into his life. He felt that the Spirit of God was upon him, that he was consecrated to preach good tidings unto the poor, to proclaim freedom unto the fettered, sight for the blind, liberty to the oppressed, to proclaim the Lord's year of favor. The Messianic era, to which the people eagerly looked forward, was at hand,[15] and he was "its principle agent and predestined head." In keeping with the general atmosphere of secrecy which enveloped Messianism, he avoided speaking of it in public, but intimated it to his trusted disciples in private. Without such a suggestion coming directly from him, it is hardly possible to explain the faith of his disciples after the tragic shock of the crucifixion. While this unique consciousness presents a psychological puzzle to moderns, it explains best the history of Christianity from Apostolic times to the present.

The oldest tradition symbolized the birth of this conviction in the mind of Jesus by the revelation made to him on the occasion of his Baptism in the Jordan. "The Tradition may have been an afterthought arising from contemplation of the later history of Jesus, although the Baptism was a definite point of departure in his ministry."[16] The beginnings of his ministry are connected with

[15] Luke 4 16–21.
[16] Loisy, *The Gospel and the Church*, p. 104. Loisy adds: "In any case,

the activities of John the Baptist. Recent reinterpretations of
the relationship between Jesus and John[17] render it plausible to
see in John's activity another manifestation of Messianism. Like
the Messenger of the Covenant of Malachi and like Elijah of old,
he heralded the coming Kingdom of God and therefore called men
to Baptism unto repentance. From both Josephus and the Gospels
we learn that his appeal met with good response. Even some Pharisees and Sadducees are said to have come to be baptized by him.
That Jesus, too, was attracted by John's prophetic idealism is
quite possible.[18]

Like Saul after his anointing by Samuel, so Jesus after his baptism by John came to feel himself transformed into a new man.
New spiritual powers were born in him. Under the influence of
John's Messianic claims, Jesus may have been stimulated to
nourish similar aspirations. He soon severed his relations with
John and proceeded to further his own mission. In other words,
this step was taken not merely because he felt himself cramped by
the rigid asceticism and by the baptismal rite of John, but possibly
also because of his nascent Messianic consciousness. None the less
he retained his high esteem for John,[19] and his disciples could,
therefore, consistently subordinate the master to the disciple in
the Messianic drama of Jesus, by recognizing him indeed as Elijah,
but in the role of forerunner of the Davidic Messiah rather than in
that of direct inaugurator of the Kingdom of God.[20]

II. MILITANT NATIONALISM AND QUIETISM

Turning from the Messianic framework of the Synoptics to the
concrete data of his ministry, we find Jesus laboring amongst his

---

the distinction that is drawn between the consciousness of Himself as the
Son and as the Messiah is absolutely without foundation. The earliest
tradition has no suspicion of it; nor would modern criticism have dreamed
of it, had there been no theological interests at stake."

[17] See note 10.
[18] Mark. 1 5; Matt. 3 7; Luke 2 7, 15.
[19] Luke 20 1–8 and parallels.
[20] Mark. 1 1–8; Matt. 17 13.

own people with devotion and determination.[21] He appears to have conceived his mission as being primarily unto Israel in his capacity not only of Messianic claimant but also of healer. Mark states that he had refused to heal the Syrophoenician woman's daughter, offering as his reason: "Let the children be satisfied first of all; it is not fair to take the children's bread and throw it to the dogs."[22] Touched by her humility, persistence and faith, he made an exception in her case. Matthew adds the explanation of Jesus: "It was only to the lost sheep of the house of Israel that I was sent."[23] According to Streeter, he had not himself "even on that occasion stepped outside the sacred soil of Palestine—for the woman had come across the border to him."[24] Matthew, while representing the compromise view of the early Church with regard to the conversion of gentiles, concedes that he charged the Twelve: "Do not go among the Gentiles and do not enter a Samaritan town, rather make your way to the lost sheep of the House of Israel."[25] While we can understand how from the standpoint of Judaism he would restrict his religious activities to Israel, we find it hard to comprehend his reason for refusing to heal gentiles or Samaritans. Montefiore comments: "We can hardly believe that, had he not said so actually, had it not been clearly known that he had said so, and that as a matter of fact his activities *were* confined to his own people, such a saying as this could even have been reported, least of all in Mark."[26]

[21] Even Talmudic legend bears witness to his devotion to the Jewish people. See *Gittin* 57a.

[22] Mark. 7 27. The term dog for gentile seems strange in the mouth of Jesus. However, see Matt. 7 6 and comp. Phil. 3 2.

[23] Matt. 15 26.

[24] Cf. *ibid.* 22.

[25] Matt. 10 6. See Streeter, *The Four Gospels*, 514, cited by Montefiore, *Synoptic Gospels* II, 358.

[26] *Synoptic Gospels* I, 167. Montefiore adds, after some extenuations: "Klausner says not untruly that Jesus' reply is 'so brusque and chauvinistic that if any other Jewish teacher of the time had said such a thing Christians would never have forgiven Judaism for it.' Yet it is historical, because 'the gospels were written at a time when the disciples of Jesus

The particularism of Jesus had nothing in common with the ultra-nationalistic aspirations of the followers of Judas the Galilean. Together with their devotion to the Torah they combined an all-consuming zeal for liberty. Under no condition would they submit to foreign rule. Josephus informs us that following the reduction of Archelaus's ethnarchy into a Roman province, Judas "urged his countrymen to revolt, and said they were cowards if they would endure to pay a tax to the Romans, and would, after God, submit to mortal men as their lords."[27] His adherents exhibited extraordinary courage. "They also make light of dying any kind of death, nor indeed do they heed the punishment of their relations and friends, nor can any such fear make them call any man lord."[28] They would recognize none save God as their ruler. Lake and Jackson may be justified in their claim that the title Zealot as descriptive of a party in Jerusalem belongs to the followers of John of Gischala, who were banded together about the year 66 C. E.[29] In that case, John only gave organized expression to the spirit which animated Judas and his followers. Galilee was the hot-bed of their patriotic zeal. It was probably due to the agitation of these Galileans at the Passover feast at Jerusalem that Pilate mingled their blood with that of their sacrifices.[30]

Born and raised in Galilee, Jesus naturally came into contact with this left wing of Pharisaism. What his attitude was towards it we are not expressly informed. However, Mark 12 13–17 (= Matt. 22 15–22; Luke 20 20–26) may throw some light on the subject. Here Pharisees, probably of this type, came together with Herodians, i. e. pro-Romans, to interview him about paying tribute to Caesar. Far from seeking to trick him, as the Gospels suggest, these contending parties may have sought to ascertain

included many non-Jews, and when no one would have put in Jesus' mouth so harsh a sentiment,' *Jesus of Nazareth* pp. 294-295. *Ibid.* p. 168." See also Montefiore's comments on page 85.

[27] *Wars* II; VIII: 1.

[28] *Antiquities* XVIII: 1, 6.

[29] The name first occurs in *Wars* IV; III: 9.

[30] Luke 13 1. See also *Ant.* XVII; IX: 3; and *Wars* II; IX: 4.

where he stood on the burning issue of loyalty to Rome and national independence. Did his gospel of liberty for the oppressed apply to his nation? His reply, to give Caesar that which belongs to Caesar and to God what belongs to God, showed that a barrier existed between him and the nationalists.

Lake and Jackson suggest that the doctrine of non-resistance (Luke 6 27—35) should be understood as the direct negation of the patriotic aspirations of the followers of Judas. The words "love ye your enemies" indeed appeared to the mind of the editor of the Gospel as he copied it out of his sources in the light of "the sufferings and persecution endured by Christians; but to the mind of the Galilean who first heard them they must have seemed to be the direct opposite of the patriotic teachings of the school of thought started by Judas of Galilee, and to be deliberately intended as an alternative to it."[31] "Israel was called on to suffer under Roman rule, and the righteous to endure violence at the hands of the wicked, for that was the will of. God, who in his own good time would shorten the evil days."[32]

On this hypothesis, Lake and Jackson account "for the failure of Jesus to convince any large part of the Galilean population," also "for his leaving even the less populous parts of the country and for the secrecy which appears to have attended his journey when he went through Galilee on his way to Jerusalem; for Galilee was essentially patriotic, far more so than Judea, which in the time of Jesus was still under the influence of the Scribes and priests, whose resistance to Rome was essentially passive."[33] The difference in patriotic fervor in the two sections must be taken as purely hypothetical. Jerusalem as the heart of the country registered every agitation and convulsion in the body of Israel.

As from the insurgents of the Pharisaic left so from the Pharisaic right, the quietistic Essenes, Jesus was separated by an impassable barrier. The points of resemblance between them dwindle into

[31] *Op. cit.*, pp. 289–290.
[32] *Ibid.*, p. 291.
[33] *Ibid.*, p. 290.

insignificance by the side of the points of difference.[34] Far from being secluded in a special brotherhood and fenced around by a high hedge of ceremonial purity, Jesus mingled freely with the people, shared in the ordinary affairs of life, and participated in joyous festivities and recreations. In contradistinction to the ultra-Pharisaic strictness of Sabbath observance on the part of the Essenes, Jesus scandalized some of his contemporaries by his conduct on the day of rest.[35] He showed great laxity toward ceremonial lustrations, which constituted an essential more distinctive of Essenism than of Pharisaism.[36] The fear of pollution kept the Essenes more than the Pharisees from contact not only with foreigners but also with fellow Essenes of inferior grades. Jesus, on the other hand, consorted freely with publicans and sinners, both male and female.[37] With the exception of celibacy, Jesus was free from ascetic habits. Therein he differed not only from the Essenes and some Pharisees but also from John. His eating and drinking drew the denunciation of his opponents as being "a glutton and a winebibber."[38] One of his first miracles consisted in turning water into wine at a wedding feast; and his last act was the observance of the *Seder*, drinking wine and partaking of the Paschal lamb. Unlike the Essenes who regarded oil as polluting, Jesus rather welcomed its use.[39] Possibly the emphasis on some of these things in the Gospels is intended to show his dissent from

---

[34] The supposed resemblances on further examination appear to come from the common stock of Jewish religious idealism rather than from direct affiliation. We refer to the elements of simplicity and brotherly love, to the prohibition of many oaths and to the respect paid to poverty. These elements appear among the *Ḥasidim Harishonim*, from whom both the Essenes and Jesus derived them. Similarly their claim to the possession of the *Ruaḥ Hakkodesh* was common to the *Ḥasidim* and even some Pharisees and was by no means limited to the Essenes. See below.

[35] Matt. 12, 1–12; Mark. 2 23—3 6; Luke 6 1–12; 14 1–6; also 13 10–17; John 5 10–18; cf. 7 22, 23; 9 14, 16.

[36] Matt. 15 1–20; Mark. 7 1–23; Luke 11 38–41.

[37] Matt. 9 10ff., 11 19; Mark. 2 15ff.; Luke 5 30ff.; 7 37ff.; 15 2; 19 7.

[38] Matt. 11 19; Luke 7 34.

[39] Matt. 6 17; Luke 7 46.

these ascetics. With regard to the sacrificial cult, too, Jesus shared none of the Essenic scruples. He accepted it as part of the religious order, shared in it personally and counselled others to do likewise.[40] The whole time of his stay in Jerusalem was spent within the pre-cincts of the Temple.[41] Though repeating the prophetic teaching (which we also find in the mouth of Rabban Joḥanan b. Zakkai) that mercy is better than sacrifice,[42] he also declares that the Temple and altar consecrated the gifts.[43] "Throughout the Gospels," observes Lightfoot, "there is not one word which can be construed as condemning the sacrificial system or as implying a desire for its cessation until everything is fulfilled."[44] Doctrinally, too, Jesus was at variance with the Essenes. He rather followed the Pharisees in the belief of bodily resurrection than the Essenes in their doctrine of the spiritual immortality of the soul.[45]

III. THE PHARISEES AND THE 'AMME HA-ARETZ

To the moderate Pharisaic center, too, Jesus stands in sharpest antagonism. The exact nature of this antagonism is not easy to discern through the fog of bitter hostility which fills the Gospels toward the Pharisees, who proved to be the strongest opponents of the claims of the early Church. Luke retains traditions of friendly relations between Jesus and the Pharisees. He dines at Pharisaic homes and is warned by Pharisees when Herod intends to slay him.[46] Generally the Synoptists present him waging a harsh polem-

[40] Matt. 8 4; cf. Matt. 5 23–24; Mk. 1 44; 14 15–18; Luke 5 14.

[41] Mark. 11 11, 15ff., 27; 12 35; 13 1ff.; 14 49 and parallels. According to Peter, he was accustomed to pay the Temple tax, Matt. 17 24ff.

[42] Matt. 9 13; 12 7. See *Abbot R. Nathan* (Ed. Schechter) I: 4, p. 21.

[43] Matt. 23 16ff.; cf. 5 23–24.

[44] *Colossians*, p. 413. See the entire analysis of the relations of Jesus to the Essenes, *ibid.*

[45] Mark. 12 18ff. and parallels. He not only followed the Pharisees in this doctrine but also their form of exegesis. Cf. *Sanhedrin* 90 b. וגם הקימותי את בריתי אתם לתת להם את ארץ כנען. לכם לא נאמר אלא להם. מכאן לתחית המתים מן התורה.

[46] Luke 7 36; 11 37; 14 1 and 13 31.

ic against them, which, if not apocryphal, violated the principle of love which he taught his disciples to apply even to enemies.[47] Instead of praying for them, he generally excoriated them as vipers and sons of Hell. Montefiore remarks: "For them he is never recorded to have uttered any prayer. The famous passage in Luke (23 34) is of doubtful authenticity and probably refers to the Roman soldiers."[48] His hostility toward them, reaching its climax in Matthew 23, can be understood only as the outgrowth of clashing views on matters that lay at the center of his being.

Their refusal to heed his Messianic claim must have been the chief source of friction between them. Tested by their beliefs regarding the Messiah, Jesus failed to qualify. Mark 12 35—37 presents Jesus endeavoring to demonstrate that the Messiah need not be of the house of David. The authenticity of this argument is established by its appearance in Matthew and in Luke, despite their incorporation of genealogies showing the Davidic descent of Jesus.[49]

In addition, they clashed in their respective attitudes towards the Law. We indeed find numerous points of agreement between them. They were of one mind in considering the Unity of God, the love of Him and the love of one's fellowman as the essence of the Torah.[50] They also agreed on the Divine origin and authority of the written Torah, on Retribution and on the Resurrection. And, as we have noticed, he accepted the sanctity of the Temple and the Temple worship. He even followed some of the older provisions of the Oral Law, such as grace at meals,[51] blessings over wine,[52] and the recitation of the *Hallel* at the *Seder*.[53] The prayer which

[47] Matt. 5 44.   [48] *Op. cit.*, II: 81.

[49] Matt. 22 41–46; Luke 20 41–44. Psalm 110 1 was interpreted in a Messianic sense in *Midrash Tehillim*; see ed. Buber, Ps. 18 29.

[50] Mark. 12 28–34. The union of Deut. 6 5 and Lev. 19 18 first appears in the Testaments of the Twelve Patriarchs, a work produced during the reign of John Hyrcanus (c. 109–106), and interpolated by an editor (c. 70–40 C. E.). E. g. Test. Issachar 5 2; 7 6; Dan. 5 3.

[51] Mark. 6 41; 8 6; 14 22.

[52] Mark. 14 23.

[53] Mark. 14 26, probably Pss. 113–118.

he is said to have taught his disciples bears close resemblance to the prayers current in Pharisaic circles. That he followed or approved the content of the then current daily ritual appears likely in view of his recommendation of the observance of the Decalogue as a means of entrance into the Kingdom[54] and of his citation of the *Shema* in definition of the leading commandment.[55] From Talmudic sources we know that the Decalogue and the *Shema* constituted the central feature of the daily service at the Temple.[56] While these passages were taken from Scripture, their arrangement in the liturgy was the work of the Scribes (*Soferic*).

In his teaching too Jesus did not wholly escape Pharisaic methods. Like the *Haggadists* among the Rabbis, he takes his lead from the text of Scripture, and pursues the general Midrashic style in developing his ideas. He spices his teachings with pointed proverbs and enforces them with poetic parables. As a Haggadist he naturally discards the prophetic "Thus saith the Lord" for "I say unto you." No self-centeredness or undue individualism need have entered into his frequent use of the first person in his preaching. He but followed the form so abundantly illustrated in the Midrashim and in the Talmud. As a Haggadist, too, he was listened to with joy. The Haggadists were great favorites with the people. Whereas the *Halachists*, like technical jurists and even theologians of today, were followed by the select few, the Haggadists spoke to eager crowds. Instead of dealing with the niceties of the Law, they generally appealed to the heart. They spoke of God, of faith, of prayer, of hope and of the mysterious future. They encouraged the people and consoled them. The Haggadic utterances appear in the pages of the Talmud like oases to the weary traveler.

Whatever difference may be noted in the content of the teachings of Jesus and of the rabbinic preachers, their form is strikingly akin. Thus his monitions concerning anger, lust, divorce and false swear-

---

[54] Mark. 10 17ff.; Matt. 19 16ff.; Luke 18 18ff.

[55] Mark. 12 28ff.; Matt. 22 37ff.; Luke 10 25ff.

[56] *Tamid* V: 1; *Berachot* 12a; *Jer. Ber.* I: 5 (8). See Rall and Cohon, *Christianity and Judaism, Compare Notes*, Part II, p. 55.

ing take the form of a rabbinic Midrash on part of the Decalogue.[57] The failure to recognize the rabbinic form in which some of the sayings of Jesus are cast, has led to much misunderstanding with regard to the teaching of the Torah concerning hatred of the enemy. Modern exegetes could save themselves a good deal of hair-splitting, if, following the late Dr. Schechter's suggestion, they would view Matthew 5 43 in the light of rabbinic models. Its correct meaning would then be: "You have heard the saying: 'You must love your neighbor.' (From this are you to infer that you may) hate your enemy? I, therefore, declare unto you: love your enemies."[58]

In Halachic matters, too, Jesus shows the influence of Pharisaic modes of interpretation. His construction of Deut. 23 19, as recorded in the Talmud, met with the approval of Rabbi Eliezer b. Hyrcanus.[59] The Gospel records of his teachings similarly exhibit "Pharisaic leaven." As a loyal Jew, he announces that he came not to destroy the Law but to fulfill it.[60] He knows of lighter and of weightier matters in the Law. However, while stressing "the weightier matters", he does not propose the disregard of the lighter. "These latter you ought to have practiced without omitting the former."[61] Like the Pharisees, he seeks to establish "a hedge for the Torah." Where he calls for a departure from the Pharisaic conception of a particular Halacha, he bases himself on a scriptural verse, on some analogy or principle laid down in another law or practice, in a manner reminiscent of some of the exegetical rules of Hillel.[62] For instance he permits anointing the head and washing the face when fasting, a practice forbidden

---

[57] Matt. 5 21–37. Cf. *Yalkut Shimoni* on Exodus 20 and Lev. 19, or *Midrash Haggadol* to Exodus (ed. Hoffmann) on Decalogue, commandments 5–10.

[58] Matt. 5 43. Schechter, *Studies in Judaism*, 2nd Series, p. 117.

[59] *Ab. Zara* 17 a and *Tos. Hulin* II: 6.

[60] Matt. 5 17. This declaration has reference to Deut. 13 1. See also Luke 16 17.

[61] Matt. 23 23; Luke 11 42.

[62] See Mielziner, *Introduction to the Talmud*, Part II.

by the Rabbis on *Yom Kippur*.[63] He dissents from John and from the Pharisees with regard to extra fasts on the ground that the friends of the bridegroom are absolved from fasting. As the Messianic King figures in the Midrashic interpretation of Song of Songs as bridegroom, both he and his disciples are not obliged to fast.[64] Similarly with regard to the Sabbath, Jesus resorts to Pharisaic arguments to counteract Pharisaic rules. He justifies his disciples in plucking ears of corn on the Sabbath by an analogy (*Gezera Shava*) from David, who under compulsion ate the shewbread, which was contrary to the Law. Matthew adds another analogy: "Have you not read in the Law that the priests in the Temple are not guilty when they desecrate the Sabbath?" and concludes (with a *Kal Veḥomer*): "I tell you, one is here who is greater than the Temple . . . The Son of Man is lord of the Sabbath."[65]

In the matter of healing on the Sabbath Jesus manifestly departed from the severe blue laws as represented in Jubilees, Chapter 50, and which correspond to the views of the Shammaites. On the other hand, the Hillelites held that where life was in danger, the

---

[63] Matt. 6 16–18 and *Yoma* VIII: 1. Mark. 9 29 shows that Jesus did lay weight on fasting.

[64] Mark. 2 18ff.; Matt. 9 14ff.; Luke 5 33ff. Rabbinic law exempts the friends of the groom from reading the Shema and from prayer during the seven days of the marriage feast, *Tos. Ber.* II: 9; *Ber.* 11a, 16a.

[65] Matt. 12 1–8, cf. *Sabbath* XII: 2. Dr. Kohler suggests that the incident referred to here was preserved most correctly in Luke. "It was not on the Sabbath, but on the first day of the Second Passover week (called δευτεροπρώτη from the Biblical expression 'the morrow of the Sabbath.' Levit. 23 11–14), when no new corn was allowed to be eaten before some had been offered on the altar, that the disciples of Jesus passed through the field and plucked the new corn, called "*ḥadash*" in rabbinical Literature. In defending their action Jesus correctly referred to David, who ate of the holy bread because he was hungry (1 Sam. 21 5–7)—an argument which would not at all apply to the Sabbath." (Article "Jesus in Theol.," *J.E.* VII, 108). See also Rudolf Leszynsky, *Die Sadduzäer*, 292, n. 1; Strack-Billerbeck, *Kommentar zum N. T.* II, p. 158. The question at issue in this incident may also be whether or not the sheaf to be waved before the Lord may be reaped on the Sabbath. If this be the case the teaching of Jesus is in agreement with that of the Rabbis. See *Menaḥot* 72a. ‏[קציר העומר] דוחה שבת‏

Sabbath laws must be set aside. They, too, believed that the
Sabbath is handed over to man, not man to the Sabbath.[66] Where
life is not at stake the only objection to healing on Sabbath is the
preparation of the medicine.[67] In the case of Jesus no such preparation was necessary. It is interesting to note the Pharisaic
character of the justification which Jesus offers for his conduct.
He argues: "Is it right to help or to hurt on the Sabbath, to save
life or to kill?"[68]

On the other hand with regard to divorce Jesus is stricter than
the Hillelites, who took a rather liberal stand in the matter.
Mark 10 2—12 (= Luke 16 18) presents him as even going beyond
the Shammaites in denying the validity of divorce under any
circumstance. Basing himself midrashically on Gen. 1 28 and
2 24 he keeps to the ideal of Malachi 2 14—16 that God hates divorce ("I hate putting away"). The compromise view of Matthew
19 1—12 and 5 32 corresponds to the position of the Shammaites,
viz. that a man may divorce his wife only in case of adultery.[69]

These agreements with the Pharisees notwithstanding, Jesus
stands out as their uncompromising opponent. The guiding principle in his radical disagreement with the Pharisees may be noted
in Mark 7 1—23 and Matthew 15 1—20.[70] Asked, "Why do not your
disciples follow the tradition of the elders?" Jesus retorts with the
repudiation of the principle underlying the tradition. The whole
body of ceremonial law as extended by the Pharisees possesses
no validity. He brands the Pharisees as rendering God lip service

---

[66] לכם שבת מסורה ואי and פקוח נפש דוחה שבת Mekhilta Ki Tissa
מפקחין פקוח נפש בשבת והזריו הרי זה Yoma 84b אתם מסורים לשבת
ואין צריך ליטול רשות מבית דין משובח. Tos. Sabb. XVI: 9-14. John
7 22-23 preserves an authentic Halacha. See also Strack-Billerbeck, Kommentar I, pp. 610-630.

[67] Sab. XIV: 2-4, XXII: 6.

[68] Mark. 3 1-6. Cf. the argument of R. Ishmael in Mekhilta Ki Tissa
and Yoma 85a. The argument in Matt. 12 11 is likewise in good Rabbinic
form.

[69] Sifre Dt. 269; Gittin IX: 10.

[70] Mark. 7 15-23 is at variance with the tradition of the early Church
as reported in Acts 15 27-28 and smacks of Paulinism. Cf. Colossians 2 20-23.

rather than the devotion of the heart, and accuses them of dropping God's commands that they might keep the tradition of their own invention. While taking over some of their older practices, he refuses to bind himself by their innovations. [71]

Rabbinic sources show that this "tradition of the Elders" was in reality a new institution in the days of Jesus. We are expressly informed that the rule of handwashing before meals was established by Shammai and Hillel. [72] Rabbi Simeon ben Elazar observes "How vastly has *Tahara* (ceremonial purity) increased, for it was but little in aforetime and has now waxed abundant." [73]

It was extended from the practice of the priests (Ex. 30 17—21) to that of the laity. Rabban Gamaliel I justified it on the ground that "not to the priests alone was the law of holiness entrusted at Sinai but unto all Israel." [74] The ceremony was indeed mechanical, [75] but like baptism or ablution in general was considered as a means of sanctification. This was in line with the general tendency of the Pharisees to assume voluntarily greater rigorism than the

[71] T. Herford writes: "If he really gave the practice of corban as an example, and if this be not due to later manipulation of the Gospel material, then the inference is legitimate that Jesus had no close acquaintance with the tradition which he denounced. The tradition of the Elders is of course the Halachah. The alleged practice of evading the fifth commandment is nowhere known in the recorded Halachah (see especially *M. Nedarim* IX: 1 and the commentaries on the passage), and is, besides, entirely at variance with the Pharisaic practice of laying the greatest stress upon honour to parents. If Jesus had any inside knowledge of Pharisaism on its Halachic side he would never have given an example so entirely beside the mark." (*The Pharisees*, pp. 205–06). If the examples of his acquaintance with Pharisaic exegesis which we cited above be correct, Herford's apprehension that this passage has been corrupted amounts to a certainty.

[72] *Sabb.* 14 b. The view is also expressed that this institution goes back to Solomon.

[73] *Jer. Sab.* I: 4.

[74] *Jalkut Shimeoni Ki Tissa* 386. Citing *Tana Debe Elijahu.* Though appearing in a later Midrash, the tradition is old. See *Tosefta Hagiga* III: 1. In *Hulin* 106 a handwashing is derived from Lev. 15 11.

[75] *Tos. Terumot* I, מהרות אין צריכות מחשבה :. For the moral aspect of Tahara see *Midr. Hagadol* to Exodus, ed. Hoffmann, pp. 208–09.

Torah requires. They are characterized in the Mishnah as שרצו
לא מפני שההלכה כן אלא שרצה להחמיר [76] and להחמיר על עצמם
על עצמו[77]. Of the House of Hillel it was said that its members
subjected themselves to extreme rigorism while permitting
others to follow a more lenient course.[78] This type of piety,
while expressing itself in every phase of religious life, was
specially stressed in Sabbath observance, lustrations and ablu-
tions and scrupulous regard for tithing—terumot and ma'asrot.[79]
It was fostered in the Pharisaic associations (Ḥaburot) as a
superior form of righteousness. Admission to these associations
was open to any trustworthy person who in the presence of
three associates (Ḥaberim) pledged himself to observe the Pharisaic requirements.[80]

While the Pharisees, as Josephus testifies, won the confidence
of the people by their austere teachings and piety,[81] there were
many who refused to submit to their restrictions. *All such were
designated as 'Amme Ha-Aretz.* They did not constitute any particular stratum in the social order. To speak of them as "men of
the soil," "farm-owning" or "farm-laboring type," the "ill-bred,"
the "common herd," or the "uncultured folk" is to grasp at the
etymology of the term and to miss its inner meaning.[82] *The use
of 'am ha-aretz as synonymous with bor is due to the sense which the
term acquired in later centuries*, when Pharisaism converted itself
into the religion of all strata of Jewry and when the name 'am ha-
aretz, as expressive of a difference from the *haber*, assumed the
meaning of ignoramus. Rabbinical literature still retains the differ-

---

[76] *Erubim* IV: 1.

[77] *B. Mez.* V: 5.

[78] *Beza* II: 6 אמרו לו [לרבן גמליאל] מה נעשה לבית אביך שהיו
מחמירין על עצמן ומקילין לכל ישראל. See also *Eduyot* III: 10.

[79] Since the reforms of John Hyrcanus special care was taken in the
discharge of these duties. See *Sota* 48a. We hear of the excommunication
of Rabbi Eliezer b. Ḥanoch for the conscious disregard of the rule of handwashing before meals. *B*. 19a.

[80] *Bechorot* 30b.

[81] *Ant.* XVIII, I: 3–4; also XIII, X: 6.

[82] Cf. I. Abrahams in C. G. Montefiore's *Syn. Gospels* II, pp. 647–669.

ence between 'am ha-aretz and bor.[83] Neither does the evidence at our disposal justify us in considering them as the poor and dispossessed. Among them we find the entire body of publicans[84] and other men of influence.[85] They probably included the whole Sadducean aristocracy. We hear expressly of priests and even of high-priests who were classed as 'amme ha-aretz.[86] Pharisees who lapsed from their discipline *ipso facto* became 'amme ha-aretz.[87]

Most of the definitions of the 'am ha-aretz, which come to us from second century rabbis, are probably not radically different from those of the first century.[88] Rabbi Elazar holds him to be an 'am ha-aretz who studied Scripture and even Mishna but did not receive personal instruction from an accredited scholar. Rabbi Meir classes a man as an 'am ha-aretz if he does not recite the Shema together with its benedictions.[89] Those who do not put on phyl-

---

[83] *Abot* II: 5. אין בור ירא חטא ולא עם הארץ חסיד. That these are not synonymous is shown by the following statement in *Bamidbar Rabba* III: 1 ישראל יש ביניהם בני תורה ויש ביניהם עמי הארץ ויש בהם בורים cf. also *Tos. Berachot* VII: 16 ברוך שלא עשני בור. For the discussion of the difference between the two see *Sota* 22a.

[84] See *Bechorot* 31a חבר ונעשה גבאי דוחין אותו מחבירתו. *Tos. Demai* II: 5; see also *Nedar.* 27b–28a.

[85] *Tos. Aboda Zara* III: 3; *Tos. Demai* III: 2. Moore correctly observes that "the notion that sometimes crops up in the books, that the 'Amme Ha-Aretz' were the humble pious in the land, in contrast to the arrogant scholars and the self-righteous Pharisees, a class corresponding to the 'anavim' of the Psalms, is without any better support than the imagination of the authors who entertain it. That among those upon whom the Rabbis and the Pharisees so liberally bestowed the name 'am ha-aretz there were many godly men and women is unquestionable, but that the genuine religion of the Jews is to be looked for in this class is an altogether different matter." Lake-Jackson, *Beginnings of Christianity*, Vol. I, p. 445.

[86] *Demai* III: 4; also *Abot R. Nathan* (ed. Schechter) I, XII.

[87] *Demai* II: 8.

[88] For a detailed study of the subject see A. Büchler, *Der Galiläische Am-Ha'Areṣ des Zweiten Jahrhunderts.* See also Strack-Billerbeck, *op. cit.*, II: 494–519.

[89] *Berachot* 47b ascribes the saying to Rabbi Eliezer and omits the word בברכותיה. This omission obscures the significance of the passage. From *Menahot* 99b we learn that the 'amme ha-aretz were opposed to the addition of the benedictions to the Shema.

acteries (*tefilin*) are placed in the same category. Ben 'Azzai considers those who have no tassels (*zizit*) in their garments as 'amme ha-aretz.[90] Rabbi Jonathan includes among them those who do not bring up their children for the study of Torah.[91] Failure to observe the Pharisaic rule of washing the hands before meals and carelessness or conscious disregard of the rules concerning priestly dues (*Terumot*) and tithes for the Levites (*maasrot*) rendered one an 'am ha-aretz.

It is significant that the term 'am ha-aretz designates men who studied Torah and even Mishnah, but who were not personally instructed by an accredited master.[92] We even hear of 'amme ha-aretz who possessed sufficient knowledge to act as teachers to the sons of Pharisees.[93] What is most surprising is to discover the application of the name 'am ha-aretz to a *hasid*. Thus the Talmud states "if the 'am ha-aretz is a hasid do not dwell in his neighborhood."[94] We are told of a prominent hasid (according to another version he was a high-priest) who, while living in accordance with the standards of *Hasidism*, had to be instructed in the true laws of ceremonial purity.[95] Accordingly Hillel teaches that "the 'am ha-aretz cannot be a hasid," claiming that true piety can be practiced only by the Pharisees.[96]

We may conclude on the basis of these facts that the barrier between the Pharisees and the 'amme ha-aretz was neither social nor cultural, but religious. It consisted in the divergent attitudes toward the so-called "tradition of the Elders," but which were in reality Pharisaic innovations. The 'amme ha-aretz were those who rejected the binding character of these regulations. The barrier vanished as soon as the 'amme ha-aretz subjected themselves to

[90] Jesus appears to have worn *Zizit*. Mark. 6 56; Matt. 9 20; Luke 8 44.

[91] *Sota* 22a. In the parallel passage *Ber.* 47b differences occur in the names of the rabbis.

[92] See also *Demai* II: 11 הבא לקבל עליו, אפילו תלמיד חכם צריך לקבל

[93] *Ibid.*, II: 15 בן חבר שלמד אצל עם הארץ

[94] *Sabbath* 63a אם עם הארץ הוא חסיד אל תדור בשכונתו

[95] *Ab. R. N.* I, XII and II, XXIV.

[96] *Aboth* II: 6; *Ab. R.N.* II: 33 presents this saying in the name of Rabbi Akiba with the important addition (פרוש) ולא עם הארץ חסיד.

the rules of the Pharisees. "An 'am ha-aretz who seeks to become a haber, if he previously followed the rules of *haberut* in private, is accepted immediately. Otherwise he has to be instructed first. Rabbi Simon says that he is accepted and taught afterwards. First he is admitted to *Kenafayim*-hand washing and subsequently to general ceremonial purity—*taharot*."[97]

Some of the 'amme ha-aretz were militant in their opposition to the Pharisees. A disciple of Shammai complained that "when you declare a utensil of an 'am ha-aretz impure, he not only disregards the ruling but turns around and says that his is pure but yours is impure."[98] The 'amme ha-aretz seem to have had their own Synagogues, where, we may conjecture, the Pharisaic innovations were not heeded. R. Dosa B. Horkinas (c. 10—90 C. E.) considered the assemblages at such synagogues most detrimental.[99] Their synagogues were mere social centers, devoid of sacredness.[100] Rabbi Akiba testified that in the days when he was an 'am ha-aretz he was ready to bite and crush the rabbis. And another statement reads: "Great is the hatred of the 'amme ha-aretz for the rabbis, far greater than the hatred of the heathen for Israel; and their wives hate even more." The 'amme ha-aretz tested the patience of the rabbis beyond endurance, and drew vehement denunciations.[101] However, the Pharisees did not give up hope of winning over all fellow-Jews to their viewpoint.[102] In *Aboth* of R. Nathan we read: "Say not love the scholars and hate the 'amme ha-aretz, but love them all."[103] "Whoever brings a single creature under the wings of the Schechina is as if he had created it."[104] Teaching the 'amme ha-aretz was, therefore, the ambition

---

[97] *Tos. Demai* II: 9.

[98] *Ḥagiga* 22b.

[99] *Aboth* III: 10. A. H. Silver suggests that the synagogues of the Judeo-Christians are meant. See "The 'Am Ha-Aretz in Soferic and Tanaitic Times," in *Hebrew Union College Monthly*, Vol. I (1914–15), No. 5.

[100] *Sabb.* 32a ר' שמעון בן אלעזר אומר בעון שני דברים עם הארצות מתים. על שקורין לארון הקודש ארנא ועל שקורין לבית הכנסת בית עם

[101] *Pesaḥ*, 49b.   [102] *Ab. R.N.* I: III.

[103] *Ibid.*, XVI.   [104] *Ibid.*, II: XXVI.

of the Pharisees. "He who teaches his friend's son Torah will merit to sit in the Academy on High; and he who teaches the son of an 'am ha-aretz Torah, even if God had issued a decree against him, He will annul it."[105] Hence Rabban Simeon b. Gamaliel rules that "laws pertaining to holy things (*Kodesh*), priestly dues (*terumot*) and tithes (*ma'asrot*) are fundamentals of the Torah (*gufe torah*), and are delivered to the 'amme ha-aretz."[106]

IV. JESUS AS AN 'AM HA-ARETZ HASID

The testimony of the Synoptic Gospels makes Jesus an *'Am Ha-Aretz Ḥasid*. As an 'am ha-aretz, he refused to subject himself to Pharisaic innovations. He deliberately broke the rules of washing his hands before meals, he partook of the food of 'amme ha-aretz without fear that it was not properly tithed, and he mingled with all classes of people without regard to ceremonial defilement.[107] Inasmuch as the term 'am ha-aretz covers all non-Pharisees, including the priestly class of Sadducees, Leszynsky is justified in pointing to a certain kinship which existed between Jesus and the Sadducees.[108] It consisted in their common 'am ha-aretz opposition to the "tradition of the Elders." Beyond that their agreement ceased. His construction of the *Lex Talionis* radically departed from their literal interpretation of that law.[109] The Gospels refer to the resurrection as the chief point of doctrinal difference between them.[110] The crucial element of friction consisted in his Messianic consciousness. Socio-political, no less than religious considerations, rendered the Sadducees impervious to his appeal. As Messianic claimant he threatened their regime, endangered the public peace and portended eventual war with Rome. While as Jews they shared the Messianic hope, they saw no more reason than

---

[105] *B. Mez.* 85a. See also *Abot R. Nathan* I: III.
[106] *Sabbath* 32b.
[107] Mark. 2 13ff.; Matt. 10 10ff.
[108] *Die Sadduzäer*, pp. 281ff.
[109] Matt. 5 38ff.
[110] Mark. 12 18–27; Matt. 22 23–33; Luke 20 27–38. See note 45.

did the Pharisees for identifying the obscure Galilean with the Messiah[111].

While he won over a Zealot and possibly a few Pharisees,[112] he recruited most of his disciples from the inferior ranks of the 'amme ha-aretz. John speaks of them as "the mob, ignorant of the Law;" and the book of Acts describes them as "uncultured persons"—*idiotai*, a term frequent in rabbinical literature for "common folk."[113] They followed the religion of their fathers, as a matter of course, without practicing the austerities and the rigorism of the Pharisees. What distinguished them from the rest of the 'amme ha-aretz was their extraordinary faith in their master. Peter recognized his Messianic character and a few others soon came to share this conviction.[114] In turn he showered his affection upon them and considered them nearer to him than his mother and brothers.[115] Though some of them were sinners, he ranked them above the righteous Pharisees.[116] He prayed: "I praise thee, Father, Lord of heaven and earth, for hiding all this from the wise and learned and revealing it to the simple-minded."[117] He spoke of them tenderly as "the little ones,"[118] and guarded them as a shepherd his flock. He taught them: "Beware of the Scribes! They like to walk about in long robes, to get salutations in the market places, to secure the front seats in the synagogues and the best places at banquets: they prey upon the property of widows and offer long unreal prayers. All the heavier will their sentence be."[119] Matthew adds to this diatribe against the Pharisees: "They make up heavy loads and lay them on men's shoulders but they will not stir a finger to remove them. Besides, all they do is

---

[111] C. G. Montefiore, *op. cit.*, I, p. CXXIII, and Torrey, "Outcroppings of Jewish Messianic Hope," in *Studies in Early Christianity*, pp. 306–09.

[112] Matt. 13 52.

[113] John 7 49; Acts 4 13.

[114] Mark. 8 27–29; Matt. 16 13–20; Luke 9 18–21. See also Mark. 10 35 ff.

[115] Matt. 12 46 ff.

[116] Luke 18 9–15; Matt. 11 17–19; 21 31–32.

[117] Matt. 11 25 and Luke 10 21.

[118] Mark. 9 42; Matt. 10 42; 18 6, 10, 14; 21 16; Luke 17 2; 21 16.

[119] Mark. 12 38–40; Luke 20 45–47.

done to catch the notice of men; they make their phylacteries broad, they wear large tassels, they are fond of the best places at banquets and the front seats in the synagogues; they like to be saluted in the market places and to be called 'rabbi' by men."[120] Whatever may be said about the genuineness of the remainder of the chapter these words ring true to the general character of Jesus as an 'Am Ha-aretz.

It is sometimes maintained that Jesus sought to break down the barrier that separated the Pharisees from the 'amme ha-aretz. It is more in accord with the evidence that he sought to overthrow the whole system of religion for which Pharisaism stood. The righteousness which he preached was supposed to have been of a higher type than that of the Pharisees. In his interpretations of the Torah, he stressed the spiritual essence underlying the ritual commands, which, according to the Gospels, the authoritative interpreters of the Torah had failed to do. While they clung to the externals of the Law, he chose to fathom its inner depths. In reality he was not as far removed from at least some of his opponents in his emphasis on inwardness as he and his disciples may have supposed.

The fine traits of spirituality which he exhibits are characteristic of the men who during Maccabean times emerge as the *Kehal Hasidim*, defending with their lives their ancient traditions and piety, and returning to their peaceful life as soon as the danger that threatened their faith was over. They continue to figure no longer as a *Kahal* but as individuals until the time of the Bar Cochba revolt, when the term *hasid* began to be used extensively by the rabbis for any "law abiding man who conscientiously practices the moral duties."[121]

As their name indicates they conducted themselves in accordance with the principle of *Hesed*, mercy. Dr. Adolph Büchler writes: "The records inform us of their love of God as the guiding principle of their actions, their humility, their active love and kindness to their neighbors as the determining features of their

---

[120] Matt. 23 4ff., cf. vss. 2–3. See also Luke 11 39ff.

[121] A. Büchler, *Some Types of Jewish Palestinian Piety*, p. 41.

character, their attachment to God and their close relation with Him expressed in their general piety, their devout prayer, their humble interpretation of their illness as a cleansing of sin, their over-great fear of unknown transgression, and the frequent atonement for such by sacrifices."[122] Dr. Büchler points to a tendency among the Hasidim to minimize sacrifice, expressed in the Proverb 16 6: "By mercy and truth (true loving kindness בחסד ואמת) iniquity is expiated (atoned for, יכפר), and by the fear of the Lord men depart from evil."

Though the Hasidim had much in common with the Essenes, we cannot find sufficient warrant for identifying the two. While some of them abstained from marriage we hear of others who led a normal family life, in homes of their own, and pursued various occupations. As pictured in the book of Daniel, in parts of Enoch, in the Psalms of Solomon and in the Talmudic sources, their piety was believed to endow them with the gift of prophecy. Rabbi Pinḥas b. Yair, a ḥasid of the 2nd century, presents the following steps of ḥasidic piety: "Care (זריזות) leads to cleanness (נקיות), cleanness to purity (טהרה), purity to [separateness (פרישות) and separateness to] holiness; holiness to humility; humility to fear of sin; fear of sin to piety (חסידות); and piety to the Holy Spirit."[123] The gift of prophecy expressed itself in the ecstatic visions familiar to us in Daniel, Enoch and other apocalyptic writings, in mystic speculations about angels, Heaven and Hell, the Judgment, the Kingdom of God, the advent of the Messiah, the Resurrection and Olam Habba.

---

[122] *Ibid.*, p. 192.

[123] *Abod. Zara* 20 b. רבי פנחס בן יאיר אומר זריזות מביאה לידי נקיות.
נקיות מביאה לידי טהרה. טהרה מביאה לידי קדושה. קדושה מביאה לידי
ענוה. ענוה מביאה לידי יראת חטא. יראת חטא מביאה לידי הסידות. חסידות
מביאה לידי רוח הקדש. רוח הקדש מביאה לידי תחית המתים. תחית
המתים מביאה לידי אליהו ז״ל. *Jer. Shek.* III, 3; *Jer. Sab.* 1: 3; *Cant. R.L.* 1–9; *Mid. Prov.* 15, 32, 41 a. *Sota* IX end, where the editions include also: וטהרה מביאה לידי פרישות. ופרישות מביאה לידי קדושה. The version in *Yalkut Shimoni* to Deut 23 10 adds: תורה מביאה [לידי זהירות, זהירות מביאה לידי זריזות. For a discussion of this passage see Büchler, *op. cit.* pp. 42 ff.

The Ḥasidim were distinguished by their high moral attainments, by their love of their fellowmen, and by their gentleness and patience. Not to reward evil with evil was one of their tenets. Both God and man they sought to serve with joy. They engaged in works of charity and of healing. Some of them gained fame as miracle workers. Various striking legends are current about Onias or Ḥoni the Circle Drawer, his grandsons Abba Ḥilkiah and Hanan, and about R. Hanina ben Dosa and R. Pinḥas b. Yair. People of all classes turned to them for aid. Even men like Rabban Johanan b. Zakkai and Rabban Gamaliel asked for their prayers. They were particularly sought in times of public distress. It is reported of Ḥanan, the grandson of Onias, that when rain was needed, the rabbis would send school children to him, who would pull him by the coat tails, calling: "Abba give us rain." Whereupon the saint prayed: "Lord of the world, for the sake of these little ones who cannot distinguish between the *Abba* (Father) who giveth rain and the *abba* (father) who can only ask without being able to produce rain, answer Thou my prayer."[124]

While some Ḥasidim, like Hillel, Hanina b. Dosa, R. Yeshobeb, Ben 'Azzai, etc. were Pharisees (חסיד פרוש), others, as we noted above, were not. Neither Onias nor his grandsons seem to have belonged to the Pharisaic ranks.[125]

His emphasis on faith, prayer and forgiveness, on love even for the enemy, and on returning good for evil, places Jesus in the company of the Hasidim who stood outside of Pharisaism. Like them he went in his Haggadic preaching beyond the letter of the Law to its innermost spirit. Like them too he claimed the possession of the Holy Spirit and manifested it in his ministry of healing and of prayer.

---

[124] *Ta'an*, 23 b. Cf. Mark. 10 18 "Why call me good?"

[125] Onias is referred to as מגים דעתו כלפי מעלה and was threatened by Simeon b. Shetaḥ, the Pharisaic leader, with excommunication, *Ber.* 19 a; *Ta'an*. 19 a. Josephus refers to this saintly soul in his *Antiquities* XIV, II, 1. He died the death of a martyr for refusing to pray against the Sadducees. Abba Ḥilkiah, too, seems to have stood at a distance from the Pharisees.

THE "PAULINE" EMANCIPATION
FROM THE LAW
A Product of the Pre-Christian
Jewish Diaspora

by
M. FRIEDLÄNDER

THE "PAULINE" EMANCIPATION FROM THE LAW A PRODUCT OF THE PRE-CHRISTIAN JEWISH DIASPORA.

THE view which I presented in my essay on " Judaism in the pre-Christian Greek World," namely, that the Jewish Diaspora of that time was divided into two opposite religious camps—one law-abiding and national, the other addicted to philosophical analysis of the original text of Scripture and advocating unlimited universalism, has failed to receive the critics' approval [1].

One very weighty authority against this view need only be named. Schürer, in his notice of my essay, says: " Such a split of the Diaspora into two opposing parties is incapable of demonstration. Certainly there were many shades and degrees of thought. But the freest and most emancipated retained certain fundamental points of ceremonial Judaism, such as the Sabbath and the elementary regulations concerning diet and hygiene. If therefore the author postulates that both tendencies were merely transferred from Judaism to Christianity, his theory is vitiated at its source. The particular renunciation of the Law which Paul started is certainly not Jewish, and the influence of Hellenistic Judaism on Christianity in apostolic times, even in those of Paul, was very moderate. On the other hand, in the post-apostolical period it must have been of considerable importance." Obviously Schürer and other eminent critics regarded my views as insufficiently supported and therefore unacceptable. I will therefore

[1] *Theolog. Litteraturzeitung*, 1897, No. 12.

make another attempt to defend and strengthen my position.

As soon as the Jews began to take root on Greek soil and became acclimatized amidst Greek surroundings, they had to mould and modify their religion in order to make possible their continued existence among the Gentiles. The narrow national and religious limits marked out by the Mosaic Law had necessarily to be expanded; and this perforce produced wide chasms and yawning gaps. That the Jews in the Diaspora soon found the national and religious cloak which they had brought away with them from their homeland too tight, and that they commenced to tear it to tatters, is demonstrated by the desperate attempts of their noblest leaders at already an early period to patch up the threadbare garment with new pieces of cloth, and refill the old bottles with new wine.

That the patches soon gave way and the old rents became wider, that the bottles burst and were utterly broken, one can learn from the history of the Diaspora, and the phenomenon is also most unmistakably repeated in Christianity soon after its birth.

In order, therefore, to adjust the Mosaic Law to the changed conditions of the dispersion, and to exhibit Judaism to the Gentiles as a system cognate with their sublimated philosophical conceptions, an act of gross self-deception was unconsciously perpetrated. The Mosaic Law received an allegorical interpretation at the hands of Jews who had quenched their thirst at the springs of Greek philosophy. Under their busy hands the whole of the Mosaic legislation was unconsciously transformed into a revealed divine philosophy. As Moses lived before the Greek sages, they must, it followed, have drawn their wisdom from him. This view was firmly held not merely by the pious allegorists of the dispersion, but also by Christianity's most eminent teachers in the first century.

That the allegorical interpretation of the Pentateuch had at an early period vogue amongst the Jews of the dispersion, is abundantly proved in every line of Philo, even if there were no other traditions to the same effect. Philo exhibits a masterly skill in this method of exegesis, such as only a long course of development could have produced. He nowhere claims to be the first inventor of the method, but regards it as a divine inspiration, and repeatedly refers to predecessors and teachers. There were indeed many exegetists of this class. One need only name Aristobulus, Pseudo-Aristeas, Pseudo-Solomon, the first of whom had exhibited prodigious feats in the use of the allegorical method.

And who will venture to doubt that from the completion of the Septuagint up till Philo's time there must have flourished, besides those already mentioned, a large band— both teachers and disciples—of allegorists.

Philo's writings are by themselves sufficient to enforce this view. This method necessarily divided the community into those on the one hand who followed the letter of the Law, and those on the other who disregarded ceremonialism.

But it may be urged that a division, such as is here indicated, is purely an assumption incapable of proof. I venture to think otherwise. Eusebius, who, on this question, had access to numerous sources, explicitly tells us: " The Judaism of the (Diaspora) falls into two divisions εἰς δύο τμήματα διῄρηται. The multitude scrupulously adhere to the Law. There are, however, also philosophical Jews who excel in virtue, have obtained a profounder insight into the spirit of the Law, and have learnt to look beneath the surface [1]."

This is clear testimony as to the existence of two religious parties, one Conservative, the other Liberal. Philo

[1] Eusebius, *Praep. ev.* VIII, 10 Ἑξῆς ἂν εἴη καὶ τόδε ἐπισημαίνεσθαι, ὡς τὸ πᾶν Ἰουδαίων ἔθνος εἰς δύο τμήματα διῄρηται, καὶ τὴν μὲν πληθὺν ταῖς τῶν νόμων κατὰ τὴν ῥητὴν διάνοιαν παρηγγελμέναις ὑποθήκαις ὑπῆγε· τὸ δὲ ἕτερον τῶν ἐκ ἕξει τάγμα ταύτης μὲν ἠφίει θειοτέρα δέ τινι καὶ τοὺς πολλοὺς ἐπαναβεβηκυίᾳ φιλοσοφίᾳ προσέχειν ἠξίου θεωρίᾳ τε τῶν ἐν νόμοις κατὰ διάνοιαν σημαινομένων· Ἦν δὲ τοῦτο φιλοσόφων Ἰουδαίων γένος ὢν τὴν τοῦ βίου ἄσκησιν καὶ τῶν ἔξωθεν κατεπλάγησαν μυρίοι.

himself is a classical witness to the marked contrast between these parties, which was forced upon his notice to his great grief. He, in vigorous terms, blames the radical party which first explained ceremonial Judaism allegorically and then rejected it. The passage which illuminates the obscurity that envelops the development of this sect reads as follows : " God said to Abraham, ' I will make thy name great.' This I take to mean that as it is excellent to be honourable and good, so is it advantageous to have a reputation for goodness. Whoever is in possession of both benefits is truly happy. For a good name is not to be despised. Only the man who observes the national laws and customs and does not attempt innovations is worthy of this fortune. There are, however, unfortunately men who, regarding the written precepts as mere emblems of spiritual truths, carefully search for the latter while contemning the former. Such individuals I cannot but blame, for they should bear in mind the hidden meaning and at the same time observe the precepts in their literal sense. They, however, live for themselves alone, as if they dwelt in a solitude or had disembodied souls. They ignore the town, the village, the home ; will hold no intercourse with others. Their ideal is to soar above the common herd and to apprehend the naked truth ; whilst the scriptures exhort us to seek a good name and to alter nothing in our laws which have been framed by uniquely gifted and inspired men.

" For, although the Sabbatical institution embodies the sublime conception, that activity belongs to God alone. While to his creatures mere passive receptivity is left, we nevertheless ought not, on that account, to permit ourselves to violate the commandment to hallow the Sabbath day by kindling fire, tilling the soil, bearing burdens, prosecuting lawsuits, administering justice, seeking the recovery of pledges or debts, or engaging in any occupation permitted on the other days of the week. Although every feast is in truth but an emblem of spiritual joy and gratitude to God, we should not therefore neglect the solemnities and customs associated with the feasts. Thus also, though the Abrahamic rite indicates the avoidance of voluptuousness and unchaste thoughts, we ought not therefore to neglect the observance of the precept. For if we resolved to retain these commandments only in their spiritual sense, we should consistently be compelled to give up the rites of self-sanctification in the temple and innumerable other necessary ceremonies. The literal sense of a precept is its body; the inner meaning, its soul. And as we take thought for the body as the mansion of the soul, so should we heed the commandments in their literal sense. Only thus can we hope to attain a clear comprehension of their true inwardness, apart from the fact that in this way alone shall we escape the censure of the multitude [1]."

Thus far Philo. Has our Alexandrian Jew in these remarks been merely addressing himself to the outside world of Gentiles? When, with sad heart, he places his finger upon a gaping wound in the body politic, is his motive anxiety to prevent a disastrous schism among his people, or is it to be regarded as adulation of the Greeks? Philo's wholesale censure upon an entire section of Jews was the cry of an anguished heart wrung from him by the peril of a complete split amongst the Jews of the dispersion. That these radical Jews, who fall under his censure, formed an influential class is indubitable. Else, why should Philo have thought it necessary to inaugurate an open, undisguised attack upon their system of life and thought, and expose the scandal of religious splits in the Jewish community to the gaze of the Greek heathen. Philo's indictment rests on a solid and unchallenged foundation of truth. What is the inference to be drawn? Surely nothing more nor less than this: *That before the dawn of Christianity there already existed in the dispersion a Jewish party, or, rather, to be more precise, a Jewish sect which, on the*

---

[1] *De Migrat. Abr.* I, 450.

ground of allegorical interpretation repudiated ceremonial
law, rejected the rite of circumcision, Sabbaths and festi-
vals, and other religious institutions; took their stand
outside national Judaism, and incurred the severe censure
not only of the masses of simple believers, but also of
liberal and cultured men of Philo's stamp.

How one can still maintain that there is no trace of
a division of the Diaspora into two diametrically opposed
sections passes my understanding. It is positively
inconceivable how, in face of Philo's positive statement,
an assertion of the following character can be made:
" Certainly there were degrees of piety ; but even the most
heterodox observed the principal ceremonial institutions,
such as the Sabbath and the elementary dietary and
sanitary regulations." Surely the passage quoted above
should convince us that if Philo severely censures a section
whose system of exegesis meets with his entire approval,
and of which he is so able an exponent, it can only be
because the party pushed the system to an extreme,
renounced all national and religious institutions, and so
provoked a reaction of resentment even among those
cultured Jewish circles who knew no better reason for
their advocacy of the observance of forms than reverence
for the illustrious dead who were their originators. This
party which, last not least, is reproached with having
severed its connexion with Judaism, must have been
Antinomians and must gradually have arrived at its
principles by an allegorical interpretation of the Mosaic
Law. A distinctly organized body who consciously expounded Holy Writ on exclusively allegorical lines and
aimed at eliciting the naked truth was the sect of Therapeutae. The characteristics with which Philo scathingly
qualifies the radicals seems to fit the Therapeutae like
a glove. The only discrepancy consists in the assumption
that these sectaries were a source of irritation to their
co-religionists. On the contrary they were looked upon
as specially pious, because of their observance of certain

ancient religious rites, to which however the allegorical
exegesis had given a foreign tinge.

Concerning the Therapeutae, Philo says: "They expounded the Mosaic Law allegorically, in the conviction
that the words were merely emblems and symbols of
mystical truths; they furthermore possessed writings of all
those sages who were founders of their sect and as such
had bequeathed to them several monuments of allegorical
wisdom which served them as aids to devotion[1]." And
in another passage he says: "The allegorical interpretation of Holy Writ helped them to fathom its deeper
import. The whole of the Mosaic legislation presented
itself to their minds as a living organism, of which the
literal meaning was the body, while the occult sense was
the soul. Reason regards the words as a mirror which
reflects with marvellous beauty and excellence an entire
range of connected ideas, gradually elucidates the inward
truths connoted by the symbols to those capable of com-
prehending them, and from apparently insignificant data
lead to an apprehension of the invisible in the visible[2]."

One may justly ask wherein lay the difference between
the Radical party attacked by Philo and the Therapeutae.
Why were the latter praised, the former blamed? Of the
Radicals, it is said that they regard the Laws as symbolic
of spiritual truths for which they search most scrupulously,
soaring above the masses in order to arrive at the naked
truth[3]. Did not the Therapeutae do the same? Almost the
identical words are used to describe their efforts—to bring
to light the real meaning of the written law[4].

The Therapeutae are praised because they compare the
Law to a living organism, whose body is the literal sense
and whose soul is the underlying meaning[5]. But the

---

[1] Philo, *De Vita Contempl.*, II, 475 f.   [2] Ibid., p. 483.

[3] Philo, *De Migrat. Abr.* I, 450 τὴν ἀλήθειαν γυμνὴν αὐτὴν ἐφ' ἑαυτῆς
ἐρευνῶσι.

[4] *De Vita Contempl.*, II, 483 γυμνὰ εἰς τὸ φῶς προαγαγοῦσα τὰ ἐνθύμια.

[5] Ibid. ἅπασα γὰρ ἡ νομοθεσία δοκεῖ τοῖς ἀνδράσι τούτοις ἐοικέναι ζώῳ· καὶ

Radicals, whom he reproaches, also teach, says Philo, that "the word is the body, the occult sense is the soul[1]." Exactly the same figure is used which suggests that it has been borrowed from the Therapeutae. Why then are the Therapeutae eulogized and the Radicals severely censured? The answer may, without much difficulty, be obtained from Philo himself. Attention should be fixed on the development of the simile. Philo continues : "Just as we take care of the body—the soul's mansion—so should we respect the laws in their literal meaning. For only by observing the latter shall we rise to a clear comprehension of the spirit; and only thus moreover can we escape popular censure." One fact is quite clear. The Radicals did, the Therapeutae did not, openly exhibit their contempt for the Law. They met, after the old-fashioned manner, in Synagogue on Sabbaths, observed festivals, conformed outwardly to Judaism; although, under the influence of their philosophical interpretation, religious ceremonies had assumed a foreign and un-Jewish aspect, which last fact, however, would by no means have been admitted by the Jewish Hellenists themselves. They were sincerely convinced that Moses would not have desired his laws to be otherwise understood than in the sense of Jewish Alexandrianism. This Philo's works sufficiently prove. To the same category belongs the religious community named in the fourth Sibylline book, whose author was a Hellenistic Jew. That community survived to a later period when Christianity had already assumed form and consistency and continued for some time to co-exist side by side with it. It was undoubtedly Hellenistic; and, like the Essenes had, by the path of allegoristic exegesis, arrived at a contempt for the temple worship and

---

σῶμα μὲν ἔχειν τὰς ῥητὰς διατάξεις ψυχὴν δὲ τὸν ἐναποκείμενον ταῖς λέξεσιν ἀόρατον νοῦν . . . .

[1] ἀλλὰ χρὴ ταῦτα μὲν σώματι νομίζειν ἐοικέναι ψυχῇ δὲ ἐκεῖνα. ὥσπερ οὖν σώματος, ἐπεὶ ψυχῆς ἐστιν οἶκος, προνοητέον οὕτω καὶ τῶν ῥητῶν νόμων ἐπιμελητέον.

sacrificial ritual, for which it substituted more spiritual exercises. The Sibyl characterizes as truly pious and happy individuals those who love the great God and praise him before every meal, while repudiating the efficacy of worship in the temple which is deaf and dumb, a pain and humiliation to mankind ; who, furthermore, bathe in flowing waters as a penance and preach repentance." These " pious Israelites " had already abjured national Judaism as well as the ceremonial law and renounced the temple service and its sacrificial cult as unworthy of the great God. In their gospel there was no room for the little word " law." Towards their brethren as a nation these pious souls showed themselves cold [1]. This sect is no doubt identical with those mentioned by Celsus and Origen, and known to the former, while in the time of the latter Church-father they were already extinct. As Origen was personally unacquainted with them he attempts to account for Celsus' Sibylline sect by the assumption that Celsus might have heard Christians blaming some of their co-religionists for regarding the Sibyl as a true prophetess, and that he therefore called them Sibyllists [2].

Moreover, Celsus' report that Sibyllists existed at his time amongst the Christians is confirmed by a contemporary, the pastor Hermas, who was also the first Christian author to mention the Sibyl. Hermas relates the following vision : A youth of majestic figure appeared to him in a dream and asked him who he thought was the old woman who gave the book. " She is," Hermas replied, " the Sibyl." " Nay," answered the apparition, " she is the Ecclesia." To Hermas' question why she is styled an old woman, the reply is vouchsafed because the Ecclesia was first in creation and the world exists for her sake

---

[1] Compare my work, *Das Judenth. in der vorchristl. jüd. Welt*, Wien, 1897, p. 56 ff.; Ewald, *Entsteh., Inhalt u. Wert der Sibyll. Bücher*, pp. 44 ff. and 51 ff.
[2] Orig., c. Cels., V, 61 f. εἶπε δέ (sc. ὁ Κέλσος) τινας εἶναι Σιβυλλιστὰς—τάχα παρακούσας τινῶν ἐγκαλούντων τοῖς οἰομένοις προφῆτιν γεγονέναι Σίβυλλαν καὶ Σιβυλλιστὰς τοὺς τοιούτους καλεσάντων.

alone [1]. This vision also indicates the mode in which, and
the period when the Ecclesia supplanted the Sibyl, as well
as the manner in which the Sibyllists were won for the
Church. Christian tradition dating from the first centuries prove the existence of Jewish sects in the Diaspora
before the birth of Christianity. Had one followed up
these traces, instead of obliterating them, as was the practice started by the later fathers of the Church and still
followed, a clearer view would have been obtained of the
origin of Christianity and of the still' obscure and unexplained function of sects within the Church.

Besides pre-Christian Jewish sects mentioned by Josephus
and in the New Testament, Justin the Martyr and Hegesippus
know others which undoubtedly belong to the Diaspora.
Next to the Sadduceans, Pharisees, Baptists, and Galileans,
he mentions Genists, Merists, and Hellenians. If we pay
regard to these traditions and do not hastily conclude that
the Genists, Merists, and Hellenians, Marbothians, &c., do
not count—as far as the history of Christian heresy is
concerned [2]—we should easily discover a relationship
between the pre-Christian Jewish heretics and Christianity
with its oldest sects.

Justin's tradition, which for our purpose is of the utmost
importance, is as follows: "If," says Justin to Tryphon
and his colleagues, " you have met with people who style
themselves Christian, but have no claim to the title, seeing
that they dare to blaspheme the God of Abraham, Isaac,
and Jacob, deny the resurrection of the dead, contend that
the soul goes direct to heaven, do not regard such as
Christians; just as little as any one with sound judgment
will allow that the Sadduceans and other heretics like
the Genists, Merists, and Hellenians were Jews; the only

---

[1] Hermas, Vis. II, 4. 1 Ἀπεκαλύφθη δέ μοι, ἀδελφοί, κοιμωμένῳ ὑπὸ νεα-
νίσκου εὐειδεστάτου λέγοντός μοι· Τὴν πρεσβυτέραν παρ' ἧς ἔλαβες τὸ βιβλίδιον
τίνα δοκεῖς εἶναι ; ἐγώ φημι· Τὴν Σίβυλλαν. Πλανᾶσαι, φησίν, οὐκ ἔστιν.
Τίς οὖν ἐστίν ; φημί. Ἡ Ἐκκλησία, φησίν. εἶπον αὐτῷ· Διατί οὖν πρεσβυτέρα ;
Ὅτι, φησίν, πάντων πρώτη ἐκτίσθη, καὶ διὰ ταύτην ὁ κόσμος κατηρτίσθη. Cf.
Vis. II, 1. 1.   [2] Hilgenfeld, Ketzergesch., p. 86.

feature these have in common with the body of their brethren is the name they bear and their descent from Abraham[1]."

The Hellenistic company in which the Genists and Merists are included clearly points to heretics of the dispersion; and surely it is not without purpose that Justin places the antinomian Christian heretics, who deny the resurrection of the body and regard the soul alone as immortal, side by side with the Judaeo-Hellenistic sects —the Genists, Merists, and Hellenians, they seem of the same class—with the sole difference that the latter are styled Jews, the former Christians. More exact traditions pointing to the pre-Christian origin of heresy we owe to Hegesippus, who introduces us to a sect omitted by Justin and called the Marbothians. He also thinks that all heresy is traceable to pre-Christian Judaism, which opposed it as much as Christianity afterwards did[2]. Jewish heresies led by a gradual transition to Christian heresies; and the arch-heretic Simon Magus constituted the link between them[3]. A marked silence concerning the sects into which the Jewish Diaspora split is observable at the beginning of the third century. Hand in hand with this studied reticence an effort is apparent to attribute all heresy to Christianity itself.

Thus the first arch-heretic mentioned is Simon Magus, who enacted his rôle during the infancy of Christianity, which he tried to counteract by heterodoxies. After Simon, *Magister et Progenitor omnium hereticorum*—as Irenaeus calls him—all bridges leading to the Diaspora were destroyed.

Heresy, as till to-day has been generally admitted,

---

[1] Justin, *Dial. c. Tr.*, cap. 80 ὥσπερ οὐδὲ Ἰουδαίους, ἄν τις ὀρθῶς ἐξετάσῃ, ὁμολογήσειεν εἶναι τοὺς Σαδδουκαίους· ἢ τὰς ὁμοίας αἱρέσεις Γενιστῶν καὶ Μεριστῶν . . . . . καὶ Ἑλληνανῶν . . . .

[2] Euseb., *Eccl. Hist.*, IV, 22. 7 Ἦσαν δὲ γνῶμαι διάφοροι ἐν υἱοῖς Ἰσραήλ, τῶν κατὰ τῆς φυλῆς Ἰούδα καὶ τοῦ Χριστοῦ αὗται, κ.τ.λ.

[3] Ibid., IV, 22. 5 ἀφ' ὧν Σίμων, ὅθεν οἱ Σιμωνιανοί, καὶ Κλεόβιος, κ.τ.λ.

developed a marked activity in the early Christian community. "In its very cradle," Hilgenfeld rightly says,
"a pair of serpents coiled round Christianity—the ethnical
and the Judaising heresies ; from infancy orthodoxy had
to battle against the monster heresy [1]." Little curiosity has
been expressed as to the origin of this monster, which is,
on its first appearance, already armed with pronounced
gnostic doctrines—surely not a product of the new creed.
One is content with the hasty assertion that pre-Christian
gnosticism was exceedingly primitive, a statement the
naïveté of which is obvious when one thinks of the high
standard attained by the Alexandrian gnosis in the time
of Jesus.

Such assertions are the necessary outcome of a reluctance
to acknowledge the influence exercised by the Jewish
Diaspora directly and immediately upon the development
of its daughter-faith.   For, after all, the first Christian
community sprang from the Synagogue of the Dispersion,
which counted among its adherents the Libertines, Cyre-
nians, Alexandrians, and the Cilicians—Asiatics among
whom Stephen developed, though at first cautiously, those
antinomian teachings which found a sympathetic hearing
with many, but were condemned by others as blasphemies
against Moses and God [2].

Here, then, we have two parties, the Conservative and
Radical. According to the Apostle Paul's opinion, as given
in the First Epistle to the Corinthians, heresy was, from
the first, an inevitable element in Christianity. The following remarkable words are put into the apostle's mouth :
"When you come together, I hear, there be divisions among
you, and I partly believe it, for there must be also heresies,
that they which are approved may be made manifest
among you"(1 Cor. xi. 18, 19)[3]. Here, then, is an authorita-

---

[1] *Ketzergesch.*, p. 2.   [2] Acts vi. 9 sq.

[3] συνερχομένων ὑμῶν ἐν τῇ ἐκκλησίᾳ, ἀκούω σχίσματα ἐν ὑμῖν ὑπάρχειν, καὶ
μέρος τι πιστεύω, δεῖ γὰρ καὶ αἱρέσεις ἐν ὑμῖν εἶναι, ἵνα οἱ δόκιμοι φανεροὶ γένωνται
ἐν ὑμῖν.

tive pronouncement concerning the existence of heresy in
the early Church, and its necessity in order that orthodoxy
should be clearly distinguished from it.

In opposition to this view, Hegesippus—who, as before
mentioned, regarded Christian heresy as a continuation of
Jewish heresy—pretends that, till Trajan's time, Christianity, where it was still untainted by futile controversies,
enjoyed uninterrupted peace, and that during the lifetime
of the apostles, heresy, if it at all existed, had not yet
dared to raise its head. Only after their death had the
reptile crept forth from its dim obscurity.

" The Church," so Eusebius reports Hegesippus [1], " was, up
to this time, an undefiled virgin ; they that sought to
falsify the pure teaching of the Gospel, if indeed there were
such, still kept in the background. But after the holy
apostolic choir had been hushed, and the generation that
had heard the divine wisdom had died out, there began the
conspiracy of a God-forsaken heresy fomented by false
teachers. When the apostles were no longer living, heresy
was brazen-fronted enough to dare to pit the Gnosis—
incorrectly so styled—against the Gospel of truth."

This account embodies much truth and affords us
a glimpse into the controversies which produced Christianity. It must, in the first place, be borne in mind that
Hegesippus speaks not merely of heretics but also of
heterodox gnosticism, which had raised its head after the
Apostles' death. The false gnosis was thus, already in
the Apostles' time, perniciously active, and it was only
their strenuous opposition which violently thrust it back
into the darkness, from which it again impetuously burst

---

[1] *Eccl. Hist.*, III, 32. 7, 8 ὡς ἄρα μέχρι τῶν τότε χρόνων παρθένος καθαρὰ
καὶ ἀδιάφθορος ἔμεινεν ἡ ἐκκλησία, ἐν ἀδήλῳ που σκότει φωλευόντων εἰσέτι τότε
τῶν, εἰ καί τινες ὑπῆρχον, παραφθείρειν ἐπιχειρούντων τὸν ὑγιῆ κανόνα τοῦ
σωτηρίου κηρύγματος. ὡς δὲ ὁ ἱερὸς τῶν ἀποστόλων χορὸς διάφορον εἴληφε τοῦ
βίου τέλος . . . . . τηνικαῦτα τῆς ἀθέου πλάνης ἀρχὴν ἐλάμβανεν ἡ σύστασις διὰ
τῆς τῶν ἑτεροδιδασκάλων ἀπάτης, οἳ καί, ἅτε μηδενὸς ἔτι τῶν ἀποστόλων λειπο-
μένου, γυμνῇ λοιπὸν ἤδη τῇ κεφαλῇ τῷ τῆς ἀληθείας κηρύγματι τὴν ψευδώνυμον
γνῶσιν ἀντικηρύττειν ἐπεχείρουν.

forth after their decease. But it had been in existence from the beginning. Gnostic teachings clearly did not spring up in a night, but had passed through a long course of evolution. What, however, was the origin of this gnosticism, which notwithstanding the Apostles' antagonism, exercised a mighty influence upon the formation of the new creed? Hegesippus furnishes a reply. It came from pre-Christian Judaism ; and, one may add, from the Judaism of the dispersion, which before the advent of Christianity already possessed a fully developed gnosis based on allegory ; and this was afterwards transferred into the Christian Church [1].

Of immense value also is Origen's remark [2] concerning the schisms in the early Christian community. "At first," he says, "the believers cherished a diversity of views concerning the meaning of the Holy Scriptures ; and this was the case at the time when the Apostles preached and men who with their own eyes had seen Jesus proclaimed his teaching."

In the epistles of St. Paul, who lived in the days of eye-witnesses of Jesus, there are passages which indicate that some doubted the resurrection and asked whether it had already taken place. And the same apostle's admonition, "Beware of profane debates and of the disputes of a spurious gnosis," shows that at the period when, according to Celsus, the number of believers was but small, there were some who misconstrued religious doctrines.

At the dawn of the third century gnosticism had made so many conquests on Christian soil, the adherents of "the spurious gnosis" had grown so numerous and invested with so much authority, that they posed as masters of the situation and played the rôle of teachers of true Christianity, which they shook to its very foundations. Then commenced a severe struggle, in the course of which the

---

[1] Compare my essay, *Zur Entstehungsgeschichte des Christenthums*, Wien, 1894, p. 8 ff.

[2] *Contra Celsum*, III, 11.

memory of the pre-Christian heretics of the Jewish Diaspora was thrust into oblivion—an oblivion encouraged by
the parties interested, who were thus enabled to represent
all heresy as an offshoot of Christianity. This attitude
was also forced upon them by learned heathen antagonists
like Celsus, who reproached the Christians with being
split up into so many sects that their religion itself was
hidden from view, or appeared nothing else than one of the
innumerable heresies which had grown up contemporane-
ously or at an earlier period.

It was therefore the Church's business to prove that it
was the mother of all heresies—new or old—which could
by any stretch be brought into relation with itself.

Christianity was the source, and all schisms were the
impure rivulets flowing from it. Tertullian strikingly
proves the success of this method in repelling the attacks
of heathens and heretics. "Surely it is unnatural," he
says, " to suppose that the true doctrine was an innova-
tion preceded by heresy, for did not the true creed foretell
the advent of heretics ?" The tares clearly sprang up after
the good ears[1]. Under these circumstances it is conceivable that pre-Christian Jewish sects which stood as
sponsors at the cradle of Christianity, though they had
till the end of the first century remained purely Jewish
sects which had made no concessions to the new faith,
were nevertheless stamped as Christian heresies by a
Church engaged in a vital struggle with external and
internal foes[2].

And even to-day, when the traces that guide one's footsteps from Christian gnosticism to its pre-Christian Jewish
predecessor have become almost obliterated, we can,

---

[1] Tertull., *De Praescr. Haer.*, 29 ff.

[2] The Pharisees, Sadducees, and Herodians, often mentioned in Josephus
and the New Testament, form an exception ; they stood quite outside the
pale of Christianity. Concerning the relation of the Essenes to that creed,
the reader is referred to my work, *Zur Entstehungsgeschichte des Christenthums,*
98–142.

amongst the innumerable Christian heresies reported by
the Church, distinguish those which sprang from Jewish
Alexandrianism. These heretics reveal themselves as the
children of the antinomian radicals of the Jewish Diaspora,
upon whom Philo passes such severe strictures. We need
only describe the Ophites, Cainites, Sethites, and Melchizedekites. The earliest history of heretics already mentions
the first three sects as belonging to the same category.
The common character of their teaching can be inferred
from the fact that the Ophites were often confounded with
the Sethites—some even maintaining that the Ophites were
called Sethites [1].

These sects were eminently antinomian. This is proved
not only from the position which they traditionally
assumed towards the Mosaic Law and from the Old
Testament figures selected by them as representatives of
their " spiritual Dynamis," but also from express testimony to the same effect [2].

The earliest accounts of the Ophites [3] can, as regards
essentials, be easily compressed into the statement that
this sect worshipped the serpent which secured for mankind the gift of knowledge of good and evil. Moses
showed his reverence for its power by making a brazen
serpent. As it opened up to man the perception of the
true and august God, the serpent is a divine force worthy
of adoration [4], an incarnation of the divine Sophia [5].

Here we have the Alexandrian doctrine of the Dynamis.
The serpent is Sophia incarnate. The Jewish Alexandrian
School, as we read in Philo, and its predecessors regarded

---

[1] Theodoret, I, 14 Σηθιανοί, οὓς ὀφιανοὺς ἢ ὀφίτας ὀνομάζουσιν . . . .

[2] Blasphemant legem et deum legis auctorem, is said of the Cainites in
Augustine, Haer., XVIII.

[3] Iren., Haer. I, 30; Pseudo-Tertull., c. 6; Philaster, 1; Epiphan.,
XXXVI.

[4] Philaster, Haer., 1 et velut aliquam dei virtutem esse eundem aestimant, atque eum adnuntiant adorandum.

[5] Irenaeus, Haer., XXX. 15 Quidam enim ipsam Sophiam serpentem
factam dicunt.

the Sophia as the power which preceded the world and
created it. This idea was founded upon the much-dis-
cussed passage in Proverbs, in which Wisdom declares,
"God created me, the first of all his works, and before
the ages he formed me[1]." The Cainites[2] adored the divine
Dynamis in Cain. This force, manifested in him in great
strength[3], overpowered the weaker Dynamis in Abel,
whom it destroyed[4]. The Cainites permitted and indulged
in all sensual excesses, teaching that none can attain to
bliss who had not indulged the bodily appetites to the full.
All should endeavour to choose a Dynamis stronger than
that weak one that created the world. The Cainites
blasphemed the Law and God its author, and denied the
resurrection of the body[5].

Could this sect have sprung from Christianity? What
is there Christian about it except perhaps its later gnostic
additions absorbed under the influence of the Christian
gnosis? All else points to the Alexandrian school, of which
it represents the extreme left section. Moreover we find
this sect clearly sketched by Philo. Cain he conceived as
the incarnation of foolish arrogance and self-conceit, which
claims everything as its own. The very name Cain, meaning possession, describes the character[6]. There are, says
Philo in another passage, two opposing views, the one
ascribing everything to individual mind, guide of all
thought, feeling and desires, the other leaves everything
to God. The one is represented by Cain, the other by
Abel[7]. Cain's challenge was only intended to provoke

---

[1] Cf. M. Friedländer, *Zur Entstehungsgeschichte des Christenthums*, pp. 8–36.

[2] Iren., *Haer.*, I, 31. 2; Pseudo-Tert., 7; Philaster, 2; Epiphan.,
XXXVII; Theodor., I, 15.

[3] Augustine, c. 18 Cainani propterea sic appellati, quoniam Cain hono-
rant, dicentes *eum fortissimae esse virtutis.*

[4] Philaster, 2 et virtutem maiorem, quae erat in ipso Cain, invaluisse
ut suum interficeret fratrem.

[5] Augustine, 18 *Blasphemant legem, et deum legis auctorem,* carnisque
resurrectionem negant.

[6] Philo, *De Cherub.*, I, 150 f.   [7] *De Sacrif.*, I, 163.

his brother Abel to a discussion and to vanquish him by
sophistries that had the appearance of truth, and when, at
the present time, Philo continues, the egoists discuss with
the moralists, they do not stop until they have subdued
and wholly destroyed them.   The evolution of their principles runs on the following lines : Is not the body the
habitation of the soul?   Must we not therefore take
exceeding care of this habitation?   Are not the eyes, the
ears, and other senses the constant companions and friends
of the soul, and, as such, do they not deserve due honour ?

*Has nature created sensuality, delights, and all the
pleasures of life for the dead and yet unborn, or rather
for the living?*   Why shall we not strive for riches,
honours, power, and other similar advantages which secure
*a safe and happy life ?   Proofs of the justice of these senti-
ments are the lives*[1] of these so-called moralists, who are
nearly all obscure, despised, wretched, and in indigent
circumstances.   With such sophistries they seem to have
vanquished those unaccustomed to casuistry.   But Abel,
whose spirit was all goodness, and who had not attained to
the specious arts of the rhetorician, ought to have refused
Cain's challenges[2].   More important still for our purpose is
the following passage.   Philo says : What is the view of
the ungodly ?   It is that *the human intellect is the measure
of everything*; a theory said to have been promulgated
by an old sophist Protagoras, an expounder and champion
of Cain's perversities[3].   How could you (philosophers)
dare to pronounce or to listen to sublime phrases concerning holiness and divine worship when you attributed[4] all
good and evil entirely or partially to mortals?   And if
anybody charges you with impiety, you boldly defend
yourselves with the statement *that you have been educated
in it by the excellent example and precept of Cain, who*

---

[1] μάρτυς δὲ ὁ βίος τούτων.

[2] Philo, *Quod det. pot. insid. solet*, I, 191, 197 ff.

[3] *De Posterit.*, 232 τῆς Κάϊν ἀπονοίας ἔκγονον.

[4] εἰ δὲ ἔχετε παρ' ἑαυτοῖς τὸν ἀντίθεον νοῦν.

taught men to honour the nearer rather than the remoter cause? Apart from all reasons it is right to follow him, as he irrefutably demonstrated the force of his teaching by vanquishing Abel, the champion of the opposite view [1].

Most striking of all is the following allegory, which shows that Philo not only knew but combated the antinomian sect of the Cainites. This remarkable passage reads as follows: *As every town consists of houses and inhabitants, so Cain regarded his proofs as structures, from which he repulses the attack of his adversaries, devising fictions instead of truth.* The inhabitants are accomplices in the crime of godlessness, self-love, arrogance, and falsehood; they imagine themselves wise without knowing true wisdom, they heap up foolishness, stupidity, ignorance, and other kindred plagues. Their laws are lawlessness, injustice, unfairness, licentiousness, impudence, audacity, lustful intemperance, and indulgence in innumerable unnatural desires. Such impious men form, in their depravity, communities, until God, incensed at their sophistries, suddenly and violently overthrows them, even though they have built not only a town, but also a town with a tower reaching up to heaven [2]. Here

---

[1] *De Posterit.*, I, 232 κἂν ἄρα τις γραφὴν ἀσεβείας ἐπενέγκῃ καθ' ὑμῶν, ἀπολογούμενοι θαρρεῖτε, φάσκοντες παρ' ὑφηγητῇ καὶ διδασκάλῳ πάνυ καλῶς πεπαιδεῦσθαι Κάϊν, ὃς τὸ πλησίον πρὸ τοῦ μακρὰν αἰτίου παρήνει τιμᾶν, ᾧ διά τε ἄλλα προσεκτέον καὶ μάλισθ' ὅτι σαφέσιν ἔργοις τὴν τοῦ δόγματος ἰσχὺν ἐπεδείξατο, νικήσας τὴν τῆς ἐναντίας δόξης εἰσηγητὴν Ἄβελ, καὶ ἅμ' αὐτοῦ τὴν δόξαν ἐκποδὼν ἀνελών.

[2] *De Posterit.*, I, 225 Ἐπειδὴ τοίνυν πᾶσα πόλις ἐξ οἰκοδομημάτων καὶ . . . . συνέστηκε· τὰ μὲν οἰκοδομήματά ἐστιν αὐτῷ λόγοι οἱ ἀποδεικνύντες· οἷς, καθάπερ ἀπὸ τείχους, πρὸς τὰς τῶν ἐναντίων ἀπομάχεται προσβολὰς πιθανὰς εὑρέσεις κατὰ τῆς ἀληθείας μυθοπλαστῶν. οἰκήτορες δὲ οἱ ἀσεβείας, ἀθεότητος, φιλαυτίας, μεγαλαυχίας, ψεύδους, δόξης ἑταῖροι, δοκησίσοφοι, τὸ πρὸς ἀλήθειαν σοφὸν οὐκ εἰδότες, ἄγνοιαν καὶ ἀπαιδευσίαν καὶ ἀμαθίαν καὶ τὰς ἄλλας ἀδελφὰς καὶ συγγενεῖς κῆρας συγκεκροτηκότες. νόμοι δὲ ἀνομίαι, ἀδικίαι, τὸ ἄνισον, τὸ ἀκόλαστον, θρασύτης, ἀπόνοια, αὐθάδεια, ἡδονῶν ἀμετρίαι, τῶν περὶ φύσεως ἄλεκτοι ἐπιθυμίαι. Τοιαύτης πόλεως ἕκαστος τῶν ἀσεβῶν ἐξ ἑαυτοῦ τῇ παναθλίᾳ ψυχῇ δημιουργὸς εὑρίσκεται. μέχρις ἂν ὁ θεὸς βουληθεὶς ταῖς σοφιστικαῖς αὐτῶν τέχναις ἀθρόαν καὶ μεγάλην ἐργάσηται σύγχυσιν. Τοῦτο δ' ἔσται, ὅταν μὴ μόνον πόλιν καὶ πύργον οἰκοδομῶσιν, οὗ ἡ κεφαλὴ εἰς οὐρανὸν ἀφίξεται . . . .

we find then a sect described as the philosophizing sect, who chose the self-worshipping Cain as the guide of their lives, their teacher and master, a sect which, in accordance with the sophist Protagoras' axiom, "The human intellect is the measure of all things," revered in Cain the supreme force. The theories of this party are based on a web of sophistry. Instead of law they proclaimed lawlessness. Orthodoxy personified in Abel was combated and defeated by the superiority of the higher Dynamis incorporated in Cain. The body, the mortal frame of the soul, is not only permitted but also enjoined to taste sensual pleasures. This is precisely Cainitism, as depicted in the earliest heresiology.

This sect, as we read in Philo, was particularly dangerous on account of the rhetorical skill possessed by its representatives, and seemed to have produced a mental ferment of an extensive and perilous character. For Philo warns all virtuous people unskilled in sophistry not to enter into disputations with them. Only those should oppose them who have mastered every device in the art of controversy. Then the pious would no longer be vanquished by their weakness in dialectics, but would easily avoid the sophist's traps. Properly grappled these sectaries would prove unsubstantial opponents. Successful in detached argument, earnest and organized controversy would discomfit them[1].

Next we come to the Sethites[2]. These are reported to have shared the chief errors of the Ophites and the Cainites. According to them, everything was created by the angels and not by the Higher Dynamis. The Superior Power which they term Mother became all-powerful, and after Abel's death gave life to Seth and bestowed upon him that heavenly spark by which the force of the creative angels was shattered[3].

---

[1] *De Posterit.*, I, 225.
[2] Philaster, 3; Epiphan., *Haer.*, XXXIX; Pseudo-Tert., c. 8.
[3] Philaster, 3 Quod providens, inquiunt, mater, quia occisus est Abel

The Sethites call Seth the Messiah[1]. The three sects here named, the Ophites, Cainites, and Sethites, undoubtedly belong to the pre-Christian Jewish Diaspora; their disciples were recruited from the Radicals. Just as the Synagogue generally everywhere counted among its adherents numerous sympathizers among Greek heathendom, so the Radical section was also joined by philosophizing heathens whom Philo dubs "the echoes of Cain's perverse theories." If an investigation had been instituted—as strangely enough has not yet been done—into the measure of influence which these proselytes—many of them adherents from the various philosophical schools—exercised upon the religious evolution of Judaism in the Diaspora, quite different views would have been accepted as to the origin and development of Christianity.

The paths trodden by Judaism in the Greek world, which have not yet been sufficiently explored, would become clear. The supreme importance of Christianity —the ripest fruit of this evolution—would remain undiminished. Even the Talmud, notwithstanding its dark presentiments, lauded as an ideal of the future the union between the Jephetic and Semitic spirits. Unhealthy symptoms undoubtedly preceded and succeeded the birth of a child, whose parents, notwithstanding the diversity of their characters, external circumstances had forced into an unnatural union; but it must be remembered that both father and mother were of originally healthy stock. The innumerable Jewish sects, from whose midst Christianity stepped to the front and by which it was accompanied like a shadow on its world-conquering path, afford evidence of the vigour of religion in the Jewish Diaspora. The principal excrescences were the sects of the Ophites, Cainites, and Sethites.

---

iustus, cogitavit ut pareret iustum Seth in quem et *collocavit magnae virtutis spiritum*, ut possint destrui virtutes inimicae.

[1] Ibid., Quidam autem ex eis non solum genus de eo deducere, sed etiam ipsum Christum esse asserunt atque opinantur.

Of the Melchizedekians I will speak later on.   Even
these spirits of infidelity, who consistently pursued evil,
nevertheless worked unconsciously for good by the prominence into which they forced Judaism and Christianity,
whose orthodox followers repelled those sects.   They were
repudiated by Philo and also by Christianity as soon as it
had become conscious of its mission.

Philaster enumerates the Ophites, Cainites, and Sethites
among the sects flourishing among the Jews before the
advent of Jesus.   Origen repeatedly and emphatically protests against the notion that the Ophites, Cainites, and
similar sects belonged to Christianity.   Thus he says:
" Celsus may possibly have heard of some sects which do
not even share the knowledge of Jesus with us.   He may
have heard of the so-called Ophites, Cainites, and other sects
who entirely renounced Christ.   But this does not justify
him in the reproach which he levels against Christianity[1]."
In another place he replies to Celsus' stricture: " That the
Christians imprecated the Creator for cursing the serpent
which brought the knowledge of good and evil to our
first parents.   Celsus ought to have known," he says,
" that the Ophites, so-called on account of their adoration
of the serpent for its good counsel to the first authors of
the human race, by which they overcame the Titans and
giants of the fable, are so little in sympathy with
Christianity that they hurl against Jesus the same
abominable charges as Celsus himself does, and refuse
to admit any one to their society who has not first pronounced imprecations against the Saviour.   It should be
noted that Celsus puts his case in his polemic against
Christianity so clumsily that he even recognizes as
Christians those who would not hear the name of Jesus
and denied that he was a virtuous man.   Can any one be
conceived more perverse than these Ophites, to whom the
serpent was the source and instrument of all goodness,
unless it be Celsus himself, who says that the charges

---

[1] Orig., c. Cels., III, c. 13.

against the Ophites were also justified against the Christians? The Greek philosopher who lived in poverty, and who sought to prove by his personal example that happiness is possible without wealth, styled himself a cynic. But these godless people act as though they were not human beings, to whom the serpent is an enemy, but rather serpents themselves. They glory in tracing their name Ophite to the reptile which is dreaded and loathed as the deadliest foe of the human race [1]."

The above three sects are not therefore in any way the offspring of Christianity. This, even apart from Philaster's and Origen's evidence, is, in our opinion, beyond question. The circumstances that they sought their *Dynamis* in the Old and not in the New Testament sufficiently indicates their Jewish origin. They are undoubtedly children of the Diaspora, and, to speak more definitely, they formed the extreme left wing of the allegorical school of Alexandria. They stood in sharp opposition to the Conservatives of this school. Here, heterodox Cain ; there, orthodox Abel ! The allegorizing Conservatives wished the Law to be scrupulously observed, although it had been disintegrated by their peculiar system of hermeneutics. They were actuated by reverence for the lofty-minded teachers who had created it. They also had regard to the sentiments of the large multitude of believers in literal inspiration. The Radicals, on the other hand, had thrown the Law completely overboard. For in their estimation it was already a thing of shreds and tatters. In the work of destruction they proceeded methodically, employing weapons with which the Law itself had furnished them. Their conception of the divine Dynamis—the instrument used by them for the process of disintegration—they borrowed from the Old Testament. From the same source was derived the idea of the serpent which endowed man with the gnosis, as well as the biblical figures of Cain and Abel, to whom the Law was yet unknown. They continued to cling to

[1] Orig., c. *Cels.*, VI, c. 28.

their scriptural ideas even after they had joined the ranks
of Christianity—a further proof that that religion had not
given them birth. Let us now consider the Melchizedekians, who, I am firmly convinced, were also a pre-
Christian sect of the Jewish Diaspora, and the Sethites,
with whom by all accounts the former were closely
connected.

The Melchizedekians, as they are termed in patristic
literature[1], regarded the Melchizedek of the Bible as a
mighty force ($\mu\epsilon\gamma\acute{a}\lambda\eta\nu\ \delta\acute{\nu}\nu\alpha\mu\iota\nu$); they place him upon an
inaccessible pinnacle of greatness, contending that he is
not only a Dynamis, but even higher than the Messiah.
" He was without father, without mother, without descent,
the real mediator between God and man, through whose
intercession alone forgiveness can be obtained from God[2]."
He was a Prince of justice and therefore was raised by the
Almighty to the condition of a spirit and Son of God.
This is essentially the creed of the Melchizedekians.

We may now ask, how did the assumption arise that
this sect was the offspring of Christianity. Nothing indicates a Christian origin, while everything points to the
Old Testament as expounded by the Alexandrian school
of Exegesis as the source of inspiration. Just as the
Ophites looked upon Ophis as the first teacher of
the gnosis, while the Cainites regarded Cain and the
Sethites Seth in the same light, so the Melchizedekians
adored the mystical Melchizedek as the representative of
their Dynamis. The object in all cases was to break
down the trammels of the Law which retarded and
hindered the spread of Judaism in the Diaspora. Their
great Dynamis, Melchizedek, did not recognize circumcision or the obligatory character of any other rite. Why,
therefore, should his reverers be bound by the external

---

[1] Epiphan., *Haer.*, LV, c. 1-9; Pseudo-Tert., c. XLVIII ; Theodor., II, 6;
Augustine, 34 ; Philaster, 52 and 148.

[2] Epiphan., c. 8 ὅτι ἄρχων ἐστὶ δικαιοσύνης. Ibid. ἐπ᾽ αὐτῷ τούτῳ κατα-
σταθεὶς ὑπὸ τοῦ θεοῦ ἐν οὐρανῷ πνευματικός τις ὢν καὶ υἱὸς θεοῦ τεταγμένος.

Law, especially as they were fully penetrated by its spirit.

When, accordingly, the time arrived for the Melchize-dekians to come to an understanding with Christianity, whose conception of the Law was entirely to their own taste, they made certain concessions, without, however, in the least giving up their own peculiar notion of the great Dynamis. Melchizedek continued to be the great Dynamis *par excellence.* Jesus was subordinated to him [1]. As the Sethites had asserted that the founder of Christianity was not naturally but miraculously a child of Seth, or Seth himself sent down on earth for the second time, so the Melchizedekians, by their firm adhesion to their own doctrine, sought to bridge the gulf between it and the new creed. Jesus, they said, had certainly been entrusted with a mission, but only "after the order of Melchizedek," to whom he is subordinate and upon whom he is entirely dependent. The Old Testament furnished them proofs for this theory, for the Psalmist explicitly said of the Messiah, "Thou art a priest of the order of Melchizedek"—which clearly shows Jesus' inferiority to the ancient King of Salem. Jesus, accordingly, was appointed in the order of Melchizedek and charged with the mission of guiding mankind out of their manifold errors and leading them to the only right path, that of the gnosis, marked out by Melchizedek [2].

Of some importance for our inquiry is the Melchize-

---

[1] Epiphan., XXXIX, 4 ἀπὸ δὲ τοῦ Σὴθ κατὰ σπέρμα καὶ κατὰ διαδοχὴν γένους ὁ Χριστὸς ἦλθεν, αὐτὸς Ἰησοῦς οὐχὶ κατὰ γένη ἀλλὰ θαυμαστῶς ἐν τῷ κόσμῳ πεφηνώς, ὥς ἐστιν αὐτὸς ὁ Σὴθ ὁ τότε, καὶ Χριστὸς νῦν ἐπιφοιτήσας τῷ γένει τῶν ἀνθρώπων ἀπὸ τῆς μητρὸς ἄνωθεν ἀπεσταλμένος. Cf. Philaster, *Haer.*, 3 De Seth autem ipso Christum dominum genus deducere aiunt. Quidam autem ex eis non solum genus de eo deducere, sed etiam ipsum Christum esse asserunt atque opinantur.

[2] Epiphan., LV, c. 8 καὶ δεῖ ἡμᾶς αὐτῷ (sc. Μελχισεδέκ) προσφέρειν φασίν, ἵνα δι' αὐτοῦ προσενεχθῇ ὑπὲρ ὑμῶν καὶ εὕρωμεν δι' αὐτοῦ ζωήν. Καὶ Χριστὸς μέν φασιν ἐξελέγη ἵνα ἡμᾶς καλέσῃ ἐκ πολλῶν ὁδῶν εἰς μίαν ταύτην γνῶσιν, ὑπὸ θεοῦ κεχρισμένος καὶ ἐκλεκτὸς γενόμενος ἐπειδὴ ἐπέστρεψεν ἡμᾶς ἀπὸ εἰδώλων καὶ ἐπέδειξεν ἡμῖν τὴν ὁδόν.

dekians' traditional conception of Jesus' mission after the
order of Melchizedek. It runs in the ecclesiastical chroni-
cler's report as follows : " Jesus is inferior to Melchizedek,
because of the former it is said, 'Thou art a priest for ever
after the order of Melchizedek.' Whilst Jesus is mediator
for mankind only, Melchizedek, being a higher and divine
Dynamis, intercedes also for the angels and heavenly hosts.
He is superior to Jesus, 'being without father, without
mother, without descent, without beginning or end[1].' " This
conception of Melchizedek explains the text—otherwise
scarcely intelligible—in the Epistle to the Hebrews, ii. 16:
" For verily he (Jesus) took not on him the nature of
angels, but he took on him the seed of Abraham."

But before we consider the Epistle to the Hebrews, which
exhibits the cult of Melchizedek in the period of its ripest
fruition, and clearly demonstrates how this scriptural hero
had, in early times, already become transformed into a
dark mystical figure[2], let us search the literature of the
Alexandrian school for traces of this cult, and thus support
our view that, like Ophitianism, Cainism, Sethianism, this
cult too was a child of the pre-Christian Jewish Diaspora.
We find, in fact, that Philo not only deified Melchizedek,
but actually identified him with the Logos. The passage
is so important that we venture to transcribe it *in extenso* :
" If any one inquires concerning the origin of the universe,
we are justified in replying that it was due to the mercy,
lovingkindness, and grace, exhibited by God to the human
race. Everything in this world and the world itself are
gifts, favours, boons from God. Thus God appointed

---

[1] Pseudo-Tert., XLVIII sed hunc (sc. Iesum) inferiorem esse quam
Melchisedech, eo quod dictum sit de Christo : Tu es sacerdos in aeternum
secundum ordinem Melchisedech. Nam illum Melchisedech praecipuae
gratiae caelestem esse virtutem, *eo quod agat Christus pro hominibus deprecator
et advocatus ipsorum factus ; Melchisedech facere pro caelestibus angelis atque virtu-
tibus.* Nam esse illum usque adeo Christo meliorem, ut ἀπάτωρ sit, ἀμήτωρ
sit, ἀγενεαλόγητος sit, cuius neque initium neque finis comprehensus sit
aut comprehendi possit.

[2] Heb. v. 11.

Melchizedek King of Salem, i. e. King of Peace, to be his own priest. This king's virtues are not named, because without preceding merits he was appointed a Prince of Peace and deemed worthy of the priesthood. He is styled king in contrast to the term tyrant; for a king rules according to law, a tyrant according to his arbitrary will. The tyrannical spirit imposes upon body and soul violent and unjust orders which bring pain and sorrow and encourage sensuality. The king does not command, but convinces. His orders guide the soul to virtue as a ship is wafted by a favourable breeze into a haven of safety. *This king is the true Logos.* The tyrant may be called Prince of War; the king—Prince of Peace—Salem. He ought to provide for the soul this ambrosia of delight and gladness, for of Melchizedek it is said, He offered wine and bread—gifts denied by the inhospitable Ammonites and Moabites, who were therefore excluded from the congregation of the Lord. The Ammonites (children of sensuality) and the Moabites (children of intellect) are types of those who strive to explain all things by the senses or the intellect, and account God as nought. Of them Moses therefore said, they shall not enter into the congregation of the Lord, because they did not present bread and water when we came out of Egypt. Melchizedek, however, might offer wine instead of water to quench the thirst of the Lord, strengthen it and elevate it to that state of divine exaltation which passeth all understanding. For he is the priest—Logos— whose inheritance is the Lord. And of the Lord he cherishes sublime and exalted conceptions, therefore is he called priest of the most high God, not as if there could be another and less high God, for God is one in the heavens above and on the earth beneath, and there is none beside him, but because, to think of God is an exceedingly lofty and exalted occupation. Hence Melchizedek is styled priest of the most high God [1].

---

[1] Philo, *Leg. Alleg.*, I, 102 . . . . . ἱερεὺς γάρ ἐστι λόγος, κλῆρον ἔχων τὸν ὄντα καὶ ὑψηλῶς περὶ αὐτοῦ καὶ ὑπερόγκως καὶ μεγαλοπρεπῶς λογιζόμενος.

We thus find that the same mystery had gathered around Melchizedek's name and personality as had enveloped the sect called after him. Melchizedek is priest by the grace of God; and without this grace he would not have obtained the priesthood. But though Philo conceived this priest as a symbol of the highest Logos, he shrinks from representing him as a second God: "For there is but one God in the heavens above, and on the earth beneath; and there is none beside him." Here, too, there are not lacking unmistakable allusions to the extreme antinomian sects. There are the Ammonites, who abandon the ways of God to wallow in sensuality; there are also the Moabites— children of intellect who interpret all things rationalistically, seeking to supersede the Almighty, and who were therefore excluded from the congregation of the Lord. Here we have the various types of schismatics, as Philo describes them; the votaries of sensuality on the one hand, the devotees of intellect on the other. Between the two Philo places Melchizedek—the Logos—as the exalted symbol of orthodoxy. Melchizedek, who harmonizes the earthly and the divine, embodies the true apprehension of God and the right worship of him. And what was the real character of moderate Alexandrian Judaism as formed on this basis? Philo, its noblest representative and exponent, has discovered its secret. He says, "However deeply we may have penetrated into the allegorical meaning of the Law; however clearly we may have grasped its higher sense, we are not justified in exclusively fixing our attention upon this higher meaning and rejecting the literal interpretation. We are not absolved from the practice of the prescribed religious ceremonies. The literal sense is like the body; the occult meaning like the soul. As we take thought for the earthly tabernacle which enshrines the spirit, so must we respect the literal meaning of the Law."

Only a short step brings us to the Alexandrian author of the Epistle to the Hebrews who stands so near to Melchizedekianism, and gives the following sketch of the

spirit of the Alexandrian school. " The law is a shadow
of good things to come, and not the very image of those
things " (Heb. x. 1)[1]. From the author of the Epistle to
the Hebrews we learn that the mystery of Melchizedek,
as taught by the professors of his cult, was not of recent
growth. For he hurls the reproach at his readers that the
mission after the order of Melchizedek, which should have
long ago been familiar to them, had to be taught them from
the beginning. Alluding to the text in the Psalms he says,
"Called of God an high priest after the order of Melchisedec.
Of whom we have many things to say, and hard to be
uttered, seeing ye are dull of hearing. For when for the
time ye ought to be teachers [2], ye have need that one teach
you again which be the first principles of the oracles of
God; and are become such as have need of milk, and not
of strong meat. For every one that useth milk is unskilful
in the word of righteousness : for he is a babe. But strong
meat belongeth to them that are of full age, even those
who by reason of use have their senses exercised to discern
both good and evil" (Heb. v. 10–14). Here it is clearly
shown that the cult of Melchizedek, concerning which the
author of the Epistle to the Hebrews might have said
much, and whose teaching he terms the mystery of the
"word of righteousness," flourished before the epistle was
written, and traced its origin to a period anterior to the
advent of Christianity. As if to leave no doubt as to
the intimate connexion between the mystery of Melchizedek
and the cult called after his name, the author of the epistle,
after prolix statements and homilies, returns to the priest-
king and expatiates on the mission entrusted to him by
God in the following characteristic fashion: " For this
Melchisedec, king of Salem, priest of the most high God,
who met Abraham returning from the slaughter of the
kings, and blessed him ; to whom also Abraham gave a tenth

---

[1] Heb. x. 1 Σκιὰν γὰρ ἔχων ὁ νόμος τῶν μελλόντων ἀγαθῶν, οὐκ αὐτὴν τὴν
εἰκόνα τῶν πραγμάτων.

[2] Heb. v. 12 καὶ γὰρ ὀφείλοντες εἶναι διδάσκαλοι διὰ τὸν χρόνον.

part of all; first being by interpretation King of righteousness, and after that also King of Salem, which is, King of
peace; without father, without mother, without descent,
having neither beginning of days, nor end of life; but
made like unto the Son of God; abideth a priest continually" (Heb. vii. 1–3). Each of these words proclaims
the Melchizedekian. One cannot but feel amazement at
the boundless eulogy bestowed upon this cult; and the
question is forced upon one—What place does the author
of this epistle assign to Jesus if it be not that accorded
him by the favour of this cult, namely, *after* the order
of Melchizedek, below that occupied by the priest-king,
and nearer that of ordinary men? Still, at the decisive
moment when a return to Jesus seems almost impossible,
the writer surprisingly swings round in the brief words,
"made like unto the Son of God; abideth a priest continually" (Heb. vii. 3). Here Melchizedek is degraded to
the secondary position of a mere copy. Notwithstanding
his greatness he is but a shadow of the true Christ, his
incomparably greater successor, whose advent had been
predicted in the Psalmist's prophecy which had been fulfilled in the person of Jesus.

With this sudden *volte-face*, the author of the Epistle
to the Hebrews saves his Christianity, raises the divine
Dynamis of the New Testament high above that of the
Old, and boldly continues his eulogy of Melchizedek in the
following instructive manner (Heb. vii. 3–12): "Without
father, without mother, without descent, having neither
beginning of days, nor end of life; but made like unto the
Son of God; abideth a priest continually. Now consider
how great this man was, unto whom even the patriarch
Abraham gave the tenth of the spoils. And verily they that
are of the sons of Levi, who receive the office of the
priesthood, have a commandment to take tithes of the
people according to the law, that is, of their brethren,
though they come out of the loins of Abraham: but
he whose descent is not counted from them received

tithes of Abraham, and blessed him that had the promises.
And without all contradiction the less is blessed of the
better.   And here men that die receive tithes; but there
he receiveth them, of whom it is witnessed that he liveth.
And as I may so say, Levi also, who receiveth tithes, paid
tithes in Abraham.   For he was yet in the loins of his
father, when Melchisedec met him.   If therefore perfection
were by the Levitical priesthood, (for under it the people
received the law,) what further need was there that
another priest should rise after the order of Melchisedec,
and not be called after the order of Aaron?"   Here the
author reaches a decisive point, and at last discovers the
supreme secret of the transcendent Melchizedek; the abrogation of the ancient Law, the proclamation of a new and
incomparably superior revelation; the vanishing of the
obsolete and decaying legislation which is but the fore-
shadowing of good things to come, but not their essence.

Let the author of the Epistle to the Hebrews speak for
himself (Heb. vii. 12-23): "For the priesthood being
changed, there is made of necessity a change also of the
law.   For he of whom these things are spoken pertaineth
to another tribe, of which no man gave attendance at the
altar. . . . And it is yet far more evident: for that after
the similitude of Melchisedec there ariseth another priest,
who is made, not after the law of a carnal commandment,
but after the power of an endless life.   For he testifieth,
Thou art a priest for ever after the order of Melchisedec.
For there is verily a disannulling of the commandment
going before for the weakness and unprofitableness thereof.
For the law made nothing perfect, but the bringing in of
a better hope did; by the which we draw nigh unto God.
And inasmuch as not without an oath he was made priest:
(for those priests were made without an oath; but this
with an oath by him that said unto him, the Lord sware
and will not repent, Thou art a priest for ever after the
order of Melchisedec:) by so much was Jesus made a
surety of a better testament."

All these expressions point to the dogma that the Law
had, in consequence of Melchizedek's mission, ceased to
exist. Their importance lies in the fact that they elucidate the relation of the Melchizedekian sect to the Law,
and authoritatively confirm what we already otherwise
knew, namely, that the cult of Melchizedek was founded
upon antinomian tendencies. For the author of the epistle
no more owes his doctrine of Melchizedek's antinomian
mission to Christianity than he derived from that creed
his Alexandrian exegeses which he treats in so masterly
a manner. Thus, too, the author of the Epistle to Barnabas
was indebted for his artistic allegories by which he endeavours to crush Mosaism as a carnal system, not to
Christianity but to the radical school of the Jewish
Diaspora from which they were imported into the faith.
The same remark applies to the Alexandrian Jew, Apollos,
a missionary to the Greek world, and later on a coadjutor
of St. Paul the Apostle (Acts xviii. 24): "An eloquent
man, and mighty in the scriptures. . . . instructed in the
way of the Lord; and being fervent in the spirit, he spake
and taught diligently the things of the Lord, knowing only
the baptism of John. And he began to speak boldly in the
synagogue [1]," i. e. his antinomian Alexandrian Judaism.
When Aquila and Priscilla, who had been converted to
the Pauline Christianity had heard him, "they took him
unto them, and expounded unto him the way of God more
perfectly"; that is, impressed upon him that the Messiah
had already appeared. Convinced by their exhortations
that the Messianic expectations had been fulfilled in the
person of Jesus, "he helped them much which had believed
through grace: and mightily convinced the Jews, and
that publicly, shewing by the scriptures that Jesus was

---

[1] Acts xviii. 24 ff. Ἰουδαῖος δέ τις, Ἀπολλὼς ὀνόματι, Ἀλεξανδρεὺς τῷ γένει,
ἀνὴρ λόγιος . . . . . δυνατὸς ὢν ἐν ταῖς γραφαῖς . . . . . κατηχημένος τὴν ὁδὸν
τοῦ Κυρίου, καὶ ζέων τῷ πνεύματι, ἐλάλει καὶ ἐδίδασκεν ἀκριβῶς τὰ περὶ τοῦ
Κυρίου, ἐπιστάμενος μόνον τὸ βάπτισμα Ἰωάννου. οὗτός τε ἤρξατο παρρησιάζεσθαι
ἐν τῇ συναγωγῇ.

Christ[1]." A striking example of the popularity achieved
by the Alexandrian exegeses among the philosophizing
heathens is furnished by Justin the Martyr, who handles
this system like a master. This facility, and his general
knowledge of the Old Testament, he distinctly does not
owe to Christianity. He himself tells us that, before his
conversion, an old man referred him to the writings of the
Jewish prophets, which he studied closely and for which
he conceived a great attachment. Thus, after long and
futile philosophical labours those gates of light opened to
him which are visible to them alone who have received
from God and his Christ the gracious gifts of insight and
discernment[2]. It is noteworthy that the Melchizedekians
did not exhibit so aggressive an hostility to the Law as
did the Ophites and Cainites. Melchizedek, the prince of
peace, asks that the carnal Law should be gently laid aside,
and the spiritual Law be taken up in its place; and this view
is held forth in the Epistle to the Hebrews. The Pauline
letter and the Epistle to Barnabas are more embittered in
their tone. They make a fierce onslaught on Mosaism,
demand that the tablets of the Law shall be shattered, and
the very fragments ground into dust. This attitude recalls
the virulence of Cainite antinomism. Paulinism continually
pushes into the foreground the antagonisms between the
Old and the New Testament, labours to cut asunder the
last links of historic continuity which the Epistle to the
Hebrews tries to keep intact.

Just as the conservative wing of the Alexandrian school—
that represented by Philo—struggled against the radical
tendency, and sought to retain the ceremonial element in
the Law, although it had been reduced to a shadow by the
discovery of its inner meaning and spirit, so the Epistle to
the Hebrews tries to rescue the old tablets from destruc-

---

[1] Acts xviii. 28 . . . . . ἐπιδεικνὺς διὰ τῶν γραφῶν εἶναι τὸν Χριστὸν Ἰησοῦν.
This passage of Acts xviii. 24-28, so much treated of and commented on,
appears to be, looked at in this light, clear and transparent.

[2] Justin, Dial. c. Tr., c. 8.

tion, though these were already shattered. To the author
of the Epistle, the Law is a shadow, but "a shadow of good
things to come." It should not be allowed to disappear
even when it had achieved its purpose, but should always
follow in the wake of the spiritual child it had long borne
in its bosom, and of whose divine origin and truth its
existence was to be a continual evidence.

The notion of a religion freed from the trammels of
ceremonial Law had thus already arisen in the pre-
Christian Diaspora, but it needed an authoritative faith
based on revelation. Certainly in limited philosophizing
circles like the Radicals mentioned in Philo, there existed
even a revelation—that of the divine Dynamis, as enunciated by the Ophites, Cainites, Sethites, Melchizedekites,
and others. But this revelation had made no headway
among the masses. At last even this was brought about
in the course of time. The divine Dynamis was incar-
nated. And the blessed message of a bodily resurrection,
sealed by the supreme exemplar, made the doctrine welcome
to the sorrow-laden.

Such a message was impossible to the antinomistic Judaism
of the Diaspora which taught the immortality of the soul, but
denied the resurrection of the body. This, too, explains the
failure of the Melchizedekians to popularize their doctrine of
the divine Dynamis. Melchizedek was too remote from the
masses. Without mother, without father, without descent,
without beginning or end, free from human temptations,
assuming a human form for a time, enthroned above the
angels and heavenly hierarchy, for whom he acts as intercessor with the most high God, Melchizedek was a mediator
for philosophers, not for the common herd who clamoured
impetuously for salvation. And this explains the passage
in the Epistle to the Hebrews which defines the essence
and mission of Jesus the true Christ (Heb. ii. 14–17):
"Forasmuch then as the children are partakers of flesh and
blood, he also himself likewise took part of the same; that
through death he might destroy him that had the power

of death, that is, the devil. . . . . For verily he took not
on him the nature of angels; but he took on him the seed
of Abraham. Wherefore in all things it behoved him to
be made like unto his brethren, that he might be a merciful
and faithful high priest." And again (Heb. iv. 15): "For
we have not an high priest which cannot be touched with
the feeling of our infirmities; but was in all points tempted
like as we are, yet without sin."

I conclude this research with the expression of my
firm conviction that sooner or later the dogma that
Christianity is founded upon Pharisaism will be abandoned;
New Testament criticism will then no longer speak of
a Jewish Christianity and a "Gentile Christianity founded
by Paul," but rather of a conservative Jewish Christianity
and a radical Jewish Christianity. That this period is
not far off is shown in Schürer's notable essay published
in 1897, entitled "The Jews in the Empire of the
Bosphorus [1]," and dealing with the inscriptions of the first
Christian century, found in *Pantikapaeum* (Kertch)
on the Cimmerian Bosphorus, *Gorgipia* (Anapa), east
of the Cimmerian Bosphorus, and in Tanais on the extreme frontier of Greek culture, in the north-east corner
of the Palus Maeotis. That Judaism had, at the latest in
the first century, and probably earlier, taken root here is
proved by these inscriptions. "The Jews of the Diaspora,"
Schürer says in his introduction, "and the Gentile world
in which they lived influenced each other in spite of the
Hebrew aloofness. The Jews assimilated the Greek
language and civilization, and adopted many heathen
habits and customs. But they, in their turn, exercised
a mighty influence on their Gentile neighbours. Many
Jewish communities had a following of σεβόμενοι τοῦ θεοῦ
who worshipped the true God, rejected idolatry, and in

[1] " Die Juden im bosporanischen Reiche und die Genossenschaften der
σεβόμενοι θεὸν ὕψιστον." *Sitzungsber. der Königl. Preuss. Akademie der Wissensch.
zu Berlin vom 4. März* 1897. Exactly at the same time—on March 5, 1897
—my work, *Das Judenthum in der vorchristl. griechischen Welt*, went to press.

part accepted the Jewish Law. Interesting illustrations are furnished by the Greek inscriptions from the Bosphorus, of which Lasyscher has published the completed edition. They show, on the one hand, that the Jews even imitated some of the Greek legal institutions; and on the other, that there were certain religious communities who cannot be regarded as Jewish, but nevertheless betray a distinctly Jewish influence by the manner in which they speak of themselves and of the God they worship."

After treating of other inscriptions Schürer continues: "these inscriptions prove the existence and influence of Jewish communities in the Byzantine Empire during the first centuries after Christ. Such an influence can most probably be traced in the religious community mentioned in the following inscription : Worshippers of the most high God who have now been received in the communion." They honour the Deity by erecting a stone tablet on which their names were inscribed.

Schürer thus sums up his conclusion: "The peculiar religious bodies in Tanais are the fruit of a Jewish propaganda in that remote region. The founders of these communities derived from their Jewish teachers the knowledge of the most high God, whose name is ineffable, and beside whom there are no other gods. But they mingled with this Hebrew Monotheism elements of the Greek Zeus idea which in its way also pointed to Monotheism. This conclusion is completely confirmed by our knowledge of similar organizations of later date, namely, the Hypsistarians and kindred communities mentioned in the Patristic literature of the fourth and fifth centuries. The Hypsistarians lived in Cappadocia, in the fourth century; they worshipped the Almighty, rejecting images and sacrifices, but nevertheless paid some reverence to Fire and Light. They rejected circumcision, but observed the Jewish Sabbath and certain Dietary Laws."

Adducing further proofs for his theory, Schürer continues : "These hypotheses enable us to understand how religious communities who exclusively worshipped θεὸς ὕφιστος could grow up in Tanais under Jewish influence. The religion of this brotherhood was neither Judaism nor Paganism, but a combination of both. From their Jewish teachers they learned σέβεσθαι θεὸν ὕψιστον. But maintaining a separate organization rather than joining the Jewish community in a secondary rank, as other adherents had done, they admitted or retained Greek elements." The utmost interest attaches to Schürer's final conclusion which shatters the view, hitherto in vogue, that Paul was the author of Gentile Christianity emancipated from the Law; for the existence is admitted of antinomian Judaizing communities in the pre-Christian Greek era.

Schürer's conclusion is as follows: "Certain indications point to the fact that the formation of antinomian Gentile-Christian communities was not exclusively due to Paul. The process in many places, i. e. at Rome, seems to have been favoured by the sympathy with which the Sermon on the Mount was received amongst the σεβόμενοι τοῦ θεοῦ. As those who had accepted only certain elements of Judaism severed their connexion with Jewish communities and formed independent organizations, it was easy for them entirely to repudiate the Law. And this is exactly the history of the Greek religious communities in Tanais. Just as these sprang from the σεβόμενοι τοῦ θεοῦ and became something distinct, so, by an analogous process, they in their turn gave birth to Christian communities."

I welcome with much satisfaction this long expelled but at length dawning recognition of the truth. It is of great promise for the elucidation of the history of the pre-Christian Jewish Diaspora and the rise of Christianity. A few more such valuable excavations and the light of the noon day will have arrived: Saxa loquuntur!

Vienna.   M. Friedländer.

Stimulated by Schürer's essay, Cumont published a pamphlet on the same subject, entitled "Hypsistos" (Supplément à la *Revue de l'instruction publique en Belgique*, 1897, 15). Cumont not only unconditionally accepts Schürer's theory, but goes beyond him in asserting the Jewish influence upon Asia Minor which notoriously had, at the time of Jesus, a numerous Jewish population. He quotes several votive inscriptions, unnoticed by Schürer ; and all referring to the θεὸς ὕψιστος ; and adds : "... combien ces milieux, tout pénétrés d'idées bibliques sans être étroitement attachés à la loi judaïque, constituaient un terrain fécond pour la prédication chrétienne, et l'on s'explique mieux, en tenant compte de cette situation, que la foi nouvelle ait opéré plus de conversions en Asie Mineure que dans toute autre région " (p. 8).

SOME OBSERVATIONS
ON THE
ATTITUDE OF THE SYNAGOGUE TOWARDS
THE
APOCALYPTIC-ESCHATOLOGICAL WRITINGS

by
Louis Ginzberg

SOME OBSERVATIONS ON THE ATTITUDE OF THE SYNAGOGUE TOWARDS THE APOCALYPTIC-ESCHATOLOGICAL WRITINGS

LOUIS GINZBERG

JEWISH THEOLOGICAL SEMINARY OF AMERICA

THE attractiveness of the novel is responsible not only for the lively interest in the Apocalyptic-eschatological literature noticeable among all students of the origins of Christianity, but also for the exaggerated claims advanced by some scholars for these literary productions of a handful of Jewish visionaries. Many an apocalypse has been discovered or made accessible only in recent times and scholars are human enough to be dazzled by sudden light. A picture drawn by artificial light will never be true to nature, great as the skill of the artist may be, and hence the failure of some really great scholars to give us a true picture of the religious life of Israel at the time of the rise of Christianity. A history of Judaism based on the Pseud-epigrapha and particularly the visions of the apocalypses could but be a visionary pseudo-history. It would, however, be impossible within the compass of anything less than a substantial volume to present an adequate criticism of the view which sees in the so-called popular literature of the Jews the true mirror of the religion of the Jewish people. In the following few remarks I intend to give some facts about the attitude of the Synagogue towards the apocalyptic writings which I hope may throw some light on the very intricate problems connected with the eschatological doctrines and beliefs of the Jews at the time of the Apostles and Apostolic Fathers.

8*

It is a well-known fact that none of the apocalyptic books
with the exception of Daniel was received by the Synagogue.[1]
The preservation of this literature is exclusively due to the
efforts of the early Church. With equal certainty one may state
that there is not one quotation from the now extant apocalyptic
writings in the vast Rabbinic literature extending over the first
six centuries of the common era. One might cite numerous
parallels to the statements, legends or phrases of the apocalyptic
authors from the Rabbinic writings, but these parallels are never
of a nature that would indicate a literary dependence of the
one kind of literature upon the other. This is best proved by
the fact that the Rabbis never mention by name any apocalyptic
writing. It is true Dr. Kohler (J. Q. R. V., pp. 400—401) finds in
an ancient Tannaitic tradition a direct reference to the Testaments of the Twelve Patriarchs. Not having however the vision
of an apocalyptic writer I fail to detect in the passages indicated
by Dr. Kohler the slightest reference to the Testaments. The
assertion of Dr. Kohler is based on an arbitrarily construed
text and on the impossible translation thereof. He quotes from
the Talmud the text dealing with the nature of the admonition
addressed by the court to the woman suspected of adultery;
the text as given by Dr. Kohler reads:

דברי הגדה מעשים שאירעו בכתובים הראשונים

כגון מעשה ראובן בבלהה ומעשה יהודה בתמר אשר חכמים ינידו

אלו ראובן ויהודה

The translation of this text by Dr. Kohler is: Words of the
Haggadah, historical facts which occur in the early writings as
the story of Reuben regarding Bilhah and of Judah regarding
Tamar, as it says in Job XV. 18 "The wise ones confess and
conceal it not; these are Reuben and Judah." The early writings,
according to Dr. Kohler, are the Testaments where the confessions of Reuben and Judah are found. We thus learn from
this tradition of the Tannaim the very interesting fact that one
of the apocalypses at least, for some time, enjoyed almost canonical dignity among the Rabbis. Before giving the true text

---

[1] The apocalyptic literature of the Gaonic period is neither in form
nor in matter a direct development of the pre-Talmudic Apocalypse.

as found in the Rabbinic sources I want to call attention to the
very strange translation[2] by Dr. Kohler of the imaginary one.
Misled by the English expression "occur in a book" he renders
שאירעו בכתובים by "which occur in the writings". But ארע ב'
has never any other meaning than "it happened to"—generally
something evil or unpleasant[3]—and accordingly our text would
speak of something that happened to the ancient writings!

Dr. Kohler, though giving three sources for the text quoted
did not state that in none of them "his" text is found.[4] Sifre,
Numbers 12 has not the sentence from מעשה to בתמר; after
כנון follows the quotation from Job;[5] in Babli, Sotah 7b where
this sentence is found it follows after the quotation from Job,
while in Yerushalmi, Sotah I, 16b the text begins with כנון as
a comment upon the words of the Mishna I, 4 and hence may
entirely be ignored in the discussion of the meaning of כתובים
הראש' found in the two other sources. The text as given in
Sifre and Babli admits two explanations. דברי הגדה ומעשים
may be taken as ἓν διὰ δυοῖν, the Haggadah concerning the events
that happened and כתובים הראשונים stands for Job which, according to the Rabbis, is the third[6] in the order of the eleven
Hagiographa. The passage is consequently to be rendered: "The

[2] Dr. Charles, who, in the introduction to his translations of the
Testaments, quotes Dr. Kohler's view with approval very likely did not
take the trouble to look up the passages quoted by him.

[3] The "happenings" consequently refer to the sins and not the confessions; why then quote the Testaments and not Genesis?

[4] The text given by Dr. Kohler is that emended by Guedemann,
Zunz — Jubelschrift, 116, in accordance with his view that Haggadah
means "story". Bacher, Tannaiten, II. 451, has disposed of the "story"
and also of the emendation.

[5] In Sifre מעשים without ו, which is probably due to some "learned"
copyist who omitted this letter on account of his inability to explain the
construction of the sentence. The reading with ו as given in the editions
of Babli is found also in Rashi, ad loc., Yalkut, I, 707, on Num. 5 15
(in the first edition: בכתובות comp. note 10), Ibn Masnut in his commentary
on Job 15 18 and in the Munich Ms. of the Talmud.

[6] According to the Massorah the three first Hagiographa are "Psalms,
Proverbs and Job", while the Tannaitic tradition in Baba Batra, 14b, gives
the order as, "Ruth, Psalms and Job". Comp. also Berakot, 57b, beginning,
"The three big Hagiographa—Psalms, Proverbs and Job".

Haggadah found in the first Hagiographa concerning the events that happened, for example: which wise men have told etc." The verse of Job is quite correctly described as a Haggadah on the narratives of Genesis about the sins of Reuben and Judah. The other explanation presupposes that the text of the Talmud though fuller than that of the Sifre is not quite complete, the words ומעשה דוד בבת שבע being omitted out of respect for the pious king. If this assumption be correct כתובים הראשׁו' stand for the Pentateuch,[7] where the sins of Reuben and Judah are told and the Book of Samuel, where the story of David's sin is given. The woman is thus admonished to confession by the court who put before her in an elaborate way, or, as the Rabbis say, in Haggadic style, the events narrated in the earlier parts of Scripture, i. e. Genesis and Samuel.[8] The second explanation has much in its favour, especially as it does away with a very great difficulty. The incident of David with Bath-Sheba and the confession of his sin by the pious king is certainly the most natural thing that we would expect the court to dwell upon in addressing the woman suspected of adultery. The omission of the reference to David in our texts can easily be explained, as according to the regulations laid down in Mishnah, Megillah, end, the "story of David" is not to be read in the Synagogue and still less to be translated by the Meturgeman, while the "story of Reuben" may be read, though not translated, the "story of Judah" only is permitted to be read and translated.[9]

Attention should also be called to the fact that the text of Yerushalmi as given in Midrash Haggadol, Num. 5, 19 (in

[7] Rashi, ad loc., understands בכתובים הר' to refer to the Pentateuch which however is very unlikely, as we certainly would expect בתורה, the usual term for this part of the Bible. Of course Rashi does not commit the error of making בכתובים dependent on שׁארעו but takes it to stand for שׁבכתובים which is quite possible.

[8] The order of the Prophets is, "Joshua, Judges, Samuel" (Baba Batra 14 b) and it is quite natural to describe the first and fourth books of the Bible as the first writings.

[9] This is in accordance with the readings of the editions. See, however, Variae Lectiones, Megillah, 25 a, note 60. It is very likely that, according to the Mishnah, the paraphrase by the Meturgeman only was prohibited, while later this prohibition was extended to the reading too.

manuscript) has באחותו אמנון ומעשה after בתמר יהודה. This reading[10] can hardly be justified, as Amnon does not belong to the repentant sinners and it can be explained only by the assumption that the original reading was: בתמר ... ראובן מעשה ומעשה דוד בבת שבע as in Mishnah Megillah, end. When the reference to David was omitted the one concerning Amnon was substituted to make our Baraita agree as far as possible with the phraseology of the Mishnah. It may be mentioned in passing that the confessions of Reuben and Judah are a very favorite subject with the Tannaim and Amoraim, comp. ᵖ. g. Pesikta Buber XXV, 159 a—159 b, Sifre Deut. 348, Midrash Tannaim 214.

On כתובים as name for Pentateuch and Prophets comp. Blau, Zur Einleitung, p. 28 sq. His explanation of the later use of the term כתובים = Hagiographa as an abbreviation of כתובים שאר is supported by the very same development of the use of ספרי "Sifre" from שאר ספרי דבי רב; comp. RSBM on Baba Batra 124b.[11]

The only quotation from an apocalypse in the Talmud[12] is found Sanhedrin 97b and reads: "Four thousand two hundred and ninety years after "creation" the world will become orphaned;[13] the wars of the dragons (תנינים, a mythological-eschatological word!) will then take place as well as the wars of Gog and Magog and after these events the days of the Messiah, but the renewal[14] of the world by God will take place after

[10] Comp. Schechter in the introduction to his Sectaries, I, 27, note 65. The emendation לאבות הראשונים suggested by him is not acceptable. It is true אבה is sometimes applied to prominent men of biblical times (comp. Ginzberg, "Eine Unbekannte Jüdische Sekte", 295, note 2), but Amnon is certainly more of an infamous person than a famous one. In Yalkut ed. princeps בכתבות (comp. note 5) is a corruption of בכתובים, not of לאבות.

[11] The objections raised by Hoffmann, Zur Einleitung, 40, note 1, against this explanation of R. S. B. M. are not very strong, but it would lead me too far to discuss them here.

[12] Prof. Israel Levi, R. E. J. I, 108 seq. has collected a number of apocalyptic passages—but not all of them—found in the Talmud. His view, however, that they prove the composition of apocalyptic writings by the Amoraim is far from convincing.

[13] I. e. there will be no pious and good men left; comp. Mekilta, Bo 16, 18b, and parallel passages given by Friedmann.

[14] חדש admits two meanings, "to renew" and "to create anew", comp. Ps. 51 ₁₂ where חדש is = ברא.

seven thousand years". This passage is quoted in the Talmud
from a Scroll "written in Assyrian script (= square) and in
Hebrew language" which a Jewish soldier is said to have found
about 300 c. e. in the archives of Rome.

The description of this apocalyptic Scroll as having been
"written in Assyrian script and in Hebrew language" is very
interesting. What is meant by this characterization of the
apocalyptic writing is that it had the make-up of a Biblical
book. Scripture defiles the hands only when written in Hebrew
language and in Assyrian script (Yadaim IV, 5), and similarly
the scroll of Esther used for public reading on the feast of
Purim had to be written in the same way, comp. Megillah I, 8;
II, 1. The claim made accordingly for the apocalyptic scroll
was that it was, if not of a canonical, at least of semi-canonical
character, written for the purpose of public reading and study.
The question whether this claim was justified does not need to
detain us since we know nothing about its merits. It is, however,
very significant that as late as the fourth century such a claim
could be raised for a non-canonical book.

This leads us to the very crucial question: did the Synagogue
at some time or another, at the joint conference of the schools
of Shammai and Hillel about 66 c. e., or later in Jabne about
120,[15] take steps to prohibit the reading of the Pseudepigrapha
and particularly the Apocalypses. This is not the place to discuss
the difficult problems connected with the history of the Canon,
but it is evident that we shall never understand the attitude of
the Synagogue towards these "outside writings" as long as we
do not know what the Tannaim have to say on this subject. The
very learned and stimulating essay by Professor George F. Moore
"The Definition of the Jewish Canon and the Repudiation of
Christian Scriptures"[16] represents the last word of Biblical
scholarship on the final delineation of the Canon. I regret however that I cannot accept the conclusion which this distinguished
scholar has reached.

The result of the thorough examination by Prof. Moore of

[15] Comp. Graetz, *Kohelet* 166 seq.
[16] Published in "*Essays in Modern Theology and Related Subjects*",
N. Y., 1911.

the Tannaitic sources bearing upon this question may be briefly
summed up as follows: The ספרים החיצונים the reading of which
is strongly condemned[17] by Rabbi Akiba, Sanhedrin X, 1 refer
to the heretical, in particular to the early Christian writings.
The ספרי המירם spoken of by Rabban Johanan ben Zakkai,
Yaddaim IV, 6 in connection with the defilement of the hands
and the reading of which books is permitted in Yerushalmi,
Sanhedrin X, 28a owe their existence to a scribal error; המירם
is nothing but a corruption of המינים. Consequently the text of
Yerushalmi is to be emended to read as follows: הקורא בספרים
החיצונים כגון ספרי בן לענה וספרי המינים אבל ספר(י) בן סירא וגו'".
The translation of this passage as given by Prof. Moore reads:
"He who reads in the arch-heretical books, such as the books of
Ben-Laana (Gospels)[18] and the books of the heretics (Christians).

[17] The words of R. Akiba are "Also he who reads in the outside
books has no share in the world to come". It may not be out of place to
remark that the rabbis were often in the habit of using emphatic language.
That the losing of the share in the world to come is not always to be taken
literally can easily be seen from the remark, Abot R. Nathan, XXXVI,
108, about the seven professions—very honorable ones—whose members
are declared to forfeit their share in the world to come; comp. also,
ibid. XXVII.

[18] The reading Laana is very doubtful. The only MS. of this part of
the Yerushalmi has לענא (comp. Ginzberg, *Yerushalmi Fragments*, 262)
and this is very likely the correct reading, as Kohelet R. XII, 12, in a
passage undoubtedly dependent on Yerushalmi has תלא and this is much
nearer to לענא than to לענה of the editions. The identification of Laana
with Jesus by Prof. Moore is neither better nor worse than the half
dozen other identifications of this name recorded by me in *Jewish Encyclopedia*, s. v. Ben Laana. When, however, Prof. Moore, in support of
his identification, points to another nickname for Jesus found in the
Mishnah I must say with the Rabbis of old: "An error once entered
remains." A Babylonian Amora in the second half of the third century,
who very likely never in his life saw a Christian nor knew anything about
Christianity had the ingenuity to find in בן סטרא—a sorcerer mentioned
in the Tannaitic source, Tosefta Shabbat, XI, 15—a nickname for Jesus.
The identification is not only without any sound basis, but hardly possible,
as has been conclusively shown by Derenbourg, *Essai*, 460 seq. and
especially Chajes in the Hebrew periodical, Ha—Gören, IV, 33—37. The
hunt for nicknames, however, continues merrily and soberminded scholars
speak seriously of Balaam, Doeg, Ahitophel, and Gehazi as being the
nicknames which the Mishnah Sanhedrin, X, 1, uses for Jesus and three

But as for the books of Ben-Sira and all books that have been
written since his time, he who reads in them is as one who reads
in a letter". The inference which Prof. Moore draws from these
premises is that the attempt authoritatively to define the Canon
of the Hagiographa was dictated by the danger that threatened
the Synagogue from the circulation among Jews of the Gospels
and other Christian books.

Personally I am firmly convinced that there never was a time
when the Synagogue had to carry on a fight against the canonicity of the Gospels,[19] but, as this is rather a matter which

---

of his disciples. If these scholars were consistent they ought to try to
identify the three kings—Jeroboam, Ahab, and Manasseh—with three
Christian emperors, since the four "private persons" mentioned and the
"three kings" are said in the Mishnah to form one class of grave sinners.
What a pity that there were no Christian emperors at the time of the
Mishnah! Numerous legends concerning these seven sinners are given in
both Talmuds in connection with the statement of the Mishnah concerning
them, and these legends can by no stretch of imagination be made to
apply to other persons than to those who bear these names in the Bible.
They show not only how the Amoraim understood this statement of the
Mishnah, but also how much the lives of these Biblical persons occupied
the fancy of the Jewish people. One may therefore state with absolute
certainty that the entire Talmudic-Midrashic literature does not know of
any nicknames for Jesus or his disciples. I may add that גליונים $= εὐαγγέλιον$
must not be taken as a mutilation or perversion, but is a very common
form of apheresis, comp. the remark on page 128 about מירום $=$ Homer.
By the way, if Ben Laana is a nickname for Jesus why not take it as
an equivalent for בן מרים, the son of Miriam? According to the Rabbis,
the name Miriam denotes "bitterness" (Seder Olam R., III, and the
parallel passages given by Ratner), and לענה "wormwood" is used in
Hebrew to describe something very bitter. Of course I do not consider
this etymology seriously. Jesus is never named in old sources otherwise
than יהושע, ישו, ישוע or Jesus the son of Pantera. Origen. C. Cels. I, 70,
shows that Pantera ($=$ פנתירא i. e. $πάνθηρ$) is a real name and not a
nickname.

[19] The passage Tosefta Yadaim, III, 4, "The Gospels and the other
heretical books do not defile the hands" has been frequently misunderstood. The defiling of the hands by a book being equal to our way of
saying that such a book is canonical, this statement of the Tosefta was
taken to mean that it needed a special ruling to declare these books as
non-canonical. The truth of the matter, however, is, that the Halakah
had to consider the possibility of the defilement by these books not on

can neither be proved nor disproved, I shall limit myself to an examination of the premises which led Prof. Moore to his conclusions. I fully agree with the view which finds in the Mishna Sanhedrin a statement by R. Akiba directed against Christians. The severe condemnation by Rabbi Akiba of the use of Exodus 15 26 in connection with medication is certainly directed against certain Christian healers,[20] as has been felt by many scholars, though they were unable to explain why just this Biblical verse was so opprobrious to the Rabbis. The answer to this question is very simple. The last three words of this verse אני יהוה רפאך have the same numerical value (three hundred eighty eight plus three for the three words = three hundred ninety one) as the name of Jesus (יהושע = three hundred ninety one). It is not unlikely that some crypto-Christians who were afraid to openly perform

account of their own merits but because of the numerous quotations from Scriptures they contain. This paragraph of the Tosefta is, as one easily sees, not a comment upon Mishnah Yad. IV, 6, where the defilement by Scripture is discussed between Rabban Johanan ben Zakkai and the Sadducees, but on Yad. III, 5, where the law is laid down that even a very small fragment of a canonical book defiles the hands. In view of this ruling the question had to be discussed what to do with those heretical writings containing copious quotations from Scriptures. The final decision was that even the most extensive quotations from Scripture lose their holy quality if embedded in an heretical writing or in a prayer book; prayers should not be written down, but recited by heart. The far fetched interpretation of גליונים in Tosefta as "margins" given in Shabbat 116a shows rather the acquaintance of the Babylonian Amoraim with the Gospels than their ignorance of the true meaning of גליונים = εὐαγγέλιον. They knew that there is no continuous quotation containing 85 letters from the Hebrew Bible in the Gospels, which number is the minimum of a fragment that might defile the hands. Accordingly the Amoraim found the statement concerning the Gospels, גליונים, given in Tosefta entirely superfluous, and solved the difficulty by explaining גליונים as margins. The Tosefta however either mentioned גליונים on account of the other heretical books with which the Gospels are ordinarily coupled together (and there very likely were heretical books that contained quotations from the Bible of more than 85 letters), or the Tosefta dates from a time when the minimum was less than 85 letters.

[20] The magical averruncation mentioned in Tosefta Sanhedrin, XII, 10, and Abot R. Nathan, XXVI in connection with this mode of healing is said in Mark 7 33, 8 23, John 9 6, to have been employed by Jesus.

cures "in the name of Jesus" would use this verse in which they found his name indicated. Professor Moore, however, does injustice to the Rabbis when he maintains that they had no scruples about using verses of the Bible in connection with medication. The prohibition against "healing by the words of the Torah" is given in the Babylonian as well as in the Palestinian Talmud (comp. Shebuot 15b, Yerushalmi Shabbat VI, 8b), and the numerous magical formulas in the Talmudim, with one exception (Shabbat 67a, top), contain no Biblical verses. The very strong condemnation of the use of Exodus 15 26 cannot, however, be explained otherwise than on account of the favour this verse enjoyed among the Christian healers. But the coupling by R. Akiba of the prohibition against the outside books with that against the use of Exodus 15 26 as a charm does not indicate that both prohibitions are directed against Christians. Tosefta Sanhedrin XII, 10 and Aboth R. Nathan XXXVI, end, add another statement concerning the Canon by R. Akiba which by no stretch of imagination can be made to refer to some Christian heresy or practice. In these sources the man who sings the Song of Songs at festival gatherings— i. e. who treats this Biblical book as if it were of a secular character—is classed among those who have no share in the world to come. We know from many other places that Rabbi Akiba was the valiant champion of the canonicity of this Biblical book, but the opposition he had to combat he met among his own colleagues and friends.[21]

The meaning of חיצונים in the statement of Rabbi Akiba is the crucial point in the entire discussion. I shall therefore try to establish its true ‚meaning. The word occurs nowhere else; Mishna Megillah IV, 8 דרך החיצון is in the correct reading[22] while החיצונים of the editions is undoubtedly due to החיצונים in R. Akiba's famous statement. The meaning of דרך החיצון is

---

[21] Comp. Yadaim, III, 5.

[22] This is the reading of Ms. Munich, Aruk s. v. אונקלי, Meïri, and R. Nissim Gerondi (*Jerusalem*, 1884) ad loc. Aruk s. v. חצן, agree with the editions, but this is certainly a copyist's error, since the explanation of the phrase given in this passage does not admit any other reading than that given in the first passage.

easily established if one considers it in connection with the expressions כשורה and לפנים משורת הדין. A correct action is
כשורה, literally "according to the line"—of the law, לפנים
משורת הדין "within the line" describes a pious action which
the strict law does not directly command and accordingly דרך
החיצון is "outside the line"—the exact regulation of the law.[23]
To say with Prof. Moore that the term חיצונים is synonymous
with מינים, but evidently carries a stronger reprobation, would
be far from the mark, even if the reading החיצונים were the correct one. The covering of the phylacteries with gold[24] or putting
them on the sleeve instead of on the bare arm is characterized as
דרך החיצונים. Now, while these practices are not quite correct
they are not at all a serious break of the Law, as pointed out
by R. Nissim Gerondi in his commentary on *Al-Fasi* ad loc.
and consequently, though censured as incorrect, are never said to
be heretical. On the other hand, the putting of the phylacteries
not on the part of the body prescribed for this practice is
declared to be an outright heresy. If therefore the reading
החיצונים in Megillah were correct it would furnish the strongest
proof against taking החיצונים in Sanhedrin in the sense of
heretics. Prof. Moore quotes Talmud Megillah 24b to the effect
that the persons described as החיצונים in the Mishna are such
as are suspected to be inoculated with heresy. The Talmud,
however, offers no comment whatever on this part of the Mishnah.
The words quoted from the Talmud by Prof. Moore refer to
something entirely different. The Mishna *ibid.* reads: "He who
says 'I refuse to step before the Tebah (perform the public
service in the Synagogue) in coloured garments' is not permitted
to do it in white gowns". The comment of the Talmud on this
Mishnah is: Because we suspect that he is inoculated with heresy.
Clemens Alexandrinus, *Instructor* II, 11, 12, as well as III, 11
likewise mentions the custom of the early Christians to dress in
white, and consequently the heresy spoken of by the Talmud in

[23] Comp. Aruk, s. v. חצון whose words are: לא עבד כדין וכשורה.

[24] This custom reminds one of the use of chrysography for the divine
names in the Holy Scrolls by the Alexandrian Jews, which was likewise censured by the Rabbis. Comp. Shabbat, 103 b, Masseket Soferim,
I, 10.

this connection refers to Christianity.[25] Professor Moore quotes
further the reading מינות הוגה חיצונה from the Munich manuscript
which he renders by "heresy and extraneous speculation". No
such reading is found there, nor does הוגה "speculation" occur anywhere else in the Rabbinic literature. The copyist of the MS.
made a mistake and wrote מינות which word he had before him
in the first clause of the Mishnah, but noticing his error he corrected it to חיצונה. Rabbinovicz, the author of *Variae Lectiones*,
thus remarks: written מינות but "corrected" הוגה to חיצונה.
The photograph of this manuscript is before me and I find that
this statement of Rabbinovicz is correct.

We may then state with certainty that there is no such
word as חיצונים "heretics" in the entire Talmudic-Midrashic
literature, and that judging by the use of the singular חיצון the
plural חיצונים could not have been used in the sense supposed
by Prof. Moore. But even granted the equation מינים=חיצונים, the
expression ספרים החיצונים "heretical books" is hardly possible
in Talmudic Hebrew. We have ספרי מינים "heretical books",
ספרי קוסמים "magical books",[26] and consequently we would
expect ספרי חיצונים the "books of the heretics" and not ספרים
החיצונים as we have it in R. Akiba's Mishnah. It is true, the
Babylonian Talmud, Sanhedrin 100b explains ספרים החיצונים
by ספרי מינים "heretical books", but the Palestinian Talmud,
Sanhedrin X, 28a, which is by far a safer guide in historical or
linguistic matters than the Babli, quite explicitly states that
Ben Sira is included among the ספרים החיצונים and thus clearly
takes ס' החיצונים to mean books "outside of the Canon", though
not of a heretical character. The attempt made by many scholars
to reconstruct the text of Yerushalmi so as to agree with Babli
is decidedly a vain effort. Before entering, however, upon the
discussion of this point it is necessary to know what ס' המירם
stand for in this passage of the Yerushalmi, as a good deal
depends upon the correct understanding of this term.

Professor Moore gets rid of this inconvenient term by emend-
ing it to ס' מינים, but while there may be some doubt as to the

---

[25] Comp. also Goldfahn, Monatsschrift 1870, 174.
[26] Yerushalmi Maaserot, I, 51 a.

exact meaning of this obscure word,[27] no doubt is possible as
to its genuineness. Midrash Tehillim, I, 9 in commenting upon
Ps. 19 15 remarks: David prayed to God that men may not
read his words as they read the books of מירום, but that they
may read them and meditate [28] over them so that they receive
reward for doing it as if they would study the most difficult
parts of the Tora ואל יהו קורין בהם כקורין בספרי מירום אלא יהו
קורין בהם והוגין בהם ונוטלין עליהן שכר כנגעים ואהלות [29] וגו'.
It is evident that מירום is the same as המירוס in Yaddaim IV, 6
and in our passage of the Yerushalmi and that by it the Midrash
understands books of a secular nature which one may read
without doing damage to one's salvation though the reading is
without spiritual benefit; one "reads them, but does not meditate
or ponder over them". To make David pray that the Psalms
may not be read by men "like heretical books" would be the
height of absurdity. A careful reading of the Mishna Yaddaim
leads to the same conclusion as to the meaning of ס' המירם.
The books which according to Rabban Johanan ben Zakkai do
not defile the hands "because they are not precious" can only
be secular books but not heretical ones. The description of
heretical books by the leader of the Pharisees as "not precious"
would be as inept as such a characterization of the Thesis of
Luther by the head of the *Index Expurgatorius.*

The earliest commentary on the Mishnah composed in the
ninth or tenth century by one of the Babylonian Gaonim—
perhaps Saadia[30]—takes המירם to be "Homer" and this is very
likely the correct interpretation of this word. Of course, we

[27] There are numerous etymologies of this word; comp. Graetz, Monatsschrift, 1870, 139 seq., Perles R. E. J. III, 114, Weil, *ibid.* 278, Kohut,
J. Q. R. III, 546, Kohler, *ibid.* V, 415, Jastrow, *Dictionary,* 355 b. Not
one of these etymologies deserves serious consideration; on the traditional
explanation of המירם = Homer see text.

[28] This passage shows conclusively that הגה is not "read" but "study"
or "meditate", comp. note 40.

[29] These laws form a very difficult section of the Mishnah and hence
are often used to describe the most important parts of the Halakah;
comp. for instance Hagīgāh, 14 a.

[30] Comp. Ginzberg, *Geonica,* 172 seq. and Epstein, *Der Gaonäische
Kommentar,* 29 seq.

must not think of a translation of Homer into Hebrew—the discussion about the "defiling of the hands" could only refer to Hebrew books—but the books of Homer[31] stand for "light literature", books one may read but which are "not precious". The apheresis of Greek loan words is quite common in Jewish writings and the forms מירוס and מירון (accusative!) offer no difficulty.[32] That some of the copyists who undoubtedly never had heard of Homer wrote המירם is not in the least surprising, if one considers that λῃστής "thief" is regularly mispelled as ליסטים, though its meaning must have been known as it occurs hundreds of times in the Talmudic-Midrashic literature.

We shall now proceed to examine the text of the Yerushalmi. We have seen that המירם must not be amended and that by it secular literature is meant, the reading of which is permitted in contrast to that of the Book of Ben Sira which is said to belong to the prohibited books. The question is of course very puzzling how to harmonize this interdict by Rabbi Akiba[33] with the fact that, of all the Apocrypha, Ben Sira is the only one quoted by the rabbis. A great Talmudist at the end of the sixteenth century[34] suggested the following emendation of the Yerushalmi: (r.: ספר) ספרי אבל לענה בן וספרי המירם ספרי כגון בן סירא וכל ספרים שנכתבו מיכן והילך הקורא בהן כקורא באיגרת. Among modern scholars it was Graetz (Kohelet 166) who

---

[31] In the Ms. of the Yerushalmi reproduced by me in *Yerushalmi Fragments*, 36 b, this word is vocalized as הומירס Homeras, comp. note 27.

[32] In Hullin, 60 b, two manuscripts have מירוס, Aruk מרון, מירון המירוס and R. Samson of Sens, in his commentary on Yadaim, III, 5, מידס which is very likely a corruption of מירוס. The reading of the Editions ספרי מינים is quite impossible as no one would ever have dared to say that there are verses in Scripture which seem fit to be burned like heretical books. The names and histories of certain nations who lived in pre-Mosaic times mentioned in Genesis—these are the verses spoken of as the Talmud, explicitly states—might be said to be superfluous, but certainly not heretical and deserving to be burned. The original reading was ס' [ה]מירום "like story books" and as מירום was later understood by many to mean heretical, a pious copyist added the words ראוין לישרף, and still later מינים was substituted for מירום. Comp., however, Baba Batra 91 a.

[33] R. Akiba himself shows acquaintance with this book; comp. Graetz, *Gnosticismus*, 119, and Bacher, *Tannaiten*[2] I, 269, note 2.

[34] R. Issachar Baer Eulenburg in his *Novellae on Sanhedrin*, 100 b.

independently proposed the same emendation which was later
accepted by Perles (R. E. J. III, 116), Joel (*Blicke* I, 75) and
Professor Moore. I do not think however that this emendation
is acceptable. The statement of R. Joseph, Sanhedrin 100b,
that one is prohibited to read the book of Ben Sira is certainly
based upon a Tannaitic tradition which counted Ben Sira among
the prohibited books. In other words this Babylonian Amora,
celebrated for his great knowledge of Tannaitic traditions (comp.
Berakot 64a, Horayyot, end) agrees with the view given in our
text of the Yerushalmi and it would therefore be against all
canons of criticism to emend it against such high authority for
its genuineness. It is true the discussion between R. Joseph
and his pupil Abbay shows that even the master was unable to
explain the reason of the interdict against the reading of Ben
Sira and driven into a lurch he had to admit: Were it not
for the prohibition against Ben Sira by the Rabbis we would
lecture on the book.[35] This, however, corroborates our view
that Rabbi Joseph was acquainted with the Tannaitic tradition
that counted Ben Sira among the הַחִיצוֹנִים 'ס and *nolens volens*
he had to submit to the authority of the Tannaim. He could not,
of course, explain this Palestinian view which is based upon
a different interpretation of חִיצוֹנִים 'ס from that prevailing in
the Babylonian academies. The Babylonians identified חִיצוֹנִים 'ס
with מִינִים 'ס "heretical books" and Ben Sira could not well be
described as heretical, while the Palestinian authorities correctly
explain the term used by Rabbi Akiba as referring to "outside
books" i. e. Apocrypha, especially those among them which were
very popular, like Ben Sira.

The above quoted remark of Rabbi Joseph with regard to
the use of Ben Sira in public lectures shows at the same time
what is meant by the reading of the "outside books". Not the
reading of the Apocrypha was prohibited by Rabbi Akiba, but
their use in the Synagogues and houses of study for public
service or instruction. More than twenty years ago I wrote:
"Akiba protested strongly against the canonicity of certain of
the Apocrypha, Ecclesiasticus for instance (Sanhedrin X, 1,

---

[35] The corruption of the text in the Editions is obvious. Read with
R. Meir Abulafia, *ad loc.*: אי לאו דנגוזה רבנן להאי סיפרא הוה דרש' וגו'.

Babli *ibid.* 100b, Yerushalmi *ibid.* X, 28a) in which passages קורא is to be explained according to Kiddushin 49a and חיצונים according to its Aramaic equivalent[36] ברייתא so that Akiba's utterance reads: "He who reads aloud in the Synagogue from books not belonging to the Canon as if they were canonical" etc. I have little to add to it, except that by reading aloud in the Synagogue I meant public study too and not liturgical recitation only. The objection raised by Prof. Moore against this interpretation of R. Akiba's statement can be easily refuted; he writes: "The principle, however, seems to have been early established that even the acknowledged Hagiographa should not be read in the Synagogue". But the very sources[37] quoted by him (Mishna, Shabbat XVI, 1 and Tosefta XIII, 1) show clearly that it needed a special ruling of the Rabbis to prohibit the public reading of the Hagiographa on Sabbath afternoon.[38] Accordingly these sources assume that but for this ordinance the reading of the Hagiographa—i. e. public study—would have been quite the thing to be expected. The interpretation of the statement of R. Akiba as given in Yerushalmi is therefore not only from the philological point of view, but also from the historical one by far preferable to that of Babli. The identification of חיצונים with מינים is, as we have seen, hardly possible and an interdict against the private reading of heretical books by R. Akiba is not very likely. Of his colleague Elisha ben Abbuyah[39] it is told that he was a passionate reader of heretical books. Later when he became an apostate his unwholesome reading was made responsible for his apostasy, but there is not the slightest indication that he was censured for his reading. The Palestinian Midrashim, even those of comparatively late

---

36 On ברייתא see my article in the Jewish Encyclopedia, *s. v.* where the origin of this term is explained differently from the traditional one. The Hebrew משנה חיצונה occurs only in late writings.

37 Comp. also the passage quoted above, page 118, from Mishnah Megillah, end; the reading of the story of Amnon undoubtedly refers not to liturgical use of this section of the Bible but to its public study.

38 Comp. Shabbat, 116b, where the view of Rab is given that the Mishnah refers exclusively to public reading.

39 Hagigah; Elisha ben Abbuyah was a younger contemporary of R. Akibah.

origin, like the Tanhumas have still the old Palestinian tradition
that the interdict against the הַחִיצוֹנִים 'ס is directed against the
Apocrypha and not against "heretical books", comp. Tanhuma
Buber IV, 59, Tanhuma Behaaloteka 15, Bamidbar R. XIV, 4 and
Kohelet[40] R. XII, 12. The last Midrash influenced by Babli
warns against taking into the house any other book than the
Bible. Pesikta Rabba III, 9a is likewise partly dependent upon the
Babli and hence distinguishes between the non-canonical and
the סְפָרִים הַחִיצוֹנִים. One of the outstanding features of the
later Midrashim is the harmonizing of the Palestinian with the
Babylonian traditions.

By an *argumentum ex silentio* one might prove too much.
We have seen that in the entire Rabbinic literature of the first
six centuries of the Common Era there is not one quotation from
the now extant apocalyptic literature, and an easy explanation
is at hand. The Jewish schools at Jabneh and Tiberias whose
literary activities resulted in the production of Talmud and
Midrash deliberately ignored the writings of their opponents,
the so-called apocalyptic Pharisees. But how about the many
other apocryphal writings, not of an apocalyptic nature of which
not the slightest trace is to be found in the Rabbinical literature?
Did the Rabbis at Jabneh detect the hidden Sadduceeism of the
First Book of the Maccabees and withdraw it from circulation?
They were certainly not Sadducees who, two centuries later,

---

[40] The present text of the Midrash is corrupt as it contains a self
contradictory statement. If the "taking into the house" of any other
book than the Bible "brings confusion", it is absurd to say that non-
Biblical books were given for "reading and not for serious study"; books
that one is not to take into the house were certainly not given for reading.
In Yerushalmi Sanhedrin, the source of Kohelet Rabba, the translation of
להגיון by "for reading" would give a satisfactory sense, as nothing is said
there about not taking into the house any non-canonical books. I have
elsewhere conclusively shown (comp. *Eine unbekannte Jüdische Sekte*, 70, 71;
see also above note 28) that הגה is always "intensive study" or "meditation".
The manuscript of the Yerushalmi in my "Yerushalmi Fragments", 262,
has the correct reading להגיון נתנו ליגיעת וגו׳. The Haggadic interpretation
of Eccles. 12 12 takes this verse to refer to Scripture which alone is said
to have been given for meditation and serious study—with the exclusion
of all other writings which are not a subject for study. Targum paraphrases
this verse in a very similar manner—on להג comp. Erubin, 21 b.

showed the Hebrew text of this apocryphal book to Origen and
Jerome. It may be profitable to remember that in the entire
Tannaitic literature only two non-Biblical books are mentioned
by name: Megillat Taanit (Mishna Taanit II, 8) and Megillat
Hassidim or Harissim (Sifre, Deut. 48 and Midrash Tannaim 42);
the former thanks to its Halakhic contents is still extant, and the
latter no longer so. The disappearance of the apocalyptic literature from among the Jews shows as little opposition on the
part of the Rabbis to it as the disappearance of the Book of
Judith shows any opposition of the Rabbis against this genuinely
Pharisaic writing. The Synagogue at the time of the Tannaim
did not use any book younger than Daniel and there is not one
apocalyptic writing that antedates this Biblical book. One might
add that, disregarding Ben Sira, which really enjoyed, at least
for a time a semi-canonical character, it would be as difficult
to prove the existence of a pre-Maccabean Apocryphon as that
of a post-Maccabean Biblical book. There is therefore very
little probability in the assumption that the Jewish schools that
survived the destruction of Jerusalem rejected writings "which
played an important part in the older religious life of Jerusalem
and the dominions of Herod Antipas in the days when the Temple
was yet standing and the Jewish state was still a reality" [41] The
Rabbis of Jabneh would never have hit upon the time of the
Maccabean revolution as the end of the period of inspiration.
This distinction must have been conferred upon the time of the
Maccabees at a very early date. It is perhaps not superfluous
to call attention to the fact that the discussion at the school
of Jabneh concerning the Canon points in the direction of a
rather liberal attitude towards it, by far more so, than that
taken by the schools of Shammai and Hillel at the time of the
Jewish state. Ecclesiastes, Esther and Song of Songs were denied
admission into the Canon by these schools, while the scholars at
Jabneh declared them canonical. But there is no book mentioned
that was excluded at Jabneh from the Canon and there is not
the least likelihood that there ever existed such a one.[42]

[41] Prof. Burkitt, "*Jewish and Christian Apocalypses*", 10.
[42] That Ben Sira was a very popular book, no one would deny, but
where are the proofs that it was considered canonical by Palestinian Jewry?

Professor Burkitt in his highly instructive lectures on "*Jewish and Christian Apocalypses*" quotes a saying by Rabban Johanan ben Zakkai which, he believes, really implies the renunciation of the apocalyptic idea, the notion that the Kingdom of God was an external state of things, which was just upon the point of being manifested and (as a corollary) that the person of insight could know something about it beforehand. This saying of Rabban Johanan reads: God revealed to Abram this world, but the world to come he did not reveal to him. In a note Professor Burkitt remarks that according to Rabbi Akiba, on the contrary, God revealed to Abram both this world and that which is to come. But, adds Professor Burkitt, Akiba unlike Johanan ben Zakkai believed that the Kingdom of God was at hand.[43]

If this however be so, one might as well quote R. Akiba's view to prove the predilection of the Rabbis for the apocalyptic idea as that of Rabbi Johanan in proof of their opposition to it. We know for certain that at the final delineation of the Canon Rabban Johanan was no longer living, while Rabbi Akiba took a very important part in the deliberations leading to it. Accordingly we certainly would expect a much more favorable attitude towards the apocalyptic writings from the school of Jabneh than from the schools of Shammai and Hillel in the year 66. That Rabbi Akiba did not stand isolated in his expectation of the imminent manifestation of the Kingdom of God is clearly shown by the "small apocalypse" found in the Mishna Sota, end, the only one of its kind in the entire Tannaitic literature. The author or transmitter of this apocalypse was no other than "Rabbi

---

[43] Genesis R. XLIV, 22, states only that R. Johanan and R. Akiba differ as to the nature of the revelation, at the "covenant between the pieces", but there is no way of telling who holds the one view and who the other, and one may doubt whether the saying attributed to R. Johanan by Prof. Burkitt does not really belong to R. Akiba. By the way, the difference of opinion between these Tannaim is of a purely exegetical nature, based upon the different interpretation of the ב in Genesis 15 18. II Baruch 4 4, and IV Ezra 3 13, 14 agree with the view that the time to come was shown to Abram, while among the Amoraim both views are represented; comp. Genesis R. l. c.

Eleazar the Great",[44] the favorite disciple of Rabban Johanan
ben Zakkai. But even the master himself counted upon the
speedy appearance of the Messiah with such certainty that one
of his ordinances regulating a certain religious ceremony had
its reason in this expectation.[45]

It would therefore not be true to the ascertainable facts to
maintain that for the leading Rabbis in the first and the second
generations after the destruction of the Temple the Messianic
hopes were not as actual and real as they were for the generation
living at the time of the great catastrophe or shortly before it.

A saying by Rabban Johanan ben Zakkai truly characteristic
of the attitude of the Rabbis towards the apocalyptic idea is the
following one; he said: "If thou hast a sapling in thy hands and
thou art told: Behold, the Messiah has come, plant thy sapling
and then go to meet him".[46] The Apocalyptics cut loose from
life, the Rabbis were the guardians and leaders of a nation and
they did not fail to see in the wild and vague visions of those
dreamers a true menace to the physical and spiritual welfare of
Israel.[47] Ethics is, if not entirely, at all events preeminently
social ethics and the apocalyptic movement that flung itself with
unrestrained imagination upon the future caring nothing for the
present concerns and perils of the individual and the community
was not only anti-social but also anti-ethical. If the Prophets
had any successors they were not the Apocalyptics who forgot
this world and with it men, but the Rabbis for whom the center
of gravity of religion was not in a world beyond—important as
that thought was—but in the actual life of man on earth. It is
true, the ethical element was not ignored by the apocalyptic
writers; with some of them it even played an important part.

---

[44] The reading: R. Joshua ben Hananaiah—another favored pupil of
R. Johanan—is not based on good authority.

[45] Comp. Rosh Hashanah, 30 a, "speedily the temple will be erected".
By "speedily" is meant there, as the content shows, the very next year.
Comp. also Taanit 17 a: אסור.

[46] II-Abot. R. Nathan, XXX, 67. Read מָלַךְ instead of לְךָ.

[47] It would be very difficult to prove the contention that the attitude
of the apocalyptic authors toward the Torah was different from that
taken by the Rabbis.

This, however, must not deceive us, any more than it did the great Rabbis, who clearly perceived that the apocalyptic view, which lacked touch with the vital problems of man, really endangered the moral element in the Jewish religion.

The "end" is the outstanding feature of the apocalyptic writings and one is apt to forget of what great importance the "beginning" was to these authors. Yet very likely the vagaries and fantasmagoria of the apocalypses about creation or, to use the term of the Rabbis, "the works at the beginning", were primarily responsible for the disappearance of this kind of literature from among the Jews. As early as the time of Rabban Johanan ben Zakkai we meet with the prohibition against discussing the "beginning" with more than one person and this prohibition was the death knell for a goodly number of the apocalypses. A matter not to be discussed becomes quickly a matter not to be read.[48]

The demonology and angelology of the apocalypses not rarely discussed by them in connection with the story of creation were again of a nature that could not but repulse those who were not blind to the danger lurking in the attempt to turn popular fancy into a system of theology. The Rabbis and, of course, still more so the people undoubtedly believed in the existence of angels and demons. But like many other popular beliefs, they meant very little in the religious life of the people and still less in that of the Rabbis. The apocalyptic writings began to make wide use of these popular beliefs, first for purely literary reasons. In describing, for instance, an ascension to Heaven one could not well dispose of the angels or the description would have fallen flat; when God commands man can only obey, with an angel one can argue and dispute. Nor are the demons to be neglected, if one strives to achieve dramatic effects, as, for instance, the author of the book of Enoch in describing the depravity of mankind at the time of the deluge. What at the beginning was merely literary form gradually became theology, angels and demons began to be considered from a speculative point of view.

[48] Comp. Mishnah Hagigah II, 1, and Tosefta, II, 1. It is worth while noticing that Daniel is one of the very few apocalypses that does not contain cosmological speculations, and this apocalypse is the only one admitted into the canon.

The true leaders of Judaism saw the danger and therefore avoided as far as possible in their sayings and writings even the mentioning of angels and demons. It is certainly not an accident that the Mishna never speaks of angels or demons and that in the other Tannaitic sources they are very rarely referred to.

Of course, it would be an error to infer from it any disregard for angels and demons on the part of the Rabbis. But it is a far more grievous error to see in the widely developed demonology and angelology of the apocalypses the religious conceptions and sentiments of the people (Volksfrömmigkeit), in opposition to the teachings of the scribes (Schriftgelehrtentum) as found in the Tannaitic literature. Whatever the Rabbis might have been, we must not think of them as a class by themselves separated from the people; they were neither monks nor professors. They were of the people, lived with the people and worked for the people. Accordingly the most pronounced feature of the Haggadah of the Tannaim is its popular character, a great part thereof being the spoken word addressed by the Rabbis to the people. The apocalyptic writings by their fixed literary forms and their obscurities were not meant for the people, but for the initiated ones. The true mirror of the religious life of the Jews we find therefore in the homely and simple sayings and the teachings of the Rabbis and not in the literary productions of the Apocalyptic writers who wrote primarily for a "class" of men like themselves and not for the people.

SPIRIT AND LETTER
IN
JUDAISM AND CHRISTIANITY

by
M. GÜDEMANN

The Jewish Quarterly Review.

APRIL, 1892.

SPIRIT AND LETTER IN JUDAISM AND CHRISTIANITY.

גיתי ספר ונחזה.—" Let us bring the book and see."
(*Talmudic Saying.*)

AMONG those whom the Mishnah (*Synhedrin*, xi. 1) declares
to have forfeited eternal life, the following are enumerated:
—He who says that the Resurrection is not taught in the
Torah; further, *he who affirms that the Torah does not come
from God* (min-ha-Shamayim); also the Epikuros This is
immediately followed by, " R. Akiba says, He also who
reads in strange books, and he who utters incantations over
wounds " (literally " wound "). Although I am here only
concerned with the assertion (italicised in the text) regarding the man *who denies the divine origin of the Torah*, I have
cited the other dicta as well, because, from their being
classed together, it is evident that, as regards their origin,
they all belong to one and the same epoch. This can have
been no other than the period which is marked on the one
hand by the party divisions of the Sadducees, Pharisees
and Essenes, and, on the other, by the birth of Christianity.
The proof of this statement lies—apart from the impression produced by the collocation of instances — in the
reference to the " Epikuros " and the " Strange Books."
Both conceptions point unequivocally to the period in
question, and can only be comprehended in connection
therewith.

If this view of the matter is kept in mind, then the assertion regarding the denier of the divine origin of the Torah has an interest attaching to that age, which I shall here endeavour to make clear. To this end it is necessary, in the first instance, accurately to define the above declaration, for, taken in the general terms in which it is enunciated, it suffers from a certain indistinctness that opens the door to the most diverse questions. What is to be understood by denial of the divine origin of the Torah? Is it that the Torah was not revealed by God, but is the work of man? This opinion is no doubt included in the statement of the Mishnah, but there is not the least justification for the assumption that in Jewish antiquity such an opinion had ever sprung up and spread so as to necessitate its resistance by the imposition of a penalty. All antiquity, including the Jews, was more inclined to refer extraordinary appearances, marvellous discoveries, teachings and writings, directly to the Deity than to contest the intervention of God in the development of the human race; and it would be an anachronism without parallel to believe that the divine origin of so extraordinary a book as the Torah had to be established by means of a law, and to be protected against the attacks of sceptics and unbelievers by threats of punishment. As a fact the contrary appears from the discussions in Sabb., 30*b* : it was easier to pronounce in favour of the divine origin of certain writings than successfully to deny such origin to others. It required no little trouble to finally establish the canon and exclude therefrom the numerous apocryphal writings, so readily were people disposed to acknowledge the divine origin of everything for which such a claim was put forth. Accordingly, the denial of the divine origin of the Torah, of which the Mishnah treats, cannot refer to the *contents*, but to the *letter* of the Torah. Its intention is to establish the divine authorship of the *text* of the Torah, and hence the denier of this claim is threatened with the loss of " eternal bliss." In this sense also the statement of the

Mishnah is explained by the Talmud (*Synhedrin*, 99a):
He who asserts that the Torah is not from God, or denies
the divine authorship of even *one single verse of the Torah*,
and affirms that not God but Moses of his own accord
pronounced it, is guilty of the transgression referred to
in Num. xv. 31, and will incur the punishment of excision
thereunto attached.[1] It is now no longer open to doubt
that the dictum of the Mishnah has for its object
to give a sanction to the verbal text of the Torah,
and that on this account it condemns the denial of its
divine origin as a sacrilegious act to be avenged by the loss
of future bliss.

II.

Herewith, however, the difficulty involved in that
dictum is rather increased than removed. While, on the
one hand, as I have shown, it was not rendered necessary by any denial of the divine character of the Torah
itself, no such attempt ever having been made, there is, on
the other hand, still less reason to believe that the divine
origin of the wording of the Torah was even questioned.
Had any such thing ever occurred, the inviolability of the
text of the Torah would have had to be affirmed much
more distinctly than has actually been the case,[2] and it
is then hardly likely that people would have been content with a legal declaration of a purely eschatological
character, such as the one under consideration or even
with the whole Mishnah in which it is found. But *textual
criticism*, especially biblical criticism, was unknown to the
ancient Jews. This fact is not contradicted by the circumstance that the greatest importance was placed upon the

---

[1] **Maimonides** הל' תשובה regards as a denier of the Law (כופר בתורה)
whosoever says אחת תיבה אפילו אחד פסוק ד' מעם התורה שאין.

[2] The views of the Talmud on this point, mainly attached to our
Mishnah, are collected in סופרים מסבחת by Rosenfeld (Wilna, 1883),
p. 6, *seq.*

preservation and propagation of the traditional text, and
that even in ancient times a special department of study,
the Soferic or Massoretic, dealt with these tasks. Such
criticism as was in vogue did not proceed from any doubt
as to the divine origin of the text, but rather presupposed
it, and nothing but the piety springing from such belief
renders the care bestowed on the biblical books explicable.
Josephus expressly says (*Contra Ap.* i. 8), "What credit we
give to these books is also well known. In all these ages
past no one has been so bold as to add anything to them,
or to take anything from them, or to change anything in
them. But it is natural to all Jews immediately and from
their birth to regard those books as the teachings of God,
and to persist in them, and, if occasion be, to die for them.
. . . . . Who among the Greeks would suffer the least harm
for such a cause, or even for the loss of all their writings ?"
If according to this evidence hardly any doubt concerning the
divine origin of the text of the Torah could ever have been
entertained, then, as I have remarked, the dictum of our
Mishnah is rather darkened than illumined by its Talmudic
explanation, and it is clear that the key to the comprehension of both passages must lie in some definite
motive which it is for us to discover, since only by this
means can we hope to overcome the difficulties referred to.

III.

Before, however, I undertake this task, I must draw
attention to another circumstance which is closely connected with our inquiry. The use which both Talmud and
Midrash make of the formula, " Read not thus, but thus "
(אל תקרי . . . אלא . . .) is well known. This formula, by
means of which, for the purpose of supporting a particular
opinion, a variant is proposed to the received reading,
keeps the Bible text in a constant state of fluctuation, and
the boldest conclusions of an arbitrary criticism do not
touch the authenticity of the text in anything like the

same measure as does its frequent and capricious use. It
will be said that in such cases no seriously-meant alteration of the text is intended ; and this is doubtless the case,
though the suggestions introduced by that formula are at
times as similar to the emendations of modern criticism as
one pea is to another.[1] Indeed, there can be no question
that many a critic of the present day, who, by his venture-
some emendations, raises a storm in theology, might, in
Talmudic times, have proposed the very same things without hesitation under cover of the formula. Be that as
it may, we must at all events allow that its use
even by way of Hagadic diversion or Halachic association, could not possibly have asserted itself to the
extent it actually has done if every alteration of the text,
however much it might commend itself and however lofty
might be the object with which it was proposed, had been
regarded as the grave sin which the dictum of our
Mishnah and its Talmudic explanation declare it to be
according to the view hitherto entertained. It is even
reported that in the *Torah of Rabbi Meir* several variations
upon the received reading had been found, presumably due
to his own hand. Granted that these remarks were only
intended as "humorous"[2] marginal notes, still such treatment of the Bible text—which, as the witty Frenchwoman
observed of chess, was too serious for play, and too playful
for a serious occupation—must occasion surprise, and all
the more so, seeing that such a proceeding is in marked
opposition with the severity with which our Mishnaic
dictum and Talmudic explanation guard the text against
all injury. Let us picture to ourselves what would be
the result if, not in some comic journal, but in serious

---

[1] Comp. *Sota* 11*b*, where, instead of עָדְי עָרִים, it is proposed to read
עָרְרִי עָרִים, which R. Samuel Edels (Chiddushe Hagadoth) seems to take
as a seriously meant interpretation of the text.

[2] In this way Graetz (*History of the Jews*, iv. 2, p. 469) understands the
" letter changes " of R. Meir there cited. Comp. Rapoport, *Erech Millin*,
p. 8.

writings, and with a good motive, the texts of ancient and modern classics were treated in the same manner as the Bible text is in Talmud and Midrash; what confusion would be certain to ensue in course of time, and what censure such license would call forth from all earnest-minded men. Out of this dilemma there is in my judgment only one way of escape, viz., the assumption that in antiquity, philological fidelity to the letter was unknown, and that men did not hesitate to sacrifice a letter here and there, when the object was to find a home in the Torah for some religious idea, and to shelter it under its sacred authority. This fact, which ought not to cause surprise, since the early students of Scripture were certainly lacking in a sense for etymology, and in a profounder appreciation of grammar, perhaps gave rise to the legend that when the first Tables of the Covenant were broken the letters flew into the air (*Pesachim*, 87*b*). Whatever view may be taken of the matter, so much is certain, that this legend could only have arisen and spread among those to whom the letter was no *rocher de bronze*. This circumstance also explains the occasional occurrence of inexact citations of Biblical passages in the Talmud (*B. Kam.*, 55*a*. *B. Bathra*, 113*a*, and *Toss. ibid.*). It has hence been inferred that many a Talmudic sage was but little conversant with the Bible (*Toss., ibid.*), an inference, however, which can hardly be sustained, seeing that searching the Scriptures formed the life's labour of the Talmudic doctors. Their minute acquaintance with the Bible text is made evident in almost every page of the Talmud. The truth is rather that they were not greatly concerned for the letter as such, and that in their *naïveté* they were free from that anxiety which fastens upon the letter of the Scripture, even the sages of the Tossaphistic age exercising a much freer and more un-biassed judgment, at least, in respect of the vowel signs, than later piety would have ventured to permit.[1]

---

[1] Comp. Rapoport in his preface to Freund's שורש דבר ומוצא דבר (Vienna, 1866). p. 7.

Now this state of things is only explicable on the assumption that our Mishnaic dictum, which, according to the explanation of the Talmud, gives especial authority to the letter, was never transmuted into the flesh and blood of the learned world, which circumstance, again, can only be accounted for on the supposition that the assertion of the Mishnah had in view a particular object which was based upon certain contemporary conditions, but which lost its significance in the altered relations of succeeding ages. Upon this object, however, the true light appears to be thrown from a quarter to which I shall now direct the attention of the reader.

IV.

In the second epistle to the Corinthians the Apostle obviously sets himself the task of proving the continuity of the old teaching and the new, or of deriving the latter from the former. One can understand the endeavour to find in the soil of the Old Testament the foundation for the teaching of Christ. Equally natural was it that such an endeavour should incur the charge of falsification. Now to attack an opponent has been from of old a mode of parading one's own innocence; on that account the Apostle levels from his side the charge of falsification against those from whom he had to expect the same accusation against himself. He designates the many (οἱ πολλοί), *i.e.*, the Jews, as corrupters of the word of God (ii. 17), and asserts of them that they do not understand the word of God at all, as "even unto this day, when Moses is read, a vail is upon their hearts" (iii. 15). But what guarantee does the Apostle offer for the accuracy of *his* conception of the divine word, *i.e.*, the Old Testament ? It is contained in the sentence, "For the letter killeth, but the spirit giveth life" (iii. 6), to which the thesis is subsequently added. "Now the Lord is that Spirit; and where the Spirit of the Lord is, there is liberty" iii. 17).

We have doubtless before us in these sentences the written precipitate of a mighty turmoil out of which the Pauline doctrine made its way to victory. If, however, we take these oft-quoted words in the simple sense that rightly belongs to them, they lose all point, and sink to the level of a commonplace, which certainly expresses a general truth, but which, on that very account, is not likely to have ever been contradicted. Does any one imagine that the idea that "the Lord is the Spirit" would have been combated by a Jewish contemporary of the Apostle? This can hardly be maintained, as it was chiefly because this same truth was so deeply rooted in the heart of the Jews, that the doctrine of the Incarnation encountered their opposition. But, further, the sentence "the letter killeth but the spirit giveth life" contains in its general sense nothing which would have been disputed by the Jewish contemporaries of the Apostle. This I think I have proved in the foregoing argument. We have seen that the Tannaim and the Amoraim used, as it were, to play ball with the letter of the Bible for the sake of the spirit, and I may here recall the Hagadah above referred to, that at the breaking of the Tables of the Covenant the letters flew into the air. What can this Hagadah mean, if any meaning is to be assigned to it at all, but that it is not the letter of the Bible but the spirit that is of value? I need not, in order to establish my contention that in Judaism undisputed precedence has at all times been accorded to the spirit over the letter, appeal to Hagadic utterances, the interpretation of which is a matter of individual taste. The history of biblical exegesis from the oldest times furnishes irrefutable proofs of this fact. How could the *jus talionis* (Exodus xxi. 24 *seq.*) have been set aside, how could the operations of the year of release (Deut. xv. 2) have been annulled, if the letter and not the spirit of the Torah had been clung to? This is also proved by the well-known traditional explanation of passages like Exodus xxi. 19, xxii. 1 ; Deut. xxii. 17, etc., all of which have reference to the administration

of justice, and on that account demanded the subjection of
the letter to the spirit. If then these assertions of the
Apostle do not in their general acceptation introduce anything which his Jewish contemporaries would not have
freely conceded, one cannot understand the irritation which
forces him to speak of the "vail of Moses" as of a bandage
which prevents the eyes of the Jews from perceiving the
truth, or the spirit of the word of God. This very irritation
is an evidence, as is also the whole treatment of the subject in the Epistle to the Corinthians, that the Apostle's
assertions are in no way intended to be taken in their
general, purely doctrinal sense. As little do they bear this
meaning as does our Mishnaic dictum which deprives of
eternal bliss him who denies the divine origin of the verbal
text of the Torah. The two declarations serve rather to
mark the respective standpoints of two opposite parties
in that conflict of opinion, which resulted in the separation
of Christianity from Judaism; they can, therefore, only be
explained by the light they mutually throw on each other,
as I shall now endeavour to show.

V.

Where, in the New Testament, the person, life and teaching of Jesus are read into the Old, or are drawn out from
it, it is by the employment of *symbolism and allegory*
that this is accomplished, neither of which was foreign
to Jewish modes of thought, the Hagadah itself making
abundant use of both methods. The הדא דכתיב of the
latter (the formula which indicates that a Hagadic
observation was based upon a Biblical passage), thus
finds its New Testament equivalent in the καθὼς
γέγραπται ("as it is written"), or ἵνα πληρωθῇ
("in order that it might be fulfilled"), by which
phrases certain passages of the Bible are directly
connected with events in the life of Jesus. This method
of exegesis was, however, the more dangerous, as being

hallowed by tradition, and beloved by the people. There is likewise no doubt that many Hagadahs, with Christian colouring, were written down, and became the common property of the people, even as there is no room to doubt that these Hagadahs, which, at the present time form a constituent part of the New Testament, led directly to an opposition against the Hagadah itself in the world of Jewish learning. We are told of scholars who most severely condemned the writing down as well as the study of Hagadahs, and who boasted of never having looked into Hagadic books.[1] However this and similar statements may be explained, it is clear that they can all be referred, partly to the recognition of the danger in which the symbolism and allegory of the Hagadah involved Judaism by favouring the intrusion of Christianity, and partly to the arrangements designed to obviate this danger. It is surely not by mere accident that R. Akiba, who in our Mishnah denies future bliss to one who reads in *strange books*, did not devote himself to the Hagadah, and perhaps even condemned it (*Synhedrin*, 38*b*, 67*b*; *Chagigah*, 14*a*). Akiba, moreover, was certainly not the first to adopt this opinion, his utterance in the Mishnah appearing only as supplementary to the preceding remarks; but, as I shall show, his name stands as representative of that mode of regarding the Scriptures, by means of which the intrusion of Christian elements could best be guarded against, and which emphasized the *letter* as the foe of all symbolism and allegory. The two latter designate the *spirit* of which the apostle, in the Second Epistle to the Corinthians (iii. 6), says that God "hath made us able ministers of the New Testament, not of the letter, but of the spirit." We only need the juxtaposition of the Jewish Tanna and the Christian Apostle in order to perceive how much depends upon the accentuation of the spirit. The Apostle was concerned, not with the spirit of the Biblical text, but with the Christian

---

[1] Comp. Zunz, *Gottesdienstliche Vorträge*, p. 335, and Rapoport, *Erech Millin*, article אגדה. § 3. *seq.*

spirit, which was to be breathed into the Old Testament. But as this could only happen by adopting the Hagadic method of regarding the letter as something unstable and movable, the Jewish teachers felt themselves compelled to retain their hold upon the letter, *not for the sake of the letter, but for the sake of the spirit.*

Herein lies also the point of the Mishnaic declaration that he who asserts the Torah is not from God (min-ha-Shamayim), *i.e.*, that he who, while acknowledging the " spirit " of the Old Testament to be Divine, yet treats the letter as symbolic or allegoric in the interest of this " spirit," would be deprived of future bliss. A vital question for Judaism was involved, viz., the purity of the Divine teaching, which could only be protected by the bulwark of the letter (*i.e.*, the literal sense of the word), from any admixture of foreign elements, and it is, therefore, comprehensible why he who threatened the very life of Judaism, was himself threatened with the loss of eternal life. It was the bulwark of the letter, or in the language of the Apostle, the " vail of Moses " which effectually warded off the invasion of Judaism by a foreign " spirit," and preserved the special characteristics of the old faith.

This explanation of the relation between spirit and letter, which, on the one hand, is represented by the Second Epistle to the Corinthians, and on the other by the Mishnah, corresponds in all respects with the doctrinal system of R. Akiba, which has rightly become of paramount influence in Judaism. R. Akiba is the exact antithesis of the Apostle Paul, and although he did not by way of opposition to the Apostle declare that the spirit kills and the letter gives life, he might well have done so, of course with the proviso that he had in his mind a " spirit " foreign to the Old Testament. For, that the sentence of the Apostle in its general sense, stripped of all notions due to religious party feeling, was accepted by R. Akiba as well as by Jewish tradition, has been, I think, convincingly established. Although R. Akiba did not make the remark just suggested, nevertheless his whole doctrinal system is based upon the accentuation of the letter, and it is well known that a Midrash[1] having reference to this subject is assigned to him. This system is not only calculated to unite the oral with the written law, and to obtain rules for new juristic cases[2]—although it must be admitted that it has been abundantly and even excessively used in this direction—but it was founded in the first instance with the object of providing in the letter a bulwark against Christian symbolism and legend. To this object point also certain mystical utterances, such as (*Sabb.*, 89*a*) that God provided the letter with crowns, etc., as well as the saying frequently to be met with in later Jewish writings, that " Letters make wise,"[3] the origin of which, it must be admitted, cannot be traced in Jewish literature. But the evidences traceable in that literature, and our Mishnah above all, suffice to prove that in the history of the origin of Christianity it was the letter which was made to enter the field, for the spirit's sake, against the spirit emphasised by Paul.

M. GÜDEMANN.

---

1 אותיות דר׳ עקיבא

2 Comp. Grätz, *History*, iv. 2, p. 56, *seq*.

3 אותיות מחכימות Comp. Dukes' *Zur Rabbinischen Spruchkunde*, p. 91.

THE JEWS IN THE WORKS
OF THE
CHURCH FATHERS

by
S. Krauss

THE JEWS IN THE WORKS OF THE CHURCH FATHERS.

FOR the history and science of Judaism, and especially for a full understanding of the Agada, the study of the Church Fathers undeniably possesses considerable importance. Naturally all of them are not of the same value. Those who lived in Italy, Spain, or Gaul, and had little communication with Jews, are of minor significance for Jewish literature, compared with the Fathers of Palestine, Syria, and Egypt. I shall therefore pay the most attention to those Fathers whose writings promise the richest results, and we can herein confidently follow the lead of Jerome, who, in his reply to his opponent Rufinus's charge, that he associated too much with Jews, quoted the examples of Origen, Clement, and Eusebius, none of whom disdained to receive instruction from teachers of the Hebrew race (Lib. I., adv. Ruff., c. 13, vol. ii., p. 469, Ed. Vallarsi). If the first notable Father, Justin, and Ephraem Syrus, Jerome's younger contemporary, be added, we obtain the following list of Ecclesiastics, whose writings are of especial interest to us : — Justin Martyr, Clemens Alexandrinus, Origen, Eusebius, Ephraem Syrus, and Jerome.

In the last four decades, since the importance of Patristic literature has obtained a gradually increasing recognition in Jewish circles, students have always sought in the Fathers for Agadic elements which they might collate with Hebrew sources. The fact has, however, been lost sight of, that these Agadas have not always come direct from the Jews. Many of those found in the Church literature must be regarded as the product of independent development. The Agadic exegesis of the Scriptures was peculiar to the spirit of the times, and flourished among the Christians as exuberantly as among the Jews. The accounts in the Church Fathers of Judaism and of Jewish conditions and modes of life are, in my opinion, no less worthy of regard than the Agadic elements there preserved. I shall, therefore, direct my main attention to this class of notices, and only speak of such Agadas as were expressly and explicitly borrowed from the Jews.

For the works of Justin, Clement, Origen and Eusebius, I have used Migne's *Patrologie* (M.); for Ephraem, the Roman edition (R.) of 1732-43; for Jerome, Vallarsi's edition (V.), Verona, 1734-42. Other editions will be quoted occasionally.

I.

JUSTIN MARTYR.

Justin Martyr was born about 100 A.D., in Flavia Neapolis, formerly called Sichem, in the country of the Samaritans. He terms himself a Samaritan, which does not, however, mean that he belonged to the religious sect of the Samaritans, but that they were his countrymen.[1] He, indeed, expressly states that he was one of the uncircumcised.[2] At a later period he came to Ephesus, the scene of his dialogue with the Jew, Tryphon (Eusebius *H. E.*, iv. 18); and here he zealously propagated Christianity among the Jews.[3] The date of the Dialogue coincides with the period of the revolt under Bar Cochba (132—135). That obstinate contest is frequently mentioned in it;[4] and Tryphon is described as a fugitive who escaped from the turmoil of Palestine to peaceful Ephesus.[5]

---

[1] *Dial.* c. 120 (vi. 755, M.), ... ἀπὸ τοῦ γένους τοῦ ἐμοῦ, λέγω δὲ τῶν Σαμαρίων.

[2] *Ib.* c. 29 (vi. 537, M.), τίς οὖν ἔτι μοι περιτομῆς λόγος . . . .

[3] This follows from several passages of the *Dialogue* ; v. Wetzer-Welte's *Kirchenlexicon*, vi. 2067.

[4] *E.g. Dial.* c. 108 (vi. 725, M.), cp. *Apol.* I. 31 (vi. 376, M.).

[5] At the beginning of the *Dialogue.*

These data alone should have sufficed to prove the historical character of the Dialogue. Nevertheless, scholars have apparently favoured the theory that it is only a literary framework for presenting Justin's views, and is purely imaginary. Emphasis is laid upon the fact that Tryphon makes concessions to Justin such as no faithful Jew would possibly have made.[1] The obvious explanation is that politeness induced Tryphon to adopt a conciliatory and yielding tone. Throughout the Dialogue he appears as an enlightened Jew, imbued with Hellenistic culture, who is anxious to exhibit extreme courtesy towards his adversary. He is introduced as a man of education and a philosopher. When Justin remarks, in the course of the interview, that he has no oratorical ability, the Jew replies with tact: "You must be jesting ; your conversation proves you a past master in rhetoric."[2] Tryphon's concessions are, moreover, in most cases, only hypothetical ; and Justin very often imitates him in this respect, admitting even once for instance, for the sake of argument, that Jesus was nothing more than a *Magus*.[3] Besides, details are given which are unsuitable to a fictitious dialogue, but have a meaning if we assume that the writer reports events which actually took place. On the first day, we are told, no strangers were present at the interview ; on the second day, however, Tryphon is joined by some Jews of Ephesus, who take a part in the discussion.[4] One of them begs that a remark which had pleased him might be repeated, and Justin complies with the request.[5] Another of those who had accompanied Tryphon on the second day, called Mnaseas, also joins in

---

[1] Weizsaecker, *Jahrb. für Theologie* XII. (1867), p. 63.

[2] *Dial.* c. 58 (vi. 606. M.), οὐ κατασκευὴν λόγων ἐν μόνῃ τέχνῃ ἐπιδεικνυσ-θαι σπεύω . . . . Καὶ ὁ Τρύφων· εἰρωνεύεσθαι δέ μοι δοκεῖς, λέγων δύναμιν λόγων τεχνικῶν μὴ κεκτῆσθαι.

[3] *Apol.* I. c. 30 (vi. 273, M.).

[4] *Dial.* c. 118. (vi. 749, M.), διὰ τοὺς σήμερον σὺν σοι ἀφιγμένους . . . .

[5] *Ib.* c. 74 (vi. 649, M.).

the debate.[1] This circumstance suggests the inference that not only Tryphon, who from the first inspired Justin with respect as a man of Hellenic culture, but that other members of the Jewish community of Ephesus were also sufficiently well educated to be able to stand their ground against the learned Church Father. Occasionally they give audible token of their satisfaction or disapproval,[2] even applauding and hissing, just as in a theatre.[3] Justin repeatedly, in the course of the disputation, bears testimony to the respect he feels for his learned opponent, and promises, when the Dialogue appears in its written form, to truthfully present Tryphon's views.[4] At the close of the debate, Jew and Christian confess that they have learnt much from one another, and part with expressions of mutual goodwill.[5] These details can only be reminiscences of a real event.

That Tryphon was the famous sage Tarphon (טרפון) is more justly discredited. Justin's description of his antagonist does not tally with what we know of R. Tarphon. The Tanaite was certainly not a philosopher of Tryphon's type. Though Tarphon and Tryphon are not identical, Graetz thinks the name was purposely chosen by the Father, so that he might be able to boast that he had won over the eminent teacher, Tarphon, to Christianity.[6] But it is questionable whether the Hebrew טרפון really cor-

---

[1] *Ib.* c. 85 (vi. 677, M.), οὐ καὶ πάλιν ἐπιμνησθήσομαι διὰ τούτου, τοὺς μὴ καὶ χθὲς σύνοντας ἡμῖν . . . . Καὶ Μνασέας δέ τις ὀνόματι τῶν συνελθόντων αὐτοῖς τῇ δευτέρᾳ ἡμέρᾳ εἶπε . . . .

[2] *Ib.* c. 38 (vi. 557, M.), μὴ ταράσσεσθε δέ, ἀλλὰ μᾶλλον προθυμότεροι γινόμενοι ἀκροαταὶ καὶ ἐξετασταὶ μένετε καταφρονοῦντες τῆς παραδόσεως τῶν ἡμετέρων διδασκάλων.

[3] *Ib.* c. 122 (vi. 760, M.), καὶ ὥσπερ ἐν θεάτρῳ ἀνέκραγόν τινες τῶν τῇ δευτέρᾳ ἀφιγμένων.

[4] *Ib.* c. 80 (vi. 664. M.), τῶν γεγενημένων ἡμῖν λόγων ἁπάντων . . . . σύνταξιν ποιήσομαι ἐν οἷς καὶ τοῦτο ὁμολογοῦντά με ὃ καὶ πρὸς ὑμᾶς ὁμολογῶ, ἐγγράψω.

[5] *Ib. ad fin.*

[6] *Gnosticismus u. Judenth.*, p. 17.

responds to the Greek Τρύφων, in which case only could Justin have intended טרפון by his Τρύφων. Jerome, in his list of the oldest Tanaim, calls ר' טרפון Telphon,[1] He would have probably written Τρύφων had the two names been equivalent.[2] Goldfahn's theory that Tryphon was selected by Justin, because it sounded like δρύπτω, needs no refutation.[3]

Accepting the historical character of the Dialogue, we naturally cannot seek for covert allusions in the name Tryphon. It was probably in common use among the Jews of that age, and there is nothing remarkable in the fact of Justin's having happened to meet a Jew with this name. The same is the case with Mnaseas, which was also frequent from an early period. We find it in Josephus (*Cont. Apion.* i. 23). ר' שמעון בן מנסיא, of a subsequent date, is frequently mentioned in Mishna, Tosefta, Talmud and Midrash; in T. Babli (Beza 30*b*) the name is spelt מנשיא. Zunz quotes a Mnasea, grandson of a Mnasea, from the Seder-ha-doroth, fol. 68*b* (Gesammelte Schriften II., p. 23). Tryphon and Mnasea were thus ordinary names among the Jews; and nothing is less surprising than that Justin's chief opponent in the Dialogue, and another Jew of Ephesus, should have borne them.

Justin's writings constitute the first attempt which has come down to us to justify Christianity before the bar of the ancient religious powers, Heathenism and Judaism. Early Christendom still clung somewhat nervously to the old faith. Christians still practised many Jewish customs,[4] and Justin feels the need of offering an excuse for the

---

[1] In Is. viii. 11.

[2] A. Geiger, *Jüd. Zeitschrift* v. 173, proposes to read instead of Delphon (a variant of Telphon) simply *Tarphon*; this is surely inadmissible; טרפון is perhaps the same as Τερπών (Fick, *Griech. Personennamen*, p. 81), which corresponds more closely to the form Telphon.

[3] Goldfahn, *Justin Martyr und die Agada* in Graetz's *Monatsschrift* XXII. (1873), p. 49, *et seq.*

[4] Smith-Wace, *Dict. of Christian Biography*, III. 581.

Christian transference of the Sabbath-day to Sunday.[1]
Judaism has no right, the Father thinks, to thrust out
its daughter Christianity, for it has also produced other
heresies which it does not disown. The Sadducees, Genistae, Meristae, Galilaei, Helleniani, Pharisaei and Baptistae
are all Jewish sects, so that it becomes a matter of some
difficulty to decide which among them represents the real
Judaism.[2] To this argument Justin attaches special importance, deeming it expedient at the same time to apolo-
gise to the Jews for the harshness of his words.[3] The
Jews, he urges, had sent emissaries in all directions to
calumniate the new sect.[4] This charge recurs in almost
every Church Father; it is also frequently asserted that the
Hebrews were zealously engaged in proselytizing. Thus
in Justin's time, we may conclude with a high degree of
probability, Judaism still retained its power of expansion.
The prophetic promise that the Word of God would reach
distant nations the Hebrews saw fulfilled in the accession
of proselytes to their ranks, the Christians, in the spread of
their own creed.[5]

---

[1] *Dial.* c. 24 (vi. 528, M.).

[2] The names of these sects are cited by Eusebius, *H. E.* iv. 22 (xx. 381,
M.), from the work of an older author, Hegesippus. There they are called
Ἐσσαῖοι, Γαλιλαῖοι, Ἡμεροβάπτισται, Μασβοθαῖοι, Σαμαρεῖται, Σαδδουκαῖοι,
Φαρισσαῖοι. In the *Indiculum Haerescon*, which is ascribed to Jerome,
the *Hemerobaptistae, qui quotidie corpora sua et domum et supellectilem
lavant* figure as the tenth sect. We recognise this sect as the טובלי שחרית
of *Berach*, III. 6c ; they must not be confused with the Essenes. Justin's
Baptistae are very likely the same as these Hemerobaptistae. Concerning the Genistae, Meristae, Galilaei and Helleneiani the views of
scholars are widely divergent, and we will leave the question open. It is
remarkable, however, that the *Essaeans* are mentioned neither by Justin
nor by Eusebius, and not even by Isodorus, *Orig. libr.* VIII. ; the Christians probably felt that they themselves had taken their origin from this
sect. and were, therefore, unwilling to designate them as heretics.

[3] *Dial.* c. 80 (vi. 665, M.), καὶ μὴ ἀηδῶς ἀκούσητέ μου πάντα ἃ φρονῶ
λέγοντος.   [4] *Ib.* c. 108 (vi. 725, M.).

[5] *Ib.* c. 122 (vi. 760, M.), concerning Is. xlix. 6, ταῦτα ὑμεῖς μὲν εἰς τὸν
Γηόραν καὶ τοὺς προσηλύτους εἰρῆσθαι νομίζετε.—Γηόρα is either גרים or
גולה.

Jewish religious teachers are frequently mentioned by Justin, usually under the title of Rabbi,[1] sometimes also simply as διδάσκαλοι;[2] in a few instances, as heads of the Synagogue, ἀρχισυνάγωγοι;[3] an insulting epithet is invariably added. The Rabbinical teachings are termed traditions, παραδόσεις.[4] Instruction was given at the conclusion of divine worship.[5] Disputations between learned Christians and Jewish Rabbis were the order of the day. Numerous specimens are found in Hebrew literature. Justin ridicules the tactics of the Jewish controversialists, who always hunted up their opponents' weak points, like the fly which settles on sore places. If, at a disputation, a multitude of well-considered and well-weighed arguments are adduced, the Jews will always discover a neglected point open to attack.[6] Such controversies might sometimes prove disadvantageous to Judaism, where expert Christian dialecticians overwhelmed ignorant Jews with arguments which they were not prepared to answer, and by which they would have to acknowledge themselves beaten. Justin strove personally for the conversion of the Jews; his efforts were, however, futile, owing to the accident that he met his match in his opponents at Ephesus. Ordinary Jews, not specially skilled in controversy, were strictly enjoined to avoid polemics with Christians.[7] And even Tryphon, who presented so bold a front to his opponent, regretted his breach of this rule.[8] By this we

---

[1] *Dial* c. 112 (vi. 736, M.). Θελόντων 'Ραββί, 'Ραββὶ καλεῖσθαι.
[2] *Ib.* c. 110 (vi. 729, M.). *et paxxim.*   [3] *Ib.* c. 137 (vi. 792, M.).
[4] *Ib.* c. 38 (vi. 557, M.). *et paxxim.*
[5] *Ib.* c. 137 (vi. 792, M.). εἰδάσκουσιν .... μετὰ τὴν προσευχήν.
[6] *Ib.* c. 115 (vi. 744, M.). "Ωσπερ γὰρ αἱ μυῖαι ἐπὶ τὰ ἕλκη προστρέχετε καὶ ἐφίπτασθε. κᾶν γὰρ μυρία τις εἴπῃ καλῶς, ἓν δὲ σμικρὸν ὁτιοῦν εἴπῃ μὴ εὐάρεστον ὑμῖν, ἢ μὴ νοούμενον ἢ μὴ πρὸς τὸ ἀκριβές, τῶν μὲν πολλῶν καλῶν οὐ πεφροντίκατε, τοῦ δὲ μικροῦ ῥηματίου ἐπιλαμβάνεσθε, καὶ κατασκευ- άζειν αὐτὸ ὡς ἀσέβημα καὶ ἀδίκημα σπουδάζετε.
[7] *Ib.* c. 112 (vi. 736, M.), ἢ καὶ ἡμῶν ἐξηγουμένων παραγγέλλουσιν ὑμῖν μηδὲ ὅλως ἐπαίειν, μηδὲ εἰς κοινωνίαν λόγων ἐλθεῖν.
[8] *Ib.* c. 38 (vi. 556, M.). καὶ ὁ Τρύφων εἶπεν .... καλὸν ἦν πεισθέντας ἡμᾶς τοῖς διδασκάλοις νομοθετήσασι μηδενὶ ἐξ ὑμῶν ὁμιλεῖν ....

may gather how the Rabbinic regulations were respected by the people at large. A Jew of Ephesus tells us that for the solution of his doubts and difficulties he often referred to the Rabbis, whom the people regarded as their appointed leaders.[1]

The differences between the Synagogue and the Church turn mostly on the exegesis of Holy Writ ; a large portion of the Agada in-the Midrash and Talmud is a polemic against Christianity. The text of the Scriptures also constituted an important subject of controversy ; the Christians usually read into the Bible more than it contained. Moreover, instead of admitting that their copies were often incorrect, they cherished the delusion that the Jews had falsified and mutilated the text for polemical purposes. This charge already occurs in Justin, who accuses the Jews of altering παρθένος in Is. vii. 14 into νεᾶνις, in order to nullify a Christological argument.[2] He quotes many passages which, he alleges, are only to be found in the old texts, but have been omitted from the new editions.[3] But he is honest enough to reject a manifest Christological gloss interpolated in the Greek version, and gives the preference in this case to the Hebrew text.[4]

In Justin we also meet with a charge which, as far as we know, does not recur in any other Church Father. He accuses the Rabbis of encouraging immorality by sanctioning polygamy among their co-religionists, and

---

[1] *Ib.* c. 94 (vi. 701, M.).   [2] *Ib.* c. 68 (vi. 633, M.).

[3] *Ib.* c. 72 (vi. 645), on Jerem. xi. 19, καὶ ἐπειδὴ ἡ περικοπὴ ἡ ἐκ τῶν λόγων τοῦ Ἱερεμίου ἔτι ἐστὶν ἐγγεγραμμένη ἔν τισιν ἀντιγράφοις τῶν ἐν συναγωγαῖς Ἰουδαίων· πρὸ γὰρ ὀλίγου χρόνου ταῦτα ἐξέκοψαν. He cites similar passages to the same effect.

[4] This gloss is the notorious ἀπὸ τοῦ ξύλου which was said to be the reading in Ps. xcvi. (xcv.). Besides occurring in Justin, *Dial.* c. 73 (vi 645, M.), this interpolation is found only in Latin Fathers, such as Tertullian, Ambrosius, Augustinus, Leo and Gregorius Magnus, who manage to talk a great deal of nonsense concerning the "a ligno."

permitting them to lust after fair women.[1] He blames the facility with which marriages are contracted. When a Jew is abroad, the first thing he does is to take another wife.[2] This matrimonial liberty was indeed, as a matter of fact, a painful characteristic of Talmudic times.

Justin, too, is the first who imputes to the Jews the crime of mocking at and insulting Jesus. This accusation was fraught with terrible consequences for them. It is repeated by all the Fathers of the first four centuries, and though the accounts have been frequently examined, the precise character and truth of this charge have never yet been definitely established. I take the liberty, therefore, of discussing this branch of our subject in some detail.

Although the Fathers are clear as to the fact of a curse pronounced by the Jews, they differ widely as to the object of the curse. Some assert that Jesus was cursed; others that the malediction was directed against Christianity or the Christians. Starting from this point of difference, we classify the weightier statements bearing on this subject under three heads.

I. Malediction against Jesus. Justin, *Dialogue,* c. 103 (vi. 720, M.), (cp. vi. 553, M.), καὶ μάλιστα τοὺς ἐν ταῖς συναγωγαῖς, καταναθεματίσαντας καὶ καταναθεματίζοντας ἐπ' αὐτὸν τοῦτον τὸν Χριστὸν; Origen, *Hom. in Jerem.* xviii. 12 (xiii. 487, M.), Εἴσελθε εἰς τὰς τῶν Ἰουδαίων συναγωγάς, καὶ ἴδε τὸν Ἰησοῦν καθ' ἡμέραν ὑπ' αὐτῶν τῇ γλώσσῃ τῆς βλασφημίας μαστιγούμενον.

II. Against Christians and Christianity. Justin, *Dialogue,* c. 16 (vi. 512, M.), καταρώμενοι ἐν ταῖς συναγωγαῖς ὑμῶν τοὺς πιστεύοντας ἐπὶ τὸν Χριστὸν. Similarly *ib.* c.

---

[1] *Dial.* c. 134 (vi. 785, M.), τοῖς ἀσυνέτοις καὶ τυφλοῖς διδασκάλοις ὑμῶν, οἵτινες καὶ μέχρι νῦν καὶ τέσσαρας καὶ πέντε ἔχειν ὑμᾶς ἕκαστον συγχωροῦσι καὶ ἰὰν εὐμορφόν τις ἰδὼν ἐπιθυμήσῃ αὐτῆς.

[2] *Ib.* c. 141 (vi. 800, M.), καὶ ὅσας βούλεται λαμβάνειν γυναῖκας, ὁποῖον πράττουσιν οἱ ἀπὸ τοῦ γένους ὑμῶν ἄνθρωποι, κατὰ πᾶσαν γῆν, ἔνθα ἂν ἐπιδημήσωσιν ἢ προσπεμφθῶσιν, ἀγόμενοι ὀνόματι γάμου γυναῖκας.

93, (vi. 700, M.)¹; Origen, *Hom. in Jerem.* xviii. 12 (xiii.
485, M.), καὶ μέχρι νῦν, ὑπὸ παρανόμου ἀρχιερέως λόγου
προστάσσομενοι Ἐβιωναῖοι² τύπτουσι τὸν Ἀπόστολον Ἰησοῦ
Χριστοῦ λόγοις δυσφήμοις.

III. Against the Nazarenes. Epiphanius, *Haeres.*, xxix.
9, Πάνυ δὲ οὗτοι ἐχθροὶ τοῖς Ἰουδαίοις ὑπάρχουσιν. Οὐ μόνον
γὰρ οἱ τῶν Ἰουδαίων παῖδες πρὸς τούτους κέκτηνται μῖσος, ἀλλὰ
ἀνιστάμενοι ἔσωθεν (*l.* ἔωθεν) καὶ μέσης ἡμέρας καὶ περὶ τὴν
ἑσπέραν, τρὶς τῆς ἡμέρας, ὅτε τὰς εὐχὰς ἐπιτελοῦσιν ἐν ταῖς
αὐτῶν συναγωγαῖς, ἐπαρῶνται αὐτοῖς καὶ ἀναθεματίζουσι
φάσκοντες, ὅτι ἐπικαταράσαι ὁ Θεὸς τοὺς Ναζωραίους. Jerome
in Isaiah ii. 18, Sub nomine Nazaræorum anathematizant
vocabulum Christianum. *Ib.* 49, 7, Christo sub nomine
Nazaræorum maledicunt. *Ib.* 52, 4, sub nomine, ut saepe
dixi, Nazaræorum ter die in Christianos congerunt male-
dicta, etc., etc.

This last group is in various ways most instructive. We
learn from it that the curse was pronounced thrice daily;
the eighteen Benedictions are obviously suggested. Epiphanius has further the important notice that it was recited ὅτε τὰς εὐχὰς ἐπιτελοῦσιν, which does not mean "at
the conclusion of the prayers,"³ but "while they read the
prayers." The commination was thus a portion of the
daily service, and has long since been justly identified with
the ברכת המינים, "the prayer against heretics." That this
blessing differed in Talmudic times from its present form is
quite clear. It must then have explicitly named the
Nazarenes, for Epiphanius gives us the definite formula,
"May God curse the Nazarenes." The Talmud, which fully
discusses this "blessing," nowhere hints that the Nazarenes

---

¹ On this v. Goldfahn, *ibid*, p. 56.

² The Ebionites, as is the case in many other respects, are here placed
on a level with the Jews; what is predicated about them applies also to
the Jews.

³ This is Schuerer's opinion: *Geschichte des jüd. Volkes im Zeitalter
Jesu Christi*, II. 387. The passage of Justin adduced there is not exactly
in place.

figured in it. Indeed, although several Christian sects are
named in that extensive literature, the Nazarenes do not
once occur in it.[1] This by no-means proves that this name
was unknown to the Talmudic doctors. Probably נוצרי
very often occurred in the Talmud, but has been erased
by the mediæval censors. There were sufficient grounds
for this. Catholic Christendom hated other Christian
heresies as much as Judaism did, and therefore tolerated
llusions to them in the Talmud. But it would not
permit mention of the Nazarenes, for these, at an earlier
period, were synonymous with the Christians. The Christians were called Nazarenes,[2] a name which they have retained in Jewish literature to this day. Our quotation from
Jerome now becomes clear : *The Jews curse the Christians or
Christ under the name of Nazarenes, i.e.,* the malediction in
the liturgy is nominally directed against the Nazarenes but
really against the Christians. From the turn of the phrase,
it is evident that Jerome thought he had made a discovery.
"How artful the Jews are," he seems to say, "they curse
the Nazarenes when they mean the Christians." This
then is established, that the so-called Benediction of the
Minim contained. in ancient times, the term נוצרי; and, in
fact, a gloss of Rashi, which escaped the censors, and is
still preserved in later authorities, makes it clear that, in
his days even, the Blessing still retained the term נוצרי.[3]

The problem still remains, Which expression is it
that has replaced the original נוצרי ? What word has
been substituted for it by the censors or out of fear of
them ? J. Derenbourg assumes that the original form of
the Benediction consisted of the following three parts :
ולמלשינים על תהי תקוה וכל עושי רשעה כרגע יאבדו וכל

---

[1] That בינצרפי in b. Sabb. 116*a* is the same as בינצרני is only a conjecture of several scholars, which. however, cannot be defended.

[2] Cp. Tertullian in *Marc.* vi. 8. unde . . . . nos Judaei Nazaraeos appel-
lant. Jerome, *On Sacr..* 143. 16 (ed. Lagarde II. p. 175) : et nos . . . .
apud veteres Nazaraei dicebamur.

[3] V. M. Bloch. *Institutionen der Judenthums*, I. 193.

אויבינו מהרה יכרתו, and that, instead of ולמלשינים,
the word ולמינים or ולמשרתיב was substituted in R
Gamaliel's days, while, at a still later date, והזדים was
added against the Romans.[1] I consider this supposition
highly improbable. We can hardly believe that the
term ולמלשינים would have been dropped, when we
reflect how much cause there was in every age for the
retention of a commination against the dangerous *Dela-
tores*. Besides, the Christians cannot, in this prayer, be
designated by the term מינים, which is manifestly the same
as μιναῖοι or Minaei; for the Christians regarded this sect
as damnable heretics, and would not have had the slightest
objection to their being cursed by the Jews. The truth
seems to be that the covert reference lies in the phrase
וכל עושי רשעה. It is with regard to these words that the
Codices of the Liturgy exhibit such numerous variations,
which proves that they were not part of the original form
of the prayer. Maimonides does not read וכל עושי רשעה,
but וכל אפיקורסים.[2] This passage, then, is the one directed
against the heretics. The modern וכל עושי רשעה, which
looks so innocent, must have been adopted as a cover for the
far more suspicious and dangerous expression נוצרים. So,
too, in another passage (*Jerusalem Berachot, 5d,* ed. Kro-
toschin) the expression רשע is used as the designation
of a sect תני כולל של מינים ושל הרשעים במכניע זדים.
Tosefta Berachot iv. 25 has, instead of רשעים, the more
forcible פושעים. *Massechet Derech Eretz Rabba* (beginning
of chap. ii.) has הצדוקים והמסורות והרשעים; *Exodus Rabba,*
c. 19, מינים ומשומדין ורשעי ישראל. In all these passages
the word רשעים can only refer to a sect. I believe that
the second phrase read originally וכל הנוצרים כרגע
יאבדו. As, however, נוצרי was primarily the title of Jesus,
the earlier Fathers were correct in asserting that the Jews
cursed Jesus, inasmuch as the expression may refer equally

---

[1] *Revue des Etudes Juives,* xiv. 30.
[2] Derenbourg, *ibid.*

to Jesus or to Christianity. As in their time Christians and Nazarenes were still identical, they had no need to explain the difference of designation. In Epiphanius' and Jerome's days the Nazarenes were only a sect, and no longer formed the whole of Catholic Christendom. These Fathers found it, therefore, necessary to say that the Jews in their formula of malediction cursed the Nazarenes, but meant the Christians.

Thus the accounts of the Church Fathers on this head are harmonised.

Returning to Justin, we note that Agadic elements are to be found in his writings in considerable quantity; most of them have been thoroughly discussed by Goldfahn in his essay, "Justin Martyr and the Agada." (Graetz's *Monatsschrift* xxii., 1873, and in a separate reprint.)

II.

CLEMENT OF ALEXANDRIA.

The writings of Titus Flavius Clemens of Alexandria offer but few materials of interest for Jewish literature. His distinguishing excellence consisted in a sound knowledge of Hellenic literature rather than of theology. His information about Judaism he seems to have derived exclusively from Greek writings, particularly from Philo and Josephus. A persecution of the Christians, which raged in Alexandria in the years 202 and 203, drove Clement to seek safety in flight, and he appears to have taken up his residence for a short while in Syria (Euseb. *H. E.*, VI. 11). Here he may have gleaned something from the Jews at first hand. Of Hebrew he was not altogether ignorant. Most of his explanations of terms are indeed unfortunate, and argue little for an intimate knowledge of the language. But that he possessed a certain acquaintance with Hebrew is proved by the prolix remarks found in his writings on the characteristics which distinguish Hebrew from other languages.[1] It should also be borne in mind that his quotations sometimes differ from the Septuagint, and this variation would seem to show that he consulted the original text.[2] Only on the supposition that Clement had a command of Hebrew can we account for the fact that he criticises adversely those who, when reading Scripture, pervert its plain meaning by their tones, and place a forced construction on clear and wise laws by their transposition of points and accents.[3] That this reproach is aimed at the Jews is obvious. And it is a valuable testimony, from a comparatively early period, to the free and unrestricted manner in which the text of Holy Writ was handled for Agadic purposes.

Hostile expressions against the Jews are not found in his writings. His essay Κανὼν ἐκκλησιαστικὸς ἢ πρὸς τοὺς Ἰουδαΐζοντας (Euseb. *H. E.*, VI., 13) may have contained some ; but the work, with the exception of a few fragments, is lost. He argues that the Jews have no right to twit Christianity with its numerous sects, seeing that Judaism is also rent by factions, but that nevertheless its professors strive their hardest to win converts.[4] He betrays his contempt by the anxiety which he expresses in his exposition not to be confounded with the vulgar Jews.[5] Apart

---

[1] *Strom.* vi. 15 (viii. 353, M.), Ἔχει δ' οὖν καὶ ἄλλας τινὰς ἰδιότητας ἡ Ἑβραίων διάλεκτος, καθάπερ καὶ ἑκάστη τῶν λοιπῶν . . . .

[2] A striking deviation in the translation of Leviticus xi. 13, 14 (Deut xiv. 12) is noticeable, Ἀλλ' οὐδ' ἰκτῖνα ἢ ὠκύπτερον μασσοφαγῆ ἢ ἀετὸν φαγεῖν φησίν . . . . *Paed.* iii. 11 (viii. 653, M.). The words ὠκύπτερον μασ-οφαγῆ are wanting in the LXX.

[3] *Strom.* iii. 4, end (viii. 1144), Οὗτοί εἰσιν οἱ κατὰ τὴν ἀνάγωσιν φωνῆς τρόπῳ διαστρέφοντες τὰς Γραφὰς πρὸς τὰς ἰδίας ἡδονάς, καί τινων προσῳδιῶν καὶ στιγμῶν μεταθέσει τὰ παραγγελθέντα σωφρόνως τε καὶ συμφερόντως βιαζόμενοι πρὸς ἡδυπαθείας τὰς ἑαυτῶν.

[4] *Ib.*. viii. 15 (ix. 524, M.), πρὸς τὰ ὑπὸ Ἑλλήνων καὶ Ἰουδαίων ἐπιφερόμενα ἡμῖν ἐγκλήματα ἀπολογήσασθαι . . . . Πρὸς οὓς φαμέν· Ὅτι καὶ παρ' ὑμῖν τοῖς Ἰουδαίοις . . . . πάμπολλοι γεγόνασιν αἱρέσεις· καὶ οὐ δήπου ςατὲ δεῖν ὀκνεῖν . . . . ἰουδαΐζειν.

[5] *Ib.* vii. 8 (ix. 553, M.), Ἰουδαίων τῶν χυδαίων.

from these isolated instances, he is a defender of Judaism
rather than an antagonist. In his Stromata an endeavour
is made to prove that the Greek philosophers obtained
their wisdom from Jewish teachers, and that the Jewish
law stands higher than Hellenic law.

Agadic elements are more plentiful in Clement's writings than the course of his studies would naturally lead us
to expect. He lays great value on the traditions of the
true and hidden sense of Scripture [1] preserved by Jewish
teachers, whom he knows as the μύσται, a term probably
current in Alexandria.[2] As he, however, usually quotes
traditions without naming the μύσται in connection with
them, it is a matter of some difficulty to distinguish in
his writings those elements which are of specifically Jewish
origin. But as a proof that his works do contain genuine
Jewish traditions I quote the following specimens. He
tells us (*Strom.* I. 23, viii. 900 M.) on the authority
of the μύσται, that Moses slew the Egyptian with a
" mere " word, φασὶ δὲ οἱ μύσται λόγῳ μόνῳ ἀνελεῖν
τὸν Αἰγύπτιον. This is identical with the well-known
tradition which explains the text (Exod. ii. 14) הלהרגני
ארה אומר as meaning that Moses pronounced the
Ineffable Name, and thereby destroyed the Egyptian task-
master. (See *Exodus Rabba*, and Rashi *ad locum.*)

Clement notes (*ibid.* viii., 897 M.), that the law-giver had
several Hebrew names besides his Egyptian one—Moses; his
parents called him at his circumcision יהויקים;[3] and after
his death he received, according to the Mystae, a new name,
Μελχί (מלכי ?). This is undoubtedly a genuine Jewish
Agada; though I cannot, at present, trace its parallel in

---

[1] *Strom.* i. 12 (viii. 753, M.), τὰς ἀποκρύφους τῆς ἀληθοῦς γνωσίως παραδόσεις . . . .

[2] *Vide infra.*

[3] This observation is also noteworthy from a sociological point of
view ; we are thereby informed that already in the second century it was
customary among the Jews to give their sons names on the occasion of
their circumcision (but see Luke i., 59).

Jewish sources. There is a discussion in T. B. *Sota*, 12*a*, and *Exod. R.* 1, between some Tanaites on the name Moses[1]; but there is no hint of Jehojakim, or of the name conferred upon the leader after his death. It should also be noticed that the phrase μετὰ τὴν ἀνάληψιν implies another Agada; that Moses, like Enoch and Elijah, did not die, but was translated to heaven. This legend is clearly alluded to in Jude, verses 8, 9. It is also found in detail in *Deut. R.*, *ad finem* Babylonian Talmud *Sota* 13*b*, לא מת משה. Cp. also *Baba Bathra*, 17*a*, where it is said that Moses belonged to those against whom the angel of death was powerless, לא שלט בהם מלאך המות. Maimonides quotes the legend at the beginning of his Introduction to the Talmud.

After these undoubted specimens of Jewish Agadas we feel ourselves justified in ascribing a Jewish origin to some of Clement's obscurer legends. Clement notes, in connection with Genesis xv. 5, that Abraham, according to the opinions of some, perceived the divine wonders of the Creation and the beautiful order of nature. This exegesis is opposed to the Christian interpretation, which sees in the text a reference to Jesus, the Son of God (*Strom.* v. 1, ix. 20 M.): Ὕστερον δὲ, ἀναβλέψας. εἰς τὸν οὐρανον, εἴτε τὸν υἱὸν ἐν τῷ πνεύματι ἰδών, ὡς ἐξηγοῦνται τινες, εἴτε ἄγγελον εὔδοξον, εἴτε καὶ ἄλλως ἐπιγνοὺς Θεὸν κρείττονα τῆς ποιήσεως, καὶ πάσης τῆς αὐτῇ τάξεως.

The Midrash, commenting on the same verse (*Gen. R.*, c. 44), says that the contemplation of the star-spangled firmament made the patriarch feel himself an astrologer, which agrees with his having realised the order of nature.[2] Even the added touch that Abraham saw an angel is not merely invented by Clement; for the Midrash remarks (on verse 7) that Michael was the saviour of Abraham and would

---

ר' מאיר אומר טוב שמו רבי יהודה אומר טוביה שמו ר' נחמיה אמר [1] הגון לנביאות.

נביא את ואין את אסטרולוגוס [2].

become ultimately the saviour of his posterity. Clement had doubtless heard this Agada, but reproduced it in the wrong place. Clement states that Buzzi, Urias the son of Samaia, and Habakkuk were Jeremiah's contemporaries. προφητεύουσι δὲ καὶ Βουζὶ καὶ Οὐρίας ὁ υἱὸς Σαμαίου καὶ Ἀμβακούμ σὺν αὐτῷ. *Strom.* i., 21 (viii., 849). Cp. *Strom.* i. 21 (viii., 872 M.), where Σοφωνίας Βουζὶ follow after Jeremiah. This notice is evidently based on an Agada. And, in fact, *Seder Olam R.*, c. xx. *ad finem*, collates the following passages :—דבר ה' אל צפניה כו' דברי

ירמיהו בן חלקיהו אשר היה דבר ה' אליו וכו' וגם איש היה מתנבא בשם ה' וכו' היה היה דבר ה' אל יחזקיאל בן בוזי וכו' כולם נתנבאו כמנד לחורבן.

According to this quotation, Zephaniah, Jeremiah, Uriah (Jerem. xvi. 20), and Ezekiel were contemporary prophets ; this is in complete agreement with Clement. We are thus also in a position to identify Clement's enigmatic Buzi— who has given this Father's editors so much trouble—with Ezekiel, *son of Buzi.* Either " Ezekiel " has dropped out, or his father is really meant, in accordance with the tradition that where a prophet's father is named, he too was a prophet.

Graetz, in his *Hagadische Elementen bei den Kirchenvätern* (Fränkel's *Monatsschrift*, III., 1854, p. 311), first drew attention to the agreement between Clement and the *Seder Olam Rabbi.* I will give one more striking instance. Clement says, *Strom.* i., 21 (viii., 842 M.), that Elisha commenced to prophesy at the age of forty, and prophesied for a period of six years. Whence is this statement, which is given with as much emphasis as if it rested on Scriptural authority, derived ? The *Seder Olam R.*, c. xix., says :—מכאן אתה מחשב כמה שנים פרנס אלישע את ישראל·······יותר משׁשׁים שנה. Undoubtedly we ought to read in the Greek, not ἕξ, but ἑξήκοντα (instead of ξ', equal to 60, ϛ', equal to 6, was written by mistake). This tradition, then, Clement has in common with the Seder Olam. That Elisha commenced his prophetic career at the age of forty we do not find in any of the Jewish sources; it must nevertheless have been a common tradition, and the same supposition would account for many other of Clement's statements. In conclusion, we may note that this Father was acquainted with many more traditions than he gives. He, for example, alludes to an exposition of the Mystae in connection with the sacrificial ritual, but does not say anything more definite about it.

III.

ORIGEN.

Origen was born, probably, in Alexandria, about 185 or 186 A.D. It is generally assumed that his parents were Christians, but this was probably the case on one side only. His father's name, Leonides, has been preserved, but not that of his mother. This omission is not accidental, but is due to the reverence of pious Christian writers for Origen's memory, which led them to suppress his mother's name on account of her Jewish descent.[1] The fact that she knew enough of Hebrew to teach her son,[2] and that he occupied himself with the study of that language, contrary —according to Jerome—to the usage of his nation and age, are strong evidence in favour of this view.[3] His impulse to Hebrew studies he probably received from his Jewish mother.[4] In his capacity as Bishop of Cæsarea, in Palestine, Origen must have come into frequent contact with learned Jews, as indeed appears from his writings. He mentions again and again his *Magister Hebraeus*, on whose authority he gives several Agadas.[5] His depen-

---

[1] *Strom.* ii. 20 (viii. 872, M.), δι' αἰτίας ἃς ἴσασιν οἱ μύσται.

[2] Jerome, *Ep.* xxxix. *ad Paulam*, c. 1, Tum vero quod in Origine quoque illo Graecia tota miratur, in paucis non dicam mensibus, sed diebus, ita Hebraeae linguae vicerat difficultates, ut *in discendis canendisque Psalmis cum matre contenderet.*

[3] Cp. Smith-Wace, *op. cit.*, iv. 976.

[4] Jerome, *De viris illustr.* 54, contra aetatis gentisque suae naturam.

[5] *De Princ.*, 1, 3, 4, iv. 26 ; in the Greek Fragment, ὁ Ἑβραιος. I may

dence on Jewish masters is already emphatically noted by
Jerome.[1] He often mentions the views of the Jews, by
which phrase he refers not to the teaching of certain
individuals, but to the method of exegesis universally
prevalent among the Hebrews of his time.[2] Those of them
with whom he cultivated personal intercourse were distinguished by their scientific attainments. The one Jew
whom he names is no less considerable a personage than
Hillel, the Patriarch's son, or Jullos, as Origen calls him.[3]
His other Jewish acquaintances were either closely related
to the patriarch's family or occupied a high position on
account of their erudition.[4] No wonder that with such
opponents Origen carefully avoids, in his polemic, offensive
expressions ; forming, in this respect, a noble exception to
the usual practice of the Church fathers. Origen fights
principles, not their representatives or exponents. Occasionally, however, a harsh sentence against his Jewish
antagonists escapes him.[5] He even ventures to assert that
the Jews of his time could no longer boast of men of real
knowledge.[6] Consistently with this adverse judgment,
Origen labours chiefly to refute the scriptural exposition
of Jewish teachers, and to establish in lieu thereof his own
exegesis. He not only had private interviews with Jewish

---

remark here that I give my quotations in Greek when the original
writings of Origen remain, and in Latin when only the Latin translation
has survived.

[1] Jerome, *Lib.* i. *adv. Ruff.*, c. 13 ; cp. the Introduction supra.

[2] *E.g., Ep. ad Africanus* § 12, φασὶ δὲ οἱ Ἑβραῖοι. For other quotations
see infra.

[3] My especial authority for this is Graetz's " *Hillel, the son of the
Patriarchs*" (*Monatsschrift* xxx., 1881, p. 433, etc.). My revered teacher,
Professor W. Bacher, in his *Hagada of the Palestinian Amoraim*, i. 92
and 107 § 2, suggests the hypothesis that Origen also had intercourse
with Hoschja.

[4] Grätz, *op. cit.*

[5] *Hom.* x. *in Jerem.* § 8 (xiii. 368, M.), βλέπετε αὐτῶν τὰς καρδίας
ζιεσθιομένας ὑπὸ τῶν δυνάμεων ἀντικειμένων.

[6] *Ib.* § 3 (xvii. 361, Gr. Text is not clear), Neque magistri neque doctores in Judaea aliqui remanserunt : et licet sint innumerabiles qui sibi
sapientiam vindicent, non est jam sermo Dei in eis.

teachers, but also engaged in public disputations in the
presence of large audiences, which included among their
ranks competent controversialists. This we gather from
several expressions in his writings.[1] The principal topics
discussed at these meetings may be summarised as follows:—

1. *The Scriptural Text.*—The copies of the Bible that
circulated among the Christians were, as we have already
had occasion to remark, corrupt in several passages. At
a disputation between Jews and Christians, the former,
naturally enough, alluded to these mistakes, and mocked
their opponents for allowing such obvious blunders. This
kind of argument, the first beginnings of which we have
traced in Justin, plays an important part in Origen. The
wish to free the Church from the just reproaches of the
Jews on this score, led him to undertake that gigantic
enterprise, the fruit of which is the Hexapla.[2]

2. *The Apocrypha.*—Another point of difference was the

---

[1] *Contra Celsum* I. 45 (xi. 744, M.), Μέμνημαι δέ ποτε ἐν τινι πρὸς Ἰουδαίων λεγομένους σοφοὺς διαλέξει χρησάμενος τοιούτῳ λόγῳ, πλειόνων
κρινόντων τὸ λεγόμενον. *Ib.* I. 55 (xi. 761, M.), Μέμνηναι δέ ποτε, ἐν τινι
πρὸς τους λεγομένους παρὰ Ἰουδαίοις σοφοὺς ἐνζητήσει ταῖς προφητείαις
ταύταις (*Jesaja* liii.) χρησάμενος· ἐφ' οἷς ἔλεγεν ὁ Ἰουδαῖος . . . . *Ib.* i. 56
(xi. 764, M.), καὶ μίμνημαί γε πάνυ θλίψας τὸν Ἰουδαῖον νομιζόμενον σοφὸν
ἐκ τῆς λέξεως ταύτης· ὃς πρὸς αὐτὴν ἀπορῶν, εἶπε τὰ τῷ ἑαυτοῦ Ἰουδαϊσμῷ
ἀκόλουθα, etc., etc.

[2] Epiphanius. *De ponderibus et mensuris*, c. 2, Ὠριγένης . . . . ἀποκα-
τέστησε τῷ ἑκάστῳ τόπῳ τὸν ἐλλείποντα λογον . . . . ἵνα μὴ παραλείψῃ
Ἰουδαῖος καὶ Σαμαρίταις ἐπιλαμβάνεσθαι τῶν ἐν ταῖς ἁγίαις Ἐκκλησίαις
θείων Γραφῶν—Ruffinus lib. v. Invect. adv. Hieronymum, c. 4, Apostatae
quidem et Judaei interpretati sunt ea, quorum lectione Judaei maxime
utuntur. Et quia frequenter si disputatio incidisset, vel immutata
esse aliquanta, vel deesse, vel abundare in nostris Scripturis mentiebantur,
veluit *Origenes* nostris ostendere, qualis apud Judaeos Scripturarum
lectio teneretur . . . . ut sciremus non quid nobis, sed quid Judaeis
adversum nos certantibus aut deesse, aut abundare videntur. Origen
recurs frequently to the Jewish method of reading, *e.g.*, *Hom.
in Num.* xvi. 4, Hebraei habere se scriptum dicunt.— *Comm. in Ep. ad
Rom.* lib. ii. § 13 (xiv. 909, M.), ipsi in Hebraeis exemplaribus habere se
dicunt . . . .

Apocrypha, to which the Church attached an exaggerated importance, notwithstanding its frequent want of taste and silliness, over which the Jews could only make merry. The history of Susanna was always derided by them for this reason.[1] The Jews had an Apocrypha of their own, which they valued; but this seems to have been distinguished from what we term Agada only in as far as it was already written down, while most other Agadas were still orally circulated.[2] Origen draws no distinction between the Jewish Apocrypha and Jewish traditions, knowing that they merged into one.[3] It is especially noteworthy that he also knew of the existence of certain mystic writings, by which he could not have meant either Apocrypha or Agada, for both these classes of literature were known to him under their proper names.[4] He must have been thinking of such works as treat of the מעשה מרכבה, or מעשה בראשית, etc., writings which, according to

---

[1] *Epistola ad Africanum de historia Susannae* § 5, 'Ασκοῦμεν δὲ μὴ ἀγνοεῖν καὶ τὰς [sc. γραφὰς] παρ' ἐκείνοις, ἵνα, πρὸς 'Ιουδαίους δια-λεγόμενοι, μὴ προφέρωμεν αὐτοῖς τὰ μὴ κείμενα ἐν τοῖς ἀντιγράφοις αὐτῶν, καὶ ἵνα συγχρησώμεθα τοῖς φερομένοις παρ' ἐκείνοις· εἰ καὶ ἐν τοῖς ἡμετέροις οὐ κεῖται βιβλίοις· τοιαύτης γὰρ οὔσης ἡμῶν τῆς πρὸς αὐτοὺς ἐν ταῖς ζητήσεσι παρασκευῆς, οὐ καταφρονήσουσιν, οὐδ' ὡς ἔθος αὐτοῖς, γελάσονται τοὺς ἀπὸ τῶν ἐθνῶν πιστεύοντας ὡς ἀληθῆ, καὶ παρ' αὐτοῖς ἀναγεγραμμένα ἀγνοοῦντας.—*Ib.* § 4, "Ωρα τοίνυν εἰ μὴ λανθάνει ὑμᾶς τὰ τοιαῦτα, ἀθετεῖν τὰ ἐν ταῖς 'Εκκλησίαις φερόμενα ἀντίγραφα, καὶ νομοτεθῆσαι τῇ ἀδελφότητι, ἀποθέσθαι μὲν τὰς παρ' αὐτοῖς ἐπιφερομένας ἱερὰς βίβλους, κολακεύειν δὲ 'Ιουδαίους, καὶ πείθειν, ἵνα μεταδῶσιν ἡμῖν τῶν καθαρῶν, καὶ μηδὲν πλάσμα ἐχόντων.—From these concessions may be observed how weak the Church felt itself at that time. Later on the victorious Church used quite a different language.

[2] *Ib.* § 9, Σαφὲς δ' ὅτι αἱ παραδόσεις λέγουσι πεπρῖσθαι 'Ησαίαν τὸν προφήτην. καὶ ἐν τινι ἀποκρύφῳ τοῦτο φέρεται. A Hagada, therefore, which existed in an *apocryphon*, *i.e.* which was established in writing. Probably it is a reference to 'Αναβατικὸν 'Ησαίου, which is mentioned several times.

[3] In Matt. xvii. 2 (xii. 1477, M.), εἴτε ἐκ παραδοσέων, εἴτε καὶ ἐπιβάλλον τες. εἴτε καὶ ἐξ ἀποκρύφων . . . .

[4] *In Matt. Comm. ser.* § 28 (xiii. 1636, M.), Ex libris secretioribus, qui apud Judaeos feruntur . . . .

the Talmud, were wont to be withheld from the uninitiated
and especially from Christians and heretics.

3. *Christian Dogmas.*—The mysterious birth of Christ
still formed a point of controversy between Jews and
Christians. Justin, who knew that the Jews could not
and would not accept Christ's divinity, also touches on
this theme.[1] Origen reports a far harsher judgment as
the belief of the Jews. He says in his commentary on
John xx. 14 (xiv., 608 M.), that the Jews spoke after the
following fashion: Ἡμεῖς μᾶλλον ἕνα πατέρα ἔχομεν τὸν
Θεὸν ἤπερ σύ, ὁ φάσκων μὲν ἐκ παρθένου γεγεννῆσθαι, ἐκ
πορνείας γὲ γεγεννημένος. Jesus' illegitimate birth was
always a firmly held dogma in Judaism, which found
clear expression in its ancient and modern literature, passed
over to the heathens of antiquity and lives to-day in the
consciousness of every simple-minded Jew, who only knows
as much on this subject as he has learnt from his parents.
Must not this conviction have found expression in the
Talmud? Has that monumental work, which contains
such valuable evidence on the events of the first Christian
centuries, nothing to tell us concerning this Jewish dogma?
Certainly it has. The Talmud here agrees with Origen.
The founder of the dominant creed it calls ישו בר פנדרא,
or ישו פנדרא.[2] What does פנדרא mean? Although much
has been written about this term, its significance and
etymology have not been fixed. I here suggest an explanation, quite different from those hitherto proposed.
In Sifri Deut., § 320, תהפוכות (Deut. xxxii. 20) is thus
interpreted, הפכפכנים הם פורנים הם, "They are a common and degraded people." פורנים is the Hebrew
transcription, with the plural suffix, of the Greek πόρνοι, as
Levy (*Neuhebr. Wörterb.*, iv. 18*a*) correctly states. The
Greek term πόρνος has become naturalised in the Rabbinic

---

[1] *Dial.* c. 49 (vi. 581, M.), ὁ Τρύφων . . . . καὶ γὰρ πάντες ἡμεῖς τὸν
Χριστὸν ἄνθρωπον ἐξ ἀνθρώπων προσδοκῶμεν γενήσεσθαι.

[2] Also פנברא, which is even written פנתרא.

dialect, in which πορνεῖον and πόρνη also occur. Now, this passage in the Sifri has, as a *varia lectio,* פרדנים. Levy gives πόρδων as its equivalent, but this has nothing in common with πόρνοι. We believe that a purely phonetic phenomenon accounts for this variant. Between the liquids "r" and "n," the dental "d" has been inserted, a procedure familiar to philologists. פרדנים is thus the same as πόρνοι. The feminine form πόρνη shows a similar phonetic trans-formation in the word פרדנית.[1] We now arrive at the con-clusion of this chain of reasoning. פנדרא and פרדנית (disregarding the feminine suffix) only differ in the relative position of the liquids "n" and "r." That these frequently change their places in the Rabbinic dialect in the case of words borrowed from the Greek is well known. It may therefore be confidently assumed that פנדרא is nothing but πόρνη, modified by phonetic influences. ישו בר פנדרא would thus mean Jesus, the son of the prostitute, or in Origen's phrase ὁ ἐκ πορνείας γεγεννημένος, or as the Pesikta Rabbathi has it ברא דזניתא. This explanation sums up the beliefs held in Jewish circles concerning Jesus.[2] This does not shut out the view that the present form of the word פנדרא, which sounds like παρθένος, may also have been influenced by the Christian dogma that Jesus was the son of a virgin. The opposition between ἐκ παρθένου and ἐκ πορνείας forms even in Origen a sort of play upon words, and Jewish popular wit was probably not slow to take advantage of the similarity of sound.

4. *Abrogation of the Mosaic Law.*—The Pauline doctrine that Jesus' advent superseded the Law of Moses encountered a lively opposition down to the third century. The contra-diction between Christ's declaration that not an iota of the Law shall be given up, and his followers' disregard of the

---

[1] This disagrees with the view of Levy. iv. 102*a*.

[2] I think it unnecessary to cite the Rabbinical passages relating to Jesus, as they are accessible in the Essay of Laible, *Jesus Christus im Talmud* (Berlin, 1891).

most essential Jewish observances was too glaring not to
be noticed and severely reprehended by impartial heathens,
who told the Christians that their spiritual conception
of the Scriptures did not justify their neglect of the ceremonial laws; for there were Jews who also conceived their
law spiritually and yet scrupulously practised all of them.[1]
Origen nevertheless pours out the vials of his contempt on
Jews "after the flesh."[2] He finds it unnecessary to wash
the hands before meals; the sole requisite is spiritual
purity.[3] The fulfilment of the laws in a spiritual sense
sometimes assumes a very comical aspect!

Origen brings against the Jews a charge already met
with in Justin; viz., that the Jews falsify and mutilate
the Scriptures.[4] He is convinced that there is a want of
agreement between the old and new copies of the Jewish
Bible, and that much which exhibited a Christian tendency
in the former, has been disfigured in the latter.[5] He is
unconscious that he is here guilty of a self-contradiction;
for he often admits that the Jews possess the genuine, the
Christians the corrupt text of Holy Writ.[6] Especially instructive is Origen's testimony to the great attraction
which Judaism possessed for the heathens. There must
have been still many proselytes to Judaism in his day;

---

[1] *Contra Celsum* I. § 1 (xi. 793, [M.), μηδὲ τοῦτο κατανοήσας, ὅτι οἱ ἀπὸ
Ἰουδαίων εἰς τὸν Ἰησοῦν πιστεύοντες οὐ καταλελοίπασι τὸν πάτριον
νόμον. Origen adds to this (§ 3), The Jew of Celsus ought rather to
have said. τινὲς δὲ (ὑμῶν) καὶ διηγούμενοι ὡς ἐπαγγέλλεσθε, πνευματικῶς,
οὐδὲν ἧττον τὰ πάτρια τηρεῖτε.

[2] *Comm. in Matt.* xi. 12 (xiii. 939, M.), οἱ σωματικοὶ Ἰουδαίοι.

[3] *Ib.* xi. 8 (xiii. 928, M.), Ὤιοντο γὰρ κοινὰς μὲν καὶ ἀκαθάρτους εἶναι,
χεῖρας τὰς τῶν μὴ νιψαμένων πρὸ τοῦ ἀρτοφαγεῖν . . . . Ἡμεῖς δὲ οὐ κατὰ τὴν
τῶν παρ' ἐκείνοις πρεσβυτέρων παραδόσιν . . . . καθαίρειν πειρώμεθα . . . .

[4] *Hom. in Jerem.* xvi. 10 (viii. 451, M.), Judaei qui exemplaria non-
nulla falsarunt.—The Greek text is here damaged.

[5] *In Matt. Comm. ser.* § 28 (xiii. 1636, M.) in Scripturis *veteribus* quae
legebantur in Synagogis eorum.

[6] *Hom. in Jerem.* xvi. 10 (xiii. 450, M.), Εἶτα ἄλλη ἐστὶ προφητεία, ἣν
οὐκ οἶδ' ὅπως παρὰ τοῖς Ἑβδομήκοντα οὐχ' εὕρομεν δὲ ἐν ταῖς ἐκδόσεσι,
δηλονότι κειμένην ἐν τῷ Ἑβραϊκῷ . . . .

otherwise there is no adequate reason for the vehement indignation with which he attacks the Judaizers, forgetting himself so far as to utter curses and imprecations, altogether unworthy of him, against those who were converted to the old faith.[1] Among the Christians, too, there were several "Judaizers." Many, especially women, 'kept the Sabbath on the same day of the week as the Jews; washed and adorned themselves in honour of the day.[2] Origen maintains that the Sabbath in the "carnal" sense, as the Jews conceive it, cannot possibly be observed; to carry out its ordinances literally, one would have to abide in the same place for twenty-four hours, without stirring. This point was often treated in controversies. It forms, even in Jerome's writings, the subject of a lively dispute between Jews and Christians.[3] Besides the Sabbath, the Passover

---

[1] *In Matt. Comm. ser.* § 16 (xiii. 1621, M.), Arbitror ergo omnem hominem qui ex conversatione gentili Judaeorum .actus est proselytus, filium gehennae fuisse et priusquam proselytus efficiatur.

[2] *Hom. in Jerem.* xii. 13 (xvii. 396, M.), Καὶ περὶ σαββάτου γυναῖκες μὴ ἀκούσωσι τοῦ προφητοῦ, οὐκ ἀκούουσι κεκρυμμένως, ἀλλὰ ἀκούουσι φανερῶς. Οὐ λούονται τὴν ἡμέραν τοῦ σαββάτου . . . .

[3] *Comm. in Ep. ad Rom.* vi. 2 (xiv. 1094, M), Quid enim tam impossibile, quam Sabbati observatio secundum litteram Legis, ut in multis saepe jam diximus? Jubetur enim non exire de domo sua, non se movere de loco suo, nihil oneris levare. Quae quia impossibilia vident Judaei, qui secundum carnem legem observant, inepta quaedam et ridicula commentantur, quibus impossibilitatem Legis sarcire videantur. Origen omits to tell us what these stupidities are. We discover them, however, through Jerome, *Ep. ad Algasiam*, c. 10 (iv. 207, ed. Martianay), Praeterea quia jussum est, ut diebus Sabbathorum sedeat unusquisque in domo sua, et non egrediatur, neque ambulet de loco, in quo *habitat, si quando eos juxta litteras experimur arctare*, ut non jaccant, non ambulent, non stent, sed tantum sedeant, sic velint praecepta servare, solent respondere et dicere : *Barachibas et Simon et Helles magistri nostri tradiderunt nobis, ut bis mille pedes ambulemus in Sabbatho*, et cetera istiusmodi. The answer of the Jew would probably in the original Hebrew run as follows : קבלה היא בידנו מפי ר' עקיבה משום ר' שמעון ר' שמעון ישאמר הלל, etc. In the Talmud and Midrash we frequently note apologetic utterance against the reproach of the Christians in reference to the keeping of the Sabbath, of which a few have been collected by N. Brüll, *Grätz Jubelschrift*, p. 191, N. 1. The laws concerning circumcision were declared by

was also kept according to Jewish rites by numerous Christians who prepared unleavened bread.[1] Origen asserts, that
this sympathy with Judaism was not spontaneous, but was
the artificial work of missionaries, who carried on a zealous
propaganda on behalf of the ancient faith, and cajoled
Christians to practise its rites.[2]

Origen has a large number of Hebrew traditions or Agadas; in this respect he stands, among the Church Fathers,
second only to Jerome. It should be noted that Origen
knows Jewish traditions which have reference to the
Gospels. He gives, in the name of the Jews, an explanation
of the term κορβᾶν, קָרְבָּן, which occurs in the New Testament.[3] Iscariot, Judas the traitor's surname, also seems to
have had a traditional, though erroneous, Jewish interpretation.[4] His account of the Tetragrammaton and of the
word pronounced in its stead, points to a genuine Jewish
tradition.[5] The Midrashim or Agadas, in the strict sense
of the terms, which Origen quotes so profusely, he probably
owed to his intercourse with distinguished Jewish friends.

Origen as impossible as those concerning the keeping of the Sabbath.
See on that point Diestel, *History of the Old Testament*, p. 27, and Bacher,
Ag. of the Pal. Amor., I. 92, N. 4.

[1] *Hom. in Jerem.* xii. 13 (xiii. 396, M.). Ὅσοι ἐν ὑμῖν (ἐγγὺς γάρ ἐστι τὸ
πάσχα) ἄζυμα ἄγετε. I quote the text with some emendations.

[2] *In Matt. Comm. ser.* § 16 (xiii. 1621, M.), [Judaei] diligenter circum-
eunt plurima loca mundi, ut advenas Judaizare suadeant.

[3] *Comm. in Matt.* xi. 9 (xiii. 929, M.), οἱ δὲ φαρισαῖοι καὶ οἱ γραμματεῖς
τοιαύτην ἐναντιουμένην τῷ νόμῳ παράδοσιν ἐκδεδώκασιν, ἀσαφέστερον ἐν τῷ
Εὐαγγελίῳ κειμένην, ᾗ οὐδ' αὐτοὶ ἐπιβεβλήκαμεν ἄν, εἰ μὴ τῶν Ἑβραίων
τις ἐπιδέδωκεν ἡμῖν τὰ κατὰ τὸν τόπον οὕτως ἔχοντα . . . . Κορβᾶν ἐστι
ὃ ὀφείλεις μοι, τουτέστι, δῶρον. The same words, but not in the name of
the Jew, are also found in *Theophylactus in Matt.* xv. 5.

[4] *In Matt. Comm. ser.* §78 (xiii. 1727, M.), Audivi quendam exponen-
tem patriam proditoris Judae secundum interpretationem Hebraicam
exsuffocatum vocari.

[5] *Selecta in Psalm* ii. (xii. 1104, M.), κύριον γὰρ ἐνθάδε ἀντὶ τοῦ Ἰαὴ
εἴρηκεν, καὶ ἔστιν ἡ ἀρχὴ τοῦ ψαλμοῦ παρ' Ἑβραίοις " Ἀλληλουΐα". ἔστι
δέ τι τετραγράμματον ἀνεκφώνητον παρ' αὐτοῖς, ὅπερ καὶ ἐπὶ τοῦ πετάλου τοῦ
χρυσοῦ τοῦ ἀρχιερέως ἀναγέγραπται, καὶ λέγεται μὲν τῇ Ἀδωναΐ προσηγορίᾳ,
οὐχὶ τούτου γεγραμμένου ἐν τῷ τετραγραμμάτῳ.

His introductions to some of these Agadas show that he had a certain respect for them.[1] Most of them are also to be found in Jewish sources. Some have already been compared by Graetz in his *Hagadische Elemente bei den Kirchenvätern.* We will confine our attention to a few selected specimens, which will serve to show how useful it would be to collect and investigate the Agadas scattered through Origen's writings.

1.—"THE GARDEN OF EDEN, THE CENTRE OF THE WORLD."

Selecta in Gen. ii. 8 (xii. 100, M.), Οὐκοῦν παραδεδώκασιν Ἑβραῖοι, ὅτι ὁ τόπος ἐν ᾧ ἐφύτευσεν τὸν παράδεισον ἢ τὸν κῆπον Κύριος ὁ Θεός, Ἐδὲμ καλεῖτα· καὶ φάσιν αὐτὸν μέσον εἶναι τοῦ κόσμου, ὡς κόρην ὀφθαλμοῦ· διὸ καὶ τὸν ποταμὸν τὸν Φείσων, ἑρμηνεύεσθαι σ τ ό μ α κ ό ρ η ς, ὡς ἐκ τοῦ Ἐδὲμ ἐκπορευομένου τοῦ ποταμοῦ τοῦ πρώτου.

A remarkable Midrash of which I have failed to find an exact counterpart in Jewish writings. It may be a conclusion drawn from the old assumption that Palestine is the centre of the earth, while Eden was supposed to be in or near to Palestine. The precise situation of Paradise forms the subject of a Talmudic controversy. T. B. *Erubin*, 19a:—
גן עדן א'ר ר'ש לקיש אם בארץ ישראל הוא בית שאן פירתחה
פירתחא גרם בית בערביא ואם. On the other hand, Midrash
Ps. xxi. 3, tells us: שערי גן עדן כמוכין להר המוריה. The
interpretation of פישון as פי אישון is unknown to me in
Jewish sources.

2.—POTIPHAR AND JOSEPH.

Origen says in a *catena regia*, quoted from a MS. in Montfaucon's Hexapla on Genesis xxxvii. 36: "Phutirpharem eundem ipsum esse tradunt, qui Josephi herus et socer

---

[1] *Hom. in Isajam* I. § 5 (xiii. 225, M.), Cur non dicamus in praesenti traditionem quandam Judaeorum verisimilem quidem, nec tamen veram .... It is a reference to the well-known tradition of the murder of the prophet Isaiah.

fuit. Narrantque Aseneth illam matrem suam apud patrem accusasse, quod insidias in Josephum struxisset, non autem ab eo insidiis appetita fuisset. Quam ille Josepho sponsam dedit"...... The same tradition is given more explicitly in Jerome, *Quest. Heb.*, in Gen. xxxvii. 36: "Putiphar eunucho. Ubi quæritur, quomodo postea uxorem habere dicatur. Tradunt Hebræi emptum ab hoc Joseph ob nimiam pulchritudinem in turpe ministerium, et a Domino virilibus ejus arefactis, postea electum esse juxta morem Hierophan-tarum in pontificatum Neilopoleos, et hujus filiam esse Aseneth, quam postea Joseph uxorem acceperit."[1]

Three features are to be distinguished in these notices, (*a*) Potiphar, Gen. xxxvii. 36, is identified with Potipherah, Gen. xli. 45, and Asenath is, accordingly, Joseph's former master's daughter; (*b*) Asenath, according to this account, felt and evinced sympathy with her father's slave before his imprisonment; (*c*) Potiphar, inflamed by the sight of Joseph's beauty, contemplated the commission of an unnatural crime, but was stricken with impotence. The whole of this tradition, with the exception of the second part, which does not really belong to it, occurs in Jewish sources. We read in T. B. *Sota*, 136:—ויקנהו פוטיפר אמר רב שקנאו לעצמו [בא גבריאל וכרכו] בא גבריאל ופירעו מעיקרא כתיב פוטיפר ולבסוף פוטיפרע. The words placed within brackets are erased by Rashi, because they are tautologous. R. Nathan, of the *Aruch*, retains them, and explains, סירסו לבצים ופירעו לגיד. This view is obviously preferable to Rashi's. The words כריס פרעה form the basis of the interpretation סירכו ופירעו. We thus have here the express tradition that Potiphar is identical with Potipherah, and was stricken with impotence as a punishment for his evil intentions towards Joseph.

The same legend is recorded in other portions of Rabbinic literature. *Gen. R.*, c. 86, פוטיפר שהיה פורע עצמו לע"ז

---

[1] This tradition is not found in Rahmer's *Hebrew Traditions in the Works of Hieronymus*, Breslau, 1861.

כיון שייד הפר לשם נעשה פוטבן כרים פרעה שנכתרם מלבד
שלא לקחו אלא להתביש וסירכו הקב"ה בנופי. Levy, *Neuhebr.*
Wörterbuch, and Fürst, *Glossarium Graeco-hebraeum*, p. 163 *b.*,
give φωτεινός as the Greek original of פוטבן. Kohut's *Aruch
Completum*, VI., 315*b*, agrees with Perles' *Rabbinische Sprach-
u. Sagen-Kunde*, p. 21, that פוטבן is derived from πουτάνα=
putana. Both explanations are incorrect; for φωτεινός would
imply a eulogy of Potiphar, where none was intended by the
Midrash, and "putana" is not Latin but Romaic. I venture
to suggest that פוטבן=σπάδων, a eunuch; σπάδων is the
rendering of כרים, which the Septuagint and Vulgate give
generally as well as Gen. xxxvii. 36, in the particular passage
under discussion (see H. Rönsch, *Itala u. Vulgata*, second
edition, p. 246). The name פוטיפרע, which sounded so
strange to the Hebrew ear demanded an Agadic interpretation. It was accordingly bisected; the first half, פוטי,
was explained in three ways: (*a*) as derived from פטם,
Gen. R., c. 86, שהיה מפטם עגלים לע"ז; (*b*) from φῶς
"light," *Tanchuma* II., וישב, § 16, למה נקרא שמו פוטיפר
שהבהיק לביתו של פרעה,[1] cp. *Jelamdenu*, quoted in *Aruch*,
s. v., פט II., פוטיאל שהאיר במעשים טובים שאת אומר ביוונית
פוטייא; (*c*) from σπάδων, a "eunuch," *Gen. R.*, ib., where the
words כרים פרעה are added to confirm the derivation. פרע,
the second component of the name, was interpreted in two
ways: (*a*) as derived from פרע, to untie or loosen, *Gen. R.*,
ib., שהיה פורע עצמו לע"ז; (*b*) from פרע, to cut out, T. B.
Sota, 13*b*, בא גבריאל ופירעו. Musafia, in *Kohut* I. 211, was
guided by a right instinct when he adds וי"מ שהוא מכרם.
He also thought of σπάδων. Our interpretation is confirmed
by a passage in *Shir R.* I. 1, בל יתיצב לפני חשוכים זה
פוטיפר שהחשיך הקב"ה עיניו וסירכו. This completely excludes the idea of Potiphar's enlightenment, or, according
to Fürst, *ibid.*, his conversion. In the *Tanchuma*, Potiphar

---

[1] The passage שנכנס לביתו של פרעה ונעשה ביתו פוטינום should be
emended into כיון שנכנס יוסף לביתו נעשה [פוטיפרע] פוטבן, according
to *Gen. Rab.* and *Yalkut.*

is not represented as the enlightened but as the enlightener, *i. e.*, the steward over Pharaoh's house, an office which has no obvious connection with *spiritual* enlightenment.

3.—DIVISION OF THE RED SEA INTO TWELVE PARTS.

Hom. in Exod. v. 5 (xii. 330, M.), Audivi a majoribus traditum, quod in ista digressione maris, singulis quibusque tribubus filiorum Israel, singulæ aquarum divisiones factæ sunt, et propria unicuique tribui in mari aperta est via, idque ostendi ex eo, quod in Psalmis (cxxxv. 13) scriptum est: *Qui divisit mare rubrum in divisiones.* Per quod multæ divisiones docentur factæ, non una. Sed et per hoc quod dicitur: Ita Benjamin junior in stupore...... (Psalm. lxviii. 28) nihilominus unicuique tribui propius enumerari videtur ingressus. Hæc a majoribus observata in Scripturis divinis, religiosum credidi non tacere. Cp. Eusebius Comm. in Ps. lxxvii. 13 (xxiii. 113, M.), φασὶ γοῦν Ἑβραίων παῖδες εἰς ιβ´ τμήματα διῃρῆσθαι αὐτὴν κατ᾽ ἀριθμὸν τῶν ιβ´ φυλῶν τοῦ λαοῦ.

Every detail of this Midrash is found with wonderful similarity in the Jewish sources.

The division of the Red Sea into twelve parts, corresponding to the number of the tribes, is recounted in the *Mechilta* (Exod. xiv. 16) נחלק לשנים עשר גזרים. In Midrash on Psalm cxxxvi. 15, in Yalkut Habakkuk, § 565, and in Yalkut Exodus, § 245, נחלק לשנים is a mistake for ב׳ ל׳ עשר. Even the verse with which this tradition is connected is the same in Origen and the Midrash. In the *Mechilta* (Exod. xiv. 15), the passage commencing מהו אומר לנוזר ים סוף לגזרים, breaks off abruptly. The expected conclusion is the deduction that the sea was divided into twelve parts. Maimonides knew this Midrash in its full form. Commentary on *Aboth* V. 4: שנבקעו לדרכים רבים כמספר השבטים והוא אמרו לנוזר וכו׳. In *Aboth de R. Nathan*, c. XXXIII. (v. I.), the circumstance is added that the tribes expressly stipulated that the sea should be divided into sections, אמר להם משה קומו עברו

אמרו לא נעבור עד שנעשה לפנינו נזרים נזרים נזרים שנאמר לנוזר וכו'.
Ps. lxviii. 28, from which, Origen says, the same tradition
is derived, is connected with it in the *Mechilta*, ibid. 6, *Sota*,
36b, Midrash on Ps. lxviii. 14, where we read that the tribes
disputed as to which of them was to be the first to pass
through the Red Sea ; the result could only have been that
they crossed simultaneously by different routes.

4.—Repentance of Korah's Sons.

Comm. in Ep. ad Rom. x. 7 (xiv. 1262, M.), Non puto
absurdum videri si ea quæ nobis de his etiam in veteri Testamento a patribus rationabiliter tradita sunt, his scilicet,
qui ex Hebræis ad Christi fidem venerunt, in medium profe-
ramus.   Aiebant ergo tres illos filios Core, quorum nomina
invenimus in Exodo (vi. 24)...... Aser...... Elchana...... et
Abiasaph......, cum pater eorum Core pecasset una cum
Dathan et Abiram..... . istos segregasse a cœtu nefario et
ab impia conspiratione sequestratos unanimiter ad Deum
precem pœnitentiæ profudisse : atque exauditos a Deo non
solum veniam pœnæ, sed et prophetiæ gratiam meruisse, et
hoc quoque eis a deo poscentibus esse præstitum, ne quid
triste aut exitiabile prophetare juberentur : et ob hoc omnes
psalmos quicunque nominibus eorum attitulati referuntur,
nihil triste adversum peccatores aut asperum continere.

Only that part of this beautiful Agada which refers to the
repentance of Korah's sons is to be found in Jewish sources.
A passage in Midrash to Ps. xlv. 4, runs as follows :—כך בני
קרח לא היו יכולין לומר שירה לפני הק'ב'ה בפיהם עד שרחש
לבם וקבלם מיד ולמה לא היו יכולין לומר שירה בפיהם לפי
שהיתה שאול פתוחה מתחתיהם ואש בלהטת כביבותיהם :
The שירה here mentioned is parallel to Origen's *preces pœnitentiæ*.   This elucidates the passage in T. B. *Sanhedrin,* 110a
(*Megilla,* 14a):—מקום נתבצר להם בגיהנב וישבו עליו ואמרו—
שירה.   That this Agada is ancient appears from the unfamiliar word נתבצר ; cp. also Midrash on Psalms i. 5,
and xlv. 1.   In the Jewish sources we miss the fine touches
of the gift of prophecy bestowed on Korah's sons, and of

the always comforting nature of the Korachide Psalms.
Perhaps others will be fortunate enough to discover these
points too.

5.—Israel's Strength consists in Prayer.

Hom. in Num., xiii. 5 (xii. 672, M.), Ut autem scias tale
aliquid cogitasser egem (Balak), ex scripturae verbis intel-
lige, quæ ego a magistro quodam, qui ex Hebræis crediderat,
exposita didici. Scriptum est ergo (Num. xxii. 4) : *Et dixit
Moab ad seniores Madjan : Nunc, ablinget synagoga hæc omnes,
qui in circuitu nostro sunt, sicut ablingit vitulus herbam campi.*
Aiebat ergo magister ille, qui ex Hebræis crediderat : Cur,
inquit, tali usus est exemplo, dicens : sicut ablingit vitulus
herbam campi ? Ob hoc sine dubio, quia vitulus ore obrum-
pit herbam de campo et lingua tanquam falce quæcunque
invenerit, secat. Ita ergo et populus hic, quasi vitulus ore
et labiis pugnat, et arma habet in verbis ac precibus. Haec
igitur sciens rex mittit ad Balaam, ut et ipse deferat verbis
verba contraria et precibus preces.

This is a well-known Midrash. *Sifri* Num. xxii. 4, § 157 ;
Num. R. c. 20, 3 ; *Tanchuma* II. ; בלק, § 4 ; Rashi, *ad locum* :
מה שור כחו בפיו אף הם כחם בפיהם.

6.—Phineas and Elijah identical.

Comm. in Joann. vi. 7 (xiv. 225, M.), Οἱ Ἑβραῖοι παρα-
διδόασι Φινεὲς τὸν Ἐλεαζάρου υἱὸν . . . . αὐτὸν εἶναι Ἡλίαν καὶ
ἀθάνατον ἐν τοῖς Ἀριθμοῖς αὐτῷ διὰ τῆς ὀνομαζομένης εἰρήνης
ἐπηγγέλθαι.

Jerome knows the same tradition, which he thinks the
Jews took from an apocryphal work. Eliam esse Phineas
Hebræi ex Apocryphis persuasum habent (V. 813 Vallarsi).
The sentence, פנחס הוא אליהו is only found in *Yalkut Num.*
772, in the name of R. Simeon b. Lakish and ascribed to a
Midrash as its original source. Its preservation in a miscellaneous collection is noteworthy. The ordinary Midrashim
seem to have purposely suppressed it, because it smacked
of Apocrypha. Its omission is particularly noticeable in

Tanchuma II., פנחם, § 3: לכן אמור לו הנני נותן לו את
ברית שלום וכן הוא אומר בריתי היתה אתו דזהיים והשלום,
which, as it stands, makes no sense. The *Yalkut*, ib., on
the basis of Malachi ii. 5, infers that the peace promised Phineas was eternal life: ונתן לו חיי העולם הזה וחיי
העולם הבא ונתן לו שכר טוב והיתה לו ולזרעו אחריו ברית
כהונת עולם. Here, too, Origen, gives the correct tradition
that Phineas' immortality is implied in the word שלום.

7.—ALLEGORICAL INTERPRETATION OF THE SERAPHIM.

De Princ. I. 3, 4 (xi. 143, M.), Ἔλεγε δὲ ὁ Ἑβραῖος τὰ ἐν
τῷ Ἡσαΐᾳ δύο σεραφὶμ ἑξαπτέρυγα κεκραγότα ἕτερον πρὸς
ἕτερον .... τὸν Μονογενῆ εἶναι τοῦ θεοῦ καὶ τὸ Πνεῦμα τὸ
ἅγιον. Cp. *De Princ.* iv. 26 (xi. 400, M.), Nam et Hebræus
doctor ista tradebat: pro eo quod initium omnium vel finis
non possit ab ullo comprehendi, nisi tantummodo a Domino
Jesu Christo, et a Spiritu sancto, aiebat per figuram visio-
nis Isaiam dixisse, duos seraphim solos esse, qui duabus
quidem alis operiunt faciem Dei, duabus vero pedes, et duabus
volant clamantes ad invicem sibi dicentes: Sanctus, sanctus, sanctus, etc. The same tradition was also known to
Jerome, in Ep. xli. (lxv.) *Ad Pammachium et Oceanum*,
who, however, rightly stigmatizes it as an odious and
godless exposition. Had it not been expressly so stated,
one could hardly believe that a Jew said it. The Christian
terms, at least, are to be placed to a Church Father's
account. I could not find this interpretation in the
Jewish sources, and none will regret its absence.

8.—DANIEL, CHANANIAH, MISHAEL AND AZARIAH
WERE EUNUCHS.

Comm. in Matt. xv. 5 (xiii. 1225, M.), Φασὶ δὲ Ἑβραίων
παῖδες τὸν Δανιὴλ καὶ τοὺς τρεῖς σὺν αὐτῷ Ἀνανίαν, Ἀζαρίαν
Μισαήλ, ἐν Βαβυλῶνι εὐνουχίσθαι, πληρουμένης τῆς πρὸς
τὸν Ἐζεκίαν εἰρημένης προφητείας ὑπὸ Ἡσαΐου ἐν τῷ "Ἀπὸ
τοῦ σπέρματός σου λήψονται, καὶ ποιήσουσι σπαδόντας ἐν τῷ
οἴκῳ τοῦ βασίλεως Βαβυλῶνος " (Is. xxxix. 7). Φασὶ δὲ ὅτι

περὶ τούτων καὶ Ἡσαΐας ἐπροφήτευσε φάσκων " Μή λεγέτω ὁ ἀλλογενὴς ὁ προσκείμενος κυρίῳ. ἀφοριεῖ μὲ ἄρα κύριος ἀπὸ τοῦ λαοῦ αὐτοῦ," καὶ τὰ ἑξῆς, ἕως τοῦ " κρείττονα υἱῶν καὶ θυγατέρων" (Is. lvi. 35). Origen gives the tradition with more fulness of detail in *Hom.* in Ezek. iv., § 8 (xiii. 703, M.). On Ezek. xiv. 15 : Audivi quondam a quodam Hebræo hunc locum exponente atque dicente, ideo hos nominatos, quia unusquisque eorum (Daniel, Job, Noe) tria tempora viderit, lætum, triste et rursum lætum...... Noe...... vidit mundum ante diluvium ......in diluvio......, rursum in resurrectione omnium peccatorum. Dicit mihi aliquis: concedo de Noe, ut tria tempora viderit: quid respondebis mihi de Daniele? Et hic ante captivitatem in patria floruit nobilitate, et deinceps in Babylonem translatus *eunuchus effectus est*, ut manifeste ex libro illius intelligi potest; vidit et reversionem in Jerusalem. Ut autem probetur quod ante captivitatem eunuchus factus sit, assumamus id quod ad Ezechiam dictum est (Is. xxix. 7)...... Job...... fuit locuples...... deinde accepit diabolus potestatem adversus eum ;...... post hæc apparet ei Dominus. *Ib.* § 5 (xiii. 700, M.). Daniel qui traditus est eunuchorum principi cum Anania, Azaria, Misaela, eunuchus fuit...... Quomodo filii Danielis docebuntur, quem eunuchum fuisse Judæi tradunt ? Verum quia fertilis et sancta fuit anima illius, et propheticis divinisque sermonibus multos liberos procreavit...... Catena Regia in Prophetas ad Ezek. xiv. 5 : Υἱοὺς ἔχει ὁ Δανιὴλ κατὰ τὴν αὐτὴν πνευματικὴν γένναν, οὓς ἐγέννησεν ἡ προφητεία αὐτοῦ. υἱοὺς γὰρ σαρκικοὺς οὐκ ἔσχεν. Εὐνοῦχος γὰρ ἦν, ὥς φασι.

The same tradition we find in Jerome lib. I., adv. Jovin., c. 25 : Superfluum est de Daniele dicere, cum Hebræi usque hodie autument et illum et tres pueros fuisse eunuchos, ex illa dei sententia (II. Reg. xx. 18)......

Jerome on Daniel i. 3 : Unde et arbitrantur Hebræi Danielem et Azariam et Ananiam et Misaelem fuisse eunuchos......Epiphanius, *de Vitis Prophetarum* (xliv. 424, M. ser gr.): Καὶ ἦν ἀνὴρ σώφρων, ὥστε θαυμάζειν τοὺς Ἰου-

δαίους πιστεύοντας εἰς αὐτὸν εἶναι σπαδόντα. Later Church
Fathers also give the same tradition, which they have
however drawn from Origen and Jerome.

This Agada is widely disseminated in Jewish literature.
All the details correspond; the statement that Daniel and
his companions were eunuchs; the verse from which this is
deduced; the question how they could have afterwards
begotten children, etc. We read in B. *Sanhedrin*, 93*b* :—

ומבניך אשר יצאו ממך אשר הוליד אשר יקחו והיו כריסים בהיכל
מלך בבל רב אמר כריסים ממש...... מאי טוב מבנים ומבנות
מבנים שהיו להם כבר ומרו ...... From which we see that
this tradition did not survive in the popular consciousness;
it is stated as simply an individual opinion. Of the many
views enunciated, the most noteworthy is R. Jochanan's,
ib. 93*a* : עלו [חנניה משאל ועזריה] לארץ ישראל ונשאו נשים
והולידו בנים ובנות. This, as Rashi remarks, stands in direct
opposition to the above. Cp. *Gen. R.*, c. 99; *Num. R.*, c. 13;
Esther R., c. 4; *Pirke de R. E.*, c. LII.

9.—Moses, Author of Eleven Psalms.

Selecta in Psalmos, p. 514 (xii. 1055, M.), Ὕστερον δὲ κινού-
μενος περί τινων λογίων Θεοῦ Ἰουλλῷ τῷ πατριάρχῃ καί τινι
τῶν χρηματιζόντων παρὰ Ἰουδαίοις σοφῶν ἀκήκοα, ὅτι δι'
ὅλης τῆς βίβλου ψαλμῶν .... οἱ παρ' Ἑβραίοις ἀνεπίγραφοι
ἢ ἐπιγραφὴν μὲν ἔχοντες, οὐχὶ δὲ τὸ ὄνομα τοῦ γράψαντος,
ἐκείνου εἰσὶν οὗ τὸ ὄνομα φέρεται ἐν τῷ πρὸ τούτων ἐπιγραφὴν
ἔχοντι ψαλμῷ. καὶ περὶ τούτων λέγων, πρότερον μὲν ἔφασκεν,
ὅτι τρισκαίδεκα εἰσὶν ὁ τοῦ Μωυσέως εἶτα δὲ ἐξ ὧν ἀκήκοα
καὶ αὐτὸς .... τὴν ἀνέφερον ἐπ' αὐτόν, ὅτι εἰσὶν ἔνδεκα, εἶτα
πυθόμενος, τοῦ παρ' αὐτοῖς δοκοῦντος σοφοῦ, ἐμάνθανον, ὅτι
εἶεν ἔνδεκα.

Jerome, *adv. Ruff.*, c. 13, quotes the whole of this passage.
He knows the tradition of Moses' authorship, gives it, however, not in the name of the Jews, but as a firmly established
and self-evident truth:—Qui [Moses] non solum nobis
quinque reliquit libros,...... sed undecim quoque Psalmos,
ab octogesimo nono [LXX.]...... usque ad nonagesimum

nonum. Quod autem in plerisque codicibus nonagesimus octavus habet titulum *Psalmus David*, in Hebraico non habetur, hanc habente scriptura sancta consuetudinem, ut omnes psalmi qui cujus sint titulos non habent, his deputentur, quorum in prioribus psalmis nomina continentur (Ep. cxl. ad Cyprianum, c. 2).

This Midrash also is found in Jewish sources; *Pesikta de R. Kahana*, 198a, ed. Buber: אחד עשר מזמורים אמר משה כנגד אחד עשר שבטים שביֵרך ואלו הן......אמר ר' יהושוע עד כאן שמעתי מכאן ואילך את מחשב לעצמך. R. Joshua's words imply that this was an ancient tradition. It is found also in Midrash on Psalm xc. 3, *Yalkut Ps.*, § 841, Rashi to Psalm xc. 1; cp. Midrash on Psalm xc. 4: אחד עשר מזמורים שאמר משה במטכסים של נביאים אבין.

10.—BEASTS AS EXECUTORS OF DIVINE PUNISHMENT.

Hom. in Ezek. iv. 7 (xiii. 701, M.), and *in Ezek.* xiv. 4: Aiunt etiam Judæi, si quando lupi homines devoraverint impetum facientes in domos, et cæteræ bestiæ, ut historia refert leones quondam in humanum genus immissos, et alio tempore ursos (II. Reg. xvii. 2) istius modi devorationes ex Dei indignatione descendere.

I have not found a parallel in Jewish sources, but the root idea is patent and needs no special tradition.

S. KRAUSS.

(*To be Continued.*)

THE JEWS IN THE WORKS OF THE CHURCH FATHERS.

IV.

EUSEBIUS.

EUSEBIUS, whose best work was accomplished on Palestinian soil, in Cæsarea, must often have come into contact with Jews, and been instructed by them on several points.

He is bitterer in tone against the Jews than Origen. "Jew," with him, is a term of opprobrium. He repeatedly calls his opponent Marcellus a Jew (*Eccles. Theol.* II. 2, 3). The phrase, "one of the circumcised,"[1] which he employs, likewise covers a world of scorn and contempt. His work, *Demonstratio Evangelica*, was avowedly written as a direct attack on the Jews.[2] He holds that, in their exposition of Scripture, the Jews are guilty of serious errors, and efforts should be made to induce them to abandon their heresies; that is to say: Religious disputations should be encouraged with the view of persuading them to give up their faith.[3]

Eusebius regards the condition of the Jews as lamentable. What they felt most bitterly was the harsh law which denied them the solace of visiting the holy city of Jerusalem. He describes the wailing and weeping of the poor Jews when they caught even a distant glimpse of Zion's ruins.[4]

---

[1] *Dem. Ec.* i. 6 (xxii. 49, M.), τις τῶν ἐκ περιτομῆς.

[2] *Ib.* i. 1, 11, οὐ . . . κατὰ 'Ιουδαίων, ἄπαγε, πολλοῦ γε καὶ δεῖ . . .

[3] *Ib.* iv. 16 (xxii. 317, M.), Διόπερ εἰκὸς τοὺς ἐκ περιτομῆς ἀποσφάλλεσθαι . . .

[4] *Comm. in Psalm* lviii. 7-12 (xxiii. 541, M.), Διὸ εἰσέτι καὶ σήμερον ἀμφὶ μὲν τοὺς ὅρους καὶ κύκλῳ παριόντες πόρρωθεν ἵστανται μηδ' ἐξ ἀπόπτου

Eusebius was as much under the influence of Jewish tradition as his predecessors and several of his successors. It
has nearly the same authority with him as the Scriptures,
and he calls it ἄγραφος παράδοσις = " unwritten tradition." [1]
Its depositaries he terms δευτεροταί, [2] and he characterises
them in the following happy fashion : " There are people
gifted with an uncommon strength of intellect ; and
whose faculties have been trained to penetrate to the very
heart of Scripture. The children of the Hebrews call
them δευτερωταί, because they expound Holy Writ." [3]
Eusebius also distinguishes between esoteric and exoteric
exegesis. The Agadas he frequently classes with the exoteric exposition. [4] Though there is no clear statement to
that effect, we may confidently assume that Eusebius enjoyed direct intercourse with Jews. Cæsarea, the Father's
residence, was inhabited by learned Hebrews ; and we
know from the Talmud that disputations between Jews
and Christians were frequent in this town. It will also
clearly appear from passages to be hereafter quoted, that
Eusebius had a Jewish teacher. His Agadas, of which we
give a few specimens, he owed to Jews.

τὸ πάλαι νενομισμένον αὐτοῖς ἱερὸν ἔδαφος θιάσασθαι καταξιούμενοι, ἔξωθεν
δὲ κυκλοῦντες, πίστιν ἐπάγουσι τὴν ... Γραφῇ (Ps. liii. 7). — *Ib.* lxix.
26—29 (xxiii. 153, M.), Ἰουδαίων δὲ οὐδένα τολμῶντα ἐπιβαίνειν τῇ πόλει.
μήτε γε οἰκεῖν αὐτόθι. ἀλλ' οὐδὲ οἴκησις Ἰουδαϊκη περιλέλειπται ἐν τῷ τόπῳ.
ὡς τινα τῶν Ἑλλήνων οἰκεῖν ἐν αὐτῇ δύνασθαι.

[1] *Hist. Ec.* iv. 22 (xx. 384, M.), ἐκ Ἰουδαϊκῆς ἀγράφου παραδόσεως.

[2] *Praep. Ev.* xi. 5 (xxi. 852, M.), Δευτερωταί ... οὕτω δὲ φίλον τοὺς ἐξηγητὰς τῶν παο' αὐτοῖς Γραφῶν ὀνομάζειν.

[3] *Ib.* xii. 1 (xxi. 952, M.), τοῖς ... τὴν ἕξιν προβεβηκόσι, καὶ πολιοῖς τὰ
φρόνημα, ἐμβαθύνειν καὶ δοκιμάζειν τὸν νοῦν τῶν λεγομένων ἐπιτέτραπται.
Τουτοὺς δὲ παισὶν Ἑβραίων Δευτερωτὰς φίλον ἦν ὀνομάζειν ὥσπερ ἑρμηνευτὰς
καὶ ἐξηγητὰς ὄντας τῆς τῶν Γραφῶν διανοίας.

[4] *Dem. Ev.* vi. 18 (xxii. 461, M.), ὁ δὲ γε Ἰώσηπος καὶ τὰς ἔξωθεν Ἰουδαϊ-
κὰς δευτερώσεις ἀπηκριβωκώς ... ἐπάκουσον. The subject here discussed
is the earthquake, the legend concerning which is to be found in the
Seder Olam., c. xx. ובעמים הוא אומר יגותים לפני הרעש ובישעיה הוא
אומר בשנה מות המלך עזיהו כו' והוא היה ביום הרעש יגאמר וינועו
אמות הספים.

F 2

1.—Abraham obeyed the Precepts of the Torah before the Revelation.

Demonstratio Evang. I. 6. Μεμαρτύρηται γοῦν τὰ προστάγματα καὶ τὰς ἐντολὰς, τά τε δικαιώματα καὶ τὰ νόμιμα τοῦ θεοῦ, πρὸ τῆς Μωσέως διαταγῆς πεφυλαγμένος. Eusebius infers this from Gen. xxvi. 3, 4, 5.

This is one of the best known Agadas, cp. T. B. Joma, 28*b*:—עקב שנאמר כלה התורה כל אברהם קיים רב אמר אשר שמע. Even the verse on which the statement is based is the same in the Father and the Talmud. Compare *Baba Meziah*, 85*b* and 87*a*, where R. Meir already asserts : אברהם אבינו אוכל חולין בטהרה היה.

2.—King Hezekiah's Sin.

Commentary on Isaiah xxxix. 1. (VI. 362 M.). συνεξετάξουσιν ἡμῖν καὶ διερευνωμένοις τὰ κατὰ τοὺς παρόντας τόπους, ὁ τῶν Ἰουδαίων διδάσκαλος ἔλεγεν νενοσηκέναι μεν τον Ἐζεκίαν, ἐπεὶ μὴ εἰρήκει ᾠδὴν εἰς τὸν θεὸν εὐχαριστήριον ἐπὶ τῇ πτώσει τῶν Ἀσσυρίων, ὡς Μωϋσῆς ᾖδεν ἐπὶ τῇ ἀπωλείᾳ τῶν Αἰγυπτίων καὶ ὡς Δεβόρρα ἐπὶ τῇ ἀπωλείᾳ τοῦ Σισάρα καὶ ὡς Ἄννα ἐπὶ τῇ γεννήσει του Σαμουήλ.

Jerome, *ad locum*, quotes the same tradition.

This Agada, which is already noteworthy for the direct statement prefacing it—that Eusebius learnt it from his Jewish teacher—is one of the most widely disseminated in Jewish literature. The reflection that Hezekiah was guilty of ingratitude in not chanting a hymn of praise to God after Sennacherib's fall, also occurs in T. B. *Sanhedrin*, 94*a*:

למרבה המשרה ולשלום אין קץ · אמר ר' רנחום דרש בר קפרא
בציפורי מפני מה כל מ״ם שבאמצע תיבה פתוח וזה סתום
בקש הקב״ה לעשות חזקיה משיח וסנחריב גוג ומגוג · אמר
מדת הדין לפני הקב״ה ומה דוד מלך ישראל שאמר כמה שירות
ותושבחות לפניך לא עשיתו משיח חזקיה שעשית לו כל הנסים

Ib., הללו ולא אמר שירה לפניך תעשה משיח · לכך נסתרב
נגאי הוא לחזקיה וסיערתו שלא אמרו שירה.

In *Exodus R.*, c. 18, and T. B. *Pesachim*, 117*a*, it is related
that Hezekiah sang a hymn of praise (Hallel) before the
destruction of the Assyrian hordes, but there is no hint of
his having been censured for omitting to sing one after the
occurrence. In *Shir R.*, on c. IV. v. 8, an excuse is put into
Hezekiah's mouth:—ראוי היה חזקיה לומר שירה על מפלת
סנחריב אמר חזקיה תורה שאני עוסק בה מכפרת על
השירה.

In *Echa R.*, c. I., the excuse takes the following form :—
חזקיה אמר אין בי כח······לומר שירה.   From all these passages it is obvious that Hezekiah's omission to compose a
special hymn of praise largely exercised the imagination of
the Agadists. In T. J. *Pesachim*, towards the end, a dictum
is found, couched in so authoritative a form that it sounds
almost like an Halacha, to the effect that a miraculous deliverance should be followed by a thanksgiving :—כשהכ"ה
עושה לכם נסים תהיו אומרין שירה.   To this the cogent
objection is raised that Mordecai and Esther did not sing
a hymn after Haman's fall. *Jalkut*, on Isaiah, § 306, quotes
a passage from the lost Jelamdenu, in which the duty of
a thanksgiving is deduced from Exodus xv. 1 : ויאמרו לאמר
לדורות.   A contrast is also drawn between the songs
of Moses, Deborah and David, and Hezekiah's culpable
negligence—a feature also dwelt upon in Eusebius. In
all the above passages, however, we miss the detail,
found in the Father's recital of the legend, that Hezekiah's sickness was a Divine punishment for his omission
of a thanksgiving. Nevertheless, this, too, comes from
a Jewish source. The following passage is excerpted
from Jelamdenu by the Jalkut on 2 Kings, § 243 :—
בשעלה סנחריב עליו והפילו האלהים לפניו הוה ליה למימר
שירה על מבלתי ולא אמר ומה היה לו והפילו האלהים במטה
כדי שיאמר שירה שנאמר מכתב לחזקיהו.
This legend illustrates the advantages that would accrue
from a systematic history of the Agada. Such a history is

however only possible after a comparison of all available
auxiliary sources, among which the Church Fathers occupy
an important place.

3.—BERODACH BALADAN AND HEZEKIAH.

Comm. in Is. xxix. 1 (vi. 361 M.) τὸν δὲ Βαβυλώνιον
ἐγνωκέναι τὴν ἀπὸ τῆς νόσου ῥῶσιν αὐτοῦ καὶ ἀπεσταλκέναι
πρὸς αὐτὸν ἄνδρας......ἐπειδὴ συνέβη τὴν ἡμέραν ἐκείνην καθ᾽
ἣν τὸ σημεῖον τῆς τοῦ ἡλίου ἀναδρομῆς ὡρῶν γεγενῆσθαι δι-
σπλασίων, μὴ γάρ λατεῖν τοῦ το τοὺς Βαβυλωνίους δεινοὺς ὄντας
περὶ τὴν τῶν ἄστρων δε ὡρίαν καὶ......συνεῖδον ὡς ὑπὸ κρείτ-
τονος περιηνέχθη εἰς τουπισὼ δυναμέως ...... ταῦτα μὲν ὁ
Ἐβραῖος.

The same Agada is given in Ephraem Syrus' work (*Op.
Syr.* I. 562, 563 R.) on 2 Kings xx. 10, as one of Jacob
Edessenus' *Scholia.* It is introduced in the following impressive phrases:—במלא הלין כוכלא מטשיא אית דלו לכל
נש ידיע ודאן זדקא דלגליא אנא אירתודי הא אמר אנא. Graetz
has discussed the latter passage in the *Monatsschrift,* 1854,
p. 383. The Agada inspires him, however, with but little
respect, because it is not given by Ephraem but by Jacob
Edessenus, who belongs to a later period. The passage in the
commentary on the parallel chapter in Isaiah, which is, indeed, given in Ephraem's name, Graetz suspects to have been
interpolated from Jacob Edessenus' *Scholion.* The historian
has however overlooked the fact that the earlier Father,
Eusebius, also has this Agada. By the time it reached
Edessenus, it had received several additions, *e.g.,* the recital
of the miracle of the turning back of the sun by the Nine-
vite Jews to the Babylonian king; and the statement that
his native Jewish subjects enlightened him as to Hezekiah's
importance. The Agada, in the form in which Eusebius
presents it, is found in Jewish sources. Thus T. B. *Sanhedrin,* 96a:—בעת ההיא שלח בראדך בלאדן......משום כי חלה
חזקיה ויחזיק שדר ליה? ורשב השמש עשר מעלות......א'ל מאי

הַאי א׳ל הזקה חלש ואיתפח אמר איכא גברא כי האי ולא בעיסא
לעדורי ליה שלמא. The detail is, however, wanting that
the Babylonians, by their knowledge of astronomy, discovered that the sun-dial had turned back. We read,
instead, in a passage excerpted from the Pesikta (*Jalkut*,
2 Kings, § 244) another account of the manner in which
the Babylonians were apprised of the miracle. מרודך בן
יבלאדן היה למוד לאכול בשש שעות וישן עד תשע שעות
וכיון שחזר גלגל חמה ישן לו ועמד ומצאו שחרית בקש להרוב
את כל עבדיו אמר הנחתם אותי לישן כל היום וכל הלילה
אמרו ליה מרי יומא הוא דהדר ביה ואלוהו של הזקיה החזירו
אמר להם איכה כי האי גברא כו׳.

We must confess that the Church Father's narrative, *viz.*,
that the Babylonians discovered the miracle by their astro-
nomical calculations, is more reasonable than the Jalkut
legend. Here is another illustration of the usefulness of
foreign sources for the purpose of rectifying the Agadas,
so many of which sound strange.

4.—THE TRAITOR SHEBNA.

Comm. in Is. xii. 10, 11 (VI. 249 M.). Ἔλεγε τοίνυν ὁ
Ἑβραῖος ἀρχιερέα γεγενῆσθαι τὸν Σομνάν (שבנא) τρυφητὴν
τινα καὶ τὸν βίον ἄσεμνον ἄνδρα, ὡς καὶ προδοῦναι τὸν λαόν.

Jerome comments on the passage "Supra diximus Sob-
nam fuisse pontificem qui Assyriis prodidat civitatem, sed
quia hoc traditionis est Hebraicæ et Scriptura non loquitur..."

All the details of this Agada recur in Jewish sources.
Thus, *Leviticus R.*, c. 5, זה שבנא כהן גדול היה. Shebna's
treachery is discussed in T. B. *Sanhedrin* 26a. Eusebius's
brief suggestion that Shebna was sensual (τρυφητής) is
repeated in T. B. *Sanhedrin, 26a,* אמר ר׳ אלעזר שבנא בעל
הנאה היה כתיב הכא לך בא אל הסוכן וכתיב התם ותהי
לו סוכנת.

This somewhat obscure passage Rashi explains in the following gloss, ‫כמשמעו וי״א משכב זכר‬. After what the Father tells us, we must decide that the explanation of the ‫יש אומרים‬ hits the correct sense of the Agada.

5.—INTERPRETATION OF ZECH. XI. 8.

The text ‫ואכחיד את שלשת הרעים בירה אחד‬ received, from a very early period, the following Christological inter-pretation: That, after Jesus' advent, the three powerful estates, Sovereignty, Priesthood and Prophecy, disappeared from Israel's midst. This explanation recurs in Eusebius, *Dem. Ev.* X. 1 (XX. 747 M.). Jerome (on Zech. xi. 8) quotes it only to reject it. His sound common sense leads him to prefer the Jewish exegesis, which applies the text to Moses, Aaron and Miriam. Strange to say, he does not give it in the Jews' name, as Graetz already noted in the *Monatssch.* 1854, p. 189. The historian has neglected to consult the older authority, Eusebius, whom Jerome follows in so many places. It is clearly evident from Eusebius, *ibid.*, that this exegesis was not specially Jewish, but was general at that period. The passage quoted by Graetz from T. B. *Taanith* 9a:—‫ואכחיד את שלשת הרעים בירח אחד וכי ביירח אחד מתו‬ ‫והלא מרים מתה בניסן ואהרן באב ומשה באדר‬, completely coincides with *Seder Olam R.*, c. X., which first mentions the distinctive blessings these three pastors brought the people:—‫אהרן = עמוד ענן ׳ משה = מן ׳ מרים = באר‬.

V.

EPHRAEM SYRUS.

In passionate hatred of the Jews, in contempt and active hostility towards the people of the covenant, Ephraem of Syria surpasses all the Church Fathers who came before and all those who went after him. His voluminous writings are filled with rage and animosity against the Jews. He would like to destroy them with the fire of his words and to draw down upon their heads, by his prayers, the avenging lightning of an offended Deity. Whence this hatred? Whence this malignant spirit of persecution? It is difficult to find an adequate reason, especially as Ephraem hardly ever came into contact with the Jews, and therefore could never have been insulted by them. His resentment seems to have been aroused and stimulated by the marvellous power of resistance shown by the old creed. In his immediate neighbourhood, Babylon, the ancient people flourished with unexpected vigour. The serious blow which Julian the Apostate dealt Christianity, and which was indirectly of benefit to the Jews, may also have contributed to the contemporary Father's prejudice. He sought to relieve his feelings by pouring out vials of wrath on the defenceless Hebrews.

Ephraem terms the Jews טעיא גזירא, the circumcised vagabonds.[1] Judaism is a worthless vineyard that cannot bear fruit.[2] He frequently refers to their wretched condition, which he regards as a punishment sent from God.[3] Because they reviled Jesus, the Lord has banished them from their land, and and now they are condemned to wander over the whole surface of the earth.[4]

The golden hopes which the Emperor Julian's policy raised in the Jews' hearts, proved vain and illusory. As soon as Christianity triumphed, it turned with redoubled fury on its indestructible foe. After Julian's death Ephraem composed four hymns: against the Emperor Julian, the

---

[1] *Op. Syr.* II. 469. Cp. Lengerke, *De Ephraemi Syri arte Hermeneutica* (Königsberg, 1838), p. 15.

[2] See Zingerle, *Bibliothek der Kirchenväter*, II., 292.

[3] In Gen. xlix. 8 (*Op. Syr.* I., 108).

[4] In 2 *Reg.* ii. at the end (*Op. Syr.* I., 523) נרישו אנון לבד כן אתרא דלהון וזרקו להון בכל פניתא דמתעמרניתא.

Apostate; against the heresies; and against the Jews.[1] We quote from these envenomed productions the following passages: "The Jewish people broke out into maddening noise; the circumcised blew their trumpets and rejoiced that he [Julian] was a magician and worshipper of idols. They saw again the image of the beast on his [Julian's] gold pieces; they again viewed the bull of shame, and danced round it with trumpets and timbrels, for they recognised in this beast[2] their ancient golden calf. The heathen bull, imprinted on their hearts, he stamped on his coins for the delectation of the Jews, who were enamoured of him.[3] The circumcised blew their trumpets and behaved like madmen.[4] Jerusalem put to shame the accursed crucifiers who had dared to announce that they would rebuild the ruins their sins had wrought.[5] Fire broke out and destroyed the scholars who had read in Daniel that the desolation would endure for ever. Look! you (Christians) live at peace, free from the 'possessed,' free from contact with the servants of the devil."[6]

What especially exasperates Ephraem is that the Jews will not give up their hopes; notwithstanding the calamities with which they have been visited, they still cherish the firm conviction that the Future belongs to them and their religion—not to Christianity. The narrative of the two concubines who appeared before Solomon for judgment, is applied by Ephraem to the rival creeds, the Church and the Synagogue. Of the latter, he says: The Synagogue continually protests that her son is the living child and pleasing to God. She, furthermore, loudly asserts that the

---

[1] על יולינוס מלכא דאחנף ועל יולפנא טע״א ועל יהודײא in S. *Ephraemi Syri Carmina Nisibena*, Ed. Bickel (Lipsiae, 1866), and Overbeck, *S. Ephraemi Syri . . . . aliorumque Opera Selecta* (= O), Oxonii, 1865. The hymns are translated into German by Hahn in the periodical *Zeitschrift für Katholische Theologie*, II. 335 (Innsbruck, 1878).

[2] An allusion on a coin of Julian with an altar and a beast, being the sign of the restitution of Paganism.

[3] O. p. 8.   [4] O. p. 12.   [5] O. p. 18.   [6] O. p. 19.

Law of Moses is endowed with eternal life. Thus the Synagogue of the misguided perpetually contends with the Church of Jesus.[1] The hopes of the Jews find still more emphatic expression in the view that, as soon as the expected Messiah shall have arrived,[2] God's people will reign supreme.

It is interesting to learn the precise nature of these hopes which dominated the Jewish mind in the fourth century. A passage bearing on this subject may here be appropriately quoted from the Sermon against the Jews:—"Now, look! this people dreams that it will return; the people which angered God in all that it did awaits and demands a time when it will have satisfaction. As soon as this people hears of a return, they lift up their voices and shout, 'Jerusalem will be rebuilt!' Again and again they listen, for they long for the return. 'The fame of the capital will be great; its name will be glorious,' they repeatedly exclaim."

Very honourable to the Jews is the testimony which an embittered foe, like Ephraem, is forced to bear to the expansive power of Judaism, even at that time of severe oppression. We learn from Ephraem, as we have learnt from Justin and Origen, that the old faith received at this period numerous accessions from heathendom. Ephraem, of course, declares that the heathens are deluded by Jewish missionaries.[3]

Christianity still felt itself called upon to defend its

---

[1] In 1 *Reg.* iii. 16 (*Op. Syr.* I. 452) הרתין נשׂין לעדתא ולכנושׁתא דֹמזן ·
כנושׁתא דין · · · · השׂא מן קעיאָ ואמרא דברא דילה הי הו לאלהא ולה
יֹפֹר · ותוב דנמוסא דמשׂאֹ דמית חיֹא דלעלם יהב ליה · הי הכיל כנושׁתא
דטצֹיֹא עם עדתא דמשׂיחא אמינאית נציא.

[2] In 1 *Reg.* i. 5 (*Op. Syr.* I. 441):—אלֹא אַך ביומתן מתחזה שׁועליה ואית
לֹיה כברא דלשׁולתגיה דתאבל נסק במאתיתה דהר משׂיחא דמסבא לה.

[3] In 2 *Reg.* xix. 1 (*Op. Syr.* I., 558): ביֹבֹא אנֹין דמכבנֹותהון דֹשׂיעֹא
הנין דבֹ:בֹין להימנות דֹהֹלי אלהא ומשׂדלין מחתחתין להון למשׁבק לעדתה
דמשׂיחֹיֹא ודיכנושׁתא דסטנא נסטון.

position against the Jews. In the Sermon against the
Jews, Ephraem exhorts them : "Come let us examine the
prophets and see whether their predictions have been fulfilled." From the course of the address we learn the chief
points of controversy between Jews and Christians at this
period. Opening with the challenge, "Let the accursed Jews
search the Scriptures and become wise," Ephraem seeks, in
the first place, to deduce from Gen. xlix. 10, 11, that the
Jews' hopes are futile. "If Judah wields the sceptre and
has an interpreter, the prophecies are not fulfilled. But
if the sceptre has departed and the voice of prophecy is
silent, then should the Jews be ashamed of their obstinacy
and stiffneckedness." Another point of controversy was
the interpretation of Zechariah ix. 9, and of Psalm viii. 3. It
is easy to understand that Ephraem indirectly attacks the
Jewish exegesis on several other points. The passages have
been collated by Gerson, *Die Commentarien des Ephraem
Syrus im Verhältniss zur Jüdischen Exegese* (Breslau, 1868),
page 8. To this brochure the reader is referred.

Intrinsically Ephraem's commentaries are incomparably
more valuable than those of the Church Fathers whom we
have already discussed. Ephraem proceeded to the exposition of the Scriptures with a sufficient equipment of pre-
liminary studies. In the first place he possessed a good
knowledge of Hebrew. This, however, is not the general
opinion. Abraham Geiger, for example, said (*Jüdische Zeitschrift*, VII. 69), "It is quite natural that Ephraem, though
ignorant of Hebrew, should have interlarded his commentaries with Midrashic elements which he learnt from his
intercourse with the Jews,'" a statement absolutely un-
warranted.

Schaf, more recently (Smith-Wace's *Dictionary of Christian
Biography*, II. 142), also seeks to prove from a few instances
that Ephraem was unacquainted with Hebrew. Although,
in itself, it does not greatly concern Jewish literature
whether any individual Father of the Church knew Hebrew
or not, still this point ought to be settled in order to enable

us to appraise Ephraem's efforts at their just value. It is
by no means the same thing whether Jewish exegesis is
criticised by a competent Hebraist or by an ignoramus. If
it should turn out that Ephraem understood the Hebrew
text, it is clearly unfair to charge him with rashly intrud-
ing into a domain in which he was incompetent to judge.

In his Commentaries Ephraem frequently refers to the
original text. This should show whether he knew Hebrew
or not. The mere reference counts for something. Neither
Clement of Alexandria, nor Basil, nor Gregory of Nazianzus
ever quotes the original text.

1. *Commentary on Genesis* i. 1 (*Op. Syr.* I. 116), Ephraem
discusses the Hebrew word את:—

הדא ברת קלא קדימות סימא עבירתא איתיה דאיתיה סוריאית
ל הנו דין לשמיא ולאירתא לו דין ית אלא את.

This remark is unobjectionable.

2. *Gen.* i. 2. He endeavours to explain the obscure
תהו ובהו, according to Severus' *Excerpts*, as follows:—

תהו ובהו · הנו דן צדיא ושהיא בצחחא דין אחרנא אמר
ארעה איתיה הות לא מתחזנירתא ולא מתקנרתא ולא מתחזנירתא
אמר איתיה הות מטל תהומא דמיא הו דקבא הוא וחשיר ליה
מן שית פליתא בדמות עולא הו דכריך בשלית אבנו מרבעא
דאמיה ולא מתהקנרתא מטל דלא גלין הוי אפיה.

Schaf sees, in this quotation, a clear proof that Ephraem
did not know what תהו ובהו meant. But when we examine the passage in question carefully, we see that the
expression צדיא ושהיא, "empty and desolate" is a correct
rendering. The next excerpt in Severus, to the effect that
the earth was invisible because of the multitude of waters
that covered it, and that this invisibility constituted an
imperfection, is the expansion of a just idea, but is not
intended to be taken as literal exegesis. Ephraem himself,
in fact, only says, I. 6:—דאיתיה הות תהו ובהו הנו דין
דשהיא הות וצדיא.

3. *Gen.* i. 21 (I. 18). Ephraem speaks of the Behemoth—
Job xl. 15 (10) and Psalm l. (xlix.) 10—as none but a sound

Hebraist could. To me it is inconceivable how Schaf can quote this passage in support of his theory. It runs as follows:—

הנינא דין רו״בא דאהבריו ואפן ללויתן נבׄא בימא מתמרין ליה אלא לבהמות איוב ביבשא משרא לא אף דוד דעבדׄא אמר דעל אלף טורׄין איהיה מרעיתיה הנודין מרבועיתיה כבר דין בתר דאהבריו אהפלגו להון אהרׄותא דלויתן נאמר בימא ובהמות ביבשא.

This rendering of Behemoth is not strange and peculiar, as Schaf supposes. The ancient translators differ as to the meaning. The Septuaginta has, in Psalms and Job, τὰ θηρία (Vulgate *jumenta*). Aquila and Theodotion, in both passages, κτήνη (Field, *Hexapla* II. 76, 173), while the *Peschito* gives in Psalms בעירא ותורא, but in Job only בהמות.

4. Schaf is guilty of a serious error in remarking that Ephraem could have had but a slight acquaintance with Hebrew, seeing that he is forced to have recourse to Syrian roots, in order to explain Hebrew words. His instance is where on Gen. xi. 29 (I. 59) the Father says:—הי דמטל שופרה אהקרית אסכה, "Sara was called Isca because of her beauty." Schaf seems to be unaware that this is an Agadic interpretation which, however, rests on the fact that in the Hebrew word a Syriac root was discerned. *Seder Olam R.* c. II., towards the end, ולמה נקרא שמה יסכה שהכל סכין ביפיה; more definitely in *Megilla*, 14*a*, and *Sanhedrin*, 69*b*, יסכה שהכל סכין ביפיה; according to another interpretation, שסכרתה ברוח הקדש. (Cp. Gerson, *ib.*, p. 19, who, however, does not cite the passage from the *Seder Olam*.) In languages as closely correlated as Hebrew and Syriac, this mode of exposition is perfectly legitimate. In the *Mechilta* on Ex. xii. 4, הכסו is explained from the Syriac (לשון כורסי). Will any one assert that the author of that interpretation did not understand Hebrew? Why then should this exegesis appear strange when employed by Ephraem, especially as it is obviously homiletic and Agadic, rather than

grammatical? Compare the Syriac derivation of the names
of Job's three daughters (Job xlii. 4).

5. *Gen.* xxxvi. 24 (I. 184):—הלף דאשכח מ״א עבריא אמר

אשכח גנבʾʾא במדברא. Ephraem's explanation here coincides
with that given by Onkelos and the Samaritan version,
as is already noted by J. Perles, *Meletemata Peschittoniana*,
page 9.

6. In the sermon against the Jews (*Op. Syr.* III. 218),
Ephraem translates the words בני ארונו (Gen. xlix. 11) " and
his ass, my son." But in his commentary (I. 108, 190) the
correct rendering, "the ass's colt" is twice given ; and in
the Sermon, too, the same rendering occurs (III. 224).
This error, therefore, proves nothing against Ephraem's
knowledge of Hebrew, as Schaf himself is inclined to
admit.

7. *Deut.* ix. 9 (I. 273). Ephraem says:—איכא גיר דאמר
דצלית דצמית כתיב בעבריא. He had, therefore, read the
original text and understood it.

8. *Joshua* xv. 28 (I. 305):—ובזיותʾʾה ׳ הנו קורʾʾה כד לא
ידעו הנון דפשקו לסורהא מנא איהוהי הי ברת קלא עבריתא
בזיותיה סמו. Ephraem exposes a mistake in the *Peschito*
and appeals to the Hebrew text.

9. At the beginning of his commentary to the Book of
Judges (I. 308), he draws a distinction between the terms
שפטים and שבטים which is irreproachable.

10. *Jud.* v. 30 (I. 316) עבריא אמר ׳ הכימʾʾתא דדרוכהאʾ עני
אכורה. It is indeed surprising that he should have understood שרותיה in the sense of concubines. This may, however, be an exegetical licence and not a real mistake.

11. On 1 *Sam.* xxi. 8 (I. 376), ברת קלא עבריהא ינעצר׳
גונירא הי לן עם עבריא ומרניאת מרהפשקא על מא דסעדין
אילין דעצרין לזיהאʾ ולעʾʾנבא. "The word נעצר is common
to Syriac and Hebrew. It specially refers to the pressing
of grapes and olives." With the imperfect sources at our
command we cannot tell that נעצר had not this meaning

in Hebrew. But our author has certainly a right to draw an inference from Syriac to Hebrew.

12. 2 *Kings* iii. 1 (I. 523), he explains the Hebrew term נקד.—נבה נבה עבריא דמן שמאהו כרבא אמר דהרכא נקדא ריש ר׳עותא דענא הנו דמתרסא סונא דענא. No objection can be offered either to the note that here Hebrew and Syriac coincide or to the explanation suggested.

13. 2 *Kings* viii. 18 (1. 539), עבריא דין הוב סוכלא אהרנא והפכא מחוא ׳ הנו ׳ אמר לא מאחא האחא. This is a studied reference to the Hebrew text.

We deem it unnecessary to give further proofs in support of our assertion, that Ephraem had a considerable knowledge of the sacred tongue.

We now turn to the question: What is Ephraem's relation to the Jewish Agada? After Lengerke, Gaertz and Gerson's thorough investigations, such a question might possibly be deemed superfluous; but such is not the case. That the Father incorporated with his commentaries a mass of Agàdas and Midrashim is clear. But how did he come by them? Were his informants contemporary Jews, or Christians of the school of Edessa or Nisibis? All the other Church Fathers, to whom we have referred in this Essay, usually quote Agadas in the name of the Jews. Ephraem never does so. We frequently meet with such phrases as :—אית ׳ מפשקונא מן אנשא ׳ אנשין מן כפר׳א ׳ אנשין מן דאמרין ׳ אנשין אמרו ׳ אנשין איך משלמנותהון ׳ אנשין אמרו ברויא ׳ דקדמיע משלמנורא מן (Lengerke, pp. 14-20), the majority of which refer to the Jews. That he never distinctly names them shows his marked hostility. Hence it is extremely unlikely that any direct communication took place between the Jews and Ephraem. He would scarcely have so far overcome his prejudices as to associate with Jews. Of course, it is conceivable that there may have been two periods in Ephraem's life; one, when he was on intimate terms with Jews, and obtained an extensive acquaintance with their views; another, when he avoided saying anything in their name. This is however, after all, a mere hypothesis, unsupported by historical facts. The question itself we have not sufficient information to settle.

The Agadas found in Ephraem's writings are too numerous to be exhaustively treated within the limits of the present essay. I refer the reader to the works of Lengerke, Graetz and Gerson, and will only quote a few specimens which those investigators have left unnoticed.

I. Comm. in *Exod.* xiv. 24 (*Op. Syr.* I. 215): מפצבא הי פשיבא הות ליה אידיה למ׳צה איך הי דהות מן בהרכן בקרביה דעמלק. Moses, at the passage of the Red Sea, stretched forth his hands in the same manner as he afterwards did in the battle with Amalek. This remark is quite in the Agadic vein, though I have failed to find its parallel in the Jewish authorities.

II. 1 *Kings* iii. 5 (I. 451): אפלא בזנא אחרנא גבׄא עבׄיא נכבו להון בנׄשא רחב ורות ומעכא ברת מלכא דגשור Ephraem defends the view that heathen women could only become the wives of Jews after embracing their husbands' creed. Rahab, Ruth, and Maacha, the daughter of the king of Geshur, are given as instances. The Book of Ruth is the authority for the statement in Ruth's case; the Agada in the case of Rahab. Thus T. B. *Megilla*, 14*a*:

חולדה הנביאה מבני בניה של רחב הזונה היתה··דאגיירה ונסבה יהושע.

T. B. *Sebachim*, 115*b*, ואחר חמשים שנה ארהגיירה.

Shir R. on I. 2, רחב שמעה וארהגיירה.

Ib. on VI. 2, *Exod. R.*, c. 26, הלא שמעה רחב ובאה ודבקה בך.

About Maacha's conversion I could find nothing in the Agada.

III. 2 *Sam.* xi. 14 (I. 408): אנׄשין בן אמׄרין דיואב אשתודע מלתא דדויד עם ברת שבע··· וידע הוא עלת קריתה דאוריא··· איתי הכיל לעבדא מדם דארתפקד אלא לאגזרתא כמה לותיה וכבר דדמה ושמה דדויד בזורה הו. "Many assert that Joab discovered David's relations with Bathsheba, and knew why Urijah had been summoned. He therefore executed the orders he had received from the king, but preserved the letter of authorisation, so as to have David's life and reputation at his mercy." Ephraem spins out the legend at great length. Joab, he tells us, wished to enact, with David, the rôle of Abner with Ishbosheth. He was also continually under the apprehension that David would call him to account for Abner's murder. The letter concerning Urijah would, he thought, save him from death and give him the upper hand. Here is undoubtedly a genuine Jewish tradition, but I have, unfortunately, been unable to trace it to Jewish sources.

IV. 2 *Kings* iv. (I. 256):— אמרין דאנתרתא הדא אנהרתא דעובדיא הות הו דביתהא דאחאב בנכסיא תלמידיה דאליא דפצי אנון למאא נבייון‧‧‧ ובכפנא תרסי אנון‧‧‧דמיא מן דבא בהו שרכא יזף כספא מן בית מלכא ודאשתבק בתר מותה חובה לאנהרתה "They say that this woman was the widow of Obadiah, Ahab's former steward and Elijah's disciple, who had rescued four hundred prophets from Jezebel's hands and maintained them during the famine. During the distress he had borrowed money of the royal household, and at his death the debt was still unpaid." The parallel of this beautiful Agada is found complete in every detail, in the Jewish sources. That the woman was Obadiah's wife is stated in the *Targum Jonathan* on the passage עבדך עובדיה בעלי מית. The steward's indebtedness is referred to in *Exod. R.*, c. 31:— כספו לא נתן בנשך זה עובדיה שהיה עשיר אפוטרפוס של אחאב והוציא כל ממונו לצדקה וזן את העניים והיה לוה בנשך מיהורם וכו'.

We notice here an even verbal agreement between the Jewish narrative and that of Ephraem.

V. 2 *Kings* v. 1 (I. 531):— ומן מלתא הדא נסבו אנשין החוירתא ואמר (ואמרו?) דהתא איהוהי הו גברא הו דקטליה ביד נארא דנפק מן אידה המימאית‧‧‧ אלא הלין מן תחוירתא שרירתא גליזין אנון. "Hence many derived the fable that this [Naaman] was the man who had accidentally slain [Ahab] with an arrow." This noteworthy Agada I could find nowhere else.

VI. 2 *Kings* iv. 35 (I. 529, 530):—אסברו אנשין מן כפ־א
דהן מנינא ראזהו דאלפא שביעיא' דבה מרנחמין כלהון מיה.א
ואמרו דזבנא דעלמא לה להנא מנינא התם ברויה' שבועא ניד
תהום אירתוהי מפרשנא דזבנא.

This view of the duration of the earth entirely agrees with the familiar Agada in T. B. *Sanhedrin*, 97a:—תנא דבי
אליהו ששת אלפים שנה הוי עלמא.

A similar tradition in Jerome is treated by Rahmer:— *"Die hebräischen Traditionen in den Werken des Hieronymos"* (Breslau 1861), p. 22. A multitude of opinions on *Chiliasm* has also been collected from the Church Fathers and Talmudic doctors by Grünwald, *Verhältniss der Kirchenväter zur talmudischen und midraschischen Literatur* (in Königsberger's *Monatsblätter*, p. 102, also separately printed, Jungbunzlau, 1891).

S. Krauss.

(To be continued.)

The Jewish Quarterly Review.

JANUARY, 1894.

THE JEWS IN THE WORKS OF THE CHURCH FATHERS.

VI.

JEROME.

THE Latin Father's comprehensive works contain a mass of data concerning the Palestinian Jews, as well as complete accounts of their political, educational, and religious status in the fourth century, which have as yet by no means been exhausted. The following pages give especial prominence to those points which, as far as my view of the literature of the subject extends, have not received adequate treatment. These are, however, so numerous that I have thought it well, for the sake of clearness and conciseness, to divide the subject into sections.

1.—POLITICAL POSITION OF THE JEWS IN PALESTINE DURING THE FOURTH CENTURY.

The Jews seem to have enjoyed the full right of domicile in Palestine and adjacent countries. We find them settled in all parts of the country. Considerable tracts were almost exclusively occupied by them,[1] while Chris-

---

[1] On. Sacr., ed. Lagarde, cxix. 15, 19 ; cxx. 6 ; cxli. 27 ; clvii. 4, etc.

tianity was only spread over that territory which was formerly called Moab.[1] In Judea itself the Christians were only here and there sole occupiers of entire localities.[2] While, however, the Jews were not forbidden by express law to settle in towns and trade centres, they seem of their own accord to have avoided large cities, where their appearance might have occasioned a tumult.[3] For the same reason they abstained from attending crowded markets[4]— so permanent and abiding was the effect of the terrible disasters which they had sustained in their last struggle with the Romans. Under Abraham's terebinth tree, where, as the story ran, thousands of Jewish captives of war had been sold into slavery in the reign of terror that followed the revolt against Hadrian, fairs were held annually and largely frequented.[5] Could the Jews help avoiding a place fraught with such sad memories? For other reasons, too, the commercial cities of the Holy Land were an abomination to the Hebrews. A Talmudic law forbade Jews from entering Ascalon, Gaza, Acco, and Scythopolis, because of their still prevalent idolatry (T. B. *Abodah Zara*, 11*b*). Cæsarea and Joppa and other towns practised the most shameful rites of heathendom as late as the fifth century.[6] We need not, therefore, wonder that Jerome was impressed by the small number of Jews who visited those cities.

Settlement in Jerusalem, on the other hand, was forbidden by an express enactment, which we learn from Jerome was still in force in the fourth century.[7] They

[1] In Is. xvi. 4, In omni terra Moab ecclesia Christi.

[2] On. Sacr. xciii. 18 ; xiv. 15; cviii. 27.

[3] In *Ep. ad Galat.* iv. 22, Vix rarus atque notabilis in urbibus Judaeus appareat.

[4] In Jerem. xxxi. 14, Idcirco execrabile esse Judaeis mercatum celeberrimum visere.

[5] In Zach. xi. 5, In tabernaculo Abraae . . . ubi nunc per annos . . . . mercatus celeberrimus exercetur.

[6] Neubauer, *Géographie du Talmud*, pp. 68, 232 ; Schürer, *Geschichte des Jüdischen Volkes im Zeitalter Jesu Christi*, II , p. 11.

[7] In Soph. i. 15, *et passim.*

were hardly permitted to wail on Zion's ruins. This was a privilege which had to be heavily paid for. Jerome dwells with satisfaction on this humiliation.[1] Every year, on the 9th of Ab, wailing and with rent garments, the Jews could be seen traversing the Temple mount, and throwing themselves upon stones pierced with a hole and daubed with oil.[2] They donned mourners' robes, walked barefoot, and rolled themselves in the dust. Even the dish of lentils, usually prepared for those bereaved by death, was not wanting.[3]

In trade and commerce no restrictions seem to have been placed on the Jews. Jewish physicians and innkeepers are mentioned by name in Jerome's works. The former were on friendly terms with the scholars;[4] the latter were accused of mingling their wine with water.[5] State offices were barred to the Jews; so was the military profession. "No wonder," says our author, with malicious satisfaction, "that the Jews have lost their manly bearing. They are not received into the army, nor are they permitted to wear swords or bear other warlike arms."[6]

2.—Social Position of the Jews.

The material condition of the Palestinian Jews must, on the whole, be pronounced favourable. They appear to have been rather rich than poor. Jerome accentuates every species of misery they suffer as proofs that they are no longer God's people; but he has nothing to say of their poverty. On the contrary, it is their wealth which

---

[1] In Soph. Compare Eusebius' account.
[2] Grätz, *Monatsschrift*, 1876, p. 4 ; Thierry, *St. Jerôme*, I., p. 253.
[3] *Ep.* xxii. *ad Paulam* (ed. Mart. iv. 27), Flent usque hodie Judaei et nudatis pedibus in cinere volutati sacco incubant. Ac ne quid desit superstitioni, ex ritu vanissimo Pharisaeorum primum cibum lentis accipiunt.
[4] Praef. in Osee, in tabernis medicorum, etc.
[5] In Amos ii. 12, Neque possunt more Judaicorum cauponum miscere aquam vino.   [6] In Is. iii. 2.

offends him. "Search through all the synagogues of the Jews," he exclaims, "and you will not find a single Rabbi who impresses on his flock the duty of despising earthly possessions, or who praises the virtue of poverty."[1] With biting scoffs he attacks their healthy, practical common sense. They do not pursue chimeras, but toil for the good things of earth.[2] This practical sense shows itself especially in their dealings with Christians. When pious pilgrims engage Jewish guides, they have to pay them heavily for their services.[3] When Christians seek the opinion of Jews in Biblical matters, they have to remunerate them substantially for their instruction.[4] When Christians wish to possess correct copies of the Bible prepared for them by Jews, they must compensate the scribes with considerable sums.[5] When, finally, a Christian, desirous of completing his Biblical education, applies to Jewish teachers, he is charged high fees for the lessons.[6]

This practical cleverness not only obtained for the Jews a good social position. It enabled them also to afford shining proofs of their inborn charitableness, even towards their Christian persecutors. Many a Gentile's wretchedness was alleviated with the money of Jews. But this generosity aroused Jerome's apprehension that the Jews' gold might corrupt the Christian, and convert him to his benefactor's creed. He therefore recommends that Jewish assistance should be firmly and persistently refused.[7] To the honour of the Church be it said that it did not forbid its adherents

---

[1] In Is. iii. 14.   [2] In Ez., iv. 13.
[3] In Naum, i. 1 ; Thierry, a. a. O. I., 236.
[4] Lib. II., *Invect. Ruff.* c. xxix. (II., 658), Judaeus . . . . verba vendat ad pretium.
[5] Lib. II. *Contra Ruff.* (II., 530), Magno sumptu sibi a Judaeis describere festinavit.
[6] Praef. in Job, memini . . . . me . . . . Lyddaeum quendam . . . . non parvis redemisse nummis.
[7] *Ep.* lii. *ad Nepotianum* (I., 263), Aut aurum repudiemus cum caeteris superstitionibus Judaeorum ; aut si aurum placet, placent et Judaei, quos cum auro aut probare nobis necesse est aut damnare.

to give alms to the Jewish poor;[1] although the almoners were only allowed a free hand when the Church members had been particularly liberal.[2] At that time, it was still admitted that God loved the Jews,[3] and that they were not outside the pale of humanity.

3.—INTERNAL ORGANISATION OF THE PALESTINIAN COMMUNITIES.

Concerning the condition of the Jewish communities in the fourth century there are but scanty notices, so that the accounts which Jerome gives us in this connection are doubly welcome.

In early times the government of the communities was vested, not in the religious teachers, but in a few influential heads elected from the laity.[4] This order of things seems to have been changed. Jerome tells us that the religious teachers were the leaders of the community. The spiritual guides were also the secular guardians. In the latter capacity they appear to have been styled *praepositi*. Before assuming office, they had to pass an examination, the object of which was to test their capacity for deciding ritual questions.[5] From one of John Chrysostom's Homilies it is clear that the Jewish Presidents, there called Archontes, were chosen at the beginning of the year, *i.e.*, in the month of September (Loening, *Die Gemeindeverfassung des Urchristenthums*, Halle, 1889, No. I., p. 69). The custom had gradually obtained of " conferring synagogal functions

---

[1] *Ep.* cxx. ad *Hedibiam* (I., 814), Non quod in pauperes Judaeos . . . . prohibeamus faciendam eleemosynam.

[2] Lib. c. *Vigilantium*, c. xv. (II., 319), Cunctis pauperibus, etiam Judaeis et Samaritanis, si tanta sit largitas, stipe porrigenda⸗.

[3] In Osee iii. 1, Quia Judaei praesens tempus diligentur a Domino.

[4] Schürer, *Gemeindeverfassung der Juden in Rom*, p. 30.

[5] *Ep.* cxxi. ad *Algasiam*, Quaest. X., Praepositos habent synagogis sapientissimos quosque, foedo opere delegatos, ut sanguinem virginis sive menstruatae, mundum vel immundum, si oculis discernere non potuerint gustu probent.

upon those who, searching in the Law of God day and night
have no part in earthly benefits, and take God as their sole
inheritance. Thus the interests of equity were served.
The good things were not unequally distributed; the superfluity of some alleviated the needs of others."[1] Jerome
notes a touching instance of Jewish tenderheartedness;
Jewish women took it upon themselves to provide religious
teachers with their livelihood.[2] Although the communal
heads were greatly esteemed by their flocks, their influence
outside the Synagogue was not very considerable. Independent jurisdiction had been taken from them. In disputed cases, the Roman magistrates decided. The Jewish
authorities were subordinated to them: "They have no
judges of their own; even the heads left to them must
submit to the decision of the Roman authority."[3] The
Patriarchate, the single institution which still shone with
some splendour in the dark days of trial, was dying.
Nevertheless messengers were still sent out to collect contributions for the Patriarch.[4]

4.—JEWISH FAMILY LIFE.

Jewish family life has always been distinguished by
affectionate tenderness. A few noteworthy details may be
gleaned from Jerome. Children were sometimes weaned

---

[1] Lib. c. *Vigilantium*, c. xiv. (II. 393), Hac in Judaea usque hodie perse-
verante consuetudine, non solum apud nos, sed et apud Hebraeos, ut qui
in Lege Domini meditantur die ac nocte et partem non habent in terra
nisi solum Deum, synagogarum et totius orbis foveantur ministeriis, ex
aequalitate dumtaxat, non ut aliis refrigerium, et aliis sit tribulatio, sed
ut aliorum abundantia aliorum sustentet inopiam.

[2] Lib. I. *adv. Jovinianum*, c. xxv. (II., 277), Mulieribus, quae juxta
morem Judaicum magistris de sua substantia ministrabant.

[3] In Is. iii. 2.

[4] In *Ep. ad Galatas* i. 1, Usque hodie a Patriarchis Judaeorum Apos-
tolos mitti. Grätz, *Geschichte der Juden*, iv.², 476, only mentions Eusebius
and Epiphanius as sources, and omits that interesting remark in Jerome,
who even tells the Hebrew name, *Slias* (שליח).

as late as the fifth year.[1] Parents carried their grown-up sons and daughters on their shoulders and in baskets.[2] In Jerome's time Jews were blessed with large families.[3] Of asceticism there was no trace. Within the limits of the law, no check was placed on good living. The meals on Sabbath were excellent. The day was passed in idleness or sleep.[4]

Jerome notes with some mortification that, as a rule, the Jews reached an advanced old age.[5] A death arouses the sympathy of the entire community. The custom still continued of employing professional wailing women who, with hair uncovered and bared breasts, summoning every one to mourning and weeping.[6]

5.—EDUCATIONAL STATUS OF THE JEWS.

For the education of the young there were elementary schools; and for the adults, Talmudical colleges. Importance was attached to the cultivation of the memory. Children had to learn by heart the alphabet in the regular and reverse order.[7] The Pharisees are reproached by Jerome with always repeating, never reflecting.[8] The strength of memory attained by this system of training arouses his admiration and chagrin. "In childhood they acquire the complete vocabulary of their language, and

---

[1] *Quaest. Hebr.* in Gen. xxi. 14.
[2] In Is. l. 18, Ridiculum est more Judaico grandaevos filios et filias in ulvis humerisque portari.
[3] In Is. xlviii. 17, Usque in praesentem diem instar vermiculorum pullulant filios et nepotes.
[4] In Is. lvi. 2, Neque enim prodest sedere in sabbatho, sive dormire aut epulis inhiare.
[5] In Is. iii. 2, Usque ad deripiam senectutem saepe venire (Judaeos) conspicimus.
[6] In Jerem. ix. 17. Cp. Moed Katan, 28*b*.
[7] In Jerem. xxv. 26, in שׁשׁך.
[8] *Ep.* cxxvii. *ad Principiam* (I., 947), Meditationem Legis in replicando quae scripta sunt, ut Judaeorum existimant Pharisaei.

learn to recite all the generations from Adam to Zerubbabel
with such accuracy and facility, as if they were simply
giving their names."[1] It gave them pleasure to annoy the
Christians by intoning[2] the long list of grandchildren,
great-grandchildren, grandfathers, great-grandfathers, and
great-great-grandfathers without a single slip. It was
quite a common feat among the Jews to recite by heart
the five books of Moses and the Prophets.[3] This strain on
the memory was not occasioned by a want of books. It
was but an additional proof of the warm love which the
Jews cherished for the ancient Law. Jerome often
mentions the "Archiva Judaeorum," by which he often
merely refers to the Canon of Scripture, but sometimes
also means libraries.[4] Jewish houses possessed shelves
loaded and cases packed with books.[5] In Palestine, an
institution analogous to our circulating libraries must have
existed. Every synagogue seems to have possessed a collection of books, from which the members were permitted
to borrow. Jerome's Jewish teacher abused his privilege,
and presented his Christian pupil with a volume lent him
by the Synagogue authorities.[6]

Jerome stood in need of a copy of the Bible which
the Synagogue regarded as authentic. Other copies of the
Scriptures that were in circulation were most untrust-
worthy.[7] But even erroneous copies of Holy Writ the

---

[1] In *Ep. ad Titum* iii. 9. The Apostle Paul also alludes to this quality
of the Jews. *Ep.* I. *ad Timoth.* i. 4.

[2] *Ib.* putant se in nominibus referendis . . . in nepotibus, abnepotibus,
avis, proavis et abavis doctiores.

[3] In Is. lviii. 2. Libros Prophetarum ac Moysi memoriter revolventes
(Judaei).

[4] *E.g.* Praefatio in Esther (ix., 1566) librum Esther . . . ego de Archivis
Judaeorum relevans.

[5] In Matt. xxiii. 5, Judaei alioquin armariae et arcae habent libros.

[6] *Ep.* xxxvi., *ad Damasum* (i. 158). Subito Hebraeus intervenit, de-
ferens non pauca volumina, quae *de Synagoga quasi lecturus* acceperat
et illico habes, inquit, quod postulaveras . . .

[7] *Praef.* in Gen. (ix. 6), emendatiora sunt exemplaria Latina quam
Graeca, Graeca quam Hebraea.

Christians could not prepare by themselves, their Hebrew knowledge was not sufficiently extensive. They had to order them of Jewish scribes, who charged heavy fees for their trouble.[1] This speaks well for the Biblical knowledge of the Palestinian Jews. Jerome assumes that in Scriptural questions, every Jew, without exception, is competent to give satisfactory replies.[2] The Jews, moreover, were acquainted, not only with the original text but also with the Septuagint,[3] the Apocrypha,[4] Aquila's Version,[5] and generally with all works relating to Holy Writ. No sooner had Apollinaris Laodicenus' writings appeared than the Jews read them and formed their opinions on them.[6] Especially noteworthy is the fact that the Jews were at home in the New Testament as well as in the Old. They could explain difficulties in it which puzzled even the officially appointed Christian teachers.[7] Jerome's Hebrew tutor even quotes Virgil.[8] That this man knew Greek, Latin, Hebrew and Aramaic, is evident from every page of Jerome's works.

6.—RELIGIOUS LIFE OF THE JEWS.

The Synagogue formed the centre of Jewish life. The Jews must have possessed several synagogues, as Jerome

---

[1] *Lib.* ii. c. *Ruffinum* (ii. 530), magno sumptu sibi a Judaeis describere festinavit . . .

[2] *Praef.* in Samuel (ix., 450).

[3] *Ep.* lvii. *ad Pammachium* (i. 234, et passim). The Jews impugn certain passages in the Septuagint.

[4] *Praef.* in Daniel, the history of Susanna is ridiculed by the Jews.

[5] *Ep.* xxxvi. *ad Damasum* (i. 165), Aquilam . . . proprie transtulisse omnis Judaea conclamat.

[6] In Eccles. v. 17, nec Judaeis placere nec Christianis.

[7] In Is. xi. 1, Illud quod in Evangelio . . . omnes quaerunt Ecclesiastici et non inveniunt ubi scriptum sit, eruditi Hebraeorum de hoc loco assumptum putant.

[8] *Praef.* in Daniel (ix. 1362), illud in sua lingua ingerente : Labor omnia vincit improbus.

234 *The Jewish Quarterly Review.*

drops a remark, in his bitter vein, on the number of them.[1]
He also knew that services were held in the Synagogue by
day and night.[2] He feels surprised that the Jews do not
kneel during prayers.[3] Among the Jewish prayers he has
much to say concerning the Benediction against the
heretics; he also occasionally quotes other Jewish prayers.[4]
The most solemn part of the service was undoubtedly the
chanting of the Psalms.[5] With especial frequency and
solemnity was the 117th Psalm, the Hallel, sung.[6]

Besides prayer and song, the sermon formed an essential
part of the Service. Concerning its popularity among the
Jews, to which the Midrash bears ample testimony, Jerome
also furnishes some data. "They say one to another:
Come, let us listen to this or that Rabbi who expounds the
divine law, with such marvellous eloquence; then they
applaud and make a noise, and gesticulate with their
hands." [7] "The Preachers make the people believe that the
fictions which they invent are true; and after they have
in theatrical fashion called forth applause . . . . they
arrogantly step forward, speak proudly and usurp the
authority of rulers." [8] Jerome was an attentive observer;

---

[1] In Is. lvii. 12. Synagogarum turba.

[2] In Jerem. xviii. 17, usque hodie diebus ac noctibus in Synagogis
invocant nomen Dei.

[3] In Is. xlvi. 2, genu flectere . . . quod Judaei mentis superbiam de-
monstrantes, omnino non faciunt.

[4] In Is. lxiv. at the end, there is the following Jewish prayer : Super
his omnibus Domine sustinebis et affliges [Var. sustinebimus et afflige]
nos atque humiliabis vehementer. I do not understand this.

[5] In Amos v. 23, Judaeorum . . . Psalmi, quos in Synagogis canunt,
tumultus (sunt) . . . Domino.

[6] *Ep.* xx. *ad Damasum* (i. 66).

[7] In Ezek. xxxiii. 33. Venite audiamus illum et illum, mira eloquentia
predicationis suae verba volventem ; plaususque commovent et vociferantur
et jactant manus.

[8] In Ezek. xxxiv. 31. Qui quum populo persuaserint, vera esse quae
fingunt, et in theatralem modum plausus concitaverint et clamores,
immemores fiunt imperitiae suae et adducto supercilio, libratisque sermonibus, magistrorum sibi assumunt auctoritatem.

the Jewish preacher's theatrical manner is also mentioned by his contemporary, St. John Chrysostom.[1] "On
certain days they recite their traditions to their pupils;
on such occasions they are wont to say: οἱ σοφοὶ
δευτερῶσιν, i.e., 'the masters explain.'"[2] From this last
remark we see that Greek terms for purely Jewish institutions had been adopted and were already fixed in
popular usage. Thus, the teachers who occupied themselves with Halacha were called in Greek σοφοί;[3] those,
on the other hand, who devoted their chief attention to
Hagada, were called δευτερωταί.[4] It is remarkable that
the title σοφός for Rabbi was maintained throughout the
Middle Ages[5] in communities of Greek origin, e.g., in
Sicily.

Jerome naturally does not approve of the Rabbinical
teachers. He reproves them for not preserving a composed
demeanour while preaching, and says they find a pleasure
in shouting.[6] Self-maceration—at that time already regarded by the Christians as a virtue—was not practised by
the Jewish Rabbis; he therefore regarded them as volup-
tuaries.[7] He does not believe that these gourmands could
bring it upon themselves to fast twice a week, on Monday
and Thursday.[8] The nature of a Jewish sermon is also
accurately defined. "The Jews," he says, "rush on certain
days into the Synagogue and pore in God's law to find

---

[1] *Opp. ed. Montfaucon* (i. 656), καὶ παίζουσι (οἱ νῦν πατριαρχαὶ πὰρ ὑμῖν)
καθάπερ ἐν τῇ σκηνῇ.
[2] *Ep.* cxxi. *ad Algasiam, Cp.* שנר חכמים or תנו רבנן.
[3] *Ep.* cxxi. *ad Algasiam* (*Quaest.* x.). Doctores eorum σοφοί, hoc est
sapientes, vocantur.
[4] So in several passages.
[5] Gudemann, *Geschichte des Erziehungswesens der Juden in Italien*,
p. 289.
[6] In Is. lviii. 3, ad orationem deferatis clamorem.
[7] *E.g.*, in Is. lviii. 3, epulis saturatus Pharisaeus . . .
[8] *Ib.* bis in Sabbatho se jejunare jactabant. This seems to be the
earliest notice of תענית שני וחמש, which will correct what Graetz says
on the subject in his *Monatsschrift*, 1854, p. 191.

out what Abraham, Isaac, Jacob and the rest of the saints
(caeteri sanctorum) may have done." [1] The narrative Agada
is here meant, such as we find it in rich exuberance in our
Midrashic literature.

The free Agadic homilies at the reading of the Law are to
be distinguished from the Sermon. The Biblical verse was
first translated, then freely expounded in the Agadic style. [2]
The tradition, or Agada, was always connected with a
Biblical verse; even a well-known Agada was always repeated whenever a passage was reached in the reading of
the Torah with which it had any relation. [3] But not all the
Agadas that were in circulation were fit to be publicly read.
The recital of several was interdicted [4] on account of their
obscenity. Here it should be noted that the Agadas must
already have been fixed in writing, as otherwise Jerome
could not have spoken of them as being read.

7.—HERETICAL MOVEMENTS AMONG THE JEWS.

Palestine was also in the fourth century an arena, where
the various Jewish and Christian sects contended for
victory. The *Minim*, who were the objects of so much
dread to the Talmudists, were disseminated among all
communities of the Orient. [5] There was a multitude of
baptised Jews, and the rigorous Talmudic teachers felt

---

[1] In Iº. lviii. 2.

[2] In Michaeam ii. 11, juxta id quod nobis ab Hebraeis est traditum
exponamus et . . . postea de eorum translatione tractabimus.

[3] *Quaest. Hebr.* In Gen. xiv. 8. Jerome speaks of the Jewish tradition,
that the first-born originally served as priests; he afterwards says, Gen.
xxvii. 15, Et in hoc tradunt Hebraei . . . The same tradition.

[4] He is speaking of the tradition that Jewish women in Babylon had
submitted themselves to certain men of guile, in the hope that they
would give birth to the Messiah. (In Jerem. xxix. 21.) Unde et a plerisque ac paene omnibus Hebraeis, ipsa (traditio) quasi fabula non reci-
pitur nec legitur in Synagogis eorum, *Cp.* N. Brüll, Jahrb. iii. 9.

[5] *Ep.* cxii. *ad S. Augustinum,* i. 741, usque hodie per totas Orientis
synagogas inter Judaeos haeresis est, quae dicitur Mineorum . . .

called upon to proceed with all possible severity against
them; so much so, that the bishops had to intervene in
their favour.[1] But these baptised Jews were by no means
an acquisition on which the Church could congratulate itself.
They either clung firmly to the Jewish enactments, even
after baptism, or they led a life which was anything but
Christian : " Take any Jew you please who has been converted to Christianity," Jerome writes to St. Augustine,
" and you will see that he practises the rite of circumcision
on his newborn son, keeps the Sabbath, abstains from forbidden food, and brings a lamb as an offering on the 14th
of Nissan."[2]

Transgressions of the Law were not uncommon among
the lower classes. Jerome reports that some Jews, on an
occasion of mourning, cut incisions in their flesh and made
their heads bald.[3] The use of Tephillin and Zizith had not
yet become general. Our author is told by Palestinian
Jews, as a curiosity, that in Babylon the Rabbis wear
phylacteries and zizith.[4] Apostates had to suffer persecutions at the hands of the Rabbis. Excommunications must
have been common.[5]

8.—SOME CHRISTIANS STRICTLY ADHERE TO JEWISH CUSTOMS.

Even after more than three centuries' separation, trium-
phant Christianity had not yet emancipated itself from
the mother religion; it was still subject to the influence
of the Jewish Law. Our author rails most bitterly at
the superstition of the Christian women (*mulierculae*),
who, ascribing to the Jewish phylacteries an indefinite

---

[1] Grätz, *Geschichte*, IV. [2] 385.
[2] *Ep.* cxii. *ad S. Augustinum*, I. 744.
[3] In Jerem. xvi. 5.
[4] In Ezek. xxiv. 15; in Matt. xxiii. 5.
[5] In Is. lix. 15, ut quicunque a traditionibus Judaeorum capierit recedere, statim pateret insidiis et persecutionibus, ita ut . . . expulerint de
Synagogis.

but vast magical power, covered up crucifixes, the Gospels, and other sacred relics with them, and thought they were thus performing a work pleasing to God.[1] The rites of the Synagogue were imitated;[2] the Christians regarded it, indeed, as holier than the Church.[3] On the occasion of a death they rent their garments after the Jewish custom.[4] About this time arose the order of the Cœnobites, who arranged their mode of life according to the old Essene pattern.[5] At this period, too, the sect of the Photinians was instituted. They adhered so closely to the Jewish Law that their dogma was termed the Jewish dogma, and yet it had to be admitted that there was much in it that was good and wise.[6] It even appears that at that time Jewish birth was considered a weighty factor in the selection of Heads of the Church.[7] But it was mainly the lower classes who could not completely cut themselves off from the Jewish Law, the enactments of which appeared to them more rational and wise than those of Christian codes.[8] The dependence of the Church on the Synagogue is best described by Ruffinus, who sarcastically observes that if a few Jews were to institute new rites, the Church would have to follow suit and immediately adopt them.[9]

---

[1] In Matt. xxiii. 5, Quae habent quidem zelum Dei sed non juxta scientiam. We have come across similar accounts in the earlier Church Fathers.

[2] In Ezech. xxxiii. 33, Tales sunt usque hodie multi in Ecclesiis.

[3] Graetz, *History*, IV.[2] 385.

[4] This is clear from a notice in Gregory of Nyssa's essay, Περὶ τοῦ βίου τῆς μακαρίας, in Oehler, *Bibliothek der Kirchenväter*, I., 188, p. 2. περιρρήξασθαι τὸ ἱμάτιον Μακρίνης.

[5] *Ep.* xxii. *ad Eustochium*, i. 118.

[6] *Chronicon*, VIII., 816, Photiniarum dogma Judaicum, qui [Photinus] multa continentia est ingenii bona uno superbiae malo perdidit.

[7] In Is. lxi. 3, Quotus enim quisque Ecclesiarum princeps est de Judaeis et non de alienigenis atque externarum gentium hominibus?

[8] *Ep.* cxxi. *ad Algasiam*, i. 878, Videntur igitur observationes Judaicae apud imperitos et vilem plebeculam imaginem habere rationis humanaeque sapientiae.

[9] Ruffini, *Invect.*, lib. I., c. v. ; II., 589, Nisi forte a Judaeis aliquibus nova nunc lege promulgatur Ecclesiae ut etiam ista discamus.

9.—CONTROVERSY BETWEEN CHRISTIANS AND JEWS.

In Jerome's time there was no lack of discussions between Church and Synagogue. The Church militant still enjoyed its youthful vigour; it had both the desire and the strength for fighting. It was considered a great undertaking to enter on a polemic with the Jews.[1] The discussions were conducted with excessive heat; they are described as regular combats.[2] Jerome says that, on the Jewish side, the efforts that were put forth in these verbal contests were appalling.[3] The Jews are charged with an inordinate love of religious disputation. They are in great distress if no opportunity presents itself of slandering and ridiculing the Christians.[4]

With regard to the Jewish method of argument, our author tells us that they never kept to the point, always introduced matters foreign to the discussion, and often wandered away to other subjects altogether.[5] The only construction that can justly be placed on this statement is that the Jews were most reluctant to enter into controversy on certain topics. The same questions also seem to have been put over and over again. The Scriptural text was a perpetual bone of contention, the Jews insisting that the Christian copies of the Bible were erroneous.[6] On some points that had been discussed *ad nauseam* the Christians knew beforehand what their opponents would

---

[1] Praef. in Psalm, Aliud Judaeis singula verba calumniantibus respondere.

[2] In Is. vii. 14, Ut cum Judaeis conferamus pedem . . . . contentioso fune, etc.

[3] In *Ep. ad Titum*, iii. 9, Ut non magnopere pertimescamus supercilium Judaeorum, solutis labiis et obtorta lingua et otridente saliva et rasa fauce gaudentium.

[4] In Is. vii. 14, Nequaquam . . . . . praebeamus eis risum nostrae imperitiae.

[5] In Is. xliv. 6, Judaei . . . . in locis difficilimis liberae disputationis excursu nascentes fugiunt quaestiones.

[6] Very frequently in Jerome's writings.

say.[1] At this time the Jews could claim, among the different sects, many adherents to their principles. Some heretical Christians, for instance, agreed with them on most questions.[2] Influential members of the Church even, who were such important personages that Jerome is afraid to name them, could not help acknowledging that, on some points, the Jews were right.[3] Victorious Christianity had still a formidable opponent in Heathendom, and it was but natural that the Heathens sometimes employed Jewish weapons in their controversy with the Christians.[4] One of the consequences of Julian's attempt to revive Heathendom was a hot attack on Christianity. Julian himself fought it with the pen, and made use of Jewish arguments.[5]

10.—MESSIANIC HOPES OF THE JEWS.

The Church continually cherished the fond delusion that it would ultimately receive the Jews into its bosom. It is noteworthy that, as early as 400 A.D., the Jews were forced to listen to Christian sermons, with the avowed purpose of inducing them to embrace the dominant creed.[6] The daughter-religion was then as much disappointed in her expectations as she has been ever since. Judaism *hoped,*

---

[1] *Ep.* xlii. *ad Principiam*, i. 236, Interrogemus Judaeos, quae sit ista filia (Ps. xlv.) . . . . non dubito, quin synagogam respondeant.

[2] Judaei et nostri Judaizantes—a formula used by Jerome.

[3] In Sophon. iii. 14, Si quis ergo Christinorum et maxime novorum prudentium quorum nomina taceo, ne quemquam laedere videar.

[4] In Matt. xxi. 21, Latrant contra nos Gentilium canes in suis voluminibus.

[5] Compare in Osee xi. 1 ; in Matt. i. 16, ix. 9, *et passim*. It has not yet been sufficiently regarded that the Jews referred many Messianic verses to Julian. We frequently find such interpretations in Jerome.

[6] *Ep.* xciii. *Jerosolymytanae Synodi* (i. 549), Atque utinam sanctorum orationibus non nos inquietarent Judaici serpentes et Samaritanorum incredibilis stultitia . . . . quorum turba quam plurima et *ad veritatem praedicationis omnino auribus obturantes* in similitudinem luporum gregeia Christi circuientes.

and this hope was a tower of strength which saved it from succumbing to the temptations of the Church. The Jews deliberately turned away from the gloomy scenes before them, to revel in the prospect of the brilliant picture which their vivid imagination conjured up. One day the Jewish people will again revive, Israel will become glorious, Israel who is so near to God, Israel who has just cause for pride, and who may confidently challenge the judgment of God and men.[1] Israel's dispersion by the Romans does not involve destruction. God, who was with him by the waters of Egypt, by the streams of Babylon, in the fire of Macedonian persecution, will not leave him when enveloped in the flames kindled by Rome.[2] It is true his numbers are diminished; but still a remnant will always survive at last to witness the arrival of the Messianic era and to experience God's mercy.[3] The outcasts of Judah will be gathered together and brought back to Jerusalem. Great will then be the prosperity of the nation. God will deliver into their hands the sons and daughters of Rome, who will be sold as slaves, not to their neighbours, the Persians and Ethiopians, but to the Sabeans, that most distant of peoples.[4] "Though history has often disappointed them, they endeavour to prove that all the prophecies must ultimately be fulfilled; they transport themselves in imagination to the Messianic times, and console themselves with the reflection that what has not yet come true will be fulfilled in the distant future. Moab,

---

[1] In Is. lviii. 3, Est alia temeritas Judaeorum, quasi fiduciae bonae conscientiae, judicium postulant istum (Ps. xxv. 12) et appropinquare deo desiderant.

[2] In Is. xliii. 2. Thus was this verse interpreted by the Jews.

[3] In Is. xliv. 6, Judaei et nostri Judaizantes dicunt Israel ad modicum derelictum, ut in adventu Christi ejus misereatur Deus.

[4] In Joel ii. 7, Promittunt sibi Judaei immo somniunt, quod in ultimo tempore congreguntur a Domino et reducantur in Jerusalem. Nec hac felicitate contenti, ipsum Deum suis manibus Romanorum filios et filias asserunt traditurum, ut vendant eos Judaei, non Persis et Aethiopibus et caeteris nationibus, quae vicinae sunt, sed Sabaeis, genti longissimae.

and the sons of Ammon, the Egyptians, as well as the
Philistines and Idumea, who now afflict the Jews, will then
receive their punishment. But why, we ask them, should
God punish just these nations? Why not the whole globe
on the entire surface of which the Jews wander? Gaul,
Britain, Spain, Italy, Africa, in fact, all nations, ought also
to be punished for the same offence, for the whole world
keeps the Jews in captivity." [1]

It was, indeed, the opinion of the Jews that all the
nations who had oppressed them would be called to account.
In order that Israel's glory might be complete, the angels
will build a new Jerusalem, a beautiful and lofty city,
ornamented with precious stones and fine gold. [2] The saints
will rise again, re-clothed in their bodily form and re-
endowed with their human qualities and capacity for
pleasures. [3] The joyous banquets of the Messianic times are
painted in the brightest colours. Christians who heard
of the delights in store for pious Jews were so attracted by
the picture, that they became converts to Judaism. [4] In

---

[1] In Sophon. ii. 8. Making allowances for the exaggeration in the
phrase "totus orbis," the above-named countries may, in fact, already
have been inhabited by Jews ; this passage would thus be the oldest testimony to the presence of Jews in Britain. It is likewise worthy of notice
that Jerome only knew this Jewish Agada in its external form. He had
no conception that by Moab, Ammon, Edom, etc., the Jews meant, not the
extinct peoples, but nations still living. It speaks well for his Jewish
teachers that their intimacy with him did not tempt them to betray to
him the esoteric significance of the Agada. However, Jerome had enough
acuteness to guess that by Edom the Jews really meant Rome : in Is. xi. 11
(דומה, רומה), Semper in Idumaeae nomine Romanos existimant demon-
strari.

[2] In Is. xlix. 14, Judaei et nostri Judaizantes putant auream atque
gemmatam (Jerusalem) de caelestibus ponendam. As well known, this
belief was, in the earliest times, one of the dogmas of Christianity, and
served to console its followers for the destruction of the earthly Jerusalem.

[3] *Ruff. Invect.* lib. I., c. v. (II. 589), Est Judaeorum vere de resurrectione
talis opinio, quod resurgunt quidem, sed ut carnalibus deliciis et luxuriis
caeterisque voluptatibus corporis perfruantur.

[4] In Is. lix. 5, Qui audiens traditiones Judaicas ad escas se mille
annorum voluerit praeparare.

their religious ecstasy, the Jews had even definitely fixed the time of Messiah's triumphal entry into the holy city. The new redemption, like the old, will take place in the middle of the month of Nissan, on the first midnight of Passover, as at the Exodus from Egypt.[1] The tradition was also firmly held, that the Messiah would first raise his standard in Babylon, would next march into Egypt and conquer it, and then would finally inaugurate his triumphal entry into Jerusalem.[2] This will, however, be preceded by the war with Gog and Magog, in which much blood will be spilt.[3] Finally, the glorious era of universal peace will set in; in the new and resplendent Jerusalem the Messiah will hold his court, surrounded by all pious nations who will do homage to his supremacy.[4] The Jews will be exclusive possessors of the sacred Scriptures; the Christians who had on account of these writings caused them so much suffering will no longer be allowed to retain copies of the Bible.[5] All disputes and misunderstandings will consequently cease; all nations will cherish the same belief, all will understand and speak Hebrew.[6] Such was the conception then current of the Messianic era.

In connection with the foregoing remarks, it is not uninteresting to inquire what conception the Jews formed of the Messiah's person. It is necessary to note first that the

---

[1] In Matt. xxv. 5, Traditio Judaeorum est Christum media nocte venturum in similitudinem Aegyptii temporis, quando Pascha celebratum est.

[2] In Daniel xii. 6.

[3] In Joel iv. 13, Judaei et nostri Judaizantes arbitrantes ultimo tempore, quando Jerusalem fuerit instaurata, sub mille annorum imperio contra Dei populum esse venturas [gentes Gog et Magog].

[4] In Joel iv. 16, Judaei et nostri Judaizantes putant, Christum habitaturum in Sion et in Jerusalem aurea atque gemmata sanctorum populos congregandos.

[5] In Micha vii. 9, Hoc sibi Judaei usque hodie pollicentur . . . . et ajunt: In die illa . . . . Scripturas sanctas . . . . quae nunc tenentur a nobis tolli de manibus nostris et tradi populo Judaeorum. Compare Exod. Rabba, c. 47, ‏כתב לך כו׳‎.

[6] In Sophon. iii. 9.

Messiah was called in Judaeo-Hellenic circles ἠλειμμένος, the " Anointed," an exact equivalent of the Hebrew משיח, but that this term must be distinguished from the word χριστός, by which the Christians denominated their Messiah. The name Christ was not pleasant to the Jews, since it had become the watchword of their bitterest enemies, and therefore they preferred to connote the same idea by the expression ἠλειμμένος. That the choice of this word was an open protest against Christianity is proved by Aquila's use of it in the Christological Psalm ii. 2, against which Irenæus made a strong protest.[1] In Jerome's time the word had obtained wide currency among the Jews, and he cannot hide his chagrin at the fact.[2] A Messiah of the tribe of Joseph is nowhere mentioned ; the Jews, however, even at that time believed, as we have already noticed, that the Messiah's arrival would be heralded by Elijah.[3] The Messiah's essential nature is defined in the sentence : He will be eternal justice (justitia sempiterna).[4] The Messiah is also the whirlwind and storm that will sweep Israel's enemies off the earth.[5] It is interesting to learn the language which was used in praying to the long looked for Messiah.   Here is a petition, clothed in Midrashic form, which, starting from Zechariah ix. 11, 12, quotes several other Hebrew texts.   " O Messiah, in whose advent we believe, thou whose dominion will extend to the corners of the earth,[6] in the blood of thy covenant,[7] in which according to Ezekiel (xvi. 6, 22), thou didst find

---

[1] Zipser, in *Ben Chananja*, VI. (1863), p. 181.

[2] We can only quote a few passages ; to quote them all would be impossible : Antichristus, ut dicitur, ἠλειμμίνος *suus*, in Is. xxvii. 13 ; Judaei sub ἠλειμμίνω *suo*, in Zach. xiv. 15 ; Referunt ad ἠλειμμίνον, id est Christum *suum*, in Maleachi iii. 1. Compare the following remark.

[3] In Mal. iii., the end, Judaei et Judaizantes haeretici ante ἠλειμμίνον *suum* Eliam putant esse venturum.

[4] In Dan. ix. 24, in the name of the Jews, according to Jer. xxxiii. 16.

[5] In Is. iv. 5, Hunc locum Judaei ad Antichristum referunt, quem per turbinem et tempestatem significari aestimant.

[6] ומשלו......עד אפסי ארץ.   [7] בדם בריתך.

Jerusalem, the defiled, and didst plight thy troth unto her (?)[1] in the covenant, which thou didst form with Abraham at the division of the calf, the ram, and the goat; thou didst release thy people Israel from captivity,[2] and from the fiery furnace of the Chaldeans who know no mercy.[3] O Israelites, vanquished (by the Romans), do ye therefore also trust in the Lord; return to the well-fortified city of Jerusalem,[4] for you still have God on your side; God who has promised that like Job you will receive a double recompense for the sufferings you have undergone in exile."[5]

11.—Concerning the Hebrew Language.

In the knowledge of Hebrew the Jews possessed an advantage over the Christians that was not to be despised. They were intensely proud of this superiority, and continually annoyed the Christians by letting them feel their ignorance.[6] "The Jews are proud of their knowledge of the Law, and parade the fact that they can correctly repeat by heart all the Scriptural names. As, however, these are foreign to us and we do not know their etymology, we pronounce them faultily. When we happen to make a mistake in the accent and lengthen a short syllable or shorten a long syllable, they laugh at our ignorance, especially if the mistake is in an aspirate or in a guttural. If we do not pronounce these surnames and the language generally— which to us is barbarous—in* precisely the same way as

---

[1] Quo compersam Jerusalem juxta Ezechielem in suo sanguine reperisti et inisti.

[2] ‫שלחתי אסיריך מבור‬.

[3] ‫אין מים בו‬. A free Agadic interpretation.

[4] ‫שובו לבצרון‬.

[5] ‫גם היום מגיד משנה אשיב לך‬.

[6] In Ezech. xxxvii. 12. Solent ridere de nobis et attollere supercilium et inflatis buccis ructare scientiam Scripturarum, si non dicam sensuum discrepantiam, qua si fuerit, jure reprehenditur, si verborum dissonantiam in nostris codicibus potuerint demonstrare. In Is. xxiv. 6, Judaei, qui se solos legem accepisse Domini gloriantur.

the Jews do, they break out into loud laughter and swear that they cannot understand what we say."[1] It must have been very difficult for the Christians to learn the Hebrew language. A friend of Jerome's, the noble Paula, a scion of the Scipio family, was so far successful in the study of Hebrew, that she could intone the Psalms in Hebrew without a trace of the Latin accent.[2] Jerome was still further advanced; he studied Hebrew so zealously, that his Latin, far from influencing his Hebrew pronunciation, was actually modified by it. Even his literary style had become changed by his devotion to Hebrew. At the end of his commentary on Haggai he says: "I entreat you, reader, forgive me for communicating my thoughts without embellishments; do not look in my writings for beauty of expression, I have lost it long ago by my study of the Hebrew language."[3] His works afford ample evidence that this apology was not a mere rhetorical figure. Hebrew idiom is frequent; he employs Biblical turns and phrases, Biblical metaphors and explanations, and continually alludes to Biblical incidents and stories.

12.—The Hebrew Language in Egypt.

Of the flourishing condition of the Hebrew language at that period Jerome gives such an astonishing account, that all who have occasion to study the history of the Hebrew

---

[1] In *Ep. ad Titum*, iii. 9, Judaei, qui in eo se jactant et putant Legis habere notitiam, si nomina teneant singulorum ; quae quia barbara sunt et etymologias eorum non novimus, plerumque proferuntur corrupte a nobis. Et si forte erravimus in accentu, in extensione, solent irridere nos imperitiae, maxime in asperationibus et quibusdam cum rasura gulae litteris proferendis. Siegfried who, in Stade's *Zeitschrift für die alttestamentliche Wissenschaft*, 1884, proposed to himself the task of fixing the ancient pronunciation from Jerome's accounts, overlooked this important passage.

[2] *Ep.* cviii. *ad Eustochium*, i. 714, ita ut Psalmas hebraice caneret (Paula) et sermonem absque ulla linguae proprietate personaret.

[3] *Praef. Libri* iii., *Ep. ad Galatas*. He complains, omnem sermonis elegantiam et Latini eloquii venustatem stridoris lectionis Hebraicae sordidatum esse.

tongue are bound to examine it closely. He tells us that, in the year 400 A.D., *i.e.*, about six hundred years after its death in Palestine, its Motherland, Hebrew, as a living language, was still surviving in Egypt. The savants who deny that the ancient Egyptian tongue is a branch of the Semitic stock, cannot refuse to acknowledge that the old Egyptian language possessed Semitic elements in abundance; this they ascribe to the contact, during a period of many centuries, between the Egyptians and the Jews settled amongst them.[1]

Suppose we went a step further and assumed that there remained in Egypt, from early times, a small portion of the Jewish population, who continued to speak Hebrew? It does not need a very lively imagination to accept this hypothesis. It is conceivable that the land which was in a sense, the cradle of Judaism, became its asylum after it had received its first terrible blow, and continued to be its home during the dissolution of the Jewish nationality.

Jerome's account, therefore, ought not in itself to be impugned. It is only a pity that, as generally understood, it does not really exist! Let us examine it more closely. " Everybody knows," he says, " that five towns in Egypt still speak the Canaanitish, *i.e.*, the Syrian language."[2] Now we ask: Is there here any mention of Hebrew? Certainly modern criticism insists that Hebrew is really the old language of Canaan. But Philo terms Hebrew the Chaldaic tongue. In Josephus and the New Testament, the Aramaic vernacular is spoken of as Hebrew, But it is quite inconceivable that Jerome, who knew that Hebrew and Aramaic were totally different and distinct should have confounded the two languages, or even, in a

---

[1] The various views have been collected by E. Meier, in *Die Semiten in ihrem Verhaltniss zu Chamiten und Japhetiten*, p. 70 ff. ; and exhaustively treated by Lenormant, *Histoire ancienne de l'Orient*, 9th edition, i. 275 and ii. 46.

[2] In Is. xix. 18, . . . Civitates, quas usque hodie in Aegypto lingua Chanaanitide, hoc est Syra loqui, manifestum est.

critical mood, have hit upon the idea that Hebrew was
the old Canaanitish dialect. Why should Jerome have
expressed himself in so peculiar a fashion, when in other
places he calls Hebrew, scores of times, as it ought
to be called — Hebrew ? If he referred to Hebrew,
why does he say in an explanatory note that he means
Syriac ? Surely the former language was as well known to
his readers as the latter ? Does not this note rather prove
that a language is here spoken of, whose existence might
not have been universally known, and that it was therefore
needful to explain the uncommon term—Canaanitish, by
one more familiar, Syriac. The Hebrew language, however, could certainly not have been meant. For the present, we will therefore merely assume that Jerome speaks
of the Canaanitish tongue. How did he become acquainted
with this tongue ? He himself explicitly tells us : " I came
to Sior, the river of Egypt ; . . . to the five towns of
Egypt which speak Canaanitish."[1] Thus, we see that, in
the course of his travels, he had visited the five cities.
The object of his journey was to visit the places named in
Scripture ; and, therefore, he only mentions those names
which there occur, and among them prefers the old to the
modern ones.[2]

Here we have the key to the enigma : Jerome uses
the old Biblical terms, and calls even the river by its
ancient name Sior (שִׁיחוֹר). Consequently, as he expresses
himself in Biblical language, he calls the language of
Egypt the language of Canaan ; and rightly so, for Egypt
even then retained its old name Cham.[3] Because Cham,
Noah's son, was Canaan's father, the language of Canaan

---

[1] *Ep.* cviii. *ad Eustochium* (xxii. 890, ed. Migne, ser. Lat.), Veniam ad
Ægypti fluvium Sior, qui interpretatur *turbidus ;* et quinque Ægypti
transeam civitates, quae loquuntur lingua Chanaanitide.

[2] *Ib.* (p. 882) ea tantum loca nominabo, quae Sacris Voluminibus
continentur.

[3] *Quaest. Hebr.* in Gen. ix. 18, Usque hodie Ægyptiorum lingua Ham
dicitur.

was the language of Egypt (Cham), and in the Bible it
alone is mentioned (שפת כנען). Nowhere in the Scriptures
do we find (שפת מצרים). Jerome was therefore compelled
to speak of the Canaanite and not of the Egyptian language.
He never thought of designating Hebrew by the term
Canaanite ; he indeed says : " The Canaanite language partakes of the characters of Hebrew and Egyptian. It is
closely related to Hebrew,"[1] but therefore clearly not
identical with Hebrew. What language could this have
been ? Every reasonable man will at once think of Coptic.
When Egypt, or at least Lower Egypt, had become quite
hellenised, it was strange to hear Coptic sounds; that this
dialect was the vernacular in five towns seemed to Jerome
a proof that Isaiah's prophecy had been fulfilled. He was
a Christian, and the population of those towns was also
Christian. That Coptic was spoken in many other parts
of the country did not greatly trouble him, or might possibly have been unknown to him, as he only visited Biblical
scenes. Isaiah's prophecy caused him to style this language
Canaanitish. And as it was unfamiliar to him,[2] he confounded it with the old Egyptian, *i.e.*, Canaanitish ; but
finding Semitic elements in this foreign idiom, he could
describe it more definitely as Syriac, *i.e.*, related to Hebrew.
It is quite time, therefore, that this notice of Jerome should
be reduced to its real worth.[3]

13.—JEROME'S JEWISH TRADITIONS.

Jerome has preserved for us a large number of Jewish
traditions. In the first place come those which aim at com-

---

[1] In Is. xix. 18, Lingua Chanaanitide quae inter Hebraeam et Ægyptiam
media est et Hebreae magna ex parte confinis.

[2] *Lib.* I., *adv. Ruff.* c. 10, Ego, philosophus, rhetor, grammaticus,
dialecticus, hebraeus, graecus, latinus, trilinguis, etc.—therefore not Coptic.

[3] Winer *Biblisches Realworterbuch*, II., 500, Anmerk. 1, writes:
" Hebrew or Syriac is said to have been transplanted by Colonists (?) into
the provinces on the Eastern boundaries of Egypt, and was the vernacular
there even in Jerome's times."

pleting the Scriptural story. Jerome usually called these
traditions "fabulae," because they are in narrative form;[1]
we might term them historical Agadas. In this class he
draws a distinction between those legends which lived in
the memory of the people, and which he therefore highly
valued,[2] and those which were only invented by individuals.[3]
The latter class of tradition was either suggested by indications in the Bible,[4] or were the product of pure fancy.
Imaginative teachers invented them for the purpose of
edification. Jerome was also indebted to his Jewish teachers
for the explanation of words and subjects.[5] Verbal exegesis
took the form either of grammatical rules,[6] or elucidations of
difficult terms; and always, of course, in the spirit of the
Agada.[7] The subjects explained are invariably connected
with the Bible, and the expositions, with the Jews, rest
partly on traditional knowledge,[8] and partly are conjectural
and arbitrary deductions.[9] This kind of Jewish teaching is,
on the whole, condemned by Jerome. He drew his Jewish
traditions and views not only from the oral communica-

---

[1] In Jerem. xxix. 21, he calls the same thing now *traditio*, now *fabulae*.
In many places, he uses the expression *fabulae* for the Agada, but then
they were always narrative.

[2] *Z. B.* in Is. lvii. 1, concerning the assassination of Isaiah : quod apud
eos certissima traditio est.

[3] In Ezech. xlv. 10, Traditionem accepimus Hebraeorum non lege
praeceptam, sed magistrorum arbitris inoletam.

[4] In Osee x. 2, tradunt Hebraei fabulam . . . auspicionem suam Scripturarum auctoritate confirmantes.—*Ep.* xxxvi. *ad Damasum,* i. 162, . . .
multis Scripturarum locis testimonia contrahentes.—In Daniel vi. 4, hoc
illi dixerint, qui propter occasionem unius verbi longas solent fabulas
texere.

[5] In Is. xxii. 5, hoc traditionis est Hebraicae et Scriptura non loquitur.

[6] In Is. xl. 9, nec de hac re apud eos ulla dubitatio est, Spiritum
sanctum lingua sua appellari genere feminino, Rua codsa (רוחא קדשא).

[7] In Ezech. ix. 3 (קסם) quum ab Hebraeo quaererem quid significaret,
respondit mihi Graeco sermone appellari καλαμάριον ab eo quod in illo
calami recondantur. The Jew, therefore, spoke Greek.

[8] In Is. xxxii. 14 (עפל ובחן) quas Judaei duas turres in Jerusalem
fuisse arbitrantur.

[9] In Is. xliv. 15, Hebraei stulta contentione nituntur asserere.

tions of his teachers and of contemporary Jews, but also
from collections of the Midrashim, *i.e.*, from written sources,
a point which deserves to be specially emphasised. I have
already quoted a passage that some Agadas are not *read* in
Synagogue;[1] they must, therefore, have been preserved in a
written form. Jerome found, probably in books, Hebrew
traditions.[2] He speaks of the secret knowledge possessed
by the heads of the Synagogue, which he wishes to reveal
to the Latins.[3] He was certainly not told this mystic
knowledge, and must, therefore, have copied it from a book.
Here I wish to point out another important fact. Jerome
translates from the Hebrew into Latin. Although the Jews
in Palestine always conversed in Greek, those Agadas were
compiled in Hebrew. In Alexandria, however, the Agadas,
or rather Apocryphas, were also composed in Greek. Translation usually implies a written original. Jerome must, therefore, no doubt, have seen many Agadas in MS. Yet certain
remarks of his point to the fact that he also translated oral
traditions.[4] However, whether Jerome had written or oral
traditions, it is at all events clear that he translated, and
in his versions, as in other translations, the original is
still discernible. Accidental agreement between Latin and
Hebrew tradition is possible; but when technical terms
of the Midrash recur in the Latin, this is not pure co-
incidence, but a conscious translation from Hebrew. Note
the oft-repeated formulas: "Hoc Scriptura nunc dicit =
הכתוב שׁאמר זה; and "Hoc est quod dicitur" = הוּדא
הכתיב, which conclude many traditions, when supported

---

[1] In Jerem. xxix. 21, nec *legitur* in synagogis eorum.

[2] In Zach. iv. 2, Haec ab Hebraei dicta reperimus.

[3] *Ib.* vi. 9, Semel proposui arcanae eruditionis Hebraicae et magistrorum
synagogae reconditam disciplinam, eam dumtaxat, quae Scripturis sanctis
convenit, Latinis auribus prodere.

[4] *Ib.* vi. 1, Haec ut potuimus, immo ut accepimus, nostrae linguae
studiosis tradimus. *Ib.* x. 11, Haec ut a Hebraeis nobis tradita sunt
nostrae linguae hominibus expressimus.

by quotations from Scripture.[1] The formula, אל תקרי, is called by Jerome, " Non debemus legere," [2] or " legi potest." [3] He also interprets a word according to the meaning of its parts (נוטריקון = νοταρικόν), but he does not seem to have a special Latin term for it.[4] Many more examples of Jerome's adherence to the wording of the Jewish Agada could be given, but what has been said exhibits sufficiently the undreamed of treasures for Jewish literature that lie concealed in Jerome's works. It is a pity that this treasure has not yet been fully opened up. Attempts, however, have been made. Besides Grätz's essay already noted, there are studies of Jerome's traditions by Rahmer. His writings on this subject are: *Die Hebraischen Traditionen in den Werken des Hieronymos I.; Quaestiones in Genesin* (Breslau, 1861); *Die Hebraischen Traditionen in dem Bibelcommentar des Hieronymos* (Ben Chananya VII., 1864); *Die Hebraischen Traditionen des Hieronymos* (Frankel's *Monatsschrift*, 1866 and 1867). Also in Grätz's *Jubelschrift*, 1887.

While giving a due meed of recognition to Rahmer's efforts, I cannot refrain from remarking that he might

---

[1] In Is. viii. 23, Et hoc—inquiunt (Judaei)—Scriptura nunc dicit. *Quaest. Heb.* in Gen. xi. 28, Et hoc esse quod nunc dicitur. Cp. in Zach. viii. 16; in Sophon. ii. 13, *et passim.* Jerome is so familiar with this formula that he employs it in an Agada which he has been told by Jewish Christians (Is. viii. 23). In a verse from the New Testament (Matt. iii. 17) is another time noticed with this formula (in Chab. iii. 5)!

[2] In Zach. xiv. 20, מצלות, Quod quum a Hebraeo quaererem, quid significaret, ait *non debere nos legere mesuloth sed mesaloth* (var. maselloth) quod significat phaleras equorum et ornatum bellicum. . . . . Similarly b. Pesach 50*a* (R. Eleazar) : כל מצילות שתחולנ לסום בין עיניו.

[3] In Nahum iii. 8, Hebraeus qui me in Scripturis erudivit, ita legi posse asseruit : Numquid melior es, quam No, Amon—et ait : Hebraice No dici Alexandriam, Amon autem, multitudinem, sive populus : et esse ordinem lectionis : Numquid melior es ab (*sic*) Alexandria populosa, sive populorum, quae habitat in fluminibus. . . . . Therefore, המון, instead of אמון. Cp. Targum *ad loc.*

[4] In Aggaeum i. 1, זרובבל, Apud Hebraeos ex tribus integris nomen ejus traditur esse compositum : Zo (זה) = iste ; rob (רב) = magister sive major ; babel (בבל) = Babylon : iste magister de Babylone. The same is found in the Midrash.

have done more justice to the theme. Rahmer does not compare other Church Fathers with Jerome; he even omits to place the parallel expressions side by side, nor does he seem to have any idea that several of these Agadas are already to be found in the so-called Hellenistic literature. The Jewish sources are also treated uncritically. The Jalkut and Midrash Rabba are not enough; the Babli, Jerushalmi, Sifre, Sifra, and Mechilta, finally the Targum, have also some connection with the subject. Here follow a few specimens.

14.—SPECIMENS OF JEROME'S MIDRASHIM.

1. *A Lost Midrash of R. Akiba.*

In Eccles. iv. 13: " Hebraeus meus, cujus saepe facio mentionem, cum Ecclesiasten mecum legeret, haec *Baracibam* (var. Baracchiban, Baracubivan = Rabbi Akiba), quem unum vel maxime admirantur, super praesenti loco tradidisse testatus est.

" Melior est interior homo, qui post quartum decimum pubertatis annum in nobis exoritur, exteriore homine, qui de matris alvo natus est qui nescit recedere a vitio et qui de domo vinctorum, de utero videlicet materno, ad hoc exivit, ut regnaret in vitiis. Quia etiam in potestate sua pauper effectus est, mala omnia perpetrando. Vidi eos, qui in priore homine vixerunt, et cum secundo homine postea versati sunt, eo videlicet, qui pro priore decessore generatus est: intellexique omnes in homine priore peccasse, antequam secundo nascente, duo homines fierent."

This Midrash is interesting, not so much for its contents as for its origin, having been composed by R. Akiba. It is a distorted version of an anonymous Midrash on Eccles. iv. 13, found in Aboth di R. Nathan, Version II., c. 4, p. 30, ed. Schechter, in the Midrash on Psalm ix. 5, in Koheleth Rabba iv. 13, and in Jalkut, Rashi, and other secondary sources. All Jerome's editors have unsuccessfully laboured to find some sense in this passage. It is corrupt simply because Jerome did not understand the Agada which was told him. Of the Jewish sources, the earliest is the Midrash on the Psalms, being the only one composed in Aramaic. Let us compare this source with Jerome's version.

JEROME.	MIDRASH, Psalm ix. 5.
Melior est interior homo qui post quartum decimum . . . . . annum in nobis exoritur exteriore homine.	טוב ילד מסכן וחכם זה צר טוב ‎······ ולמה צווחין ליה. ילד דהוא מזדווג לבר נש מן תלת עשר שנין ולעילא‎······זה יצר הרע
Qui de matris alvo natus est.	דהוא מזדווג לבר נש מן טליותיה עד סיבותיה :
Qui nescit recedere a vitio—qui . . . ad hoc exivit, ut regnaret in vitiis.	דכל איברים שמעין ליה ‎······ ולקרה צוותין ליה מלך דכל איברים שמצין ליה ‎······ למה צוותין ליה
Qui . . . . pauper effectus est, mala omnia perpetrando.	כסיל דהוא מכוון בריותא‎······לארחן בישן :

It is obvious that here we have the original Midrash; but Jerome had not understood it, and makes the best sense he can of it. His further explanations of the passage should be read in conjunction with the Agada he quotes. Moreover, in the Midrash itself there reigns confusion, the cause of which is the attempt to bind together disconnected verses in one interpretation. The passages should be read in the original, and this view will become clear.

2. *An Historical Tradition.*

Quaestiones Hebraicae in Gen. xxii. 21 (בוז). Et ex hujus genere est Balaam ille divinus, ut Hebraei tradunt, qui in libro Job (xxxii. 2) dicitur Eliu, primum vir sanctus et prophetes dei, postea per inobedientiam et desiderium munerum . . . . divini vocabulo nuncupatur (privatur?) diciturque in eodem libro : *et iratus Eliu* . . . . de hujus videlicet radice descendens.

The popular legend that Job, Balaam and Jethro, lived at Pharaoh's court (Sanh. 106ᵃ), brings Balaam into connection with Job. An apocryphal addendum of the Sep-

tuagint to the book of Job identifies Job with Jobab, son
of Joktan. Various opinions, some similar to and others
divergent from the foregoing, are found at the beginning
of Bar-Hebraeus' Scholion to Job, printed in Bernstein's
Chrestomathia Syriaca (Leipzig, 1832, p. 186). Ibn Ezra
regards this legend as Karaitic, originating with יצחק
הטקביל (Isaak ben Jasas) whom he ridicules. (See M. Sachs,
Beiträge zur Alterthumskunde II., 11 Note.) Jerome knows
it also, but not as of Jewish origin; he rejects the apocrypha. But in his view that Elihu and Balaam are identical,
he stands quite alone. This isolation sufficiently confirms
our view that here, too, Jerome had made a mistake. He
seems to have got hold of the Talmudical legend) Sanh.
105ᵇ) that Balaam was descended from Boaz and Ruth;
confused by the various traditions, he confounded Boaz
(בעז) with Buz (בוז).

3. An Halachic Midrash.

In Ezek. xlv. 13, 14 : Traditionem accepimus Hebraeorum
non lege praeceptam, sed magistrorum arbitrio molitam :
qui plurimum, quadragesimam partem dabat sacerdotibus,
qui minimum, sexagesimam, inter quadragesimam et sexagesimam licebat offerre quodcunque voluissent. Quod
igitur in Pentateucho dubium relictum est, hic specialiter
definitur propter sacerdotum avaritiam, ne amplius a populo
exigant in primitiis deferendis, id es ut sexagesimam partem
offerant eorum, quae gignuntur e terra.

Jerome makes a calculation which is either original or
part of the tradition received by him, in order to show how
this interpretation was derived from the verse in Ezechiel.
The Talmudic computation of what constitutes עין יבה,
עין רעה and בינוני is also derived from that verse
(J. Therumoth VI., 1, 42ᵈ), but it is much less simple (compare Tosafoth, Kidduschim 41ᵈ, *s.v.* תורם). Jerome's calculation seems to be the only correct one. Epiphanius also
knew of this enactment. The Pharisees are said to have
offered τριακοντάδες τε καὶ πεντηκοντάδες. Compare Hil-

genfeld, *Judenthum und Juden-christenthum* (Leipzig, 1886),
p. 73.

4. *Seventy Noachide Precepts* (?).

In Zech. xi. 13, Judaei istum locum malitiose interpre-
tantes, triginta argenteos, triginta legis mandata com-
memorant quae facere jubeantur in lege et rursum triginta
sex alia, quae prohibeantur in lege.   A remarkable Agada !
Grätz (*Monatsschrift*, 1854, p. 192) refers to T. B. *Chullin*,
92*a*, where the same verse is explained as enjoining thirty
precepts on Noah's descendants.   He writes as follows :
Jerome has certainly misunderstood the Agada if he thinks
it refers to enactments imposed upon the Jews, and speaks
of thirty affirmative and thirty or thirty-six negative precepts."   It appears to me that we ought first to understand
the Agada in its Jewish form before we complain that Jerome
recites it incorrectly.   Is the reason quite obvious why T. B.
Chullin, 92*a*, suddenly speaks of thirty Noachide commandments, whereas usually we know of seven such precepts ? It
is better to confess with M. Joel (Grätz, *Jubelschrift*, German
portion, p. 174) that here we have an insoluble enigma.   The
riddle will, however, be solved if we take a totally different
road to that followed by Grätz in his attempt to elucidate
the passage.   Among the 613 precepts of Judaism we find
in various places that certain of them are grouped together.
Thus, besides the division into affirmative and negative
precepts, we also find the following classification in *Pesikta
di R. Kahana*, p. 51*b*, Buber :

(Hosea iii. 2) ר' יוחנן פתח ואכרה לי בחמשה עשר כסף
בחמשה הרי חמשה עשר • וחומר שעורים הרי שלשים • ולתך
שעורים הרי מ״ץ • הרי ששים • אלו ששים מצות שכתב לנו
משה בתורה ואמר ר' יוחנן בשם ר' שמעון בן יוח' שלוש
פרשיות כתב לנו משה בתורה וכל אחת ואחת יש בה ששים
מצות • ואלו הן פרשת פסחים ופרשת נזיקין ופרשת קדושים •
ר' לוי בשם ר' שילא דכפר תמרתא אמר משבעים שבעים
מצות • אמר ר' תנחומא ולא פליחי מן דעבד פרשת פסחים

שבעים כולל עמה פרשת פרשת תפלין ‏•‏ וכן מאן דעבד פרשת נזיקין
כולל עמה פרשת שמטה וכן מאן דעבד פרשת קדושים שבעים
כולל עמה פרשת עׂרה :

Much ingenuity has been expended on the interpretation
of the division here given, with but dubious results. Moses
Tobias, of Hanau, believes it to mean that in *the whole Thora*
there are sixty enactments with regard to Passover. This
is certainly wrong, as the Midrash speaks of פרשיות, and
not of the whole Thora. Heidenheim, in the *Pesach-agada*,
enumerates sixty *sections* bearing upon Passover; but this
view is opposed to the literal meaning of מצות. These
opinions are justly discarded by M. Bloch, in the *Revue des
Etudes Juives*, I., 201, who thinks the exact number is not
to be pressed, as a round number was given. S. Buber, in
his edition of the *Pesikta*, note 163, adopts the view· that
the Midrash speaks of the number of *verses* contained in the
portions relating to Passover. He accordingly endeavours
to show that the number, if referring to verses, would work
out right. But a close examination reveals the fact that
this is not the case. We must also avoid the fallacy of
assuming that R. Simon ben Jochai had the same verse
division as we have in our Bibles. It is therefore advisable
to keep to the literal sense of the Midrash. The Agadists
found sixty or seventy precepts, מצות, in the specified sections. Is this number correct? We reply, Yes, though
according to our calculation a different number might possibly be obtained. It might be worth while giving in detail
the calculation which yields the above number. We refrain
from wearying our readers with a dry list of sixty or
seventy precepts. However, let us examine ten precepts;
if the calculation should prove correct in the smaller, it will
probably also be so in the larger number. The פרשת
שמטה, it is said, contains ten precepts. The reference
here is clearly to Exod. xxiii. 10-19. There we find:
(1) שמטה, (2) שבת, (3) שם אלהים אחרים, (4) חג המצות,
(9) לא תזבח, (8) חגיגה, (7) זׂג האסיף, (6) חג הקציר, (5)
בשׂר בחלב. (10) בכורים,

We willingly concede that the Agadist's meaning may not have been fully grasped in detail; but it will be seen that, on the whole, the calculation agrees. We have thus gained a sure result : all the precepts, affirmative and negative, are counted which are found anywhere in any section of the Thora.

We now return to Jerome. He says : " Triginta legis mandata quae facere jubeantur in lege." Those words sound like the Midrash : ‏מצות······ שכתב לנו משה בתורה‎ Further : " Rursum triginta sex alia, quae prohibeantur in lege," which in Hebrew would be rendered ‏וכננדן כתב‎ ‏לנו ל״ו מצות לא תעשה‎. Accordingly we must not connect these traditions with the remark in *Chullin*, 92*a*, as Grätz has done, but with the passage quoted from the *Pesikta*. A group of precepts is discussed as a separate code. If it were permissible to suggest that Jerome was in error when he gave thirty-six as the number of precepts, when really it was only thirty, we could simply compare Jerome's tradition with R. Simon ben Jochai's view ; thirty of these sixty precepts would be affirmative and thirty negative. The Scriptural sections in question contain both classes of commandments. The deduction from Zech. xi. 12, 13, would thus also be intelligible. The number thirty appears twice ; the phrase ‏ואב לו‎ (ver. 12) would suggest ‏מצות לא תעשה‎. But if the number thirty-six, and therefore a total of sixty-six is correct, the existence of three traditions may be assumed ; one tradition found in that portion sixty precepts, the other seventy, and the third compromised the two and accepted sixty-six as the right number. The characteristic distinction, however, between affirmative and negative precepts shows that Jerome's account gives the original tradition, which is wanting in the Jewish sources, and proves its authenticity, though Grätz is unwilling to acknowledge it. The difficulty, that Jerome speaks of precepts imposed on the *Jews*, whilst the Talmud refers to *Noachide* laws, disappears when we remember that Jerome was thinking of another Midrash altogether. An old Agada is given in the T. J. *Aboda Zara* II., 1, where שלשים כסף are explained to refer to thirty pious men on whom the moral order of the world depends. Diverse Agadas were attached to this verse. Amongst them one told by Jerome might also have been in circulation. As regards the thirty commandments given to the Noachides, we note, first, that this Agada is found in the following passages: B. *Chullin*, 92a; J. *Ab. Zara*, II., 1; *Leo Rabba*, c. 24; Midrash Psalm, II., 5; *Jalkut Exod.*, § 307; *Jalkut Hosea*, § 519. Between these different sources we give the preference to the Jerusalem Talmud, which is distinctly different from the rest. There the following statement is made in the name of מב בר הונא בשם רב : "These are the thirty commandments which the sons of Noah will *one day* take upon themselves" (שעתיד ידין בני נח). The golden Messianic age is here spoken of. The meaning of the Agada thus becomes clear. In olden times the Gentiles were only expected to keep seven commandments; but when the human race will have attained perfection, they will observe thirty. This distinction removes the discrepancy between this Agada and the ordinarily accepted canon of שבע מצות בני נח. To what class do those thirty commandments belong? This is indicated by the T. Jerushalmi, in which הכלין וציצית are mentioned, and by a Midrash on Psalms which gives כוכה ולולב. In this Midrash we read:

ננתקה את מוסרותימו אלו שבע מצות שנצטוו בני נח ונשליכה ממנו עבדתימו אלו שלשים מצות שהן (Manuscript by Buber)
קולעין בהן כגון סוכה ולולב שהן נקראו עבות.

The meaning of קולעין is not quite clear, but the sense is, "These are the thirty commandments which they break." (Cp. B. *Chullin*, 92b, above.) Some positive cause of complaint must have occasioned this remark. We do not think we shall be far out in conjecturing that this passage contained a veiled attack on certain heresies concerning Zizith and Tephillin, Succah and Lulab. Of the former definite accounts are extant; concerning the latter, Succoth and Lulab, only vague suggestions and hints have come down to us. It was a long time before the use of the phylacteries became general. In T. B. *Berachot*, 47*b*, this is said to constitute the difference between *idiotai* (עם הארץ) and scholars (חבר). The latter alone wear Tephillin; the Am-Haaretz does not wish to have anything to do with Tephillin and Zizith.[1] The lament at the neglect of Tephillin is echoed in T. B. *Sabb.*, 130*a*,[2] and resounds in the Rabbinical literature of Spain throughout the Middle Ages.[3] The use of Tephillin was often perverted by superstition, as the Greek name phylacteries already evidences. They were regarded as charms to ward off evils. The Mishna (*Erubim* x. 1) complains that the Tephillin are sometimes used for superstitious and not religious purposes; and we often encounter the expression קמיע = charm, talisman, in connection with Tephillin.[4] Those who did observe the precept seem also to have endowed them with a magical power.[5] According to an old Bóraitha, the women shared this superstition;[6] even Christian ladies, in Jerome's times, made use of Tephillin as charms, as already noticed. So much about Zizith and Tephillin. With Succoth and Lulab something similar must have happened. The difference between the Pharisees and Sadducees with regard to the *Ritual* of the Feast of Tabernacles is known to history. This antagonism may have been revived. The Agada, therefore, which rele-

---

[1] Cp. B. *Sota*, 22*a*; B. *Gitt.* 61*a* ; B. *Pesach*, 49*b*, and Rosenthal, *Four Apocryphal Books*, p. 26.

[2] וכל מצוה שלא מסרו ישראל • עצמן עליה······כנון תפלין עדין היא מרופה בידם. Cp. *Tosaphoth*.

[3] S. T. J. Reifman, in *Beth-Talmud* II. (1881), p. 52.

[4] Especially in *Masecheth Tephillin.* Kirchbein, *Septem Libri Talmudici*, p. 19.

[5] B. *Erub*, 96*b*, אמר רבא וכי אדם טורח לעשות תפלין כמין קמיע. What Raba in Babylon regarded as improbable might have been the case in Palestine.

[6] B. *Berachoth*, 30*b*, מעשה באישה אחת שהיתה ב׳ שאת לחבר והיתה קוטעת תפלין על ידו where the expression קדמעת must be noticed. Possibly in the Midrash on the Psalm, which we have quoted, we should read קומעין instead of קולעין, " They are superstitious about it."

gates the universal observance of Tephillin, Zizith, Succoth, and Lulab to the *Messianic times* started from the indisputable fact that that consummation had, at all events, not yet been reached. "The Noachides" designates the uncultured populace. It is to be regretted that those commandments have not been written down, so that we are unable to discover the historical background of this remarkable Agada; however, we venture to think that, if not altogether, we have at least partly discovered it. It is to be hoped that an investigator will soon arise who will treat the immense field of the Agada according to the requirements of historical criticism.

S. KRAUSS.

NOTES ON THE RELIGIOUS VALUE
OF THE
FOURTH GOSPEL

by
C[LAUDE] G. MONTEFIORE

NOTES ON THE RELIGIOUS VALUE OF THE FOURTH GOSPEL.

My title sounds presumptuous. It is not, however, pre-sumptuously meant. I merely wish to indicate the limits of my intention. It would be foolish and unnecessary on my part to attempt to give any systematic representation of the religious doctrine contained in the Fourth Gospel. In the case of St. Paul it was almost obligatory, even to a writer who was bold enough to print his first impressions, to cast them into the form of exposition. The readers for whom he specially wrote were not only, as he imagined, un-familiar with the actual wording of the Pauline Epistles, but from upbringing, association and temperament, were unable, without effort and assistance, to understand or appreciate their meaning. On the other hand, though the Epistles of Paul are not fully to be explained or understood without a study of the religious and in-tellectual environment of their author, they can, never-theless, to some extent be expounded from themselves, or, at any rate, from data known to the average Jewish reader of magazines. But as regards the Fourth Gospel the case is different in both directions. It is at once harder and easier than the Epistles. Let a fairly-cultivated Jew, ignorant of the New Testament (the two qualifications are at present quite compatible), read the Epistles to the Galatians and the Romans, and I believe his main sensa-tion will be one of bewilderment; let him read the Fourth Gospel, and he will at all events *think* he understands a fair amount of it. Moreover, in a sort of way he will under-stand it; for the oppositions between " spirit " and " flesh," or " of this world " and " not of this world," the meta-phorical and spiritual use of words like " bread," " light,"

" life," and many others, have become familiar to him in other ways. Yet, *per contra*, he who would fully understand " St. John " must understand two of his predecessors. It is true that the Jewish outsider can *partially* understand and *partially* appreciate the Fourth Gospel far more readily than he can appreciate and understand St. Paul. And yet *properly* to understand that Gospel you must in the first place understand Paul. And, secondly, to properly understand that Gospel you must be acquainted with and even understand Philo. But Philo, though, as I imagine, no savour of unorthodoxy attaches to his name, is necessarily no more than a name to all but the professed student.

It would not be difficult to assign other reasons for the comparative comprehensibility of the Fourth Gospel, in spite of its dependence upon two obscure or even unknown quantities. For one thing there is the style so lucidly clear and simple, so different from the involved and excited utterances of Paul. Then, again, just because the Fourth Gospel is so much further removed from Judaism, it is easier for a Jew to understand it. The period of conflict and creation is nearly over ; the Gentile Church is fully formed. The Law is no longer a burning question ; the opposition of faith and works, no longer prominent, is even partially reconciled, for " faith " has become the supreme " work." The Pauline paradoxes have done their duty ; they have been absorbed and disappeared. In spite of the subject and its tragedy, we have passed into a serener air. Again, as the books on " St. John " fully explain, the death of Christ is no longer the main feature of the Gospel. There is a sense in which that death and its effects are still a stumbling-block to the Jew, even as they were when first enunciated by the daring genius of St. Paul—a stumbling-block in two senses : impossible to accept, difficult to appreciate or understand.

Once more putting questions of authorship on one side, there seems much more agreement among theologians as regards the Fourth Gospel than as regards St. Paul. There seems less room for endless diversities of interpretation. Even on the critical side the commentators on St. Paul differ a good deal one from the other, so that much time is taken up by one man in pointing out the degrees of error in others. But in explaining St. John, the exponents of the critical school show a much greater unanimity. Of course, there are varieties, and you learn things in one book which you do not find in another. Still the views of Pfleiderer, and Thoma, and the two Holtzmann's, and Scholten, and Martineau, and Cone, all bear a very marked likeness to each other; and there is a fair amount of repetition as you pass from the first book to the second, and from the second to the third and fourth. The consequence is that anybody who will work a little at Philo, should be able with the help of some two or three of these scholars to get a very fair idea of the contents of the Fourth Gospel.

A principal question which I have set before myself in reading, and in reading about, the "Gospel according to St. John" is, What is the religious value of this book to those who have not been brought up in Christianity, and who do not believe in some of its most distinctive dogmas? What is its religious value to the average modern Jew?

For a Jew to ask this question is partly but not entirely equal to asking without qualifications "What is the religious value of the Fourth Gospel?" Such an identification is only conceited in appearance. Each one of us in estimating the religious worth of another creed, is bound to regard his own belief to a considerable extent as a fixed standard of value. The Christian judges Buddhism favourably by its real or supposed resemblances to Christianity, and so on. But this identification need nöt and should not be complete. To the more philosophic believer at any rate, no religion (his own included) is ever perfect, and none is without its partial though perhaps temporary defects. One religion may be onesided in one respect, a second in another. A third may have the defects of its qualities. The exaggerations of one religion may be of a certain use to the opposite exaggerations of another. It is, therefore, quite possible that certain points in the Fourth Gospel, themselves perhaps not wholly true or accurate, may be of religious value to a Jew. He may realize their onesidedness, while they help him to correct his own.

It must at once be allowed that this method of approaching the Fourth Gospel is the one of all others which would probably be least sympathetic to its author. I *assume* that the main contention of the Gospel—the contention or argument laid down in its opening prologue (*e.g.*, i. 1-14) or in its closing verse (xx. 31)—is false : and then I coolly proceed to ask, What is its religious value ? As the believer would answer, "Infinite," so might he maintain that the unbeliever must answer, "Nil." For the object of the Gospel is not to teach ethics ; it is not to teach any aspect of religion, or any phase of the spiritual or moral life, which may be independent of or only mediately connected with its supreme and central propositions, that the Eternal and Divine Word became flesh, that Jesus was the Christ, the Son of God, and that he is the Way, the Truth, and the Life. As Thoma most rightly says, " *Die Lehre des Johannesevangeliums ist eigentlich nichts anderes als Christologie*," [1] " The doctrine of the Fourth Gospel is pure Christology." Does it not seem ridiculous that any one should find religious value in a book the essential and all-pervading object of which he, *ab initio*, assumes to be untrue ? If we want a florilegium of ethical and religious sayings, we should go elsewhere than to the Fourth Gospel, where almost every verse is made subservient to and dependent on the main doctrine and purport of the whole. " Take away the *Godhead* of Christ," says Dr. Martineau, " and there is not an incident or a speech in the Fourth Gospel which does not lose its significance." [2]

---

[1] Thoma, *Die Genesis des Johannes-Evangeliums*, 1882, p. 302.
[2] Martineau, *The Seat of Authority in Religion*, 1890, p. 426.

What, then, can be the value of this book to the Unitarian or the Jew? Is it not almost an affront to the book and almost an insult to its author to ask the question, when you defiantly shut your ears to the very thing they have to say? Yet the Unitarian, Dr. Martineau, can find in this same Gospel at least "one vital element" of permanent value. And so, perhaps, may a Jewish reader, though (putting the central proposition on one side) he finds some things that are ethically and spiritually dangerous, and as he hopes erroneous, find also others which are ennobling, beautiful and true.

Few persons, at any rate, be their religion what it may, can read the Fourth Gospel through without yielding to its spell. Few persons, I imagine, can remain proof to its remarkable fascination. May I briefly indicate wherein probably (to the outsider) the causes of this fascination consist?

First of all there comes the beauty of the manner, apart from the matter of the book. Its simplicity and elevation of style, the sustained dignity and, occasionally, the dramatic power, all hold the interest of the reader. The greatest subjects in heaven or on earth are dealt with, and while the sentences are clear and unadorned, the sense of grandeur is usually well maintained. We feel that we are reading the work of a genius, and, moreover, the work of one who has full control over his material, his thought and his words. How delightfully the shortness and pointedness of St. John contrast with the diffuse rhetoric of Philo. The very same ideas sometimes offend us in the one writer which charm us in the other. A single crisp verse takes the place of pages of involved and florid rhetoric. The taste of the one was doubtless excellent for his own age and environment; the taste of the other still seems excellent to our own. A thought strangely expressed in Philo fails to arrest our attention. The same thought in the Fourth Gospel compels reflection or astonishment. Again, the Fourth Gospel, like so many other books, both of the

Hebrew and the Christian Scriptures, is alone of its kind. It is very short; but there is no other book exactly resembling it. Like the Prophets, the Psalms, or the Epistles of St. Paul, it has a uniqueness and isolation of its own.

But these reasons have only skimmed the surface. Others lie deeper. Most fairly cultivated persons, who are not naturally indifferent to one important side of our complex humanity, will be attracted by the spirituality of the book, by its idealism. This Fourth Gospel has, I suppose, gone a good way to form the religious consciousness of civilised humanity such as it now exists, and we have not yet, I imagine, got beyond—it may be hoped that we never shall get beyond—these oppositions between the seen and the unseen, the outward and the inward, the flesh and the spirit, which our Gospel has helped to make a permanent item in the forms and categories of cultivated, and even uncultivated, thought. When Plato talks about the true beauty and the true goodness, unseen and yet real, more real far than the world of sense, when he speaks of a life that is death, and of a death that may be life, though his ideals be often "vacant forms of light," they will always awaken a sympathetic response from our higher nature —a yearning, sometimes vague and untutored, but not phantastic or spectral, towards a truth and goodness of which we could not dream if they were not real. So with the Fourth Gospel. On the purely religious side it has been the great source for those spiritual antitheses and truths with which mankind is now familiar. And great primal phrases such as "God is a spirit," the "Bread of Life," "Peace not as the world giveth," in their striking simplicity and at their fountain source, will always, I should imagine, continue to attract and fascinate the spiritual and religious consciousness of man. Connected with this spirituality, or only another expression of it, is the symbolic language of the Gospel. As artistic limits of length and degree are not outstripped, the double meaning with which the actions and words of

Christ are often charged cannot fail to cause pleasure and profit. The scene where Christ washes his disciples' feet is in itself striking and beautiful, but its inner and symbolic meanings, half concealed and half revealed, add materially to its effect. As sometimes we feel that the respondents in the Platonic dialogues are made to misapprehend the meaning of the questions too clumsily, so sometimes the gross misconceptions of Christ's auditors are exaggerated in the Gospel. But the spiritual use of such words as light and darkness, slavery and freedom, bread and water, life and death, through their very background of material application, moves our admiration and quickens our discernment. The spirituality of the Gospel liberates and appeals to what is spiritual in ourselves; we are not reminded of or impelled to any particular duty, but we are rendered alert and responsive to that ever-recurrent opposition of sense and spirit, on which much that is best and noblest in life seems to depend. There is a possible danger in this. A mere tickling of the spiritual instincts, a mere spiritual palpitation, may be of little use or even of positive harm to our moral nature, and may not make us fulfil the better, but even the worse, our definite duties and obligations. It is much better to fulfil these well and not to appreciate the ethereal spirituality of the Fourth Gospel, than to succeed in the latter and to fail in the former. Moreover these sundered capacities are quite possible and probably not unfrequent. But the fascination, beyond which at this stage I should perhaps not have gone, is independent of the question of ethical profit and loss.

What has been said of the spirituality and symbolism of the Fourth Gospel applies in even greater measure to its mysticism. Putting aside the religious *value* of mysticism, whether generally or for the average modern Jew, there can be no question of the fascination which mystic religious sentiment, if expressed with adequate simplicity and conciseness, exercises upon the mind and the feelings. These qualifications are eminently complied with in the Fourth

Gospel. The eternal need of a God within as well as a God without, of breaking down or bridging over the gulf which seems to separate the human from the divine, and of yet maintaining the separateness and "personality" of both — these needs are felt and realised in the Fourth Gospel with considerable power and penetration, and for the believer of its main hypotheses, they are largely satisfied and appeased.

To these causes of fascination there may perhaps be added, not only the beautiful use of the ideas of love and sacrifice, a use so beautiful that we are apt to overlook the limitation of their range, but also the fact, however unconscious the average reader may be of it, that the author of the Fourth Gospel is a philosopher, and that his book is a form of popularised, or rather religionised, philosophy, transfigured by his genius and by his faith. The simplicity of this Gospel is not the simplicity of nature. It is the elaborate simplicity of art. It is carefully wrought out and worked up. Even while we admire, we feel that our admiration puts us into the category and fold of the elect. We are initiated into the mystery, and those who accept the Gospel become, as it were, the chosen few out of the condemned mass—in the world, but not of the world. Unconsciously to ourselves we philosophise, and this philosophy may truly be called divine. More even than with Plato, we are elevated and carried out of ourselves. In Plato we are invited to side with Socrates; in the Fourth Gospel we are invited to side with Christ. The distinction fascinates. We seem to breathe a purer and rarer air, and this higher atmosphere quickens and gladdens us. We are free and even bidden to enter within the holy place, to take our seats and be enrolled in the spiritual aristocracy of the world.

Such might be said to be some of the causes of that fascination which the Gospel of St. John is likely to exercise upon most cultivated and religious minds even outside the pale of believing Christianity. And these

causes of its fascination are partly the causes of its abiding
religious value. Nevertheless, emotional fascination is one
thing, critical appreciation is another. And upon this a
due appraising of the Fourth Gospel must largely depend.

Religious belief, while not without its intellectual
basis, is notoriously different from belief in matters of
science or history. I believe that in the year 841 A.D.
a battle was fought at Fontenay. Firmly as I believe
this, it has not, as an isolated fact, any effect upon
my thought, feelings, character, actions, happiness, or
power. I believe that there is a good God in the ordinary
sense of that word; or I believe that there is a devil into
whose power I may fall for all eternity, or I believe that
an aspect of God became flesh at a particular time, and
while I believe these things to be facts, just as true as the
occurrence of the battle of Fontenay in the year 841,
they may also have a tremendous effect upon my life and
character.

The power and influence of true belief are intensely prominent in the Fourth Gospel. In its emphatic insistence
on truth, as in its frequent use of the very word, it is
at once separated from the Synoptics (ἀλήθεια occurs
between twenty and thirty times in John, once in
Matthew). The true knowledge of the only true God, and
of Jesus Christ, his Son, is in itself eternal life : the lack,
still more the rejection, of that knowledge, is in itself the
absence or the forfeiture of that life. The whole man is
transformed by his belief.

We shall, I think, find that the Fourth Evangelist
goes beyond even this, and here we shall probably part
company with him. To all Jews, presumably to all
liberal Christians, the action of God on man is not determined by the accuracy of his belief about God. We
do not believe that the relation of God to man is different
in the case of a Jew and in the case of a Christian. We
realize that varying religious beliefs may and do have
varying effects upon character, but so far as God is con-

cerned we do not believe that he has other laws of influence and judgment for those who believe concerning him more truly or less truly, or even for those who have failed to find him altogether. Least of all do we believe that these variations of belief affect the destiny of the soul beyond the grave. And in these negations, which can also be presented as the most solemn affirmations, we find comfort and consolation, even as we find glory and rest. But inconsistently, as we believe, with the justice of God and the universalism of his providence, the author of the Fourth Gospel did presumably believe that the result of true belief is not merely the moral and spiritual transformation of the believer, but the bestowal on him by God as a gift of his grace, the prerogative of eternal life, the special influx of the divine spirit.

Once more. Not merely is it true that religious belief may ethically transform, but it is also true that the essential character of your belief, as realised and appropriated by you, is partly dependent upon your prior or present ethical condition. The interaction and interrelation of morality and religion are notoriously complex in the extreme. Every man, good or bad, is at once capable of believing that a great battle was fought at Fontenay in 841. As the belief in the battle has no effect upon him hereafter, so it makes no demand upon him beforehand. But the belief in God—and here is one aspect of its solemnity—is not as easy as the belief in the battle. At all events there is, I apprehend, a sense in which it is true to say, that though a scamp can believe in God as well as a saint, his belief must be of a different texture and complexion. He may believe; he cannot realise. He may say that he believes in communion with God, but that belief in it which is more than verbal, because based on experience and feeling, he cannot possibly possess. Without goodness a man cannot sound the depths of belief in God. A man may be very good, and not believe in God —and this is where the Johannine writers (like Philo) were naturally in the wrong—but he cannot adequately realise God and not be good. "He that loveth not, knoweth not God; for God is love." It is a great saying.

While we shall have to reject the Fourth Gospel's dualism, and its identification of the good man and the believer, we must always bear in mind that it was written when Christianity was still comparatively new, and fresh adult adherents, drawn from Paganism, were continually coming in. We can hardly appreciate the ethical effect which the discarding of heathenism, and the adoption of Christianity, may have had upon such persons. The recollection of it may also serve to partly excuse the peculiar dogma of the Evangelist, that he who rejected Christianity was morally bad. Among ourselves religion and morality grow up together, and their intermixture and interaction are far more subtle and complicated than anything which the writer of the Fourth Gospel could possibly have conceived.

Proceeding now from these points of view to the main religious ideas of this remarkable book, we perceive that what it contains is a new revelation of God in his own nature and in his relation to man. And by God must be also included those other aspects or phases of him, which are known as the Word or the Son, and as the Holy Spirit or the Spirit of Truth. We are told that before the advent of the Incarnate Son none knew the Father, for none can come unto the Father but through the Son. So tremendous an assertion, that the true nature of God was unknown before Christ, makes us ask what fuller revelation of God is given in this Gospel than we had known before, whether through the Old Testament, Philo, or the Synoptics? Now, apart from the metaphysical question of a distribution of the divine nature and function among double or triple aspects within the Godhead itself, there is very little in the Fourth Gospel to make good this claim. There is, indeed, far less than in the Synoptics, where Jesus, with perhaps one exception, never casts so overwhelming a disparagement upon the religious knowledge of the generations which had preceded him. We find one statement of grand simplicity and permanent value: " God is spirit, and they that worship him must worship in spirit and truth." It cannot be said that the statement contains a truth which was wholly new, for it is already implied in Isaiah and Philo.[1] But in its setting, in its final overthrow of that dangerous localization of deity which still attached to the temple of Jerusalem, in its bold and distinct denial of the notion that God can be nearer to one spot than to another, its value is undoubted and abiding. It takes its place with the 139th Psalm as one of the great spiritual possessions of humanity. With this exception, the Fourth Gospel contains little that is of value to the outsider about God, even as regards the more metaphysical relations of his being. In v. 17: " My Father worketh until now," we get the idea of God's ceaseless activity, which, however, is more clearly enunciated by the Evangelist's predecessor, Philo.[2] On the moral side we notice that the appellation Father is used far more to mark the relation of God to the Word than to man. Scholten has pointed out that the use of the term is reserved for the Logos: man may be the *child* of God; Christ is his *son*.[3] Passing over the restricted character of God's beneficence, of which there will be more to say later on, it is also true, as Cone observes, that the Evangelist " shows no predilection for dwelling on the goodness and mercy of God, and in this respect he is not to be compared with some of the prophets and psalmists, and even with Philo."[4] It is not unnatural that the Jew, familiar with a catena of

---

[1] Cp. Reuss : *Historie de la Théologie Chrétienne au siècle Apostolique.* Vol. II. p. 433.

[2] Cp. especially I. *Alleg.* III. (M. I. 44) : "God never ceases to create, but as it is the property of fire to burn, and of snow to be cold, so also it is the property of God to create."

[3] Scholten : *Das Evangelium nach Johannes*, 1867, p. 82.

[4] Cone : *The Gospel and its earliest Interpretations*, p. 275. Why "*even* with Philo"?

the best and noblest sayings about God in those psalmists
and prophets, rejects with something like indignation
the right of the Fourth Evangelist, whose divine hero
prays not for the world which he has come to save,
to assert that the Father was not known before the
coming of the Son, or to teach the Jew something more of
the nature and goodness of God than he already knew and
revered. If the Jesus of the Synoptics claims this right,
there is something to be said for its accuracy. Challenged
by the Fourth Gospel I deny it. But it must not be overlooked that the First Epistle of St. John has succinctly
summed up in a single formula or epigram the ethical
truths about the nature of God already enunciated by
earlier writers. " God is love," on the ethical side, ranks
worthily with " God is spirit," on the metaphysical side.
For both we are grateful. But I have sometimes wondered
whether, if goodness or righteousness had been used instead of love, and if it had been said, therefore, " God is
righteousness," or " God is goodness," rather than " God is
love," the religion of Christ would have been stained by
so many sins and cruelties committed in his name. Perhaps, however, human nature, in its corruption and blindness, is indifferent to the meaning of words.

When we pass from God as he is in himself, to God in
his relation to the world, we are at once plunged into
the theory of the Logos. It is true that the Logos constitutes part of the eternal nature of God, as well as the
predominant factor in his dealings with the universe; but
to the Evangelist the importance of the Logos centres in
its incarnation and in its relations with humanity.
Consistently with my special purpose, I do not propose
to give any analysis of the doctrine of the Logos or of its
genesis. I am only concerned with its value. Seeing,
then, that the doctrine may be represented as an adap-
tation of the Philonic theory to the person and story of
Christ, we can hypothetically regard it under two aspects,
distinguishable in our thought, though not in its author's,

first as a division or separation of the single Godhead into divers aspects or phases; secondly, as the incarnation of one particular aspect in the person of Christ.

Now to those who stand outside the Christian pale, these various aspects of God are only ideal. We make them for our purposes because we conceive that they may approximately answer to that which we think must be *included* in God's own nature, and in his relation to the world. With our human capacities and knowledge, we do not presume to take the immense further step of constructing any hypothesis as to the relation of these ideal aspects to each other. Most of us would, I think, feel that any introduction of such human relationships (for they can only be human) between the aspects of the one and only true God, would be an infringement of the Unitarian point of view, a violation of monotheistic purity. What we lose thereby in warmth and colour we gain in truth, sublimity and self-restraint.

But even the strictest monotheist may recognize that the ideal separation of the Divine unity into various aspects may have had in the past, and may have in the present, a religious value of its own. It is in the change of aspects into persons that the danger begins; in the second part of the Athanasian creed rather than in the first. For the theory of a Logos, or of a spirit, or of both, represents one way of realising to ourselves, whether popularly or philosophically, that relation of God to the world and to man which we not only *want* to be true, but which we also trust *is* true; that relation, in other words, which not only satisfies our feeling, but our thought. The metaphysical difficulties, for which the Logos seemed a solution to Philo, no longer press so hardly upon us. God in his lonely greatness must be kept apart from the world; God, in his perfect purity and abstractedness, is unapproachable and unknowable by man. And yet a way there must be in which God and the world, and God and man, must be brought together, just as a way there must

be in which the self-sufficing God must be conceived to
have created both the world and man. These oppositions
and difficulties, of which we can easily find traces in the
Fourth Gospel, scarcely hamper and trouble us to-day as
they troubled and hampered the Alexandrian divines and
philosophers of eighteen hundred years ago. For one
thing, we are less worried by the conception of matter as
something in itself opposed or resistent to God. For
another, we are perhaps less sensitive of logical difficulties
in matters of religion, more willing to leave them unsolved,
but to believe them soluble. But, perhaps, also, we are
less easily taken in by the creations of our own thought.
We do not suppose that we have really bridged the gulf
or solved the puzzle by any theory of a Divine " Word " or
a Divine " Spirit." We merely put back the difficulty
another step. Just as, on the moral side, the theory of a
devil, with which the Fourth Gospel thinks it can take
away from God the responsibility of giving over to evil
the souls which he himself has created, merely removes the
problem in one form to raise it more sharply in another,
so the theory of the Logos does not really *harmonise* the
dual aspects of the Divine nature, it merely expresses them
more clearly.

Nevertheless, a Logos theory is not an arbitrary and
even immoral hypothesis like the theory of a devil. We
feel that while God is omnipresent and infinite, he must
also be self-conscious. Not less than " personal," we say,
however much he may be more. He is something in himself, to himself, and for himself; above and beyond the
world. We call him " transcendent." But then comes the
recoil. He is also something for the world and for ourselves. We are not wholly without God. " Whither shall
I go from thy spirit, and whither shall I flee from thy
presence ? " God is omnipresent. Moreover, there is reason
in the world, and above all there is self-conscious reason in
man. There is a relation, partly constant and partly
variable—constant as regards God, variable as regards our-

selves—between us and him. He is "there," though we
see him not. He is within us, though he is also without.
We grope for words to express this realised feeling and this
believed truth. The psalmist speaks of the Holy Spirit
within him; Philo speaks of the Logos. Some such
hypothesis, some such method of verbally expressing in
separate terms this aspect of the Divine, we may perhaps
always stand in need of. It is possible that a too exclusive
consideration of God as the transcendent cause (though not
without its justification), a too complete avoidance of those
other appellations of him, the manysided One, which the
Hebrew Scriptures, the Alexandrian philosophers, and the
older Rabbinical writers created or employed, may have
reacted not without prejudice upon the religion of our
later Judaism. It may to some extent have robbed us of
those elements of "personal religion" which are partly
conditioned, or, at least, aided by emphasizing more
markedly, through the help of separate words and titles,
the "immanent" aspect of God's complex personality and
being.

We feel at any rate that a theory such as that of the
Logos has a distinct value in helping us to realize that
aspect of God turned outwards to the world and to man,
which seems as much a part of him as any other. Human
thought and human love are not merely the gift of God,
but as the product of reason are themselves partly divine.
Man is created in the image of God, says Genesis : through
thy light we see light, says the Psalter. We can commune
with God and aspire towards him, because, in however
fragmentary a degree, we are akin to him. And if akin to
him, this means that there is a sense in which, though we
are we and God is God, he may be said to be within us as
we may also be said to be within him. "There is a sense"
in which these seductive words have a meaning and a
value: although let it never be forgotten that there is a
sense, only too easily reached, in which they can become
dangerous, immoral and untrue.

For these reasons such a theory as the Philonic Logos has not only an historical interest, but also, as I venture to think, something of permanent and religious value. Perhaps its value is not wholly out of relation to its vague and floating character, to its inconsistencies and contradictions. We feel that the theory cannot be hardened into a fixed dogma ; it is always more or less metaphorical or symbolic —a way of expressing the inexpressible. For these reasons too the Logos of the Fourth Gospel may also have its value even to outsiders. Whether *for them* it has greater *religious* worth than the Logos of Philo may well be doubted. They cannot accept a human relationship between the two aspects of the one God, and therefore the love of the Father to the Son, and the love of the Son to the Father, however movingly and delicately expressed, is for them meaningless and inapposite. The single and complete incarnation of the Logos at a particular time and place gives the theory, to their eyes, something of that hard and fast character which the fluid nature of Philo's Logos avoids. Instead of a constant divine and spiritual operation, we have—at all events for the period of the incarnation—something mechanical, sensuous, spasmodic, magical. It seems as if the work of the Logos before Christ had been a failure, and a new and miraculous method was conceived as necessary. The gradual development of God's purpose in human history seems interrupted by a divine interposition, which comes athwart and between the relation of God to man both before it and after. Such considerations will seem both unphilosophic and unmeaning to those who take their stand upon the dogma of Christ's divinity ; but I think they may partially explain the impression which that dogma makes upon those who have been from their very childhood brought up in a different environment and with different notions of the divine nature and rule.

If we pass to the relation of the Evangelist's Logos— that is, of Jesus Christ—to man, and of man to the Logos, we are immediately confronted by the intense Johannine

dualism. The main object of the incarnation is to save;
but then there is only a certain number for whom salvation
is possible. Those who are potentially good attend to the
words of Christ, and believe in him and in his works; those
who are potentially children of God, become so *de facto* by
the life and death of the incarnate Logos and by the Spirit
which he sends. But more than the children of God are
the children of the Devil. For them no salvation is possible. Their life is no true " life," and with the end of their
earthly existence their separate personality is concluded.
For the children of God the " life eternal," begun on earth,
is continued in heaven ; for the children of this world, that
is, for the children of the Devil, there would appear to be
no hope. Their end is not eternal punishment, but sheer
annihilation. In no other point is the Fourth Gospel more
antipathetic to the outsider than in this. We object to this
dualism, both in itself and in its test. That it is but the
culmination of a tendency does not make it truer or more
acceptable. There is a dualism discernible in the Psalter
and in other portions of the Hebrew Scriptures ; but it is
not so theoretic and complete as the dualism of " St. John."
It is more natural and ordinary ; the dualism of the average
hot-blooded patriot, not the thought-out dualism of the
philosopher in his study. Jewish particularism is very
objectionable ; to identify the enemies of your people with
the enemies of God, the Gentile with the wicked, is utterly
repugnant to our modern notions of justice and religion.
But this particularism was happily not part and parcel of
the real Jewish creed. It could be, and has been, easily got
rid of. The Johannine doctrine involves a particularism
more deadly than the Jewish form of it, because it is more
intertwined with the very essence of the Evangelist's creed,
and receives a more theoretic and logical basis. It is, therefore, less easily got rid of.

   Philo too teaches a dualism analogous to the dualism of
" St. John." But as Réville, in his admirable pamphlet, *La
doctrine du Logos dans la quatrième Evangile et dans les œuvres*

de Philon, has well pointed out, Philo's dualism is less sharply defined, less consistent and less irreversible. Between the two extremes there are various shades and modifications of character, partly inclining towards the flesh, partly aspiring towards God. Moreover Philo admits the possibility of a passage from one division to the other; he finds a place for Repentance. But in the Fourth Gospel, those who belong to Christ's flock believe and are saved, those who do not belong to it cannot believe. The "world" cannot receive the spirit: it knows him not. Those who are not of God cannot hear his words. He that is of the "earth" cannot receive that which comes from "heaven." The Fourth Gospel knows nothing of Repentance. The very word μετάνοια is not found in it. Those who receive the words of Christ no longer include a contingent of publicans and sinners; they are morally good.[1] A forgiveness of sins is only cursorily mentioned: it is inconsistent with the main doctrine, an importation from without, or rather a survival of a rejected element. It is true that the wrath of God abides on the unbeliever, but this would seem to be not so much because the unbeliever can help his unbelief, but because God, as pure light and goodness, must by his own nature be eternally hostile to what is corrupt, evil and diabolic. The intense dualism of the writer is finally and consummately revealed to us in the great prayer in the seventeenth chapter, where Christ is made to say, "I pray not for the world, but for those whom thou hast given me." Surely the defenders of the Gospel's authenticity and historical character do Jesus of Nazareth an evil turn. Surely "I come to call sinners to repentance," "Father, forgive them, for they know not what they do," were more characteristic of the historic Jesus than all the elaborate speeches of "St. John."

For the exquisite beauty of the Fourth Gospel tends to

---

[1] Oscar Holtzmann, *Das Johannes Evangelium*, 1887, p. 89.

blind us to the full meaning and implication of its dualistic doctrine. We do not realise that all the love which God and the Logos, God's son, bear to the world is only to an elect portion, and that the sublimer pity of the Synoptic Gospel to the outcast and the sinner is wholly and ne- cessarily wanting. Nor do we easily realise that the human reflection of that love is only to be exercised within the brotherhood of believers. If it be charged against the Rabbis—with some truth and with some falsehood—that they interpreted the love of one's neighbour enjoined in Leviticus to mean the love of one's fellow-Jew, it may with better accuracy be said that the love enjoined by the famous " new commandment " of St. John is restricted to fellows in faith. Is love restricted by race much more objectionable than love restricted by creed ?

Moreover, the moving splendour and calm assurance of language, which adds so greatly to the Gospel's perennial charm, has tended to make men think that its dualism, if not justified in itself, was justified by the environment and age in which the author lived. I find this excuse for the Evangelist in Thoma,[1] and I find it also, where it seems far more surprising, in Dr. Martineau. He speaks of the " inevitable but imperfect dualism forced upon human thought by the contrasts of experience." " A new religion," he goes on to say,

gives birth to an entrancing affection, and, going apart with its own enthusiasm, sees all else at variance with it, and needing either con- version or rejection. It cannot live without its outcasts : the Israelite has his Gentiles : the apostle Paul his false " brethren," that " make the cross of Christ of none effect " through their " dead works " ; and now the mysterious evangelist, who finds in union with Christ the whole spiritual distance annihilated between the life of man and God, looks upon a world made up of dissolute Paganism and embittered Judaism as in the mass delivered over to the power of evil. Between the low passions that reign there of greed and lust, of ambition and envy, and the aspirations and trust, the humility and love that breathe through the prayers and sweeten the inner life of a true Christian

---

[1] **Thoma,** *Die Genesis des Johannes Evangeliums,* 1882, p. 283.

community, the contrast presents itself to him as little less than
infinite ; so that only now does the genuine history of humanity open,
with the planting of a sacred colony in the midst of the dark continent of earthly sin and shame.[1]

Now, in the first place, the immense ethical difference
between " conversion " and " rejection " is somewhat ignored
by their close juxtaposition in this passage; but in the
second, what right has Dr. Martineau even to *imply*
that the world upon which the author of the Fourth
Gospel " looked forth " was not only seemingly to the
Evangelist, but *really* made up of a " dissolute paganism "
and an " embittered Judaism " ? Within the Christian
pale, nought but aspirations and trust, humility and love ;
without, nothing but greed and lust, ambition and envy !
At the very period when the Fourth Gospel was composed,
Paganism was not without its spiritual revival and its
ethical nobility. Surely there were many Pagans who
rejected Christianity and yet led lives of purity and goodness ; and as for Judaism, was there no spirituality among
its martyrs and heroes who perished in all the sublimity of
perfect faith at the scaffold and by the sword ? It is a
mournful fact that the good men among the Jews thought
that the good men among the Christians were bad, and
vice versâ ; but it is still more mournful to perpetuate
their error, and to think that either side could arrogate
to itself an exclusive possession of goodness, humility and
love.

A number of points relative to the moral and religious

---

[1] *Seat of Authority*, p. 493. Still more one-sided is a passage on
p. 434 : " This intense moral dualism in the Johannine writings, which
allows no gradations, drives all antitheses into contradictions, and
invokes God and devil to settle every disputed cause, doubtless indicates
that the interval had become practically hopeless between the spiritual
ideal of life and character reached by the Christian conscience, and the
low types of motive and conduct into which the unconverted Judaism
and heathenism had set." If one met this sentence in any unorthodox
German Protestant divine, one would pay no notice. It seems to belong
to their business to misrepresent Rabbinic Judaism ; it lies, perhaps,
in their blood. But from the English Dr. Martineau it is amazing.

condition of the world before and at the advent of Christ
are left obscure. Those who " come to the light," that is,
believe in Christ, are good. Did then the Incarnation not
increase the capacity of human goodness ? Did it merely
give the means of acquiring " truth," the chance of a
fuller bliss, a purer enlightenment, but not the power
of becoming more good ? The command to love one
another is described as new. Were then people not
really good before Christ, but only potentially so,
seeing that the only definition of goodness recognized by the Evangelist seems to be love ? If they
were in any true sense good, why should they have been
in danger from the devil ? The redemption of the good
seems less urgent than the redemption of the evil, and yet
the purpose of the Incarnation is for the sake of the good
and not for the sake of the evil. The Logos shone into
the world before it became flesh. The darkness did not
apprehend it. But was that darkness universal both
among the Jews and among the heathens ? Were there
good men who died before the Incarnation, and in
what sense ? What knowledge of God, what light
had they, whether in Judæa or outside it ? One
of the best features in the Gospel is its universalism,
for on this point the author is no inept disciple of
St. Paul. Gentiles rather than Jews come readily to the
light. Other sheep there are not of this fold. But what
then of all the great mass of heathen who died before
Christ came ? Was the pre-Christian action of the Logos
too feeble to generate in them the spiritual life ? Was
nobody born anew, or born from above, whether Gentile
or Jew, in all that immense period of waiting and preparation ? If yes, why did not this normal action of the Logos
and the grace of God suffice ? If not, and if no man was
" spiritual," could any have been good? Are we to suppose
that the new birth and the true goodness which it includes
were coincident with Christ ? And lastly, was everybody before Christ annihilated at death, or are we to

believe with Dr. Martineau that two or three obscure and doubtful passages refer to a resurrection and a judgment both of punishment and of reward for the endless generations of the dead?[1] Just in proportion as the Fourth Gospel leaves us with no clear answer to questions such as these its religious value seems to me to halt and fail. If you set up a great religious theory, involving mighty miracles and tremendous presuppositions, you should at least make that theory complete. A religious *Weltanschauung*, which intellectually and morally is fraught with difficulty, should at least be co-extensive with the world which it seeks to interpret. If in crucial points of urgency and moment, it leaves us in the lurch and in the dark, if it not only does not satisfactorily explain the facts of history and human nature, but even ignores them, its religious value, both theoretically and practically, is, I venture to think, most seriously impaired.

We pass from these unexplained and unsolved difficulties to consider how "eternal life," in the bestowal of which are contained both the prerogative and the mission of Christ, is won, and wherein it consists. So far as it is bestowed *ab extra*, as a gift from without, it does not concern us. So far as it is conditioned by the fact of Christ's death and by a participation in baptism and the eucharist, it also lies outside our sphere. Whatever spiritual meanings the author attached to these material processes, he would apparently have believed that they exercised upon the rightly disposed person a special and semi-miraculous influence. He would probably have objected to any abolition of these ceremonies, just as Philo objected to a merely spiritual interpretation of the Pentateuchal laws.[2] But the details of his views do not affect our present enquiry, just as the degree of atoning or sanctifying efficacy which he assigned to the death of Christ is of little importance to the outsider

---

[1] *Seat of Authority in Religion*, p. 439, n. 1.
[2] Cp. Pfleiderer, *Das Urchristenthum*, p. 774.

except historically. What we want to know is how this eternal life can be won by man. We have already seen that the attainment of it is, partially at any rate, predetermined. Those who have not the spiritual germ within them can not be quickened by the spiritual sun. For them darkness is light and light is darkness. The opportunity of salvation to the one class is but the means of completer damnation to the other. Therefore it is that the "judgment" of Christ is one of sifting : the rejected become worse and worse as the light shines brighter and brighter. But in addition to all this, human effort is needed for the acquisition of life eternal, and there is a method by which it can be won. This may not be wholly logical, but it is certainly more in accordance with experience and fact. So in Philo all spiritual attainment is due to the grace of God, and Philo's insistence on this point, implying man's incapacity to move upward without divine help and the necessity of humility, is quite parallel to John v. 41-44 and vii. 18 ; but, nevertheless, there is room and need for moral effort and endeavour. You are reborn by the spirit, and the spirit is given you from above; and yet you may struggle to attain the spirit, or at any rate to develop the potentialities of the divine gift. Any obscurity and inconsistency here need not surprise us : no one can precisely allocate to man and God their exact share in the moral and religious development of the human character. Yet most religious persons feel that there are both human and divine agencies helping towards the ultimate product.

Now, in most of the higher religions, the attainment of the best life is supposed to depend upon two main elements. One of these elements is moral and one is religious. These separations are somewhat misleading, but nevertheless they have their uses. The elements may also be described thus : eternal life is partly won by works and partly by faith.

Which element comes first in time and in importance ? The modern and Jewish view is that the ethical element

comes first. What society needs is the most developed
goodness ; with what fashions and dogmas of religious belief this goodness is combined is of inferior moment.
That belief is of the greatest value to society which has
the best ethical effect upon its believers. Moreover, we
recognise that in faith, do and say what we will, there
does enter an intellectual element which is not wholly
under the control of our will. We are aware, though Philo
was not, that a man may be very good who is an Atheist
or an Agnostic, though we are far from thinking that
society would not morally degenerate if Atheism and
Agnosticism were immensely to increase. That we become
good by doing good is still true. And the content of
"life eternal" is interpenetrated by morality. Remove
morality and it is vague, ascetic, selfish—a refined egoism.

But this ethical element is not unaffected by the other
element, which consists in man's attitude towards God, in
his belief in him, his love of him, his more or less constant sense of his abiding omnipresence. "Solet enim
dei amator illico etiam hominum amator esse." Yet while
these two elements influence and interact upon each other,
we feel that the primary one of the two is morality. If
we may separate inseparables, we might say : Through
morality to religion.

And in the Fourth Gospel the need of these two elements
is also recognised. But, on the whole, the emphasis seems
placed on the wrong factor, on faith rather than on
morality. Through religion to morality, rather than
through morality to religion, is the tendency of the Gospel.
In this respect, the First Epistle of St. John takes a saner
and more ethical line. But both Gospel and Epistle incline
to identify the one element with the other or to gloss over
the difference between them.

As we have already seen, the man who believes in
Christ is at least potentially good. The bad man is an
unbeliever, and even the reverse holds also true—the unbeliever is a bad man. Now, apart from his metaphysical

and à *priori* dualism, what reason has the Evangelist to say that the unbeliever is morally bad ? " Every one that doeth evil hateth the light." " Except ye believe that I am he, ye shall die in your sins." The second quotation seems, with doubtful consistency, to imply that even in spite of sin, belief may be won and sin destroyed (cp. v. 14). You might argue that only those who were hardened to good-ness could be insensible to the moral beauty of Christ's words, or doubt that he was inspired. The argument is plausible though not convincing. But even if admitted, it does not suit the case. For what the moral beauty of Christ's words can never prove is that the speaker of them was metaphysically connected with Deity, the In-carnation of the eternal Word.[1]

It is, however, also true that the Gospel teaches morality as the condition precedent of faith. " If any man willeth to do his will, he shall know of the teaching, whether it be of God, or whether I speak from myself." " He that doeth the truth cometh to the light." " He that keepeth my commands, loveth me." And this teaching is whole-some and sound. Let God and duty prove themselves to you in your life by living on as if they truly were.[2] The Epistle is more definite still on this point. " If a man say, I love God, and hateth his brother, he is a liar"; through the love of man we pass to the love of God. Prac-tically this teaching comes to this : theoretic belief is of no spiritual value ; the test of true faith is that it should rest on a moral basis and issue in a moral life. Through morality to religion, and when there, from religion to morality. These excellent utterances of the Epistle (*e.g.*,

---

[1] Cp. Chavannes' *La Religion dans la Bible*, II. p. 183 :—"Certes Jésus me révèle la veritable vie ; mais en quoi cela me prouve-t-il qu'il est un être divin incarné? Pourquoi veut-on absolument que je le croie pour aimer la vie qui mène à Dieu? . . . Cette théosophie est un hors-d'œuvre dangereux. C'est elle qui est cause que notre auteur se soit si malheureusement exprimé, par exemple, lorsqu'il écrivait : ' Quiconque croit que Jésus est le Christ, est né de Dieu.'"

[2] T. H. Green, "Address on Faith." *Works*. III.. p. 273.

"whosoever doeth not righteousness is not of God, and he that loveth not knoweth not God"), suffice to give it value to the outsider as to the insider, to the Jew as to the Christian.

But, as we have seen, neither Epistle nor Gospel stops there. They do not merely say, morality shall be the test of your faith, and the method by which you reach it. They have led the way to the dangerous doctrine that unbelief is necessarily as much moral as intellectual. If you can win faith by goodness, you miss it because of vice. The unbeliever is a sinner. It seems to me that for the terrible consequences of this doctrine, the Johannine writings are partially responsible. Their matchless beauty tends to hide the danger and the cruelty of the doctrine which they preach. For let us pass from the work of a great genius such as the Fourth Gospel to the writings of a soulless fanatic, and what do we find there? The fanatic would be reprobated now by all; nevertheless, views such as his have had great influence in the world, and if he had been asked to justify them, he could have quoted the Fourth Gospel with great cogency and aptitude for his uncharitable purpose. That Gospel undoubtedly maintains that moral evil is the root of unbelief. And is not this what Dr. Cumming, as quoted by George Eliot, in that striking essay of hers, on Evangelical Teaching, in the *Westminster Review* of October, 1855, also maintained?

I once met with an acute and enlightened infidel, with whom I reasoned day after day, and for hours together ; I submitted to him the internal, the external, and the experimental evidences, but made no impression on his scorn and unbelief. At length I entertained a suspicion that there was something morally, rather than intellectually wrong, and that the bias was not in the intellect, but in the heart. One day, therefore, I said to him : "I must now state my conviction, and you may call me uncharitable, but duty compels me ; you are living in some known and gross sin." The man's countenance became pale ; he bowed, and left me.

One point more. The author of the First Epistle of St. John is urgent to impress upon his readers the importance of morality. In simple adages of great power and beauty he preaches, as we have seen, the noble doctrine that the doer of righteousness is begotten of God, and that the lover of God must be also a lover of man. But there is another side to this picture. Even with him the element of faith frequently overcomes and predominates over the element of morality. That he should be blind to goodness outside his own community is natural. But what of the sinners within its pale ? He cannot consistently maintain the paradox that the man who calls himself a Christian is not a Christian if he be a sinner. It conflicts with language and experience. He therefore equivocates. The Christian sins, but it is a "sin not unto death." What is a sin unto death ? It is clearly apostasy. Therefore the intellectual sin of abandoning a belief in Christ would seem to be more unpardonable in the author's eyes than a moral sin of indefinite intensity. Here again we are confronted with a false doctrine which has worked grievous evil in the history of the world. The believer's sins are judged by a different standard from the sins of his unbelieving neighbour. No longer "Ye are my people: *therefore* will I visit upon you all your iniquities." But rather, "Whosoever believeth that Jesus is the Christ is begotten of God ; and whosoever is begotten of God doeth no sin." The individual who is proudly conscious that he so believes and is so begotten, may rapidly become convinced that he is incapable of sin. Take care of your faith, and your deeds will take care of themselves—a perversion doubtless of the Epistle's general doctrine, but not without possible support from the ambiguous language of a document which exalts faith at the expense of morality even while it attempts indissolubly to combine the two.[1]

The content of eternal life, according to the Fourth Gospel, we have already heard defined as the knowledge of the only true God and of Jesus Christ, the Divine Word

---

[1] Cp. Chavannes' *La Religion dans la Bible*, p. 184.

made flesh. But it would be improper to infer from this
single passage that no ethical elements entered into its composition. With equal or greater injustice the same attack
might be made on Philo when he defines this life as a taking
refuge with the true God (ἡ πρὸς τὸ ὂν καταφυγή); or
where in many other similar passages he gives to it an
exclusively religious character. The moral element is
certainly not wanting in the Fourth Evangelist, though by
the very purpose and object of his Gospel moral teaching
as such is very slightly dwelt upon. But in the flush and
glow of his spiritual enthusiasm, faith in Christ seemed
necessarily to involve a regeneration of the whole man.
Man receives by it the fullest truth and highest knowledge, and it so transforms his character as to bring out its
best and divinest possibilities. Personal devotion and
emotional love are part and parcel of that knowledge of
the Son and of the Father wherein life eternal consists. To-
day we are bound to separate, at least in language, our
moral and religious life more clearly, and the intellectual
element in "faith," through its very difficulty, presses
itself the more strongly and distinctly upon our attention.

All the same, the ethics of the Fourth Gospel are certainly its least original part. If you subtract all that
seems a reproduction of Paul and all that seems a reproduction of Philo, you have little left that is at
once admirable and new. So, for example, with the conception of spiritual freedom and the slavery of sin (viii.
31-36). So also, in the main, with the conception of self-
glory as preventing the possibility of spiritual enlightenment. As with Socrates the vain man who thinks he
knows but is really ignorant is intellectually hopeless and
helpless, so to our Evangelist they who love the glory of
men more than the glory of God are also those who think
they see but are really blind. " If they were blind they
would have no sin ; but now they say We see ; therefore
their sin remaineth." To this conception also there are

several parallels, both in the Epistles of Paul and in the treatises of Philo.

Yet everyone who reads the Gospel and Epistles of St. John with a fair measure of sympathy, will probably find in them a certain ethical elevation. They are not only spiritual in religion, but also in morality. And when in this essay the word "morality" has been used, and all things in heaven and earth have been appraised by a moral standard, I have always had in mind the fullest connotation that could possibly be given to this expansive term. I was not thinking only of mere work-a-day and *bourgeois* morality (though this, as Rauwenhoff says, includes a good part of man's moral worth), but of the morality which is exhibited in self-sacrifice and devotion. Morality does not stop short of love; and, though the highest morality to our modern notions does not consort with useless asceticism or isolation, it does, I should imagine, always include that antagonism to the "world," in one specific and spiritual sense, which is characteristic of the Johannine writings. The precise meaning which their authors gave to the word κόσμος has doubtless passed away. We do not approve their antithesis between this world and another world when they mean by it that this world is under the sway of diabolic agencies. Nevertheless, softened and modified though our notions of the "world" may be, there is a sense in which we do find ethical meaning and religious value in the famous sentences: "Love not the world, neither the things that are in the world. If any man love the world, the love of the Father is not in him. For all that is in the world, the lust of the flesh, and the lust of the eyes, and the vainglory of life, is not of the Father, but is of the world. And the world passeth away, and the lust thereof; but he that doeth the will of God abideth for ever." So far as these words are true, they are true for those without, as well as for those within, the limits of Christianity ; and, seeing that the measure of abiding truth which they contain is nowhere else, to my knowledge, more simply and effectively expressed, the outsider, as well as the insider, may rightly render them both gratitude and admiration.

Ethics certainly owes more to the Epistle than to the Gospel. It is undoubtedly true that in the long speeches in the Gospel, " the ethical teaching of the Synoptic Christ falls wholly into the background."[1] Not unconnected, I should imagine, with this lack of ethics is another fact pointed out by the same acute commentator, that the predominance of the Fourth Gospel in the Christian Church has regularly produced a tendency to asceticism and mysticism, from the days of Clement of Alexandria to those of Schleiermacher.[2] The one positive moral command of the Johannine Christ is that contained in the word ἀγάπη, or love. " A new commandment I give unto you, that ye love one another." But is not this, it may pertinently be asked, sufficient and all inclusive ?

Without attempting to depreciate in a nasty or grudging spirit the value of so famous an injunction, it must be pointed out that this love is merely reciprocal. It is restricted to the fellow disciple, and is thus in sharp and violent contrast to the bidding of the Synoptic Jesus. The particularism of race is exchanged for the new and more dangerous particularism of creed. Leviticus xix. 18 is perhaps supplemented by Luke x. 33, and enlarged by Matthew v. 44 ; it is not improved by John xiii. 34. That is no new command which does not go beyond the old. Enlargement fulfils, and therefore Matthew v. 44 does not (it may be contended) contradict Matthew v. 17, but John xiii. 34 is not only in conflict with Leviticus xix. 18, but with Matthew v. 17 as well. And the supplementary

---

[1] "'Die sittliche Verkündigung des synoptischen Christus tritt vollkommen in ihnen zurück." (O. Holtzmann, p. 89.)

[2] " Das Hervorheben des johanneischen Christusbildes vor dem synoptischen hatte in der Kirche regelmässig ein Ueberwiegen des weltfremden Lebens der Christen zur Folge, in Askese und Mystik, von Clemens Alexandrinus an bis auf Schleiermacher und Luthardt." (O. Holtzmann, p. 136.)

command of Leviticus xix. 34 finds no parallel in St. John.
The stranger in creed need not be loved. Too accurately
has Christianity recognised the difference : too closely has
she followed the Christ of the Fourth Gospel rather than
the Christ of the First.

Nevertheless within the limit of the brotherhood, the
force and beauty with which the command of love is urged
and emphasized, cannot be gainsaid. All of us may be
grateful for such passages, and can apply them in our own
way. As a picture of the love which lays upon itself
willingly the lowliest duties, the scene where Christ washes
the feet of his disciples will always retain its power.
This service of love is to rise to the heights of sacrifice.
" Greater love hath no man than this, that a man lay down
his life for his friends." But it is again characteristic of the
Evangelist that whereas to Paul the supremacy of Christ's
sacrifice consisted in his dying for sinners, those whom his
death benefits in the Fourth Gospel are no longer ἀσεβεῖς,
but φίλοι, not the ungodly, but the good. The dualism is
preserved unto the end.

One integral portion of the Evangelist's conception of
love has thus far been omitted. The followers of Christ
are to love one another. But wherefore ? By what force
or example is this love to be set in motion, stimulated,
maintained ? Here we come to the great and distinctive
ethical motive characteristic of the Fourth Gospel. The
love of man to man is conditioned by the love of man
for Christ, and of Christ for man. It may also be said to
be partly conditioned by the love of God both for Christ
and man. (But we must always remember that neither
God nor Christ has love for the man who will not or cannot
be saved by faith in the Incarnate Son.)

No outsider would dream for a moment of denying the
ethical power which the love of man for Christ and the belief
in the love of Christ for man have exercised in human history. This is not the place to consider how far that power can
be, has been, or is supplied by Judaism with its more direct

appeal and immediate relationship to God the Father. It is probably harder to love God, and to feel the joy of loving him, than to love Christ; and it must not be forgotten that this emotional feeling of love and of joy in loving— reaching up to and passing into a mystic feeling of union and communion with the beloved and Divine object—may, within certain limits, have excellent ethical results. Now, as Rauwenhoff has so clearly pointed out, every excitement of feeling, however noble the feeling may be, partakes to some extent of the character of enjoyment. This enjoyment is easier if the spiritual is clothed in sensuous forms. An image impresses us much more keenly than an abstract conception. For how, he adds, could the worship of Jesus and the worship of Mary have so obscured the worship of God in Christianity if it were not that the humanised God appeals so much more to the feelings than the Infinite One ? [1]

It is certainly true that one element in the love of Christ and also in the conception of God, produced by the Christian theory, can never be filled up by concentrating our love upon God alone. It is the element of sacrifice. Christians are convinced of God's love for man, because he sent his Son to save them. They love God the more because they think he so sacrificed himself. And the exemplar of human love is given them to all time in the divine sacrifice of Christ. It has been said in this Review by a gentle and gifted Christian writer, that if we say that self-sacrifice is the greatest of the virtues, but that it has not been or cannot be displayed by God, then God's character is less noble than man's. This argument appears to me to assimilate the divine and the human nature too closely. To resist temptation is a human virtue, but it cannot be attributed to God: the same might be said of other virtues that imply effort. Is there not still a truth in the Aristotelian dictum, that we praise virtue (and virtue is

---

[1] Rauwenhoff, *Wijsbegeerte van den Godsdienst*, 1887, pp. 175, 176 (German translation, p. 117).

human), τοὺς θεοὺς δὲ μακαρίζομεν? At any rate the
"inner contradiction" of which Hausrath speaks in the
conception of a being who is *both* God *and* man, the vivid
feeling that "human life becomes an empty phantom (*ein
leerer Schein*) if it is lived by a God," prevent those who
stand without the Christian pale from realising how the
notion of a Divine sacrifice, offered at a given moment in
time and once for all, can be assimilated with the idea of
God, or what exact meaning it can convey.[1]

It may be questioned whether the Fourth Gospel, though
it lays so much stress upon the love which Christ bore to
his disciples, has been the Gospel which has chiefly contributed to create that wonderful figure of the pitying and
suffering martyr, the divine ideal of humanity, in whom
so many countless souls have found comfort in trouble,
strength in temptation, light in darkness, and love amid
hate. "Inasmuch as ye did it unto one of these my
brethren, even these least, ye did it unto me." Such
sayings, and others like them, are more characteristic of
the Synoptic than of the Johannine Christ. Are they not
also more characteristic of a conception of Christ in which
he reveals the love of God and the "divine image" of man,
inasmuch as, though inspired, he was, nevertheless, human,
and not God himself, incarnate and complete? It would
be very interesting to consider what share the human or
Unitarian conception has really had in the motive power
for good which the worship and love of Christ have produced in the course of the ages. Or is that motive power
dependent upon a belief in his absolute divinity? Can we
have no Father Damiens without the Incarnation?

Putting these ultimate questions on one side, let us note
some peculiar features of the Fourth Gospel's conception
of human and divine love, and how these are partially
modified in the first Epistle. In the Gospel the Logos, still
more than in Philo, occupies the position of intermediary

---

[1] Cp. Hausrath, *Neutestamentliche Zeitgeschichte,* iv., p. 493, *fin.*

between God and man. Through the Son to the Father; other approach there is none. Where such a theory is merely metaphysical, as we may say it is in Philo—for whom the aspect of Deity revealed in the Logos is the means whereby man may ultimately pass to the fuller knowledge and love of the absolute God—it is not objectionable. The danger of its presentment in the Fourth Gospel is that the Logos is no longer merely a philosophical aspect of God, but a " person " in our modern sense of the word, who became flesh for a definite period of time. If you say " only through the Son to the Father " with this definite and personalised sense attaching to the Son, you run near to saying that the Father cannot be known except by those who may have heard of, and hearing may believe in, the dogma of the pre-existent, incarnate and resurrected Son. And this implies, as it seems to me, an improper and intolerant limitation of the knowledge and love of God to the followers of a particular creed.

In the Gospel the love of the Father is mainly directed to the Son. That love is insisted on several times with marked emphasis. On the other hand, the love of the Son for the Father is only once alluded to (xiv. 31). The love of the Son is directed mainly to his disciples. The love of the disciples is directed to the Son. The love of God by man is only once alluded to (v. 42). The object of Christian love in this Gospel is not the Father, but the Son. Yet it is only fair to say that the Father's love for those who are capable of loving the Son, and hence of winning life eternal, is the motive of the incarnation. " He that loveth the Son will be loved of the Father. The Father loveth you because ye have loved the Son." Finally the love of the Son for them conditions and causes the love of the disciples for each other. " A new commandment I give unto you, that ye love one another; even as I loved you, that ye may also love one another."

In contrast with this markedly mediatorial position of

the Son in the Gospel stands the relation of the believer to God in the Epistle. That relation is more immediate, and therefore more sympathetic with the Jewish point of view. Professor Pfleiderer would, of course, be outraged to hear that what he calls, " *die tiefsinnige Erfassung des Kernes der christlichen Religion,*" and the immediate relation of the human soul to the Divine Father—*enger und einfacher* in the Epistle than in the Gospel—is essentially Jewish. And yet, outraged as he and his friends would be by such a statement (as if Rabbinic Jews could possibly know anything of an immediate love of God by the individual believer), it is nevertheless strictly true. Moreover, this love of God is brought into direct relation with the love of man. None can love God if he love not his brother. When Professor Pfleiderer asks whether it would not have been possible for the Church to have abided by the teaching of the Epistle in this respect, and whether it could not have thus avoided many quarrels, useless alike for piety and for morality, his Jewish readers are in full accord with him.[1] Such has ever been the contention of Judaism, to put no separable divine "person" between man and God. It is running on the same unconsciously Jewish lines when Cone, quoting and following Pfleiderer, remarks that the author of the Epistle "establishes an immediate relation of the soul to God, which Christian theologians since Paul have unhappily disregarded, apparently solicitous lest the person of Christ should not be sufficiently exalted and his mediatorial office magnified."[2]

One more characteristic and essential feature of "life eternal," according to the Johannine conception of it, remains. That element may fitly be called mystic. It is the glad and keen consciousness of God and of his love, the sense of nearness to him, by our being in him and his being in us, which is often supposed to constitute

---

[1] Pfleiderer, *Das Urchristenthum*, p. 799.
[2] Cone, p. 326.

the core of the inner religious life. In the Fourth Gospel this consciousness is once more strictly limited to the Christian believer. It is so limited because it partly depends on a definite and supernatural act, namely, the bestowal of the Spirit to the disciples after the death of Christ. The gift of that Spirit is not granted in various measures to those who seek God by many creeds and divers pathways. It is rigidly restricted to those who seek the Father through the adoration of the Son. They only are capable (through their incipient spiritual nature) of receiving it. It is therefore necessary, before the doctrine of the Fourth Gospel can be appreciated by the outsider, to disentangle it of the narrow and circumscribing form in which it is presented. As it stands, it is too closely connected with a miraculous dispensation of a supernatural gift at a particular season, and too limited in its application and its sphere, to be true generally and for all time. The parallel presentment of the theory in Philo may be arid and rhetorical, yet it is more human, because it is consonant with a variety of creeds. Many of those who have extolled the Johannine mysticism seem to forget its narrowness. But mysticism above all things should be broadly human.

It is "the intimate relation between God and man" which the Fourth Gospel teaches—at least for the believer. "If a man love me, he will keep my word; and my Father will love him, and we will come unto him and make our abode with him." "He that abideth in me, and I in him, the same beareth much fruit." "I will pray the Father, and he will give you . . . . the spirit of truth . . . . he abideth with you, and shall be in you." "Even as thou, Father, art in me and I in thee, that they also may be in us; that they may be one, even as we are one; I in them, and thou in me, that they may be perfected into one; . . . . that the love wherewith thou lovedst me may be in them, and I in them"—in other words, God's immanence in man, and man's glad consciousness of that immanence and love of it.

As an introduction to the study of this subject, many people might find it useful to read those pages of Rauwenhoff's book which deal with what he calls the Psychological Forms of Religion, Intellectualism, Mysticism, and "Moralism."[1] To the Understanding, to the Feelings (or rather to *Gemüt*), and to the Will, are there assigned their proper part and function both in the religious history of the past, and in the religious life of the individual. He shows that of these three forms, "Moralism," which lays the stress of religious life on moral action, is on the whole the most important and the most wholesome.

Judged from the outside, moralism presents little attraction, especially when compared with mysticism (*Mystik*). Putting aside everything which savours of emotion, God is considered as the supreme Lawgiver, and the test of piety is exclusively sought for in virtue. Man's future is usually regarded as a reward or retribution of the use to which he has put his life on earth.[2]

There is an undoubted onesidedness in "Moralism," but nevertheless that onesidedness is not religiously so dangerous as the onesidedness of "Intellectualism" and "Mysticism."

In a onesided emphasis of Morality lies an adequate means to prevent the practical character of religion being misconceived —an error into which "intellectualism" so readily falls—and at the same time a means to prevent religion being made sensuous, which is the besetting danger of mysticism. If for a "Moralist" religious life becomes little more than a discharge of what he thinks to be his duty, he is at least preserved both from sterile orthodoxy and from an immoral running riot of the religious emotions. The discipline of the moral consciousness may never lead to the sunny heights, whereon the purest life of religious sentiment is passed: it keeps men at any rate upon the right path. No such sins can be charged to the school of Kant as to the school of Calvin or of Spener.[3]

---

[1] Pp. 109—124, in the German translation.
[2] Rauwenhoff, p. 180, German translation, p. 120.
[3] Rauwenhoff, p. 182, German translation. p. 122.

Nevertheless, religion needs and implies something more
than mere "moralism" can supply :—

The one-sided conception of religion as a sanctifying power which
acts upon the will is unable to perceive that there is also something
else in religion which can never be dispensed with without harm.
The *unio mystica*, the yearning of the heart to a more intimate relation with Deity, for that " Thou in me and I in thee," which forms
the fundamental thought of the theology of the Fourth Gospel, may
easily lead the way to hurtful aberrations. It, nevertheless, always
remains a truly religious phenomenon and an essential constituent of
the normally-developed religious life. To this mystic union and
yearning, "moralism," to its own great loss, can do no justice ; for it
thereby fails to realise that in these emotions lies the great motive
which lifts morality above legalism, and so ennobles the consciousness
of duty till it becomes a mighty impulse and passion towards moral
perfection. " Thou shalt " will presumably always remain the basis
of all morality ; but when religion transforms it into "God wills,"
and God is no longer a mere lawgiver, but the object of heartfelt love
and spiritual desire, you reach the " Da quod jubes et jube quod vis,"
which unites religion and morality, and brings morality to its highest
possible perfection.[1]

This *unio mystica* of which Rauwenhoff here speaks is
the source or the content of those blissful experiences
wherein, according to Oscar Holtzmann, the perennial
value of the Fourth Gospel consists. He says :—

The blissful experiences which Christ declares concerning himself
in Matthew xi. 25-30, and to which Paul briefly alludes (Gal. ii. 20),
are described in the Fourth Gospel as the permanent possession of the
Christian community (x. 14, xiv. 20-24, xv. 10, 11-15, xvi. 12-15,
33). They are, in short, the experiences which accrue to the individual from his consciousness of the love of God and the redemption
through Christ. In its expression of this thought lies, to my idea,
the absolute and eternal value of the Johannine Gospel.[2]

Now, if Rauwenhoff be right, and if the yearning of the
spirit towards a closer relation and communion with God be
in truth an essential constituent of the properly developed
religious life, the presentment of that yearning and of its

---

[1] Rauwenhoff, p. 18J ; German Translation. p. 121.
[2] *Das Johannesevangelium*, p. 90.

satisfaction in the Fourth Gospel will probably always retain its attraction and its value, however unnecessary and even intolerable Jews and Theists may find it to split up the Deity into two so markedly personal aspects as the Father and the Son, and however repugnant it may be to them to put any mediatorial agency—human and divine in one—between the human soul and God. Philo's less personal Logos is in this respect far more universal and less restrictive than the Johannine Christ.

"Nearer, my God, to thee" is a true and fundamental feeling of the religious mind. Their sense of the nearness of God is the stepping stone on which men have risen to the consciousness of the "Unio mystica." This nearness is fully recognised and asserted in the Hebrew Scriptures. God is described as near, because, in the first place, he is lovingly omniscient. "The Lord is nigh unto all them that call upon him, to all that call upon him in truth." "The Lord is nigh unto them that are of a broken heart, and saveth such as be of a contrite spirit."

This certainty of God's saving solicitude, his ever present and watchful care of those who pray to him in truth, passes over into a glad sense of communion. It is not merely that the Old Testament psalmist believed in God's *protective* nearness, but he also felt that nearness as a possession and a joy. This feeling was partly, as we know, conditioned by the Temple, but it was perfectly real, and it reaches classic and forcible expression in such Psalms as the 63rd, the 73rd, the 84th, and several others. It is quite a mistake to suppose that this living sense of communion with God was lost by the Rabbis. Both in the Old Testament and in the Talmud it is, however, purely popular. It has not been given any foundation in religious psychology or metaphysics, showing how this sense of communion *with* God and nearness *of* God is based upon a theory of man's nature and God's immanence. It could, as I imagine, only receive such a foundation by the fructifying contact of Greek philosophy.

And I believe that it is this union of practical Hebrew religiousness with Greek philosophy which has produced that religious mysticism, that idea of " Thou in me and I in thee," which constitutes a main conception of the Fourth Gospel. So, too, in the famous speech attributed to St. Paul in the seventeenth chapter of the Acts, we may notice, I believe, this union of Greek and Hebrew. " That they should seek God, if haply they might feel after him, and find him, though he is not far from each one of us," is a Hebrew thought, hardly going beyond what might have been said by a Psalmist or a Rabbi. But the philosophical justification of the divine nearness passes beyond the Hebraic limit. And it is just this philosophic justification which is, to our modern notion, the kernel or essence of the whole—ἐν αὐτῷ γὰρ ζῶμεν καὶ κινούμεθα καὶ ἐσμέν: " In him we live and move and have our being." It may be noted that J. Holtzmann in his Commentary cites a curious parallel from the Greek rhetorician Dion Chrysostom. One could, perhaps, find other parallels in Philo.

The Hebrew had no definite theory of man's nature or of God's ubiquity. He was not in the least disturbed by any philosophical difficulties about a God outside the world who must be "far" from man. He had no difficulty in finding God: or rather he had no doubt as to the road. Through goodness unto God: but not through perfection. Pride stood in the way : to the repentant sinner the path lay open. " To them that repent he granteth a return, and he cheereth them that fail in hope." He had no theory of God being within him and of himself being in God, but without the theory he practically realised its results.

I do not say that for the Jew reared mainly on the Old Testament, the Liturgy and Rabbinical excerpts, there is nothing in this respect to be gained from Philo and the Fourth Gospel. We want the justification as well as the simpler and more popular expressions of that faith which it seeks to justify. Nor can we afford to lose this union of Greek and Hebrew thought as exemplified in the Johannine Gospel. For it is no mere union : it is religious genius working upon its twofold material with majestic effect and thrilling beauty. Nor again would I for a moment deny that, owing to the absence of this union between Greek and Hebrew, and also to the greater difficulty of loving God and feeling him near than of loving and feeling near the less abstract Christ, the Jewish religion, at any rate from the days of Moses Mendelssohn, the rationalist, has been somewhat exposed to the dangers of " Moralism." Hence it is that a sympathetic study of the Johannine writings may help some of us (without the least infraction of our purer monotheism) to a more vivid and habitual sense of communion between ourselves and God, and a keener consciousness of the Divine presence.

Dr. Martineau, the great Unitarian philosopher and divine, goes further than this, and becomes, as I think, not only unjust to the Judaism, whether Palestinian or Hellenistic, which had preceded Christianity, but exaggerates the debt we owe to the Fourth Gospel itself. In the Johannine theology he tells us " there is contained one vital element, which, however questionably reached, transcends in truth and power the level of the Synoptists' Gospel."

It so construes the personality of Christ, so avails itself of his characteristics, as to abolish the difference of essence between the Divine and the human nature, and substitute for the obedience of dependence the sympathy of likeness and the fellowship of trust. In appearance, it unites the qualities of God and man in *one* case only, and centres the blended glory in a single incarnation. But there it does not end. The unexampled spectacle of such " grace and truth," of heavenly sanctity penetrating all human experiences, startles and wins hearts that never were so drawn before, and wakes in them a capacity for that which they reverence in another. This attraction of affinity there could not be, were there not divine possibilities secreted and a divine persuasion pleading in each soul. There cannot be a chasm of forbidding antipathy and alienation, rendering for ever inaccessible to man the very " beauty of holiness " which he already adores ; nor is there any hindering curse to be bought off, before he can enter on the new life of self-consecration. There is no longer need of despair at the seemingly hopeless task of climbing the heavens and finding the unapproachable God. For He himself comes unsought, and lifts the latch of our nature when we thought the door was shut, and makes his abode with us (John xiv. 23), seeking us with his love, finding us with his truth, and claiming us with his righteousness. Thus does the Paraclete perpetuate and universalise the impersonation of the Son of God in the Son of Man, and carry it through the spiritual history of the world, and convert the life of Humanity itself into a Theophany.[1]

He emphasizes the newness of the Johannine teaching in another passage more definitely still—

And so the great end is reached, that the mingling of the Divine and the human in Christ is not there on its own account, as a gem of individual biography, unique and unrepeated ; but as the type and the expression of a fact in the constitution of our nature. The intimate relation between God and man, which declared itself in the utterance, "I am not alone, but the Father is with me," belongs to the essence of the soul and consecrates every human life. Nor is it anything but simple and indisputable truth to say that the consciousness of this has taken its commencement from the experience and religion of Jesus, and has imparted to Christendom its deeper tone of feeling, its higher conception of purity, and its inextinguishable hope for humanity.[2]

Now I think it is nothing but "simple and indisputable truth" to *deny* that the consciousness of the intimate relation between God and man took its commencement from the experience and religion of Jesus. He probably felt that relation with intense keenness, but the relation itself, as a known joy and satisfaction, is far older. It existed among the men who wrote the Psalter, and, *mirabile dictu*, it existed among the men who wrote the Talmud. "The chasm of forbidding antipathy and alienation, the hindering curse to be bought off," never existed for the Jewish consciousness at all, and therefore it was not the Fourth, or any other Gospel, which did away with them. There never existed as a dominant feature in the Jewish religion, from Isaiah to Jesus, or from Jesus to Mendels-

---

[1] *Seat of Authority*, p. 449.　　　　[2] *Ibid.*, p. 509.

sohn, any "despair at the seemingly hopeless task of climbing the heavens, and finding the unapproachable God." Therefore, it was not the Fourth, or any other Gospel, which had to annul a non-existent despair.

Whether we indeed can say that there is no difference of essence between the Divine and the human nature, so that we should be grateful to the Fourth Gospel for abolishing it, is another and more doubtful question. So far as this merely means that "there are divine (*i.e.* rational) possibilities secreted and a divine persuasion pleading in each soul," that there is an affinity between the human and the divine reason, and *therefore* between human and divine goodness, we may admit it; but in that case the double theory of the Fourth Gospel, first, that only a select number of men possess this affinity, and secondly, that the sense of it was never wakened and the power of it never realized before the teaching of Christ, or since his advent by unbelievers, is wholly and radically false. When, therefore, it is said of the Fourth Gospel that it is *one* writing out of others, which teaches this affinity and its possible issues, however "questionable" the manner of its presentment of the doctrine may be, we accept and register the claim. But when the discovery and the sense of glad communion with God, and of the intimate relation between the human and the divine, is asserted to be the patent and prerogative of one religion only and of a single book, we are bound to demur and to protest. We render our homage to the genius of the Fourth Evangelist: we recognise his great contribution to the spiritual store of humanity, but, in homely, though pregnant language, we must not give him more than his due, nor in order to pay our debt of gratitude to the Hellenistic Christian, rob the Jew, whether from Palestine or Alexandria, of all we owe him and still shall owe.

Of the Fourth Gospel an outsider can say and feel what a student of philosophy can feel and say of the great philosophers. Such a student may learn and profit from

E 2

them all, though he be a disciple and follower of none. So Dr. Martineau says of the philosophers whose teachings he expounds so lucidly in his *Ethical Theories*, that there is none to whom he is not grateful for intellectual service or delight. So to the outsider a great work of genius such as the Fourth Gospel must always be suggestive, helpful, stimulating. There must be many ways of expressing the inexpressible, many ways, in other words, of setting forth by and to our human minds the nature of God and of his relation to man. One way will seem truer to us than another, but the less true in one respect may be the more true in another; and in whatever form a theory of God may be presented, and however unacceptable it may seem, it may yet contain aspects and germs of valuable truth, which in another form, though, as a whole, purer and truer, are either wanting or less prominent. So from the doctrine of the Logos, as it is presented to us both by Philo and the Fourth Evangelist, we may find something to learn and to cherish, some religious profit and truth for the nurture and benefit of our souls. The Logos of Philo is more abstract, but also more impersonal; far less capable of rousing emotion and enthusiasm, but at the same time less invasive of the Divine unity. There is nothing in the Philonic Logos to stimulate affection or move to self-sacrifice; no ideal of love and pity to imitate and adore; but at the same time no devolution of the Divine perfections upon any aspect of Deity separate or separable from the self-sufficient and infinite Father. For these reasons the two presentments of the Logos theory have, for the outsider, each its own merits and each its own defects. The identification of the Logos with Jesus, and the plenary incarnation of the Godhead in the person of Christ, were fraught, as it seems to him, with peculiar danger. The Jew as well as the Unitarian can, I should imagine, largely appreciate and concur in the judgment of Dr. Mackintosh, who says:—

The moment the Church, by recognising the divinity of Christ, abandoned the position of monotheism pure and simple, it placed itself on an inclined plane, or on what a popular preacher has called the "down grade"; and that it should descend, sooner or later, to the worship of the Virgin and the saints was inevitable. Nothing but the evangelic doctrine in its purity and freshness—the living conception of God as our heavenly Father—could deliver the soul of man from the spirit of fear and diffidence before the Unseen Power so as to enable it to dispense with the Logos idea, and, consequently, with all inferior and subordinate agents of the divine will. The monotheistic doctrine, in its physical or non-moral aspects, is to this day, and always has been, the strength of Mahometanism. In the moral and humane aspect of it, as presented by Jesus, it has yet to prove the strength of Christianity by the overthrow of all competing cults, and of superstition in every shape.[1]

But this moral and humane aspect of the monotheistic doctrine is nothing but the purest Judaism. What seems to one student a return to the best and earliest Christian teaching seems to another a return to the best and most developed presentation of Judaism. The doctrine of Jesus may be regarded either as pure Christianity or pure Judaism. Either way of looking at it contains a truth.

Nevertheless, though men may possibly learn to dispense with the "Logos-idea," they will scarcely without detriment to the richness and variety of their religious life, dispense with some of the thoughts which it fostered and diffused. To the Jew the Evangelist's " Even as thou, Father, art in me, and I in thee, that they also may be in us" will seem to involve a false and needless subtlety of distinction in the Divine nature. But the Epistle's simpler doctrine: "If we love one another, God abideth in us;" " he that abideth in love, abideth in God, and God abideth in him," remains, and the Jew and the outsider may seek to appropriate and realize its truth as well as the Christian believer. "Love" is more universal than "wisdom," and therefore the Epistle's doctrine is in this sense wider and nobler than the equivalent and parallel teaching of Philo, for whom

[1] *The Natural History of the Christian Religion.* By Dr. William Mackintosh. 1894. p. 503.

the soul of the wise is inhabited by God. The fool may transcend the philosopher: Parsifal is nearer God than Faust. And with these sayings of the Johannine epistle we may fitly combine the adage of the Acts: " In him we live and move and have our being." For this more abstract statement, which, as we have seen, gives an Hellenic and philosophic justification to the Hebrew idea of God's nearness and omniscience, goes also beyond the notion which it justifies. Its value to many persons consists in this, that without destroying or infringing upon the idea of God's transcendence, it uses the omnipresence of God in such a way as to make man himself contained in that Divine ubiquity. Of course it does not really *explain* the true relation of God to man, and it is liable to perversion. If we are in God, we are a part of God, and if we are a part of God, every aspect of ourselves is equally divine. What then becomes of goodness and sin ; and where is their difference ? What becomes of human responsibility, without which no moral life is possible, and the facts of morality incapable of explanation ? If God is *in* nature, we may try to believe that its horrors are really beneficent, its cruelty imaginary, its malignancy merely apparent; but what we must not try to believe is that our own sin and our own vileness are only apparent too, or that they can be explained away by any theories of "absolute idealism " or of divine immanence. These lead perilously near to many pantheistic aberrations. The Jewish conception of God and of his relation to man will take its stand upon the separate self-consciousness of both man and God. Judaism will, I imagine, thoroughly concur with that splendid chapter of Dr. Martineau's "Study of Religion," in which he deals with Pantheism.

The voluntary nature of moral beings must be saved from Pantheistic absorption, and be left standing, as, within its sphere, a free cause other than the Divine, yet homogeneous with it . . . . Are we then to find God in the sunshine and the rain, and to miss him in our thought, our duty, and our love ? Far from it. He is with us in both ; only in the former it is his *immanent life*, in the latter his *transcendent* with which we are in communion. It is not indeed *He* that, under the mask of our personality, does our thinking, and prays against our temptations, and weeps our tears ; these are truly our own ; but they are in presence of a sympathy free to answer, spirit to spirit, neither merging in the other, but both at one in the same inmost preferences and affections.[1]

But within these limitations, the doctrine, " In him we live and move and have our being," or " Thou in me and I in thee," has still its value. It is a way of expressing this further truth, not only that God helps man as from without, but that in the Psalmist's phrase the Divine Spirit helps him from within. It means that man is only then most free when he may most fitly be called the child of God, and that at his best the difference between his action and the action of God in him falls away. He is then most himself, when he is most at one with God : " Not my work, but God in me." It implies not merely that God, if you are good and humble, helps you in your toil, sustains you in your struggle, and lifts you to himself, but that all your best work and striving are part and parcel of the divine process of things, links in the chain of evolution, lapped round and embraced by the divine infinitude, but yet a portion of it, however infinitesimal, fulfilling its allotted space, and necessary to the whole. It looks away from sin and lust and madness, and thinks only of the good, whether in failure or success, and it finds in this thought of man's best life as lived in God—the everlasting arms beneath us and around—a consolation and a solace, a sustainment and a strength, which no mere outward God, however wise, powerful and good, could possibly inspire.

I feel inclined to ask in conclusion whether there is anything in these selected excellencies of the Johannine writings which is not in full accord with Judaism, or which is out of harmony with the main drift and current of its teaching. The answer, I believe, is " None."

---

[1] *Study of Religion*, 2nd ed., Vol. ii., p. 167, 179.

For certainly the spiritual or symbolic use of words like life and death, light and darkness, bread and water, is not un-Jewish. We find it in the Hebrew Scriptures. That "God is a Spirit," is, as we contend, in easier accord with Jewish than with Christian orthodoxy, and the true method of his worship, indicated by the Evangelist, is now as axiomatic in the Jewish as in the Christian Church. If the adage that "God is love," may be looked upon as a brief summing up in three words of such verses as Psalm cxlv. 8 and 9, and other parallel passages; if love is goodness raised to the highest power, then is the doctrine of the Johannine Epistle the doctrine also of the modern Synagogue.

Nor is there any reason why the Immanence of God, so far as we hold it to be true, should not be taught and maintained by Judaism. It suits certain theologians to caricature the Jewish "transcendental" or "outside" God, but Jews need not be irritated by these foolish misrepresentations. So long as we suffer no violation of the Divine unity and spirituality, we are free to teach, as even orthodox Jews throughout the ages have taught, an immanent as well as a transcendent aspect of the Divine Being. So long as we keep rigidly within the limits of Theism, we may include within our conception of God, and of His relation to man, whatever truth we can find in the idea of the "Divine within the human." The oldest historic Theism of the world is serviceable still. And lastly there is one more point in the catalogue of the Fourth Gospel's merits which we may also with, I trust, increasing accuracy, accept as consistent with Judaism—I mean its universalism. Indeed, the Judaism of to-day is far more universal than the Gospel. For we have attained to a universalism of creed, as well as of race, and the famous "other sheep I have, which are not of this fold," if we only interpret the Shepherd as God, is nowhere now preached more earnestly than from Jewish pulpits. I trust that in God's own good time it will become a principle of action, as well as of faith, so that when the bond of race shall be recognised as obsolete, the bond of religion shall wax firmer and still more firm. Community in religious practice shall yet, perchance, be wedded to community in religious belief, and in this union shall lie the Jewish kinship of the future. Τὸ συγγενὲς οὐχ αἵματι μετρεῖται μόνον, πρυτανευούσης ἀληθείας, ἀλλὰ πράξεων ὁμοιότητι καὶ θήρᾳ τῶν αὐτῶν. We may well take to heart and apply, with due measure of enlargement and difference, these striking words of the Alexandrian sage.

NOTE.—From some friendly hands, through which this article passed in proof, I received certain criticisms upon it, of part of which the following is the substance :—

" You are not so sympathetic a critic of the Fourth Gospel as of Paul. Parts of it, at any rate, you interpret in too narrow and literal a way. For example, your judgment of the writer's ethical point of view is not as wide and scholarly as it should be. You touch his weak points, it is true, but you do not distinguish finely in doing so. A fuller attempt to search for the *humanity* of the author, his character, the possible influences round him, and the purpose with which he wrote, would not have altered your main conclusions, but would yet have given a more sympathetic tone to your criticism, and have been more impressive to your readers.

" You isolate the Fourth Gospel too severely ; you criticise it rather too much as if its sayings had been written yesterday for our special edification. Now, in the author's day, there would have been probably far fewer examples of a belief which was a mere intellectual assent, and so, too, the divorce between belief and action would not have been as common as it is now. 'In the glow of the moment,' to use your own words, while not forgetting the wideness of God's mercies, a man might yet have asserted that between the believer in Christ and the non-believer, not as a matter of intellect, but in a moral and spiritual sense, the difference was real and wide. It was the very spirituality and idealism of the author which drove him to assume that the whole man was transformed by his belief, so that ' believer ' and 'unbeliever' tended to become synonymous with 'righteous' and ' unrighteous.' And if, on the other hand, he asserted that only the good could believe, that in a sense is accepted by you also, for you say that the scamp cannot realize God. You seem readily to perceive and allow for enthusiasm and excitement in Paul, but not in the Fourth Evangelist. But perhaps there is excitement, though of a different kind, in the Evangelist too. It is a sort of intellectual white-heat. Thus throughout it seems as if the criticism was a little harder and cruder than it should, or need have been, because you have not taken a sufficiently historical and understanding view of the whole.

"Perhaps the new truth (as it seemed to him) came upon the writer of the Fourth Gospel like a dazzling blaze of light, which half-blinded him, as Paul, some think, was physically half-blinded, by its very excess of splendour. He looks out, ever after, with what one might perhaps rather oddly call a dualistic vision upon the world. But he was not a philanthropist like Paul. Keenly anxious that the light which he saw should shine throughout the world, he was impatient and incredulous of those who passed it by. Possibly, nevertheless, you might have been more accurate had you shown more tenderness for the man who said so much about love; but who in his intense antagonism to sin, or to what he too rashly thought sin, seemed unable, or was afraid to let love come in."

How far this criticism is cogent I cannot now inquire. It is at any rate interesting and suggestive. Any stray reader of the article will, I am sure, be glad to read its Note.

C. G. MONTEFIORE.

RABBINIC JUDAISM
AND THE
EPISTLES OF ST. PAUL

by
C[LAUDE] G. MONTEFIORE

THE
JEWISH QUARTERLY REVIEW

JANUARY, 1901

RABBINIC JUDAISM AND THE EPISTLES OF ST. PAUL[1].

IT is with great diffidence that I venture to address the company whom I see before me this afternoon. It was, indeed, with much reluctance that I accepted the kind and liberal offer which was made me that I should speak to the St. Paul Association on a matter so delicate and difficult as that which is my subject to-day. First of all, I am no learned scholar, and if it were not that I have had a learned friend upon whose unstinted assistance I could rely, I should have been unable to accept the task at all. But without wearying you further by dwelling in detail upon personal deficiencies —" protesting too much " has an evil sound—let me pass at once to the difficulties inherent in my subject, difficulties which would and should be felt by every honest scholar, however learned and however industrious he might be.

The most exact title for my lecture would, I fancy, be : " The relation of St. Paul's Epistles to the Jewish religion." And Jewish should be understood to mean Rabbinical. Hence, what I have to do, so far as one lecture can do it, lies, as it were, in between the provinces of two other lectures,

[1] An Address delivered before the St. Paul Association on November 21, 1900.

which are closely related to, but not exactly equivalent to
my own. Mine partly overlaps the other two, but is not
wholly coterminous with them. The one of these two
other subjects would be : " The Jewish religion of the first
century after Christ." *That* lecture is far wider than mine.
It would deal with the Jewish religion as a whole, and
deal with it apart from St. Paul. It is a lecture, or rather
it is a book, which needs doing because you will not get
a fair and full estimate of early Judaism until this constant
reference to the dominating figure of Paul is cleared out of
the way. But I am speaking to a St. Paul association, and
therefore your interest in Judaism is rightly and properly
relative to its bearing upon the great apostle. Thus in
preparing this lecture I had to keep one eye fixed upon the
epistles, and one upon the Rabbinical literature. That is
a position alike unnatural and unwholesome, and my lecture,
like many other writings and books upon the Rabbinical
religion, will bear upon it the traces of a squint.

Now the other lecture, with which my own largely but
not absolutely coincides, would be called: " The Jewish
background in the Epistles of St. Paul." I have imagined
that you want something a little wider than that, or, at all
events, that you want me to look at the matter from
a slightly different point of view. I shall not minutely
inquire how great that Jewish background may be.
That also would involve a long discussion, more suited
for a book than a lecture. I shall not ask, though the
question is of grave importance, and has not yet been
completely and satisfactorily answered, how far did Paul
exaggerate his Judaism, more especially his Rabbinical
Judaism, when it suited his purpose and his rhetoric to do
so. Nor shall I inquire, though the subject is full of interest,
how far Paul's Judaism was rather modelled on the
Hellenistic Judaism of Philo than on the Rabbinic Judaism
of Hillel, Gamaliel, or Akiba. I have to take the six
central epistles as I find them, and without discussing the
past influences which went to their production, to consider

their general relation to the Rabbinical religion of the time.

But alas! "The Rabbinical religion of the time" was my phrase, and clearly that is what we want to consider, but where are the sources, where is the material? Roughly speaking there are two kinds of literature available. The first kind consists of books, most or many of which were originally written in Hebrew, but which are now only preserved in Ethiopic, Greek, Latin, or other translations. These books comprise what is known as the Apocalyptic literature, of which Daniel in the Old Testament is the prototype, and the Revelation of St. John in the New Testament the most famous and widely known example. This apocalyptic literature, for reasons upon which I cannot now dwell, may only be used with great care and caution in dealing with the Rabbinical religion[1]. Moreover, written not in unpointed and unfamiliar Hebrew, or in equally unpointed and still more unfamiliar Aramaic, and far smaller in compass, it is more known to and studied by Christian scholars, and its contents and teaching are more easily available. For this present lecture it may safely be neglected. The other kind of literature from which our knowledge of the Jewish religion may more rightly and properly be drawn is the Rabbinic literature, and consists of the many volumes of the Talmuds and the Midrashim. Now this literature is, nevertheless, not so hidden away as many people imagine. A considerable bulk of that very portion of it which has most direct bearing upon the Rabbinic religion as a whole, has been translated into German or French. And if certain distinguished scholars would make a more frequent, prolonged, and impartial use of these humble but useful "cribs," they would, I think, make fewer mistakes about the Rabbinical religion than, unfortunately, is now the case.

This, however, is but a hint, and perhaps a rude one, by

[1] Cp. Schechter, "Some Aspects of Rabbinic Theology." *J.Q.R.*, vol. **VI**, pp. 407, 408 (July, 1894).

the way. The serious thing I have to point out is, that though the Talmudic and Midrashic literature is of vast extent, its dates are very dubious and confused. Much of it was not only written down, but even said or composed long after the death of St. Paul. Especially for the first century are the certain sources doubtful and few. Of Gamaliel, the reputed teacher of Paul, we know hardly anything, for his activity is merged in that of the "School of Hillel [1]." Much or most of the Talmudic material belongs to the third, fourth, and fifth centuries of the Christian era. Nevertheless, with caution and prudence, we may rightly use these late ill-dated sources as material for our subject, and for the following reasons.

The main elements of the Rabbinic religion underwent little change from 50 to 500 A.D. Above all, the central position of the Law was not shaken or altered. If the religion was "nomistic" in 50, it was assuredly no less nomistic in 500. The formative period was already over in the age of St. Paul. While, therefore, the strangest results would ensue from attempting to depict the Christianity of the first century out of the literature of the fifth and sixth, the same untoward results need not be feared from using Jewish material on similarly anachronistic lines. Christian scholars of to-day are wont to draw a sharp distinction between the Jewish religion before and after the Maccabean revolt. As the Psalms are now commonly ascribed to the post-Nehemian era, and as these sacred lyrics scarcely show the awful consequences of legalism, it is customary to say that all the immoralities and irreligiousness of the Rabbinic religion only began to bloom and flourish after the death of Judas the Maccabee. They were in full swing by 50 A.D., but I have never read in the work of any German theologian that between 50 and 500 there was any improvement whatever. And here I entirely agree with the theologians. The general effects of the Law, both for good

---

[1] For Gamaliel, the student may consult Graetz, *Geschichte der Juden*, Hamburger's *Real-Encyclopädie des Talmud*, Hastings' *Bible Dictionary*, &c.

and evil, were (with one exception) the same in 500 as in 50; in both directions, indeed, if both directions there be, it is probably true to say that while those effects were deepened and hardened at the later date, their main character and tendency remained throughout these centuries the same. If I use the material by which some Christian scholars give so one-sided a picture of the law and its results, in order to present what I believe to be a truer and more historic, though a far less picturesque and harmonious statement, I cannot reasonably be called to book. What is usable on the one side is usable on the other.

Not that I want to give you an hour of apologetics. Heaven forbid. I shall freely recognize the limitations, the dangers, and the shortcomings of the Rabbinic religion, just as I shall freely recognize the greatness and the truth in the religious teaching of St. Paul. But where I differ from most speakers or writers on this subject, whether Jewish or Christian, is, that I apply these substantives to both sides of my subject ; I recognize the greatness and the truth in the religious teaching of the Rabbis, and—if you will show an English toleration in listening to such words— the limitations, the dangers, and the shortcomings in the doctrine of St. Paul.

Let me here say, before closing more nearly with my subject, that Paul means for me to-day those six epistles, the genuineness of which is recognized by the vast majority of scholars [1]. I will not discuss whether the remaining epistles (or the speeches in the Acts) are or are not genuine. Those who hold that they are do not the less admit the authenticity of the central six, and these six contain enough material, or rather suggest sufficient considerations and difficulties, for our purpose to-day.

In the writer, then, of those six epistles there are four separate strands to be distinguished. I will mention them in the wrong order. There is first of all the originality of

[1] 1 Thessalonians, 1 and 2 Corinthians, Galatians, Romans, Philippians.

the great man, the flash of genius which illumines and
transfigures. But upon what did this genius work? We
have, then, as the second strand, Christianity, by which
I mean whatever came to Paul by revelation, tradition,
or any other means, concerning the life and death and
resurrection of Christ. Then there is that with which
these two former strands intermingled. For, thirdly, we
have Hellenism, an element in the Pauline Epistles, the
extent of which is still under discussion. This Hellenism,
whatever its amount, had a double source. On the one
hand, there was the direct contact of St. Paul's mind with
the Hellenism of his day. How far that went is debated,
and perhaps unascertainable. On the other hand, there
was the influence of Hellenism refracted through a Jewish
medium. If there is one thing certain about the Epistle
to the Romans, it is that its author had read and used
the Wisdom of Solomon. Now that book is saturated
with Hellenistic elements. This single fact gives rise to
many reflections; it suggests possibilities which cannot
be pursued here. I will only just say this: Philo, who was
a contemporary of St. Paul, uses, as you all know, the letter
of the Pentateuch for elaborate philosophical allegorizing.
The real value of the Law lies for him not in what it says,
but in what it implies; not in its literal meaning, but in its
underlying spiritual significations. Philo nevertheless was
a strictly observant Jew. But there were others who went
beyond him, and whom he sharply censures. "There are
some," he says, "who, when they have discovered the
spiritual meaning of the law, think that they are free from
the letter, and need no longer observe the ordinances."
Hellenistic Judaism must have produced more than one
type of mind, and there may have been Paulists before
Paul. But into the mazes of this obscure and controversial
subject I cannot enter [1]. There is lack of knowledge as well
as lack of time. Last of my four strands comes Judaism,

---

[1] Cp. M. Friedländer, *Zur Entstehung des Christenthums* (1894), and *Der
vorchristliche jüdische Gnosticismus* (1898).

the Rabbinical Judaism with which we are immediately concerned.

Now I do not want to imply that only one-fourth of Paul is Jewish, or to be accounted for by Judaism. Such arithmetical calculations would obviously be absurd. But true it is that there is much in Paul which, while dealing with Judaism, is inexplicable by Judaism.

Please do not misunderstand me. I am only giving you my personal opinion, and all the great Christian theologians would say that I am hopelessly and childishly wrong. They would tell you that I am blinded by prejudice, and utterly unable to see or to appreciate the facts of the case. So all I would say is : keep an open mind, and—if the subject interests you and you know French and German— *read the cribs.* You will be horribly bored by them (their form is usually so repellent and their matter frequently so dull), but I think they will give you pause before accepting the judgments of the theologians on the relation of St. Paul to the Jewish religion.

As my own individual opinion, then, I repeat that there is much in Paul which, while dealing *with* Judaism, is inexplicable *by* Judaism.

Paul has been called by Wellhausen the great pathologist of Judaism [1]. I venture to assert that this is just what he was not. The Jesus of the Synoptic Gospels *was* a critic and pathologist of Judaism. *His* criticisms are real : they are flesh and blood. There are, be it observed, parallels to and illustrations of them in the Rabbinical literature. Jesus put his finger upon real sore places : upon actual dangers, limitations, shortcomings. But the author of the Epistle to the Romans fights, for the most part, in the air. He sets up imaginary evils, and with superb eloquence and admirable rhetoric he brushes them away. His conception of the Law—for we are all agreed that everything turns on this—is unreal. The Jews must have understood the diatribes of Jesus well enough. Even if they thought them

---

[1] *Prolegomena zur Geschichte Israels* (fifth edition), p. 430.

exaggerated—and in the form in which we have them
perhaps they are so—they would yet have known well
enough what he was driving at. The spurious Pharisees—
of whom the Talmud speaks as well as Jesus—knew where
the shoe pinched. But Paul's criticisms of the Law would
have glided off a Jewish reader like water off a duck's
back. They do not touch the spot.

Let us consider for a moment the real evils and defects
which Jesus found and censured in the religion of his
time. They were mainly three. There was, first, the putting
of ritual in the place of morality. Secondly, there was
self-righteousness or pride. Thirdly, there was a certain ill-
directed intellectualism. With divers passages of Romans
and Corinthians before your minds, it may seem to you
a ludicrous statement if I venture to say that with none
of these evils has Paul any prolonged or vital concern.
Yet modern exegesis has established the fact that Paul's
attack upon the Law *as* Law does not differentiate between its moral and its ceremonial elements. Nowhere
in connexion with his elaborate argumentations about the
inefficacy of the Law, does he make the charge that
the Jews or the Pharisees were keen to obey its ritual
but neglected its moral ordinances. The Law is the
strength of sin, not in virtue of its containing a number
of purely ritual enactments, but because it is law and all
that law implies. Again, though Paul has a vast deal to
say about boasting, that which he censures is in reality
quite different to the practical and everyday evils which
are so nobly castigated by Jesus. Many of his remarks
about "boasting" are directed against the assumptions
and actions of his Jewish-Christian antagonists, with the
validity of which we have nothing to do ; but where they
are directed against Jews, they are far more theoretical
than practical. They refer not to the evil characters of
living men, boasters of flesh and blood, but to that theoretical boasting, which, according to the Pauline theory,
must inevitably accompany any attempt to seek justification

by the works of the Law. It is the theological opposition
between human merit and divine grace which is the dominating subject before the writer's mind, not an actual
society of men. And so as regards intellectualism. There
was a marked intellectual element in Rabbinic Judaism ;
it constituted both an excellence and a defect, a strength
and a weakness. Jesus criticizes it from the point of view
of its weakness, its real living weakness in relation to the
lives of his contemporaries. But Paul's depreciation of
wisdom and of knowledge springs from different roots and
has different implications. He is partly alluding to strife
within Christian limits, and partly to the old theoretical
opposition between human achievement and divine grace.

Hence it is that, with one tremendous exception to prove
my rule, the defects of Rabbinic Judaism are little illustrated by St. Paul. So to explain him, or stand to him
in the relation of a dark foil, compared to which, like
" star i' the darkest night," his brilliance shall shine more
nobly, the commentators and theologians have had to make
up a Rabbinic religion of their own, to point the moral and
adorn their tale.

Every great religion has the defects of its qualities. It
may be difficult to recognize them in our own religion, but
at all events we can easily discern them in the religions of
our neighbours. Such defects there clearly are both in
Protestantism and Catholicism. Such defects, too, there
were and are in Rabbinic Judaism. But while these evils
explain and illustrate the sayings and sermons of Jesus,
they only very partially explain and illustrate the Epistles
of St. Paul. This daring statement I ought to make
good. For lack of time I can do little but dogmatize : but,
given the time, the task could be achieved.

Here I must put in two saving clauses. If my thesis
were true, the puzzles and difficulties in the Epistles of
St. Paul would certainly be increased. But it does not,
therefore, follow that the thesis must necessarily be false.
Truth is often complex and difficult. Secondly, I must not

be understood to mean that the Pauline Epistles as a whole cannot be illustrated and illuminated in a hundred ways by a reference to Rabbinic literature and religion. It is obvious that there are numerous elements in St. Paul's theology on which Rabbinic Judaism throws the greatest light. Paul's monotheism, his use of the Old Testament, his conception of the Messiah, his doctrine of angels and devils, the central place occupied in his system by eschatological considerations—all these and many other interesting points are illustrated by and stand in close connexion with parallel or analogous doctrines in the Rabbinic religion. Just because these are the more obvious and the safer points, I shall say nothing about them in the present lecture. I have to concentrate my attention and yours upon the Rabbinic doctrine of the Law as illustrating or *not* illustrating Paul's conception of it as the strength of sin.

It is possible that one or two of those here present may read some of the German and French translations from the Rabbinic literature, or they may read Weber's standard book on "Jewish Theology." May I suggest two cautions, both of which are germane to our present purpose? First of all to compare St. Paul with the Midrash would be unfair. St. Paul was a religious genius of the first order, who writes in the flush of a fresh enthusiasm. The Midrash is a confused jumble of sermons, parables, sayings, and anecdotes, without system or plan. There are indeed occasional flashes of genius, but most of it is of very second and third rate order of literary merit. You must (I imagine) compare the writings of the Rabbis not with the New Testament but with the Fathers.

My second caution is of far greater importance. It is also more difficult to realize and explain, and it deserves a whole lecture for its adequate justification and support. *St. Paul is far more systematic than the Rabbis.*

There are indeed contradictions and antinomies in the Pauline theology, but yet the main lines of argument are

firmly maintained. We have certain central theories carefully and insistently worked out. But with the Rabbis
it is all very different. You can make a digest and system
of their law, but a system of their theology you can only
make with the utmost caution and with many reservations.
It is in their theology that they let their exuberant
fancy run wild. There all is incidental, casual and unsystematic. A deliberately playful and fanciful exegesis
is pushed to the wildest extremes. Earnest and jest go
cheek by jowl; wayward exaggeration and stern simplicity
intermingle. Opinions on the one side are met by opinions
on the other; the widest latitude is freely allowed. It is
all familiar and among friends; there is no effort or
restraint; you see the speakers at their worst and best.
Here, then, is the obvious danger of such a book as Weber's,
which cuts up the Rabbinic theology into ordered chapters
and paragraphs, and makes a system out of confusion.
Even if a book on those lines were written by a South Sea
Islander who did not care a brass farthing what the
Rabbinic religion was, whether for good or for evil, it would
be dangerous. The subject is full of pitfalls. But when
written by an Evangelical Christian who is constantly
thinking of the Epistles of Paul, and is haunted by
parallels and contrasts, it becomes more dangerous still.
Indeed, after lately reading Weber's book three times
through, I am astonished that such a book written on
such lines by such a writer should be as good as it is.
His very honesty enables us often to correct Weber
by Weber. But even so it must be read with caution.
For he who wants to make a system where system
there is none, inevitably falls into error. And so it is
with Weber. He presses some passages to mean more
than they can bear; he minimizes others which qualify or
contradict them. He neglects contexts; he takes jest for
earnest, the elegant antitheses of a sermon for the ordered
pronouncements of dogma. Paul is doubtless illustrated
by Weber's book, but instead of a real religion full of

inconsistencies, yet palpitating with life, you have a one-
sided and artificial system of dry theological opinions.

You would, I think, be in error if you suppose that
I have laboured this point too lengthily. It is of more
importance than at first sight it seems. Paul, according to
my assertion, is more systematic than the Rabbis. Illustrate
this and its consequences by the juridic elements in the
epistles. If Paul is more systematic in his theology, he is
also more juridic. Now you will always find in the textbooks that the juridic elements in the Pauline teaching are
those which he owes to Judaism. Juridic, moreover, is
a very convenient word. It is almost as good as legal.
It means transitory, unmystic, hard, irreligious, immoral.
That element, then, in Paul which is juridic, and therefore
implies all these dreadful things, is the Jewish element—
the element which he inherited from Gamaliel and the
Pharisees. That which remains is Hellenic, Christian,
original. But the truth is that Paul, in his dogmas about
the Law, is far more juridic than the Rabbis.

Modern Christian scholars, with certain honourable
exceptions, neglect the unjuridic elements of the Rabbinic
religion, while the juridic elements they harden and
exaggerate. It is more convenient and dramatic to do so,
but the question is: Should even the history of religions
be written in order to find picturesque facts and contrasts?
The desire works unconsciously. Paul must not be responsible for any defects; they must merely be remnants of the
old leaven. Do not imagine that I wish to exaggerate
Paul's defects, or to minimize and cheapen his great contribution to the development of true religion. I only ask
that we play the game fairly. Whether we criticize Paul
or the Rabbis, let us always be sure that we are hitting
above the belt. The caution is quite as much needed for
Jewish as for Christian theologians. And yet one might
have supposed it to be wholly superfluous. For surely we,
both Jew and Christian, have reached a loftier platform, and
breathe a purer air. For us, not only are there many

mansions in God's house, but there are many pathways by which to reach it. Paul could not understand that those rigid Rabbis were on the road, nor they that he was, and each must have been vastly astonished to meet the other. But for us such misunderstandings and astonishments have passed away.

In making the Law the pivot of my remarks to-day, I shall not be unfair either to the Rabbis or to Paul. For, as Weber rightly sees and affirms, the Law is the centre of the Jewish religion; all radiates out from the Law, and from it all depends. And, in another fashion and for different reasons, you can make the Law a centre for the treatment of the Pauline religion likewise. It is in opposition and antagonism to the Law that the apostle reaches the fundamental propositions of his theology. God and Christ, the divine scheme of salvation, human morality, past and present, are all related to the Law, so that in an inverted sort of way the Law may be said to be as important in Paul's system of religion as in the Judaism of the Rabbis.

What would the Epistle to the Romans be without the Law? Though the Law "came in between," its importance is tremendous. We have to remember the fragmentary shortness of human history in the Pauline conception of it. There is the period between Adam and Abraham about which the facts are few, there is the period from Abraham to Moses, and there is the period from Moses to Christ. *With Christ the end of this world was near at hand.* Though the Law only came with Moses, the third period of human history was more actual and living than either the second or the first.

What, then, was the Rabbinic conception of the Law, and of Israel's relation to God as conditioned by the Law, which we may assume to have been common and current in the days of Paul? For simplicity's sake I will here assume that the Hebrew word *Torah* is equivalent to the Pentateuchal Code, though in reality the *Torah* had a wider

connotation and a more far-reaching significance. But for
our present purpose the equivalence will do no harm. Let
us also remember and press the words: the *Rabbinic* conception of the Law. How far *Hellenistic* Judaism deviated
from that conception, and how far Paul before his conversion was a *Hellenistic* Jew, we are not to inquire.

God, then, in his perfect wisdom and goodness, has given
the Law to Israel for the divine glory and for Israel's
benefit. It is the good God who has given it, the God who
is not only just but also merciful, the God whose own
glory is closely connected with the fortunes of Israel. In the
gift there was no deception and no *arrière-pensée* or mental
reserve. God did not say one thing and mean another.
When he said that the Law should be Israel's wisdom,
Israel's honour, and Israel's good, he meant what he said.
Nor did he say it with the unexpressed idea at the back of
his mind, " Yes, the Law is all this if you obey it, but you
never can obey it, and you are not meant to obey it." He
gave it in sincerity and not in craft. The Law is the will
of God, the expression of his wisdom. Partly by those
powers of his which are themselves God-given, and partly
by the special aid of God, man, if he try his best, can
do the good God's will. It is true that God has made him
frail; it is true that God has created within him—why we
do not entirely know—two impulses, one towards good and
another towards evil, and it is true that man never passes
through the years of his pilgrimage upon earth without
yielding from time to time to the baser impulse, and breaking some of the commands of the good God's law. But
God is gracious and forgiving, and though he punishes as
well as rewards, yet there is no need for despair. Perhaps
the struggle to avoid sin, and to do and to be good, was
divinely intended in order to enable Israel the more
worthily to live the second life, the life after death, which,
in his infinite goodness and mercy, God has prepared for
them. The commands of the Law are necessarily good
and wise, for they are given by and are the direct outcome

of infinite wisdom and goodness. We ourselves can see the wisdom and the goodness of many of these laws. Some we may regard as greater than others, and God himself has told us of those on which he lays the greatest stress. But all the laws are his, and it is not for us to cavil where we, in our limited wisdom, are, likely enough, unable to understand. For the Laws are the will of God, our Father in Heaven, and to study and to accomplish that will, so clearly and so graciously revealed to us, is at once our holiest duty and our supremest joy.

That in barest outline is the Rabbinic conception of the Law. *That* was the conception of it in the days of Paul; *that*, I beg you to observe, is the conception held by many a simple Jewish believer at the present hour. It is perhaps in many ways a too easy and childish conception of religion, but if it is accurate, if, that is to say, my picture is correct, you can already realize how irrelevant to the ordinary Jew Paul's attack upon the Law must seem. And if Paul seems irrelevant, far more irrelevant, yes and far more absurd, seem those elaborate bogies of the Law decked out in mock horrors by the hands of Christian theologians.

The outline of the Rabbinic conception must now be filled up. The Law was given for Israel's benefit. In what sense is this word "benefit" used? In every conceivable sense, might be the answer. The different senses jostle upon each other in the Rabbinical literature, and certainly they are not all in perfect consistency with each other. The first and greatest of them undoubtedly is that through the Law Israel obtains eternal life. The life to come is the "reward" of a faithful observance of the Law upon earth. But faithful observance is far from meaning complete observance, and we may even go so far as to say that the merits and efficacy of the Law will in one way or another secure the life to come to almost every Israelite. I put this benefit first, because, though the eschatological motive and hope are less prominent in the rabbinical than in the apocalyptic literature, yet in some

respects they dominate and transfigure it almost as strongly
and vividly as they transfigure and dominate the epistles
of St. Paul. But what are the Law's benefits on earth?
What are its present rewards?

Oh, this terrible bogey of reward! German theologians
are wont to regard *Lohnsucht* as the main motive of the
Jewish religion. *Lohnsucht*, the search, the lust for reward.
A more cruel libel it would be impossible to imagine.
Because Paul declares that destruction will be the lot
of those who reject Christ, and eternal bliss the lot of
those who accept in glad faith the sacrifice of his death,
is *Lohnsucht* the motive of the believer? Because you
believe that there is a difference made after death between
the believer and the infidel, or between the saint and the
sinner, does that make your religion mercenary and
servile? Nay, even if you believe that in the last resort
God has so ordered the world of earth that honesty is the
best policy—and for the Jews this has been very hard
to believe even from Paul's days to our own—do you
necessarily serve God for hope of pay? Must true and
pure religion be attended with every kind of misery both
here and hereafter?

Over and over again do the Jewish teachers speak of the
rewards of the Law, but frequently do they tell their disciples that the motive for observance must not lie in the
desire to obtain them. Jewish scholars have pointed this
out time after time, but never a whit do the theologians
heed. "For its own sake" the Law must be observed;
the true Israelite should delight in the commandments
themselves more than in their rewards[1]. And what funny
rewards some of them are. Though the Jewish teachers
strongly held the view that the earth is good, and that
God has formed man to be happy upon it, to rejoice in his
portion, they did not shut their eyes to the actual lot of

---

[1] Cp. Schechter, "Some Aspects of Rabbinic Theology," *J.Q.R.*, vol. VI,
p. 642 (July, 1894), and the "Doctrine of Divine Retribution in the
Rabbinical Literature," *J.Q.R.*, vol. III, October, 1890, p. 49.

themselves and their contemporaries. Thus one of the greatest rewards of the Law are the sufferings received in its service. "Beloved are sufferings, for through sufferings Israel obtained three great gifts—the Law, the land of Israel, and the life to come [1]." Some of the supremest benefits of the Law are spiritual. By the Law Israel becomes a wise and holy nation, an exemplar to the world. By the Law and through the Law Israel finds happiness. But what sort of happiness? Surely one that cannot fairly be called mercenary. It is "the happiness of the commandments" to use the common Jewish phrase, the joy in doing God's will, the rapture in fulfilling the ordinances of God [2] Through the Law the Israelite draws near to God; he enters into communion with him. It is then that he feels the *Schechinah*—the presence of God—to be near him and about him [3].

How much we read in the theologians of the Law being external. It is a task-master ordering from without; it says "Thou shalt" and "Thou shalt not" but it supplies no inward force with which to obey these cut and dry commands, these cold, severe, and terrorizing ordinances. It was, indeed, given by God, but by a God distant, gloomy, and rigid, a Lawgiver and a Judge, not a Father and a Friend. I wonder if there is the smallest chance that you, unlike the theologians, will believe me when I say that all this business of the severe Judge and the stern Lawgiver is a figment and a bugbear? God to the Rabbis is certainly both Lawgiver and Judge, and even the Pauline Christian recognizes that there is such a thing as justice and judg-

---

[1] Cp. Weber, *Jüdische Theologie*, (2nd ed.), p. 322. Schechter, "Doctrine of Divine Retribution in the Rabbinical Literature," *J.Q.R.*, vol. III (October, 1890), pp. 45-49.

[2] Cp. *Bab. Talmud, Sabbath,* 30 *b*; *Pesachim*, 17 *a* (Wuensche, *Die haggadischen Bestandtheile des babylonischen Talmuds*, I, pp. 126, 241. But the passage from *Sabbath* 30 *b* is more fully translated in L. Goldschmidt's new translation (not yet completed) of the *Babylonian Talmud*, vol. I, p. 387.

[3] Cp. Weber, pp. 30, 31.

ment both in this world and in the next. But how can
you call that Lawgiver stern and cruel who gives the Jaws
for the benefit of his creatures, and who is ceaseless in his
love for them, who pities them in their sorrows, and on the
smallest pretext of repentance hastens to forgive them their
sins? Yet that is the Rabbinic conception of God, and endless passages of the Rabbinic literature are full of nothing
but proofs of it [1]. How can you call that Law external,
which is believed to be the will of God and, like God
himself, perfectly wise and perfectly good? It is no more
external than the Moral Law to the philosopher. Even
Dr. Cone, usually so fair and honest, seems to think that
a lawgiver and judge cannot also be gracious and loving.
Holtzmann, in his admirable exposition of Paul's theology, feels bound to speak of a "servile service under the
yoke of the Law [2]." "Servile service!" Wherein lies
the servility of serving God? It seems to me almost an
insult to common sense that I should have to show that
such a service, willingly offered, is not slavery but freedom. But because Paul says so, therefore it must be so.
Though the entire Rabbinic literature is one huge denial,
though the hypotheses on which Rabbinic Judaism rests,—
that God is infinitely good, that he loves Israel, that
he has given his Law to Israel out of love; that Israel,
believing in this doctrine about God, finds in the service of
God its greatest privilege; that the Law was originally
freely offered and freely accepted, and that this free offer
and free acceptance is continued from generation to
generation—though all these hypotheses are absolutely
inconsistent with the supposed servility, though there are
thousands of Pharisaic Jews to this day who live under
the Law and find in it no servitude—all this counts for
nothing. One would have thought that history would

---

[1] Even Weber gives some hints of this : cp. pp. 51, 52, 57-9, 61. But
the passages he quotes are mere drops from the ocean.

[2] Holtzmann, *Lehrbuch der neutestamentlichen Theologie*, II, p. 137. Orello
Cone, " Paul : the Man, the Missionary, and the Teacher " (1898), p. 348.

show how cautious we ought to be in accepting for literal truth what the man who has gone over to another faith, or experienced a great religious convulsion, says about the religion he has rejected or his own spiritual condition before his conversion, but, where Judaism is concerned, history has no voice or lesson for the Pauline theologians.

The Law to the Rabbi holds in many respects the same place as Jesus Christ to the Christian believer. Let me take the "servile service" as an illustration. It is freedom according to the Rabbinic teaching which is secured by the Law. Playing upon the word *Charuth* (graven) in the sentence, "And the writing was the writing of God graven upon the tables," a Rabbi observes : "Read not *Charuth*, but *Cheruth* (the Hebrew word for freedom), for none is free but he who is occupied in the learning of Thorah." Or again : "Every one who busies himself in the Thorah, he is a free man." Or again : "Happy art thou, O land, when thy king is a free man. And when is a land in this happy case ? When its king busies himself in the Law, for there is no free man but he who occupies himself with the Law." And again : "When law entered into the world freedom came with it [1]."

In any great religion the question is, Are you going to expound and assess it by its ideals and successes or by its defects and its failures ? Are you going to judge it by its sinners or its saints? But no such questions are asked about Rabbinic Judaism when it is used to illustrate St. Paul. According to Canon Gore, of whom I shall have more to say, it seems to have been one mass of "moral hollowness and rottenness, of pride, stagnation, conventionalism and hypocrisy." That is a pretty good list, especially when thrown in by the way, and so far as I

---

[1] Cp. *Aboth de R. Nathan*, II, p. 10 (ed. Schechter) ; *Bemidbar Rabba*, X, Wuensche's translation, p. 226 ; ibid. XVI, Wuensche, p. 426; *Shemot Rabba*, XLI ; Wuensche, pp. 291, 343 ; *Bereshit Rabba*, LIII ; Wuensche, p. 253 ; *Abot*, VI, 2 (ed. Taylor), &c.

can make out, *not* the result of patient and laborious perusal of the original authorities. Rabbinic Judaism has no ideals of excellence ; the darkness which is to throw Jesus and Paul into higher light must clearly be unrelieved. But would it not be fairer to deal with Rabbinic Judaism as you would deal with Catholicism or Calvinism ? In other words, not to rely exclusively on the works of converts and enemies for your judgment upon these great religions and on the men who lived under their sway, but while not neglecting such authorities, to study in the first instance their own literatures, and to make *these* your main sources and your chief tests ? What are the ideals ? What are the defects of those ideals ? How far did the actual men and women live up to the ideals ? How far did they fall victims to the defects ? Are you seriously able to believe that Rabbinic Judaism could send martyrs to the sword and the stake by hundreds and thousands, and yet be one mass of " pride, stagnation, conventionalism, hypocrisy, moral hollowness and rottenness "? Have the Jews never had any religious or moral virtues ? If so, whence did they obtain them except from the Law ? Or did some wonderful change for the better come over them after the days of Paul ? And if so, how did it come except by the Law ? Or was it the spectacle of Christian toleration and Christian love ?

The Law, then, as the wise and broadminded Dr. Taylor says, is " a charter of freedom[1]." That is the ideal. But can the Law be fulfilled ? And what does the attempt at its fulfilment involve ? I have no doubt that you are familiar with the two great, and to my mind contradictory, charges which are commonly brought against the Law. The first is that the Law as a whole is incapable of fulfilment. Failure provokes despair. The very multiplicity of its enactments—here the ritual side is mainly thought of—is an intolerable burden. There are laws to left of

---

[1] Taylor, C., "Sayings of the Jewish Fathers " (i. e. Abot). 2nd ed. Note on III, 8, p. 46.

you, laws to right of you, laws in front of you, thundering forth their orders and threats. Perpetual is your anxiety lest even inadvertently you may have transgressed or have omitted to fulfil. The second charge is that the Law causes pride. You are proud of its mere possession, and an easy outward conformity can well go together with " moral hollowness and rottenness " within. Some writers emphasize the first charge ; others the second. Thus Weber takes the line that the life of Judaism was a constant terror, Canon Gore insists mainly on the self-righteousness and the pride. The really ingenious thing to do is to ride on both stools at once, like Holtzmann who bravely accuses the Pharisees of *Selbstzufriedenheit* on the one hand and of *Friedlosigkeit des Gewissens* on the other.

It may be well to ask how far Paul himself is responsible for these charges and in what form. A careful reading will show, as I have already pointed out, how very different his position towards the Law is from that of Jesus in the Synoptic Gospels. The first charge is Pauline, but with a difference. The famous seventh chapter of the Romans has to do with moral and not with ceremonial ordinances. The point is that the Law, which orders from without and supplies and stimulates the consciousness of sin, provides no inward force with which man can resist and quell his sinful lusts and desires, and thus do the right or avoid the wrong. The dead letter is contrasted with the life-giving spirit. This spirit can only come to the believer who accepts in loving faith the atoning efficacy of the death of Christ. The conception of the Law as a burden is scarcely Pauline. He is sometimes disposed to regard its ceremonial enactments as belonging to an elementary stage of religion which has passed away; the Israelite under the Law is in a state of bondage, and the Christian who allows himself to be bothered and harassed by times and seasons and days is foolishly unappreciative of the spiritual freedom which Christ has given him. But the notion that the mere weight and number of the ceremonial

enactments constitute a grievous trouble and a baneful
burden can hardly be illustrated from the six genuine
epistles. Paul's objections to the Law are always relative
to his own theoretical or theological system ; they are
evolved from his own consciousness. The second charge—
that of self-righteousness and pride—is also only partly
illustrated by Paul. Here, however, the apostle is far
nearer to reality. For the Jew, humble towards God, was
guilty of pride towards the gentile. Particularism was
the great weakness and defect of the Rabbinic religion,
though it was accompanied by qualities too commonly
overlooked or denied in the customary descriptions of
Judaism. But the charge of easy, outward conformity
and self-righteousness is not Paul's. To him the Law is
almost always a whole. It is not from him that we get
the picture of the proud Pharisee who does the light things
of the Law and neglects or transgresses the essentials.
For that you must go to the Gospels and—don't believe
me if it sounds too queer—to the Rabbinic literature itself[1].

But, once more, can the Law be fulfilled? Is man expected
to fulfil it? The Rabbinic reply is simple. It does not
perhaps go deep enough to satisfy a consistent theorist;
it is not without its difficulties if you choose to dig for
them ; but it is practical, it works. It is the reply according to which ordinary life seems to be carried on.

God has given man capacities in virtue of which he can,
to a considerable extent, fulfil the Law. There are good
men, even saints. That is a fact; it was a fact in the
days of Paul, and it remained a fact in all the generations
which succeeded him. As God has given man the power
to fulfil the Law, he is expected to fulfil it. God punishes
failure, he rewards success. But God has so constituted
man that he not only is possessed of powers—God-given
powers—by which he can fulfil the Law, but he also contains an impulse, an inclination, a desire, leading him to

[1] Cp. *Babylonian Talmud, Sota,* 22 b. Wuensche, *Die haggadischen Bestandtheile, etc.,* II, 1, pp. 297, 298.

transgress and disobey it. This is the famous *Yetzer Ha-Ra*, corresponding to Paul's "Law of sin which is in the members." But God has taken care—so far at least as Israel is concerned—that the *Yetzer Ha-Ra* shall win no necessary or inevitable triumph. He helps the good in their struggle against evil. He sustains them by his spirit and his presence, and by the promise of resurrection and the life to come. And if from time to time men fail and lapse and sin—for the saints are few—even then God does not leave or forsake them. He provides means by which their sin is forgiven, and better still, means by which they themselves are led back to rectitude and goodness. For the best gift of God is repentance.

This abstract of the Rabbinic doctrine may perhaps suffice to show that the Pauline opposition of works and faith, and of merit and grace, is inapplicable to the Rabbinic religion. Rabbinic Judaism is an unsystematic mixture of works and of faith, of grace and of merit. You will find passages about faith which sing its praises quite in the Pauline manner, but no Rabbinic Jew reading these passages would either find anything odd in them or anything inconsistent with the predominating doctrine that "by his works shall a man be judged." Man cannot neglect for long the many-sided demands of his own nature. Cone admirably shows how works crop up again and again even in Paul, and so—only far more naturally and unsurprisingly—is it with faith and the Rabbis. "Through the reward of faith," as it says in the *Mechilta*, "the Holy Spirit rested upon Israel, and they sang the song by the waters of the Red Sea. Abraham our father only inherited this world and the world to come by the merit of faith. Every one who accepts even one command by faith is worthy that the Holy Spirit should rest upon him [1]." Of course, Weber tries to belittle the Jewish conception of faith by calling it a *Leistung* (a work, an action), but, call it by what name you will, it means

---

[1] *Mechilta*, 33 b. Cp. Weber, pp. 304, 308.

just simply an absolute trust in the goodness and wisdom
of God. Faith and trust are used interchangeably, as
where it says in the Midrash that whoever trusts in God
is worthy to become like him, or that Joseph only once
lost his trust in God (and the lack of faith brought him
two more years in prison), when he besought the chief
butler to remember him, and did not think that God alone
was adequate for his deliverance [1].

But does man perform the Law by his own merit and
covet his reward from God by right and not by grace?
Yes and no. It is a doleful answer, but if you limit
me to three words, no other can truthfully be given.
Let me use Paul as a parallel. According to his doctrine
there can be no question of merit between God and man.
The parties are not equal and independent. Unless and
until you believe in the atoning efficacy of Christ's death
upon the cross, you can neither be good by fulfilling the
Law, nor, even if you did fulfil it, would you be good. For
the very fact of having fulfilled it in the flesh and by your
own will would rob the fulfilment of all ethical and religious value. But after the act of faith has been accomplished, and the death of Christ has wrought in you its
mysterious grace and power, then, though theoretically
you should sin no more, yet practically the old leaven
still works. There are differences between believer and
believer, and while the one may be a saint, the other may
be something very closely resembling a sinner. On the
results of man's action after the acceptance of Christianity
God judges, and it would seem that there may even be
Christians for whom destruction and not eternal bliss will
be in store. Now the Law is the Jewish Christ. It was
given in pure grace, and it is only through the Law that
man can work his way to heaven. God has bestowed the
Law upon Israel for Israel to win its spurs. You cannot
therefore speak of man's independence. The laws constitute

[1] *Bereshit Rabba*, Wuensche's translation, p. 435; *Debarim Rabba*, V,
Wuensche's translation, p. 69.

the rungs of the ladder which God has planted for man to climb. But because God loves Israel, and because his own glory is involved in the praise which Israel renders him, therefore he says, " Earn what you can by your own effort and by my help, and what is then lacking I will supply."

You will find a great deal in Weber about the important conception of *Zechut* or Merit. But it must be read and accepted with the utmost caution. It is throughout written with the desire and design of enlarging the contrast between Rabbinic merit and Pauline grace. I cannot, unfortunately, deal with the subject in detail, for it would need a lecture to itself. But without detail the subject cannot satisfactorily be explained. The first point to remember is that there is no equality of relation. That is Weber's capital error. If man can earn merit, he can only do so because God has given him the Law by which to earn it. The father is glad when the child executes his will. But the rewards which the father gives are not a bargain. Nor *as towards the father* is there any place or opportunity for pride. The true and genuine Rabbinic attitude is shown in the following prayer, which every orthodox Jew still repeats day by day : " Sovereign of all worlds ! not because of our righteous acts do we lay our supplications before thee, but because of thine abundant mercies. What are we ? what is our life ? what is our piety ? what our righteousness ? what our helpfulness ? what our strength ? What can we say before thee, O Lord our God and the God of our fathers ? Are not all the mighty men as nought before thee, the men of renown as though they had not been, the wise as if without knowledge, and the men of understanding as if without discernment ? [1] " There does not seem much pride or insistence upon merit in *that* prayer ! There are many passages about divine grace in the Rabbinical

---

[1] *Authorized Daily Prayer Book of the " German and Polish " Congregations of the British Empire*, ed. Singer (Eyre and Spottiswoode), p. 7. The prayer is referred to in *Bab. Talmud, Yoma*, 87 b. The date of the prayer is at latest the second century A.D.

literature, and even honest Weber is bound to quote a few of them. He naturally wants to weaken them if he can. He does not appreciate their almost childish simplicity. Thus the Midrash makes one of its untranslateable grammatical jokes upon a word in Zechariah (ix. 9), and observes : " Even if there are no good works in your hands, God will redeem you for his own sake." Upon which Weber solemnly remarks that " Grace is merely *faute de mieux*; God first asks, ' Is there merit ?'[1]" But the Midrash draws no such fine distinctions. It is simple and unsystematic. Where there is no " law," God will act by " grace," as indeed he did with all the generations betwéen the creation and the redemption from Egypt, for they had no good works by which they could " live." But with the revelation of Sinai, God gave to Israel the merit of the Law,—the privilege of becoming worthy through the fulfilment of its commands. This high privilege was in itself an act of grace, and can never produce a sense of pride and independence against God. There is no virtue on which the Talmud lays greater stress than humility ; none against which it speaks more vehemently than pride. God himself is said to be humble, and even for humility man can find in God his pattern and example. Though God may choose to reward man for his good deeds, and to let his lot, both here and hereafter, depend partly upon himself, that does not involve pride, and the Rabbi would agree with the poet that " merit lives from man to man, and not from man, O Lord, to thee." " He in whom is the spirit of pride," say the Rabbis, "is as bad as an idolater." " Man may learn of God, for God let his *Shechinah* rest upon Sinai and not upon the higher mountains, and he avoided the grander trees but let his *Shechinah* rest upon the thornbush." " The humble are regarded by Scripture as if they had offered all the sacrifices of the Law [2]." Like to these

---

[1] Weber, p. 304.

[2] *Sota*, 4 *b*, 5 *a*, 5 *b* ; Wuensche, *Die haggadischen Bestandtheile*, II, 1, pp. 243. 245, 247.

are the constant utterances of the Rabbis about humility and pride. Are they the sayings of men who thought much of their own achievements?

The Rabbis were far from assigning too low a position to the Evil Impulse—the *Yetzer Ha-Ra*. Though it is possible, by earnest effort, by prayer, and by the help of God, to triumph over the incitations and temptations of evil, the task is difficult. It needs constant watchfulness; man must be ever on the alert to quell the suggestions of sin as they arise. On the whole, Weber gives a fair account of the *Yetzer Ha-Ra* in the Talmudic literature; his main fault seems to be that he too much ignores the help from God which man receives according to the Rabbinic theory, and that he describes the general Rabbinic attitude of mind in colours too dark and gloomy. The seventh chapter of the Romans is too constantly before his mind. The rule of the Law and the help of the Spirit do not exclude one another. "Whatever the righteous do," it says in *Tanchuma*, "they do through the Holy Spirit." Nor is it true to say that God's help is only given to exceptional piety. The general doctrine is accurately expressed in the saying: "He who wants to be pure is helped to be pure; for him who wants to pollute himself the door is opened [1]." If the help of God were not believed in, of what use and point would be those frequent prayers in the liturgy for guidance and help: "O bring us not into the power of sin or of temptation; let not the *Yetzer Ha-Ra* have sway over us; make us cling to the good *Yetzer* and to good deeds; subdue our *Yetzer* so that it may be made subservient unto thee [2]." Whatever the mysterious process may be by which, as most religious persons believe, God helps us on towards goodness— whether you call it the gift of his Spirit or what not—the Rabbis believed in it, and they were strengthened and comforted by the belief. Why Paul does not refer to this

---

[1] *Yoma*, 38 b fin., 39 a; Wuensche, *Die haggadischen Bestandtheile*, I, pp. 367, 368.

[2] *Authorized Prayer Book*, p. 7.

current dogma of his time is one of the many puzzles which his writings suggest.

The question of fear must, however, be looked into a little more closely. I do not wish to ignore the defects of a nomistic religion. There is a danger lest rectitude be cut up into fragments, and the unity of virtue be lost in a multiplicity of separate enactments. It would not seem unlikely that the breezy simplicity of a noble character might soon be injured or never be achieved. Life and character must not be carved up into atoms. The late Master of Balliol has said : " Strange as it may appear, it is nevertheless true, that scruples about lesser matters almost always involve some dereliction of duty in greater and more obvious ones. A tender conscience is a conscience unequal to the struggles of life. At first sight it seems as if, when lesser duties were cared for, the greater would take care of themselves. But this is not the lesson which experience teaches. In our moral as in our physical nature, we are finite beings, capable of only a certain degree of tension, ever liable to suffer disorder and derangement, to be over-exercised in one part and weakened in another. No one can fix his mind intently on a trifling scruple, or become absorbed in an eccentric fancy, without finding the great principles of truth and justice insensibly depart from him. He has been looking through a microscope at life, and cannot take in its general scope. The moral proportions of things are lost to him ; the question of a new moon or a Sabbath has taken the place of diligence or of honesty." Doubtless into some of these evils and pitfalls Rabbinic Jews occasionally fell.

It is commonly said that the Law compelled a certain externality in the relations between God and man. The Jew had the feeling that there were a heap of little things which he must do, and a heap of little things which he must avoid doing, in order to win God's approval. And God judges by a system of book-keeping. Your good deeds are added up on the one side, your bad deeds upon the other. Then the balance is struck by subtracting the one from the other. Hence an anxious scrupulosity, a sense of burden, of obligation unfulfilled, a constant and harrowing uncertainty. "The difference," says Prof. Sanday, "between the man whose rule is one of faith and the man subject to law is that while for the latter there are definite and often minute regulations he must follow, for the former the only laws are great and broad principles." Nothing is so destructive to character as constantly to be thinking whether this is right or that is wrong, whether here you have transgressed or there you have obeyed.

I admit these dangers, though let me again point out that they hardly consort with that "self-satisfaction" which Prof. Sanday, without any reference to or support from the original authorities, tells us "was ingrained in the Pharisaic temper," because "the performance of Pharisaic righteousness was too well within the compass of an average will[1]." I admit the dangers and the defects. Weber has rightly called attention to them, and the passages which he quotes in support are worthy of the utmost consideration[2]. But you will not gain a true idea of the Rabbinic religion and of its attitude towards the Law without bearing in mind another side to the picture. That side is not wholly ignored by Weber, but he does not set it in its proper light. Moreover, it is exceedingly difficult for those who have not lived under the Law (I speak as one of them) to appreciate the Rabbinic point of view.

First of all one has again and again to repeat that the Law was regarded as a privilege and a joy. "The more the merrier" is the Rabbinic attitude towards the number of legal enactments. Because God loved Israel, therefore he gave them so many commands. From a lower point of view these commands were the means by which the Jew could earn reward—the reward of the future life. From the higher point of view they were the ornaments of Israel,

[1] Sanday and Headlam, *Epistle to the Romans*, pp. 183, 387.
[2] Weber, pp. 278–288.

his crown of glory, his links of union and communion with the God who gave them. And remember that the Rabbis who say these things, so simply, unaffectedly, and devoutly, are no priestly class. They were the sons of the people; many of them artisans and craftsmen; in close touch with their contemporaries, sharing with them their sorrows and their joys. Weber and others lay stress on a verbal metaphor. The Rabbis speak of the yoke of the Law. But the yoke of the Law is used in conscious opposition to the yoke of worldly care or the yoke of political subjection. You might as well argue that Paul felt his relation to Christ to be burdensome because he speaks of himself as Christ's bondman. As we have already seen, the yoke of the Law is the highest and the fairest freedom.

Again, the commandments of the Law were a sanctification of life. From the Rabbinic point of view it was a grand thing that even the ordinary actions of every day—eating and drinking and sowing and ploughing—were hallowed by commands [1]. All could be done to the glory of God; and the thought of him, and of his love for Israel, could accompany the pious Israelite at every step. For Israel is God's beloved, his bride, and when the commands of the Law are being fulfilled by Israel, then the divine presence rests upon them. The enactments of the Law are the adornments in which the bride enters within the presence of her Lover [2]. It is very difficult for us to realize all this, but many things in other people's religions are difficult to realize, yet none the less are they real. The sanctification of every-day life through the Law has been of immense service to the Jews. Think what a sordid life theirs has been. But the Law has illumined it with a radiant light. The theologians talk of the burden of the Sabbath. Why this Sabbath has been the poetry of many a forcedly

---

1 Cp. *Bemidbar Rabba*, X, Wuensche's translation, p. 201 ; *Canticles Rabba*, on V, 16, Wuensche's translation, p. 149.

2 Cp. *Canticles Rabba* on I, 15, Wuensche, p. 49; ibid. on IV, 1, Wuensche, p. 101 ; ibid. on VII, 7, Wuensche, p. 171.

prosaic life [1]. The Sabbath a burden—the bride, the fairy! Heine's *Prinzessin Sabbat* should give the theologians pause.

Thirdly, one has to remember that somehow or other there was a good dose of common sense in these old Rabbis which often shows itself in various ways. They were well aware that in God's eyes as well as in man's there must be an obvious difference between the value of command and command. It is true that all must be obeyed and none must be cavilled at, but it is also true that the moral laws culminating in the famous "Thou shalt love thy neighbour as thyself" were regarded as far outweighing the importance of all the others. The Talmudic ethics are lofty and delicate. Again, even Weber can show you that the Rabbis were well able to distinguish between outward act and inward thought, between intention and deed. While they recognize that "'tis one thing to be tempted, another thing to fall," yet from a different point of view they condemn the impure thought as worse than the impure deed, while the intention to do right, though hindered by *force majeure*, counts equally with performance. Nor do they really hold that God judges by one hard and mechanical method and by no other. Especially does this come out in their stories about repentant sinners. Not infrequent is the saying "Many obtain the kingdom of heaven in an hour, while many require a lifetime."

But what, it may be asked, about those pages and passages in Weber, wherein he shows that the life of the pious Jew was passed in one long round of terror, in a perpetual dread of the punishments which might befall him upon earth and of the punishments which might befall him after death [2]? Did not the scrupulosity which the Law engendered also engender fear, the restless fear of a conscience that was never at ease, never assured that it was at peace and reconciled with God?

---

[1] Cp. Schechter, "The Law and Recent Criticism," *J. Q. R.*, vol. III, July. 1891, pp. 754–766.

[2] Weber, pp. 248-250, 256–259, 281, 284, 288, 235-337.

The true reply would, I think, be that Weber's conclusions
are obtained partly by concentrating attention upon
certain passages and wholly neglecting others, partly by
exaggerating or misinterpreting the import of those passages. The Rabbinic literature contains almost every
conceivable variety of opinion. One has to ask: what is
the *usual* opinion, what is the prevailing or predominating
note? Jewish apologists on their side make the same kind
of mistake that Weber makes on his. For instance, you
can collect a number of sayings by which to prove that the
Rabbinical literature teaches toleration and universalism.
These sayings have been collected in various elegant extracts, and they have done duty in many a sermon and
controversy. But the truth is that the Rabbis were no
more tolerant than Athanasius, and they peopled Gehenna
with their enemies as thickly as ever Dante peopled Inferno
with his.

The predominant note of the Rabbinical literature,
so far as its relation to God is concerned, is one not of
fear but of joy, not of doubt but of faith. The greater
danger lay in the opposite direction, and it is against this
danger that the Rabbis had more often to preach.

There is, indeed, a whole crop of superstitions to be
gathered from the Rabbinic literature, but Weber makes
too much of it. The Talmud and the Midrash are a
repertory of religion and law, but also of folklore and
superstition. The world to the ordinary Jew was as full
of demons and genii and fairies and spirits as it was to the
ordinary Christian. The Jews, who are an extremely
assimilative people, picked up superstitions wherever they
went. But in reality they sit as loosely to Judaism as
to Christianity. To say, as Weber does, that the Jew
"believed himself to be surrounded on all sides by evil, by
death and by the power of demons," so that "constant fear
was his portion," is nothing less than a libel. Again I say,
read the cribs: most of Weber's quotations come from
books which Wuensche, himself a Christian scholar, but

of a very different stamp, has translated. .Those who choose to read the 5000 pages of Wuensche's translations will, I believe, come to a very different conclusion from Weber. They will perhaps rather be inclined to think that the Jews were somewhat too confident that they would inherit the glories of " the world to come."

Weber quotes passages to show that the Jews feared to die. For a nation of martyrs this is pretty strong to begin with. But let us look at the matter a little more closely.

The Rabbis—let me use this opportunity to make the observation—were burdened by the sheer mass and authority of the Old Testament. Alas, through the prejudiced and foolish attitude which they took up towards all other literatures, and especially towards the wisdom of the Greeks, the Bible was their only book. And it was all true, all good, all divine. To be sure, it could be interpreted, and they did interpret it with a vengeance. On the whole they read into it a good deal of fine and wholesome religion. But some of its lower and impurer elements could not be explained away. Among these was the prevailing doctrine that calamity implied iniquity, and that death was the punishment of sin. As we have seen, the doctrine was frequently softened and changed. Calamity or suffering was often regarded as a blessing in disguise. It was a trial, a discipline, a purification, an earthly indication *per contrariam* of heavenly beatitude. But the evil side of the doctrine was not entirely overcome. Thus we are told that such and such sins are visited by famine, or such and such by pestilence and so on. The false and horrible doctrine is formulated that " for three " (purely ritual) " transgressions women die in childbirth," and I am ashamed to say that this atrocious rubbish defames and pollutes the Jewish liturgy to the present day [1]. Now it is implied in Genesis that death was the punishment of Adam's sin; in the Psalms the prayer for length of days is constantly offered up, and in the

[1] *Authorized Prayer Book,* p. 121.

Pentateuch long life is often declared to be a reward of right doing. Under these circumstances the Rabbis, though, by a belief in a future life, their religious centre of gravity had been entirely changed, could not wholly shake off the burden of the doctrine that in some way or other death was a punishment. But for them the doctrine was far more theoretical than practical, and their conviction that the death of the righteous or the repentant would be ultimately followed up by the beatitude of the world to come, could not but make an immense difference in their real genuine attitude towards earthly life and its inevitable close.

True, then, it is that the angel of death is often spoken of as an enemy, but it is also true that in other passages death is spoken of as "very good" because it leads from trouble to rest or from sorrows to joy. The same Rabbis who invented the pretty legend of the reluctance which Moses showed to quit life before he had entered Palestine, and of his long dialogues with God and with the angel of death, also invented the conception of the *Neshikah*, the kiss by which the souls of the righteous are removed from their bodies. Why, in Weber's opinion, did the Jews fear death? Because they were afraid, so runs the answer, of the judgment which might befall them. Their anxiety throughout life as to whether they had fulfilled the Law culminated in their fear as to what after death might be their fate. For instance, Weber says "The constant fear of death permitted no joy in life." As proof he quotes a passage from *Tanchuma* which runs thus : "God has said : Death does not allow man to rejoice in this world, but in the world to come death shall be swallowed up for ever." The context clearly shows that the meaning is : "The sadness of life and its transitoriness permit no joy upon earth, but in the eternal security of the life to come joy will be unending." The passage merely repeats the conventional commonplace that in comparison with that future existence which will be the lot of every virtuous or repentant Israelite, the present life is one of gloom and sorrow. With several other passages Weber is hardly more successful [1].

His great object, of course, is to show that there was no confidence, no trust in God, no assurance of salvation, no *Heilsgewissheit* in the German phrase. If proved, the charge would throw a flood of light upon the Epistle to the Romans. But the truth is that the Rabbis sought to observe the proper mean between easy security and needless fear. It says for instance in the Midrash : "The righteous, so long as he is on earth, must have no self-assurance." Or again, it says, (quoting the verse in Proverbs "Happy is the man that feareth always"): "That is the manner of the pious. Even although God gives them confidence, they never cease to fear." The meaning is that the righteous are not to get into a state of torpid confidence, as if they had nothing more to do, or as if there was no danger even for the best of them that they might fall a victim to temptation and sin. There is no implication that the righteous are to live in constant terror of God's judgments. Elsewhere the Midrash quotes the verse "Trust in the Lord and do good," and it observes : "It is like a market-master who went about testing weights. One saw him and hid. The master said : Why hide ? Keep fair weights and fear not. So says the text : do good and have trust in God." Though Weber gives us no passages like these, that is no reason that such passages do not exist [2].

But then Weber would reply : Can a man say that he *has* done good ? It is true that the Rabbis have some very strong passages about the constant assaults of the *Yetzer Ha-Ra*. On no virtue do they lay greater stress than on chastity, but like most oriental nations they believed that there was no virtue harder for man to secure. But does not the Christian too think it needful to pray : " Bring us not into temptation and deliver us from evil " ?

---

[1] Weber. p. 335.
[2] Weber, p. 284 ; *Yalkut. Deuteronomy*, § 892.

To whichever side the unfortunate Rabbis incline, the
theologians are down on them. Thus Weber says: "The
Jew lived in constant terror as to what might befall him
after death." And he quotes by way of proof the following passage from the Midrash: "When R. Jochanan was
dying, he said: Bury me neither in black raiment nor in
white, but bury me in grey raiment, in order that if I have
to stand among the pious, I may not be ashamed, and if
I have to stand among the wicked, I may not be put to
shame." Immediately following this story about Jochanan
is another story about R. Joshua. When R. Joshua was
dying, he said to his disciples: "Bury me in white raiment,
because I am not ashamed of my deeds and I am worthy to
enjoy the presence of my Creator." Weber does *not* quote
this story: it would not suit his purpose, but I should not
be surprised if another Pauline theologian has cited it in
order to prove the pride and self-righteousness of those
intolerable Rabbis and Pharisees[1].

It is observed in the Talmud: "The Rabbis have taught
that a man should always regard himself as half guilty and
half innocent." The inference which you are intended to
draw is, that while it is never too late to mend, it is also
never too late to sin. The right attitude of mind is therefore
one between careless confidence and a despairing fear. But
the predominant stress is undoubtedly laid upon the folly
of the second alternative. Whoever reads what the Rabbis
have to say about Repentance can never believe that their
religion was one of fear, or their deity a God who was
believed to deal out in awful severity the irrevocable
judgments of measure for measure. All that we can justly
say is that the defects of a legal religion occasionally
made themselves felt. Man was sometimes looked upon
too much as a bundle of deeds and intentions. By some
teachers he was perhaps too little regarded as a whole,
possessed after a time of a certain fixity of character, which

---

[1] Weber, p. 384; *Bereshit (Genesis) Rabba*, § 96, § 100, Wuensche's translation, pp. 475, 501.

is little likely to change. The "I" tended to be lost in, and confused with, the external actions which it produces. Perhaps this defect is more noticeable on the side of the righteous than on the side of the wicked.

The Rabbis were well aware of the increasing power of sin, and how every yielding to temptation makes the next solicitation more difficult to resist. "The *Yetzer Ha-Ra* is at first weak as a woman, but at last strong as a man. At first he is as weak as a spider's web, but at last he is as strong as a ship's rope. At first he is but a wandering guest, at last he is the master of the house[1]." They are also well aware of the psychological puzzles of sudden conversion from evil to good, and they are never weary of accentuating the possibility of repentance. Yet perhaps it is but a false logic which led them to lay not indeed equal but yet considerable stress upon the uncertainty of the good. They did not adequately realize that man is more than his actions, and that to obtain his worth you cannot strike a balance between his good deeds and his bad. They did not perhaps adequately realize the complexity of character or appreciate the mystery of personality. They felt to the full the joy which religion could give; they believed in a God of mercy, and by none has God been more deeply loved and more gladly served, but, whether it was that they had not enough varied intellectual interests or because of an inadequate psychology which the legalism of their religion suggested to them, they did not sufficiently realize that the righteous lover of God cannot fall away into mortal sin, that though he may not be sinless, he may yet reach a calm confidence a serenity of soul, a freedom from temptation, which is nevertheless altogether different from carelessness or pride. They did not perhaps sufficiently realize the truth of that profound saying of Goethe's: "Ein guter Mensch, in seinem dunklen Drange, ist sich des rechten Weges wohl bewusst."

---

[1] Weber, p. 233.

Yet when by pure accident I chance to read the odd interpretation which the Midrash gives to the verse in Proverbs, " She laugheth at the time to come," I wonder how far what I have just said may be correct and accurate. " God," says the passage on which my eye happened to fall, " in the hour of their death shows unto the righteous their reward and gladdens them. For the Psalmist says : Precious in the sight of the Lord is the death of his pious ones. When, then, does God reveal to the righteous the precious gift which he has appointed for them ? In the hour of their death. Then they see it and laugh. Therefore the verse runs : She laughs at the time to come." (The Midrash translates : " She laughs at the last hour.") Not less interesting is the following : " According to R. Chija bar Abba, R. Jochanan said : If the majority of a man's years have passed without his having sinned, he will never sin. And R. Shila said : If a man has once or twice had the opportunity to commit a certain sin, and has not committed it, he will never do so." Truly one cannot easily get to the bottom of the Rabbinic theology [1] !

It may be said that in all the foregoing I have largely missed the point. The new confidence of the Christian is not because of works, but because of faith. The very nature of his confidence precludes the possibility of pride. If you can only win " confidence " or _Heilsgewissheit_ by works, you must either despair, if you have not got it, or swell with pride, if you think that you have.

It is here that the unsystematic nature of the Rabbinic religion again comes in, together with its saving common sense, its strange combinations, and its childlike faith. God and Israel are on terms of intimacy and friendship. By one means or another—this is really a dominant note of Rabbinic Judaism—all but the truly unrepentant sinners and heretics must and will be " saved." God loves Israel too deeply to allow them to perish without making every effort and

[1] _Shemot (Exodus) Rabba_, LII, Wuensche's translation, p. 345 ; _Yoma_, 38 _b_, Wuensche, _Die haggadischen Bestandtheile_, I, p. 367.

arrangement he can to secure their salvation. He gave them the Law in order that wherever possible, by glad obedience to its behests, they might secure the life to come at least partially by their own "merits." But where this method fails, he has others. For he can always give "for nothing": he is glad to show grace and forgive.

As God's glory and promises are inseparably connected with Israel, he saves and delivers "for the sake of his name." This divine motive, already familiar to Biblical writers, is maintained and appropriated by the Rabbis. This is also the case with the merits of the fathers. Here too a Biblical motive is carried on and expanded. The simple way in which these two methods or motives of the divine compassion are familiarly used may be conveniently illustrated by the following Rabbinic prayer, which early found a place in the liturgy and is still retained: "With abounding love hast thou loved us, O Lord our God, with great and exceeding pity hast thou pitied us. O our Father, our King, for the sake of thy great name, and for our fathers' sake, who trusted in thee, and whom thou didst teach the statutes of life, be also gracious unto us and teach us. O our Father, have mercy upon us; put it into our hearts to learn and to fulfil in love all the words of thy law. Blessed art thou, O Lord, who hast chosen thy people Israel in love [1]."

But I pass from this point of the merits of the fathers, and also from that of the service wrought to average or sinful humanity by the special righteousness of exceptional heroes and saints (Weber, p. 298) to the fundamental and immensely important subject of Repentance.

In no other respect do the Epistles of St. Paul more clearly show their curious lack of relation to the actual religion of his contemporaries. And yet it is just here where the very hinge of his whole theology is fixed. I am

---

[1] Daily Prayers: Spanish and Portuguese and Italian Rites. The German Rite happens to omit "for the sake of thy great name." Cp. *Babylonian Talmud, Berachoth,* 11 b. The date is the second century, at latest.

at a loss to explain the puzzle. But all I have to do now is to show that the puzzle exists.

The theologians make the matter easy by ignoring the difficulties, and (I regret to add) by a strange inaccuracy. I will take Holtzmann as an example. In his excellent account of the Pauline teachings he says : " Ancient thought in general, but in particular the religious consciousness of the latter Judaism, regulated the relations between the Deity, who represented the moral requirements and avenged the transgressions of them, and men, from the axiom that on the one hand compensation must be made to requiting justice for guilt incurred, a sacrifice must fall, but on the other, an innocent person may intervene for the atonement of the offence, and thus take the penalty upon himself." Dr. Cone seems taken in by this unhesitating assertion ; he quotes Holtzmann's clear statement in a footnote (I have borrowed his translation), and himself says: "It must not be forgotten that Paul thought of God's relation to man in accordance with the judicial idea of Judaism, to which the Law was inexorable. It was an expression of God's attitude toward sin, and must take its inevitable course of retribution unless an atonement was provided. The thought never appears to have occurred to Paul that God could arrest the penal operation of the Law on any other condition, but must allow it to proceed on its remorseless infliction of death and destruction[1]." Dr. Cone is right: "the thought never appears to have occurred to Paul," but that is just the extraordinary part of the matter.

But first of all let us return to the Rabbis. Vicarious atonement is not unknown to them. The passages cited by Weber (p. 328) are quite accurate. "There lies atoning efficacy in the death of the righteous." "When there are righteous men in a generation, God lets them die (or suffer ?) for the sake of others, and when there are no righteous, then the innocent school children are taken[2]."

---

[1] Cone, p. 258.   [2] Weber, p. 328.

But all such passages, and for the matter of that, all passages relating to the "merits of the fathers" or to the "merits of the righteous," are but as a drop in the ocean compared to the overwhelming mass of passages about Repentance and Forgiveness.

God has put into man's hands the key by which he can always open the door which sin may temporarily have shut between himself and his Maker. "Great is the power of repentance for it reaches to the throne of glory." "If a man has slandered his neighbour publicly, and wishes to be reconciled to him, his neighbour says, First summon those before whom you have slandered me, and then I will be reconciled to you. But God acts not so: man stands and reviles him and blasphemes in the street, and God says, Repent in secret and I will receive you." "The angels sought to shut the windows of heaven, that Manasse's prayer might not be heard, for they said unto God, Can a man who has set up an idol in the temple repent? But God said, If I receive him not in his repentance, I shut the door upon all penitents. So God bored a hole under the throne of glory and heard his supplication!" "Repentance is like the sea, for as the sea is always open, so too are the gates of repentance." "What shall be the punishment of the sinner? Wisdom answered, 'Evil pursueth sinners'; prophecy answered, 'The soul that sinneth it shall die'; the Law answered, 'Let him bring a guilt-offering, and atonement shall be made for him.' But God answered, 'Let him repent and *that* shall be his atonement.'" "Whence do we learn that of him who repents, God reckons it as if he had gone up to Jerusalem and rebuilt the altar and offered upon it all the sacrifices? From the verse, A broken and a contrite heart, O God, thou wilt not despise, for this is followed by, Do good to Zion, build thou the walls of Jerusalem: then wilt thou delight in the sacrifices of righteousness." "Where the penitent stand, the righteous cannot stand." It is idle to multiply these quotations. For mere con-

venience I have taken all except the last adage from
a single section of a single Midrashic book[1]. But there
can be no question that they represent the regular doctrine
of the Rabbis. There is no ultimate need of sacrifice or
vicarious atonement, or of personal merit, or of the merits
of others. All these things are good, but repentance is
better. It is the more excellent way.

But what does repentance imply? Weber uses a mere
phraseological idiom, without religious or moral significance, to try to prove that Rabbinic repentance has no
ethical worth. I am bound to add that his editors have
themselves called attention to his error while leaving it
in the text. Weber says that the very phrase for "repent,"
namely "do repentance," shows that it is a *Leistung*, a
mere outward deed or rite, no change of heart, no μετάνοια.
But Weber himself admits that Rabbinic repentance
includes shame, contrition, and sincerity. He is aware
that it implies a *return* from evil deeds, and that the
Rabbis, while extolling repentance, pour out their scorn
upon those who attempt to cheat God by a merely verbal
or resultless contrition. Weber cites two Midrashic legends
about Adam and Cain. According to this story God
urged Adam to repent of his sin. But Adam refused.
Twice did God repeat the summons to repentance, and
twice did Adam refuse. Then only was punishment
pronounced upon him. In the case of Cain the difficulty
occurs: Why was the murderer let off so easily? The
Midrash can only explain this on the assumption that he
had repented of his sin, though it is also suggested that
his repentance was merely outward and deceptive. But
why these legends show the worthlessness of Rabbinic
repentance I am at a loss to understand.

The real danger of the Rabbinic doctrine was somewhat
different. The teachers were well aware that, in order to
have any religious value, repentance must be sincere and
effective, but their constant praises of its powers and

[1] *Pesikta Rab Kahana*, XXV, Wuensche's translation, pp. 224-239.

their incessant iteration of the ready forgiveness of God were not without their perils. "God says: Open me a gate that is as wide as a needle's eye, and I will open you a gate which horses and chariots can pass through." Such doctrine, however beautiful and true, had obvious dangers when it was linked to and associated with an institution like the Day of Atonement. The Rabbis were careful to lay down the teaching that the Day of Atonement only secured God's forgiveness on the terms of repentance, and even then only for sins committed against God. For sins against your neighbour no forgiveness could be obtained unless and until you had made good to your neighbour the injury you had done him. And if a man says in his heart, "I will sin, and the Day of Atonement will secure my forgiveness," for such a one, say the Rabbis, the day brings no forgiveness. With wonderful tact they chose for the prophetical lessons of the day, first the fifty-eighth chapter of Isaiah, describing the *moral* character of the true fast, and secondly the book of Jonah, concerning which they are at pains to point out that God paid no heed to the sackcloth and ashes, but that when the Ninevites turned from their evil way and God saw their *works*, then he forgave them [1]. Nevertheless the Day of Atonement, with its implied doctrine of a big national forgiveness year after year, inevitably tended to certain immoral superstitions; against these Jewish teachers in every age have had to fight. But these superstitions and the too complacent acceptance of the doctrine of repentance are all on the line of making sin too easy and God too lenient. So far from erring on the side of severity, they err on the side of compassion. The Jews were perhaps a little too inclined to think that God must inevitably pardon their transgressions. As Heine said, *C'est son métier.* He can no other.

It is surely a most extraordinary thing that of all this

---

[1] *Mishnah Taanith*, **II**, 1. Wuensche, *Die haggadischen Bestandtheile*, **I**, p. 436.

Jewish scheme of justification St. Paul says never a word. According to the Jewish mind, the entire scheme of Pauline theology was absolutely unnecessary. God had already provided a reconciliation, and he had so constituted the nature of man that he was able, if he chose, to take advantage of it. So far as man failed to fulfil the divine commands, he could yet be reconciled to God by repentance and by the Day of Atonement. Instead of the Law " working wrath," it worked reconciliation, peace, forgiveness. The deliverance from sin is wrought by human repentance and divine pardon.

Paul's theology substitutes another manner of justification, another method of reconcilement, which it is quite possible to argue is higher, more satisfying, more permanent. Franz Delitzsch, great scholar, keen conversionist, and noble soul that he was, readily realized and acknowledged the difference between the Jewish and Christian point of view. He quotes the section of the Pesikta from which my own quotations about repentance are mainly culled, and says: "According to the Jewish doctrine, God lets himself be reconciled through repentance; according to the Christian doctrine, he is reconciled (*versöhnt*) through the mediation (*Mittlerwerk*) of Christ, and the individual man is reconciled to God (*versöhnt*) when in faith and repentance he accepts the mediation, which is common and general for all mankind. The New Testament method of salvation (*Heilsordnung*) has the same sound as (*lautet auch wie*) *jer. Maccoth*, I, 6 יעשה תשובה ויתכפר לו (' *let him repent and receive atonement* '), but repentance is not the factor which atones (*das Sühnende selbst*), but only the way to receive atonement (*der Weg zur Versöhnung*)[1]." In other words, Rabbinic Judaism requires and postulates no intermediary between God and man.

Dr. Cone rightly says of the Pauline theology: "Justification as God's act is negatively the non-imputation of their sins to men, which is equivalent to forgiveness.

---

[1] Delitzsch, *Translation of the Epistle to the Romans into Hebrew.*

Satisfaction for sin having been rendered on the Cross, forgiveness is not prominent in the Apostle's thought[1]." The very word μετάνοια (so far superior, in Weber's judgment, to the Hebrew תשובה), together with its derivatives, is only met with about four times in all the six epistles, and even on those occasions it has little or no doctrinal importance. So too Ménégoz most aptly says : "Jésus-Christ n'a pas été pardonné : il a expié les péchés et il a été justifié. Le croyant qui s'identifie avec Christ est de même considéré comme ayant expié ses péchés par la mort, et comme ayant satisfait ainsi à la justice divine, il n'est pas pardonné, mais justifié." "La justification n'est pas un pardon, c'est une justice nouvelle[2]."

It may, then, be that the new justification is a far higher thing than the old repentance and forgiveness ; but is it not strange that Paul, in criticizing the Law, or in arguing with the Jew and with Jewish-Christians, should never touch on this fundamental point of difference ? Is it not strange that he should not mention a matter which to every Jew was of such absolutely vital importance, never seek to anticipate a reply which the Jews would infallibly make to his attack upon their creed, and to the need of another and better means of reconciliation with God ? The old doctrine, like the new, is susceptible of criticism ; what religion, what theology is not ? It might have been argued that the old method was on the one hand too facile, on the other too ineffective ; that the process of sin and forgiveness was repeated again and again with no permanent and satisfying result ; that what was wanted was not a mere outward pardon for sin, but a method by which pardon would be necessarily and mysteriously followed by a change of heart and a regenerate life. Such a criticism, while quite capable of receiving a rejoinder, would at any rate have compelled attention. But, instead of this, St. Paul beats

---

[1] Cone. p. 360.
[2] Ménégoz, Le péche et la rédemption après St. Paul, pp. 271, 274. The passages are quoted by Holtzmann, II, p. 127, n. 2.

the air with words, which, magnificent as they are, seem out of relation to the actual Jewish religion. They leave the impression: either this man was never a Rabbinic Jew at all, or he has quite forgotten what Rabbinic Judaism was and is.

According to the rigid theory of St. Paul's theology, no Jew should be anything but a sinner, and no Christian should be anything but a saint. "In the passage from the sphere of law to the sphere of grace, the dominion of sin has come to an end. The believer can sin no longer." "Such," says Holtzmann, "is the theory." But the "evil reality does not answer to the excellence of the construction. As a latent force sin still operates, so long as man lives both in the spirit and in the flesh together [1]." It is still necessary (though on paper or by theory it should be superfluous) to warn believers to cleanse themselves from defilement in the fear of God. Salvation has still to be worked out with fear and trembling. There are men who believed in Christ, and yet, after the new life had begun, became guilty of covetousness, of drunkenness, of extortion, of fornication, of incest. No man can say Jesus is Lord but in the Holy Spirit: yet the old leaven is still not entirely removed.

No one would desire to press these facts too hardly. Christianity is not less great because from the very beginnings of its history there have been many bad men who called themselves Christians, or because there were many sincere Christians who, in this point or in that, were yet guilty of error and of sin. Nor shall we, standing on the eve of the twentieth century after Christ, value the nobility of St. Paul's Epistles the less, because we have to realize that there are weak points in his armour or that his theory is rather an ideal than a fact. But if we recognize that the Christian was not necessarily a saint because he believed in Christ, shall we not play fair and recognize that the Jew, because he lived under the Law, was not necessarily a sinner?

[1] Holtzmann, II, p. 152 fin.

On the Pauline theory a sinner he must be. Theoretically there could never have been and there can never be a really good man under the Law. The Jew must indeed be not only as bad as, but he ought to be far worse than the gentile. For the Law is the strength of sin. Not only is the quality of sin worse—for without Law there is no transgression—but, as Holtzmann quite properly points out, in quantity of sin also the Jew must be superior. From Moses to Paul there must have been nothing but sin; the constant consciousness of failure must have perfectly corresponded with reality. Is this consequence of Paul's theory in consonance with the facts? Or is this another instance of my contention that there is much in Paul which, while dealing *with* Judaism, is inexplicable *by* Judaism?

We are naturally concerned most nearly with Paul's own contemporaries, but, on the theory, so long as men and women live under the Law, the Law must produce its inevitable results. There is no reason why the Jews of A.D. 500 should have been a whit better than those of A.D. 50; nor is there any reason why those who live under the Law in 1900 should be other than those who lived under it in 190. But even within the limits of St. Paul's own age, the matter is serious enough to demand the most careful consideration. Has this consideration been shown? Has the Rabbinical literature been adequately read by those who pronounce judgment? Is it fair to take the New Testament as the sole authority? Are we not all of us enough critics to see that so far as Paul is concerned it is eminently to his advantage, it is part of his case, to paint Jewish morality as darkly as he can, or that (so far as the Gospels are concerned) a preacher's sermons and a religious reformer's speeches, reported by prejudiced parties at second-hand, cannot and must not be taken, without the most careful testing and sifting, as incontrovertible evidence of the moral lives and religious ideals of the great bulk of his contemporaries? How that testing and sifting is to be effected without a prolonged study of the Rabbinical literature, I fail to understand.

Even English theologians (and surely *English* theologians should be fair) seem to me to blame in their hasty and unqualified condemnation of the Rabbinic religion. Is it not possible to be loyal to the Master without throwing mud at his race? Thus Dr. Sanday writes, "The Jews were at the head of all mankind in their privileges, but morally they were not much better than the gentiles. The truth must be acknowledged; as a system, Law of whatever kind had failed. The breakdown of the Jewish Law was most complete just because that Law was the best[1]." Where is the evidence? None is offered, except the *ipse dixit* of St. Paul. But if the breakdown were so complete, is it possible that both the practical and theoretical ethics of the Rabbis would be as noble and as delicate as they are? If the Law broke down—and remember that it was the Law and nothing but the Law which was the religious motive f all Jewish life for centuries after Paul—would those famous words of Zunz, which George Eliot has immortalized, be true: "If there are ranks in suffering, Israel takes precedence of all the nations—if the duration of sorrows and the patience with which they are borne ennoble, the Jews are among the aristocracy of every land—if a literature is called rich in the possession of a few classic tragedies, what shall we say to a national tragedy lasting for fifteen hundred years, in which the poets and the actors were also the heroes?" No, if morally the Law had broken down, these martyrs and nobles, these poets, actors, and heroes would never have existed at all.

The main attack of St. Paul upon Jewish morality is confined to the second chapter of the Epistle to the Romans. Elsewhere we have little, beyond casual expressions about his Jewish antagonists on which no sensible person would lay any stress (for who would trust an excited man when he speaks about his enemies?), or theoretic

---

[1] Sanday and Headlam, p. 188.

statements about Jewish pride and the rejection of Christ. The first two chapters of the Epistle to the Romans show many peculiarities. The special dogmas of Paul are conspicuous by their absence. A refined justification by works is the doctrine preached, culminating in the superb close. In fact, Paul introduces his dogmatic letter with a sort of sermon or diatribe, and fine as the sermon is, it has all a sermon's wonted exaggerations. It contains a tremendous castigation of existing society, whether Jewish or heathen. The heathen world is described much as in the Wisdom of Solomon or as in many passages of the Rabbinical literature. Idolatry is regarded not as a misfortune but as a crime, and every kind of moral offence is made to spring from it. This is familiar enough; the same statements meet us in Jewish sources. But then Paul turns the tables upon the Jews (and proves the point so vital to his coming dogma that all the world without exception is under the power of sin) by roundly asserting that the Jews are no better than their gentile neighbours. Even apart from coming dogmatic necessities which cast their shadows before, the sermon, taken with the proper grains of salt, was a good and useful sermon, not without its seasonable sting and justification. For, as I have already pointed out, the Jews, humble before God and among themselves, were proud towards the gentile. They did plume themselves upon their privileges, upon the special love which God bore to them as his children and his chosen. The theologians are quite right there, though, while they are glad to accentuate the Jewish pride in imaginary privileges, they do not like these privileges, even in the Jewish view of them, to include the loving friendship of God, because then all other useful counts of the indictment would *ipso facto* disappear. If the Jews were proud, they were also slavish and timid. For two religions of love there cannot be, according to these particularist theologians. Thus Jewish pride towards the gentiles is rightly censured by St. Paul. The Jews spoke of themselves as the righteous, the saints, the elect, precisely as Paul plumes himself towards his enemies, but is humble towards God. Or again, just as Paul calls the Christians " saints " in relation to the outer world, while he is fain to acknowledge that the saints were not all saintly, so too was it with the Jews. There were among them. as among every nation and community, black sheep; there were formalists and hypocrites; there were doubtless also robbers and adulterers. Who denies it? Certainly not the Rabbis, for none attack the hypocrites or the unchaste more bitterly, more openly than they. But it would be no less absurd to make Rabbinic Juda. m responsible for these black sheep, than to make St. Paul responsible for the vicious elements in his own communities. All we can rightly say is that just as Paul's doctrine could degenerate into antinomianism, so the Rabbinic doctrines could degenerate into hypocrisy and formalism. No religion can escape the defects of its qualities. But to ignore the qualities and make the whole thing a mass of defects is as false to logic as it is false to fact.

Thus. as a sermon, what St. Paul says of the Jews in the second chapter of the Romans (ii. 17–29) is not unreasonable. Its grand and noble teaching of the true Jew and the true circumcision recalls the best utterances of Amos and Isaiah. It is likely enough that many of the black sheep were foremost in contempt and hatred of the gentile—that besetting Jewish sin, so soon to be paralleled in the Church by contempt and hatred of the heretic. Rightly enough does Paul say to them: " Thou therefore that teachest another, teachest thou not thyself?" But to suppose that the religious Jews of the time were a mass of hypocrites, adulterers, and robbers seems to me absolutely grotesque.

Canon Gore, as we have seen, does not agree with me. As his book on the Romans will probably be widely read, let us hear what he has to say. Paul, he declares, was " certainly right in his estimate of Jewish religion." There is no clear sign that Canon Gore has read the Talmud and the Midrashim, or even the 5,000 pages of Wuensche. The New Testament seems enough for him. The religion of the Jews was, he says, "a matter of public opinion—with all the stagnancy which belongs to the public opinion of a compact society—not a matter which lived with ever fresh life in the inner relation of the conscience to God." This is a most extraordinary statement about a people who set God before their eyes and hearts with exceptional pertinacity and continuity, but much stronger statements are still to come. Canon Gore proceeds to quote the Gospels to show that what Paul attributes to the *religious* Jew (mark the word and its sting, though the italics are mine) is fully confirmed.

"Avarice," he says, was "a notorious sin of Jews." Do you mean to tell me that because a great preacher was to attack avarice to-day, therefore it would be right to say that avarice was a notorious sin of Christians, and of religious Christians to boot? If Canon Gore would even read that one book of Wuensche's, in which he has collected some of the Rabbinic parallels to the Gospels, he would know that the Rabbis themselves condemn the very same sins as Jesus. Charity and simplicity were two marked Jewish virtues, the offspring and product of the Law. Then, in spite of what Dr. Schechter and other scholars in easily available and accessible works have shown, the Jews are next accused of trying by means of religious craft "to evade the righteous claims of parents." As if the honour and love due to parents was not an almost exaggerated feature of the Rabbinic religion and of the Jewish character. Then, on the flimsiest of evidence, the charge of adultery is also brought home. And so, without any appeal to their own history and literature, we are concisely told that "the 'religious' Scribes and Pharisees (though not of course the best of them) were, in fact, as a body truly hypocrites, as our Lord summarily said they were."

P 2

For my part, I do not believe that Jesus ever said any
such thing, but if he did he exaggerated. But note the
qualification: "though not of course the best of them."
But why *not* the best of them? Were they subjected to
any other and higher influences? Were they not lovers of
the Law? Would they not have given their lives rather
than, as sign of apostasy, infringe the smallest of its
precepts? Will Canon Gore go the length of saying that
"the best of them" were good not because but in spite of
their religion?

In a later passage Canon Gore returns to the charge.
He wishes to explain what Paul really meant by
"seeking to be justified by works of the law." It was,
he says, "the attitude of the Jews, especially as they
appear in St. John's Gospel." Observe the words "especially as they appear in St. John's Gospel." Would it
not be fair to remember that almost all critical scholars
regard that Gospel as written not only long after the death
of Jesus, but written with an intense hatred of the Jews
and with a wonderful dramatic power? In it the Jews are
the men of darkness; the believers are the men of light.
But let that pass. The Jews, our author proceeds to say,
"were proud of their divine law and of belonging to the
chosen people. They knew how to make good their
standing ground with God. By keeping the law, as the
law had come to be understood among themselves, they
could accumulate merits altogether out óf proportion to
their failures or demerits. They could even be helped by
the merits of the old saints. Thus they could stand before
God as the basis of a certain engagement or covenant, into
which God had entered with his people, and claim their
due reward. This utterly demoralizing attitude—leading
as it does to formalism and hypocrisy, or, at the best, un-
progressive stagnation—this attitude, which left out of sight
all the higher and infinite elements in the Old Testament,
was the actual attitude of contemporary Pharisaic Jews."

Now, I have already declared that the Jews were proud

of their law, that, moreover, they were proud of their moral and religious superiority to the gentiles, that, as the defect of its qualities, their religion, like Calvinism or Catholicism, might and did lead to hypocrisy and formalism, but with these qualifications Canon Gore's statements are inaccurate. He has not attempted to prove his assertions ; I will not attempt to prove mine. I will ask any candid person to read Wuensche through and to judge between us.

Canon Gore would have you believe that the law, " *as the law had come to be understood among them*," meant nothing but ritual. It was thus easy " to accumulate merits " by observing it. Not even Weber would venture to go as far as this. Nothing but ritual : when over and over again we are told that its greatest elements are humility and charity and justice and chastity and love ! " Claim their due reward : " when even so far as the Jew *can* observe the law, he .knows that it is only God who, in his love for Israel, has given him the glorious power and privilege of observing it; when the Talmud again and again warns its hearers and readers against pride and self-- righteousness, when every day humble prayers are poured forth to God for strength to do his will and for the pardon of sin. Surely we ought to know enough history and exegesis to realize that it was not *necessarily* " self- satisfied stagnation, slavery to convention, and moral hollowness and rottenness " which made the Pharisaic Jews " utterly resent the new light of the Gospel and reject the Christ." If it was these things then, will you say of us that it is these things now ? For, as the Christ, we reject him still.

But the most singular of all the connotations given by Canon Gore to that "seeking to be justified by the works of the law " of which the contemporaries of Paul and all the subsequent generations of Jews were guilty is still to come. " By ' works ' or ' works of the law,' St. Paul means an attitude towards God which left a man largely independent of him. Under the divine covenant the man

of the covenant has a certain task to do, a certain law
to keep; that kept, especially in its external requirements as contemporary authority enforces it, he is his own
master. He is entitled to resent any further claims upon
him. This religious ideal means, as we have seen, pride,
stagnation, conventionalism, hypocrisy. And the more it is
considered, the more unnatural it appears. For—

(1) It ignores the fundamental relation of man to God,
viz. that, as a creature, he depends absolutely and at every
stage on God. He has no initiative in himself. Thus
the only attitude towards God which expresses the reality
is one in which God is recognized as continually supplying,
or promising, or offering, or claiming, and man is continually
accepting, or believing, or corresponding, or obeying.

(2) It ignores the ineradicable taint of sin in man, and
the accumulated guilt of particular sins. A man may
gloss over his inward sinfulness, and cloak and ignore
his secret sins ; he may live outwardly in high reputation ;
but if he comes to know himself, he knows himself as a
sinner, who depends, at starting, absolutely on God for
forgiveness and ' deliverance from coming wrath.'

(3) It is quite contented to leave all mankind, except a
small elect body, out of all the conditions of acceptance
with God [1]."

To any one who (like myself) has even a casual and un-
learned acquaintance with Rabbinic religion, this passage
is almost funny. What the Rabbinic Jew, independent
of God ! still more the Rabbinic ideal—independence of
God ! The Jew his own master, whose pride was that
every action of his life was wrought as in the presence of
God ! No words, indeed, could more aptly and succinctly
describe the Rabbinic frame of mind and religious position
than to say that " man depends absolutely and at every
stage on God," and that he is " continually accepting, or
believing, or corresponding, or obeying." Of this sup-

[1] Canon Gore, *St. Paul's Epistle to the Romans*, vol. I, pp. 96-8,
164-7.

posed independence it is safe to say that the Rabbinic
literature shows not a single trace. And does Rabbinic
Judaism ignore sin? What about the doctrine of the
Yetzer Ha-Ra? What about the stress on repentance?
Does Rabbinic Judaism know nothing of the doctrine that
man must "know himself as a sinner" who depends upon
the forgiveness of God? Let Canon Gore on the next
Day of Atonement go into any little synagogue in Russia,
whose worshippers have grown up under the very shadow
of the Law, and there let him hear and find the answer.

But how about the last short paragraph of the indictment? Was Rabbinic Judaism " quite contented to leave
all mankind, except a small elect body, out of the conditions of acceptance with God." In this charge there lies
truth; but before I deal with it further, one single remark.
Canon Gore deduces this charge from the law. It was the
direct consequence of seeking justification by legal works.
But is it not then an extraordinary thing that that phase
or section of Christianity which has been most "contented
to leave all mankind, except a small elect body, out of the
conditions of acceptance with God," has precisely consisted
of those who most utterly rejected works, had the deepest
sense of the "ineradicable taint of sin in man," and most
absolutely denied the possibility of any human initiative?
So cautious must we be in religion of deducing one thing
from another, or of a wholesale condemnation of another's
creed. Human religions are as complex as human characters. Because a man believes *this*, it seems to you
necessary that he must believe or be *that*, or because he
holds *this*, it is therefore impossible that he should accept
that. But the human mind can do wonderful things in the
way of antinomies and contradictions, and the Rabbinic
mind in this respect was one of the most wonderful.
Canon Gore, for instance, observes that it "seems to be
true to say that a really Christian theism, and a really
Christian doctrine of human freedom, are inseparable from
the belief in the possibility of wilful sin leading to final

ruin[1]." Now to me such a belief seems utterly incompatible
with a belief in the love of God and in the goodness of
God, and yet I am as convinced that Canon Gore believes
in the love of God and in the goodness of God as that
I wrote this lecture with pen and ink.

The grave fault of the Rabbinic religion from the ethical
point of view was its particularism. Though it is not *quite*
true to say that it " was contented to leave all mankind
except the Jews out of the conditions of acceptance with
God," it is very largely true. The heathen were the
enemies of Israel and of God, and though many teachers
in Israel desired their conversion and believed that many
of them would ultimately be converted to the true faith,
the majority of Rabbinic Jews doubtless believed that the
Resurrection would be limited to themselves. By what
shifts and artifices and false reasonings and unnatural
limitations and self-deceptions they arrived at this horrible
conclusion, those translations, to which I have already
referred, will clearly tell. For the Midrash shows Rabbinic
Judaism in undress : its best without affectation ; its worst
without apology.

Without belittling the splendour and magnificence of his
universalism, we may yet observe in St. Paul a measure
of limitation. The idea of human souls "appointed to
destruction" does not seem to fill him with horror. Is
it certain that he believed that his enemies, the Jewish
Christian agitators, all those who rejected Christ or rejected
the Gospel, would assuredly share in the coming resurrection ? It is open to doubt whether he held that there was
any salvation or future life for the mass of heathen and of
Jews who had died before Jesus was born. He prepared
the way for that Christian particularism of belief which
was so soon to grow up as a rival and competitor to
the Jewish particularism of race.

But think not that I would not wish to add my grain of
admiration and of gratitude for him who wrote : " There is

---

[1] Canon Gore, op. cit., vol. II, p. 214.

no distinction between Jew and Greek." "There is no respect of persons with God." " And the greatest of these is love." Not till St. Paul had written did the prophetic universalism attain its goal. It can be appropriated, and I am glad to think it *has* been appropriated, by Jew as well as by Christian, and there can be added to it the further virtues of toleration and mutual esteem. I trust that nothing which I have said or implied about those great though human documents which you are leagued together to study has done violence to those virtues, whether in the letter or in the spirit.

C. G. MONTEFIORE.

CHRISTIAN WRITERS ON JUDAISM

by

GEORGE FOOT MOORE

HARVARD THEOLOGICAL REVIEW

VOLUME XIV   JULY, 1921   NUMBER 3

CHRISTIAN WRITERS ON JUDAISM

GEORGE FOOT MOORE
HARVARD UNIVERSITY

I. To the End of the Eighteenth Century *

CHRISTIAN interest in Jewish literature has always been apologetic or polemic rather than historical. The writers of the New Testament set themselves to demonstrate from the Scriptures that Jesus was the expected Messiah by showing that his nativity, his teaching and miracles, the rejection of him by his people, his death, resurrection, and ascension, were minutely foretold in prophecy, the exact fulfilment of which in so many particulars was conclusive proof of the truth of his claims, and left no room to doubt that his own prediction would be fulfilled in the speedy coming of the Son of Man to judgment, as Daniel had seen him in his vision. In the Pauline Epistles and Hebrews and in the Gospel according to John the aim is not so much to prove that Jesus was the Messiah of Jewish expectation as that the Lord Jesus Christ, in whom Christians believed that they had salvation from their sins and the assurance of a blessed immortality, was a divine being, the Son of God, the Word of God incarnate; and this higher faith also sought its evidence in the Scriptures. The apologetic of the following centuries, especially that which addresses itself to Jewish objections, has the same chief topics: Jesus was the Christ (Messiah), and Christ is a divine being. Others, which also have their antecedents in the New Testament, are accessory to these,

---

* The following pages are not meant to be a history of the literature or even an introduction to it. The author's aim has been to show the influences which have determined its character in successive periods and to illustrate these stages by certain outstanding works, laying thus the foundation for a critical examination of modern representations of Judaism to which the second part of this study is devoted.

particularly the emancipation of Christians from the Mosaic law, or the annulment of the dispensation of law altogether, or the substitution of the new law of Christ; the repudiation of the Jewish people by God for their rejection of Christ, and the succession of the church, the true Israel, the people of God, to all the prerogatives and promises once given to the Jews.

The volume of anti-Judaic apology still extant or known to us through titles and quotations is considerable.[1] The earliest, a discussion between Jason, a Jewish Christian, and an Alexandrian Jew called Papiscus, written probably not long after the Jewish revolt under Hadrian and attributed to Ariston of Pella, is lost. Not much later comes the best known of the Greek apologies of this type, Justin Martyr's Dialogue with the Jew Trypho. The literary form of dialogue was chosen because it enabled the writers to combat Jewish objections as well as to develop their own argument in the way best adapted to their purpose. No doubt there was abundance of real controversy between Jews and Christians, through which the apologists were acquainted with the points of their opponents' argument, but in the apologies the Jewish disputant is a man of straw, who raises his difficulties and makes objections only to give the Christian opportunity to show how easily they are reso'ved or refuted, while in the end the Jew is made to admit himself vanquished. This of itself shows that the authors did not write to convert Jews but to edify Christians, possibly also to convince Gentiles wavering between the rival propaganda of the synagogue and the church. The argument for the divinity of Christ turns largely upon the theophanies of the Old Testament and the appearances of the Angel of the Lord, in which Philo had already recognized the manifestation of a divine being, the Logos, distinct from the transcendent Supreme God. Of Latin apologies the most noteworthy is Tertullian *Adversus Judaeos*. The occasion of the work, the author tells us, was a protracted discussion between a Christian and a convert to

---

[1] The most recent conspectus of this branch of Christian apologetic down to the fifth century, with the modern literature, will be found in Juster, Les Juifs dans l'Empire Romain (1914), i, 53–76. For a general survey of the whole field reference may be made to L. Blau, 'Polemics and Polemical Literature,' Jewish Encyclopedia, x, 102–109.

Judaism; but the argument is not conducted in the form of disputation.[2]

All the early apologies have much in common both in the topics and in the scriptures adduced. Later authors undoubtedly made free use of their predecessors, and collections of *loca probantia* from the Old Testament were made expressly for the use of controversialists. The argument is purely biblical; the interpretation, in large part symbolical or allegorical, is fixed in a tradition and repeated by one after another. There is more reality in the homilies of Aphraates directed against the Jews and in Chrysostom's sermons *Adversus Judaeos*. In the former we see that an aggressive Jewish polemic in the Persian Empire made necessary a vigorous defense, and in the latter that many Christians in Antioch were so strongly attracted by Jewish festivals and other ceremonies, especially by the great fast of the Day of Atonement, as to arouse apprehension that their Judaizing predispositions might carry them farther than the spectacular. The last important representative of the older species of apologetic is Isidore of Seville, *De fide catholica ex Veteri et Novo Testamento contra Judaeos*. The first book sets forth the catholic doctrine of the Person of Christ, the Son of God begotten of the Father *ante saecula ineffabiliter;* Christ *deus et dominus;* the Trinity; the incarnation, passion, resurrection, and ascension. In the second book the author deals with the rejection of the Jews and the passing of the gospel to the Gentiles, the abrogation of the Old Testament with all its institutions, and the establishment of the New with its sacraments. Isidore thus sums up and systematizes the Latin apologetic which he transmits to the early Middle Age, fundamentally doctrinal and still strictly biblical.

Of early Jewish apologetic and polemic we have hardly any knowledge except what is narrated in the Talmud of Palestinian Rabbis, chiefly of the third and early fourth centuries, who engaged in discussion with Catholic Christians about points of

---

[2] Joseph Scaliger's estimate of these apologies is not unfair: Judaei hodie cum disputant, sunt subtiles. Justinus Martyr quam misere contra Tryphonem scripsit, et Tertullianus! Debet esse valde peritus Judaismi, qui Judaeos volet reprehendere et refutare. (Quoted by Wagenseil, p. 89.)

interpretation, or controverted the doctrines of the church, particularly about the person of Christ.[3] The objections which are hereditary in the Christian apologies bear no mark of derivation from Jewish writings. That there were such in the second century is intrinsically probable, and it is possible that Celsus drew upon them in his True Account. More than this cannot safely be said; of a Jewish literature in Greek or Latin there is from that time on no trace. After Christianity became the established religion of the Empire and the conversion of Christians to Judaism was made a high crime, writings directed against the church and its doctrines or intended to make propaganda for Judaism are not likely to have been numerous. The situation was different in the Persian Empire, as we have seen in the case of Aphraates, and after the Arab conquest in the countries under Moslem rule, where Jews and Christians were upon an equal footing and some of the Caliphs were entertained at court by discussions of the merits of the three religions; but there Christian apologetic had a more urgent task in defense against attacks from the Moslem side.

In the Oriental revival of learning, in which the Jews had an active part, scholars arose among them who were well acquainted with the New Testament and the intricacies of Christian doctrine. The controversies of the tenth century between Rabbanite and Karaite Jews presently led both to include Christianity and Islam in their apologetic. Saadia (d. 942), the protagonist of the orthodox and the first to undertake a systematic exposition and defense of Jewish theology, disputes not only the Christian arguments to prove that Jesus was the Messiah, particularly that drawn from Daniel 9, 24–27, but the doctrines of the Trinity and the Person of Christ, on the last of which topics he specifies four distinct theories, including the most recent. His contemporary, the Karaite Kirkisani, sets the belief and teaching of the immediate disciples of Jesus in contrast to the doctrines of the church; according to him it was Paul who was the author of the doctrine

---

[3] Some illustrations are given by Blau in the Jewish Encyclopedia, x, 103; see also Bacher, Die Agada der Palästinensischen Amoräer, i, 555 f. (Simlai); ii. 115–118 (Abahu); and the indexes under 'Christen, Christenthum.'

of the Trinity and the divine Sonship. In general it may be said that the Jewish apologists of the following centuries not only endeavor to refute the Christian arguments drawn from the Old Testament, but carry the controversy over into their opponents' territory by criticism of both the New Testament and the dogmas of the church.

In the following period the intellectual hegemony of the Moslem world passed to the West, where learning and science were eagerly cultivated, and philosophy engaged some of the best minds. The Jews participated in this movement, and in all spheres some of them stood in the front rank. There was much discussion among the adherents of the three religions which divided among them the mixed populations of the Iberian peninsula concerning the foundations of their respective faiths and the truth of their doctrines. When Christians entered into such controversy with Jews they were in a very different position from their apologetic predecessors. They had to deal, not with fictitious opponents, but with real antagonists who stoutly defended themselves and struck back hard. Moreover, the defenders of Judaism now compelled their adversaries to meet them in the biblical argument on the ground of the Hebrew Scriptures, not of a disputable Greek or Latin version. They had not only a traditional knowledge of the language but, following in the footsteps of the Arab philologists, had made serviceable Hebrew grammars and dictionaries; they possessed commentaries on the Old Testament in which the text was interpreted on a sound philological method and frequently with historical and critical insight, and they distinguished clearly between the literal sense and homiletic improvements. They were learned also in the traditions of Judaism preserved in Talmud and Midrash, and in its normative teaching and practice. They defined and systematized its beliefs and doctrinal tenets, harmonized them with Scripture and philosophy, and undertook to prove them both by authority and reason.

Christian controversialists, if they were not henceforth to beat the air, were thus put under the necessity of knowing Jewish literature, ancient as well as modern. It did them no good to *assert* their interpretation of their Old Testament proof-texts; they had to *demonstrate* it. One of the most effective ways to do this was to show that their interpretation, though denied by contemporary opponents, had the support of ancient tradition — Targum, Talmud, Midrash — whose authority the Jews could not dispute, or that it was conceded by more recent Jewish exegetes of high repute. Thus to array the ancients against the moderns, is, as we shall see, a favorite piece of tactics in this new style of apologetic. Whatever its value otherwise, it had at least one good result — it led to a much more zealous and assiduous study of Judaism than any purely scientific interest would have inspired. Converted Jews naturally made themselves serviceable in this new apologetic; they brought the knowledge with them, and in defending their new faith or assailing the old they were excusing their own apostasy and giving proof of a sincerity which was often suspected by both sides.

The earliest of this type which has been preserved is the Dialogue of Petrus Alfonsi (died 1110), physician to King Alfonso VI of Castile, who stood sponsor at his baptism (1106) — hence the name, "Alfonso's Peter." In his new character of Peter the Christian, the author confutes and eventually converts himself in his former quality of Moses the Jew. The argument is chiefly philosophical and biblical; Jewish lore is brought in principally by way of exposing to ridicule the absurdities of the Haggada, particularly its anthropomorphisms. Only rarely (e.g. on Gen. 49, 10) is Jewish interpretation alleged in confirmation of Christian.

Converts became more numerous in the thirteenth century.[4] As the Christian kingdoms grew stronger and more secure, the policy of the government became more consistently unfavorable to the Jews, and the Church promoted these measures. At the same time the missionary efforts of the Dominican friars, whom Gregory IX (1227–1241) had particularly charged with this work, were prosecuted with persistent and well-directed zeal. Raymund de Pennaforte (died January, 1275), the general of the order, sought to win Moslems and Jews to the catholic faith by conviction rather than to force them into

[4] See below, note 21.

the church by persecution, and to this end established a college in which promising members of the order selected for the task studied the Arabic, Hebrew, and Aramaic languages, the Moslem and Jewish Scriptures, and their philosophical and theological literature. Among these students was Raimundus Martini, whose *Pugio Fidei* is the great monument of this endeavor. Of his life, a large part of which was passed in a convent of his order in Barcelona, little is chronicled. In 1264, in the sequel of the disputation at Barcelona in the preceding year before King James I of Aragon between the convert Pablo Christiani and Rabbi Moses ben Nahman,[5] Martini was one of a commission appointed by the King to examine Jewish books, with instructions to expunge passages injurious to Christ or the Virgin Mary. He had thus the best imaginable opportunity to become acquainted with Jewish literature of all periods down to his own day, and to acquire copies. For the rest, we know that in 1278 he was in the midst of the second of the three parts into which his work is divided (II. x. 2, p. 316),[6] and that he was still living in 1284.

The first of the three parts of the Pugio is a refutation of the errors of the philosophers, that is chiefly the Arab Aristotelians, whose three fundamental errors are that the world is eternal, that God's knowledge does not embrace particulars, and that there will never be a resurrection of the body. In these chapters he shows himself familiar with the Moslem authors and Arabic translations of the Greeks. Averroes, as might be supposed, is the most obnoxious of the philosophers; Algazel a welcome ally.

The second and third parts have to do with the Jews. In the former the proofs that the Messiah is already come are marshalled, and the contrary arguments of the Jews are combatted. The third part has three subdivisions (*distinctiones*). The first

---

[5] An account of this discussion, written by R. Moses ben Nahman, may be found in Wagenseil, Tela ignea Satanae. The three subjects appointed to be debated were: Whether the Messiah has already appeared; Whether the Messiah of the prophets was divine or human; Whether Judaism or Christianity is the true religion. In the report we have, the controversy ends with the Trinity.

[6] The year 1278 is often given inexactly as the year of the completion of the whole work.

deals with the unity of God and the distinction of persons in the Godhead; the second with man, the fall and its consequences; the third may be denominated Christology, closing with chapters on the rejection of the Jews and the ultimate conversion of the remnant. In the argument addressed to the Jews, Martini meets them on the ground of the Hebrew Bible, and quotes extensively from Jewish authorities. His quotations are given at large in the original, with exact references according to the method in use in his time, accompanied by a Latin translation and interpretation. The range of his learning is very wide; he quotes the Targums, both Talmuds, the Seder Olam, the various Midrashim which are commonly called Rabboth, the Midrash on Psalms, the Mekilta on Exodus, and others. Of commentators he uses Rashi (d. 1105), Ibn Ezra (d. 1167), David Kimchi (d. 1235), and his own contemporary R. Moses ben Nahman, and frequently cites the Moreh Nebukim of Maimonides (d. 1204). Some of the works from which he drew have perished and are known only through his excerpts; one such from which he frequently quotes was the Bereshith Rabbah attributed to R. Moses ha-Darshan, who flourished in Narbonne in the middle of the eleventh century.[7] Mention may be made further of extracts from Josippon, and the Toledoth Yeshua. It is important to observe, on the other hand, that the Pugio contains no quotations from the Zohar or other cabalistic works. The Cabala had, in fact, made little headway in Spain against the current of Aristotelianism when Martini wrote, though Azriel, who is regarded as the founder of the speculative Cabala, belonged to the generation before him and Moses ben Nahman, who is said to have been inducted into the Cabala by Azriel, was his contemporary.

The Pugio is a controversial work, and the manners of serious theological controversy, one observes, are seldom perfectly

---

[7] The texts as Martini quotes them sometimes differ materially from the manuscripts and printed editions in our hands, and his good faith has consequently been called in question. Where the text has really been tampered with in Christian interest, it is more likely that the copies he used had been interpolated by Jewish converts than that he falsified them himself. The judgment of recent Jewish critics is in general favorable to his honesty.

urbane; but it was composed for the purpose of converting Jews, not of vilifying them, and compared with much more recent anti-Judaic polemic it might almost be called gentlemanly, notwithstanding the suggestion of the assassin in the title. But its proper praise is that it is a genuine work of learning. In an order like the Dominicans, which counted among its members numerous Jewish converts, some of them men of rabbinical education, there were great possibilities of coöperative scholarship, and it is probable that Martini availed himself of them; but whatever assistance he may have had in gathering his material, it is evident that he had made it completely his own. The Pugio is not merely remarkable as a first enterprise; it still remains within its scope an admirable monument of erudition. A large part of what today constitutes the common stock of references in this field derives ultimately from Martini, though the source has long been forgotten, and not infrequently the references have got wrong in the long chain of borrowers borrowing from borrowers. Some characteristic examples of this will be given further on. In recent books the Pugio has a traditional place in the bibliography, but of first hand knowledge of it there is seldom any evidence.

Martini's work, in three great volumes, was in another sense *too* monumental. Copies of it are not, and probably never were, numerous. References to it in the following centuries are infrequent. Very early, however, a good deal of its contents was transferred to the pages of a handier book, the *Victoria* of Porchetus de Salvaticis, completed in 1303. The author, a Carthusian, native of Genoa, explains in the introduction that he names his work Victoria, *eo quod per eum Judaei facile convincuntur, ac eorum conscientiae non modicum penetrantur.* He acknowledges his obligation to Raymund Martini, *a quo sumpsi hujus libelli materiam in plerisque compilandi.* The long extracts from the rabbinical sources in the original Hebrew are omitted, and much besides which Porchetus evidently did not regard as essential to his purpose. On the other hand, Porchetus not infrequently introduces *de suo* matter not found in the Pugio, for example, a discussion of the pronunciation of the

Tetragrammaton (*Johouah*).[8] Porchetus's Victoria was printed in Paris in 1520 under the editorial direction of A. Giustiniani, the first professor of Hebrew and Arabic in the university of Paris.[9] It evidently had considerable circulation in its day; it is quoted, for example, by Luther, who in fact translated from it passages of some length in his pamphlet, *Vom Schem Hamephoras und vom Geschlecht Christi*, appended in the collective editions to his *Von den Juden und ihren Lügen* (both of the year 1543).

Two years before Giustiniani printed the Victoria, Petrus Galatinus, a Franciscan, with the encouragement of Pope Leo X and the Emperor Maximilian, published a folio volume under the title, *De arcanis catholicae veritatis*,[10] the immediate motive of which was to support Reuchlin in his strife with the Dominicans about the books of the Jews [11] by showing that the distinctive doctrines of Christianity can be proved from these same books. The argument is conducted in the form of a discussion in which Reuchlin (Capnio), Hoogstraaten (Prior of the Dominicans in Cologne), and Galatinus himself take part; Galatinus being the chief speaker, Reuchlin the interrogator, who humbly sits at the feet of Galatinus, Hoogstraaten an occasional objector.

The resemblances between Galatinus and Porchetus were early remarked in a sense uncomplimentary to the former,[12] but it was left for Joseph Scaliger to discover that the De Arcanis was an enormous plagiarism from the Pugio, a manuscript of

[8] On the pronunciation *Johouah* in Porchetus, see my Notes in The American Journal of Semitic Languages and Literatures, xxviii (October 1912), pp. 55–57, and on Luther's use of Porchetus, *ibid.*, pp. 60 f.

[9] See Appendix, p. 254.

[10] See Appendix, p. 254.

[11] The Dominicans, instigated by a baptized Jew named Pfefferkorn, had got from the emperor in 1508 an edict that the Jews should deliver all their books to be examined, and that such as contained things injurious to the Christian religion should be burned. The emperor was induced to reconsider this action, and called upon Reuchlin for an expert opinion as a Hebraist and a jurist. In his report Reuchlin distinguished seven classes of Jewish books, of which at the outside only one, such scandalous writings as the Toledoth Jeshua, and direct attacks on Christianity like the Nissahon, merited destruction. Thereupon he himself became the object of a venomous attack.

[12] E.g. by Jean Morin, Exercitationes Biblicae, lib. i, exerc. 1, c. 1 (p. 9 f.), 1660.

which he had seen twenty years before in a library in Toulouse.[13] In fact, though the plan and disposition are different, most of the learning in the Arcana was conveyed direct from Martini, The critical comparison made by the Dominican editors of the Pugio a half century later gave an exhaustive demonstration of the Franciscan's fraud; the long annals of literary theft record no more egregious case. The numerous material additions in Galatinus are chiefly cabalistic, derived from the Zohar and other supposititious writings of Simeon ben Yohai. He also quotes frequently from a work called *Gale Razaia* (Revealer of Mysteries) which professed to have for its author no less a person than R. Judah ha-Kadosh. Though more than one book bearing the same title (from Dan. 2, 29) is recorded by bibliographers, Galatinus's is none of them, and it has even been suspected that the alleged quotations from it were a pure fabrication of Galatinus himself, who was presumably as capable of inventing fictitious sources as of concealing real ones.[14] The suspicion does him no injustice, though it perhaps overrates his creative imagination, but in this case it is erroneous. The real author was Pablo de Heredia (d. 1486), a Spanish Jew, who signalized his conversion to Christianity by a series of impudent forgeries.[15]

Large as was Galatinus's surreptitious conveyance of learning from the Pugio, the purpose and plan of the Arcana are very different. The primary object of Galatinus, as has been already remarked, was to uphold the cause of Reuchlin against the Dominicans; Hoogstraaten is throughout the opponent whose attack on the whole Jewish literature is to be repelled. Galatinus does not, however, confine himself to that task. When he takes upon him to prove in long discussion (Book vii) the immaculate conception of the Virgin Mary against Hoogstraaten and Hoogstraaten's authority, Aquinas, he is prosecuting the long-standing controversy of his order with the Do-

[13] In letters to Casaubon, August, 1603, May, 1604; see Carpzov's edition of the Pugio, pp. 106 f. Scaliger erroneously supposed that the author was Raymundus Sebon.

[14] Morin broadly hints as much; and a half century earlier the elder Buxtorf wrote: Galatino saepissime hic liber laudatus et citatus, de cujus fide multi dubitant.

[15] A note on Heredia's fabrications will appear in another number of the Review.

minicans, and his occasional quotations from (spurious) Jewish writings hardly suffice for a pretext. In the two centuries and more between Martini and Galatinus both Christian theology and Jewish polemic had brought new points into prominence, as may be seen in the chapters on the Mother of the Messiah. The Arcana is adapted to a new situation.

Galatinus's Arcana was several times reprinted (Basel 1591, Frankfurt 1603, 1612, 1672), and many who came after him derived much of their learning directly or indirectly from it.

The Pugio itself was first printed in 1651.[16] It had waited long, but had the good fortune at last to fall into hands worthy of the task. The names of those who in different ways encouraged or furthered the enterprise are recorded on the title-page, and their respective parts in it defined in the ample prefatory matter. The principal editor, Joseph Voisin,[17] not only collated four manuscripts for the text, but appended to the several chapters of the second and third parts *Observationes* containing additional quotations from the sources employed by Martini and from later authors, including some from the Zohar and cabalistic commentators such as Behai, notes on differences between the text of the Talmud and other books as adduced in the Pugio and the current printed editions — differences in part accounted for by the subsequent activities of the censorship — and the like. To Martini's *Proemium* Voisin attached, at a length of nearly a hundred and fifty folios, prolegomena, treating first of the *Lex non scripta* and the whole subject of Jewish tradition, including a complete analysis of the Mishna; the thirteen norms of halakic deduction; on the Talmuds, Midrashim, and commentators, with a short chapter on the Cabala, etc.; then of the *Lex scripta* and its contents; the commandments, positive and negative; the divisions of the Pentateuch; the rules for copying the Scriptures and the defects which render a copy unfit for use; the disputed question of the age of the vowel points; the canon, and the authorship of the several books according to Jewish tradition; on Hebrew poetry; the lections from the Prophets and the

[16-17] See Appendix, p. 254.

divisions (*sedarim*) of the prophetic books; the translations of the Old Testament, etc. Particular note may be made of an extensive collection of quotations from the Old Testament (arranged in the order of their occurrence in the New) which were interpreted by the Jews in a way similar to the interpretation and application given them in the New Testament, and rabbinical parallels to New Testament ideas and expressions — a precursor, in a limited field, of the Horae Hebraicae of succeeding scholars.

Voisin's account of Jewish teaching and opinion is compiled, with large quotations in Hebrew and translation, from the best reputed authors, including Maimonides (*Mishneh Torah* and *Moreh*), Joseph Albo (*Ikkarim*), Azariah de Rossi (*Meor Enayim*). The whole is a work of admirable learning, and a most useful introduction to Martini. The greater part of it might still be studied with profit by many who profess to write on the subject in the light of "the attainment of modern research"; incidentally they might learn how a genuine scholar does his work. Voisin's edition of the Pugio was reprinted in Germany in 1687 under the direction of Johann Benedict Carpzov (the second of the name; died 1699), Professor in Leipzig, who prefixed to it a long *Introductio in Theologiam Judaicam et lectionem Raimundi, aliorumque id genus autorum.* The author's attitude toward his subject is illustrated by the title of one of his subdivisions: *Theologiae Judaicae modernae Autor principalis, Satanas; Ministerialis, Rabbini.* Nevertheless — probably by some oversight of Satan — even in it, he admits, there are vestiges of the true doctrine of the Old Testament which may be turned against the Jews; such were collected in the Pugio, whose author, *refutandam sibi caeteroqui proposuit theologiam Judaicam modernorum, apostatarum, reprobatorum, excoecatorum,* etc. It is this edition that is commonly in the hands of scholars; Voisin's is seldom found.

New and welcome sources were opened to Christian apologists in the Cabala, which purported to be an esoteric tradition of immemorial antiquity.[18] The eccentric genius Raymund Lull (died 1315) was the first Christian scholar whose

[18] See L. Ginzberg, 'Cabala,' Jewish Encyclopedia, ii, 456–479.

writings give evidence of acquaintance with the Cabala, but he employed his knowledge chiefly in his great scheme for a new science. It was two centuries later before the vogue of the Cabala in Christian circles began. Pico della Mirandola (died 1494) took it up with enthusiasm. He found in it a philosophy which he easily identified with his own Neoplatonic ideas, coming with the authority of revelation; it contained all the distinctive doctrines of Christianity: "The mystery of the Trinity, the incarnation of the Word, the divinity of the Messiah, original sin and its expiation through Christ, the heavenly Jerusalem, the fall of demons, the orders of angels, purgatory, and the punishment of hell." And all this in an esoteric tradition which, preserved among the Jews for many centuries orally, was reduced to writing by Ezra! It thus not only offered confirmation of the Christian faith, but enabled its defenders to confound the cavils of the Jews by the authority of their own books: "There is hardly a point in controversy between us and the Jews on which they cannot be so refuted out of the books of the cabalists that there will not be a corner left for them to hide in." [19] Reuchlin (died 1522), whose interest in cabalistic studies had been awakened by Pico during a temporary residence in Florence in 1490, entertained a similar estimate of the Cabala, both the speculative and the practical branches of which, in his view, centered in the doctrine of the Messiah. Of Galatinus, what is necessary has been said above.

From this time on the Cabala has a prominent place in Christian apologetic and anti-Judaic polemic, taking its place beside, or before, the testimonies from the Targum, Talmud and Midrash, and Jewish commentators and philosophers, such as Raymund Martini had adduced. The first introduction of Christian scholars to cabalistic literature was through recent authors like Recanati (flor. ca. 1300), whose commentary on the Pentateuch Pico della Mirandola translated into Latin, and Bahya ben Asher (Behai; died 1340); but students soon found their way to the Zohar, which passed for the highest authority in this sphere. The Zohar, in form a Midrash on the Pentateuch, professed to be the secret instruction imparted by R. Simeon

[19] De hominis dignitate ed. Basel 1592), pp. 329 f.

ben Yohai to a select circle of disciples, Simeon himself having received the doctrine by revelation. Whatever reservations Christian scholars may have made on the point of Simeon's inspiration, they did not doubt the age or the authenticity of the Zohar; nor that in substance it perpetuated a tradition much more ancient than the time of its reputed author, the middle of the second century of our era. Indeed, the great antiquity of the cabalistic tradition has been maintained by some orthodox Protestant theologians as late as the middle of the nineteenth century.[20] What could be accomplished in the way of proving Christian dogmas from the Zohar is well exemplified by G. C. Sommer, *Specimen Theologiae Soharicae cum Christiana amice convenientis, exhibens articulorum fidei fundamentalium probationes, e Sohare, . . . petitas*, etc. (1734), in which a complete system of orthodox Protestant doctrine, formulated in twenty 'theses,' is established, article by article, by *loca probantia* from the Zohar instead of the Bible, the extracts being duly exhibited in the original and translation, with explanatory and illustrative commentary.

The exchange of polemics between Jews and Christians increased in volume and violence in the fourteenth and fifteenth centuries, not alone in Spain, where converted Jews demonstrated their zeal for their new faith by the vehemence with which they impugned the old, and provoked equally vehement replies, but in France and Germany.[21] The replies did not restrict themselves to the defense of Judaism against its assailants, or to a refutation by exegetical and historical arguments of the Christian interpretation and application of the Old Testament, or to disputing the doctrines of the church on rational or philosophical grounds, but directed their criticism against the Gospels and other books of the New Testament, with which the authors show themselves well acquainted. An indication of the temper in which some of them were written is given by the title *Niṣṣaḥon*, 'Triumph,' which more than

[20] Notably Tholuck and Hengstenberg.

[21] The most prominent of the Spanish converts were Abner of Burgos (Alfonso of Valladolid, or of Burgos), died ca. 1350; Solomon ha-Levi of Burgos (Paul de Santa Maria, or Paul of Burgos), died 1345; Joshua ben Joseph ha-Lorki (Geronimo de Santa Fe), body physician of Pope Benedict XIII.

one of them bears, precisely as Porchetus had named his book 'Victoria.'

One of these Triumphs, the work of an unknown author who appears to have lived in the Rhineland, perhaps at Speier, in the thirteenth century,[22] gives considerable space to an examination in detail of passages from the Gospels, beginning with the genealogy of Jesus in Matt. 1, and its conflict with the genealogy in Luke. The writer is familiar with the Vulgate, whose words he frequently quotes in Latin (done into Hebrew letters) and sometimes criticizes its renderings of the Old Testament. Another work under the same title was written by R. Lipmann-Mühlhausen, about the beginning of the fifteenth century. Its author, who also was well acquainted with the Latin Bible, offers a detailed refutation of Christianity, divided into paragraphs, three hundred and forty-eight in number, each of which begins with a passage from the Old Testament. A compendious answer in poetical form to the Christian contentions and a summary of Jewish polemic is prefixed.. In the *Hizzuk Emunah* of the Karaite Isaac Troki (died 1594),[23] the argument ranges over the whole of the New Testament, from Matthew to Revelation, and is always on the offensive. The polemic is of a completely modern type, and the change of the times is evident also in the fact that the book was not only widely circulated in the original Hebrew but was translated into modern languages. The growing aggressiveness of the Jewish controversialists was met in a like spirit by those who hastened to defend Christianity and repel the calumnies of the Jews. To expose these 'calumnies' they printed the Jewish polemic treatises with Latin translations, comments, and refutations, thus ensuring their preservation and wider publicity, in the act of exciting prejudice against the Jews.

Wagenseil, who published a thick volume of such texts (including the *Toledoth Jeshua*) and replies, gave it the significant title *Tela ignea Satanae*, The Fiery Darts of the Evil One (1681). Wagenseil's principal 'Confutatio' is annexed to the

---

[22] Commonly cited as Nizzachon Vetus, to distinguish it from the work of Lipmann-Mühlhausen. Printed in Wagenseil.

[23] Troki's work is also in Wagenseil.

little Carmen Memoriale prefixed to Lipmann's Nissahon. The poem itself, if printed solid, would hardly fill more than a page or two; the reply occupies 413 pages in quarto. The author takes up Lipmann's twelve issues of controversy — chiefly Messianic — article by article and almost word by word, going into detailed discussion especially of Messianic prophecies, such as Gen. 49, 10 (63 pages), Isaiah 7, 14 (47 pages), etc., and incorporates long extracts from other authors, e.g. Amyraldus on the proof of the Trinity from the Old Testament, Chrysostom on the vain attempts of the Jews to rebuild the temple in Jerusalem, a catalogue of false Messiahs from the *Shalsheleth ha-Kabbala*, several specimens of Jewish synagogue sermons (in German), an epistolary altercation in Hebrew between Rittangel (d. 1652) and a Jew, Jewish computations of the time of the future advent of the Messiah, and the like (also from the Shalsheleth ha-Kabbala). The Toledoth Jeshua is also honored with a lengthy refutation; and the volume closes with a Mantissa on the Seventy Weeks of Daniel, directed against the recent interpretation of the English scholar, John Marsham. Nor should the hundred pages of formidably learned preliminaries be ignored.

Still more violent against the Jews and everything Jewish is Eisenmenger's *Entdecktes Judenthum* (1700, 2 vols.). [24] It is a malignant book, if ever there was one, but it is doubtful whether any man ever gave himself so much pains to gratify his malignancy. The book describes itself, in a title-page as long as a modern preface, as a "thorough and truthful account of the way in which the hardened Jews horribly blaspheme and dishonor the most holy Trinity, Father, Son, and Holy Ghost, defame the holy Mother of Christ, jeer and scoff at the New Testament, the Evangelists and Apostles, the Christian religion, and utterly despise and curse all Christian people," etc. The author promises to expose, besides, the gross errors of Jewish

[24] On the complaint of the Jews, this first edition of Eisenmenger's book was suppressed by the emperor as prejudicial to public order (see Wolf, ii, 1024). It was reprinted under the auspices of Frederick I, King of Prussia, and published in 1711, at Königsberg (or Berlin; see Wolf as above), in two volumes quarto, together nearly 2200 pages. A facsimile of the title page and other information about the work will be found in the Jewish Encyclopedia, v, 80 f.

religion and theology, together with its ridiculous fables and
other absurdities — all this by extracts in their own words from
their own books, of which he had read through a great many,
"mit grosser Mühe und unverdrossenem Fleiss." To give him
his due, he had read prodigiously. The annotated bibliography
of Hebrew books from which his quotations are taken, prefixed
to the first volume, fills more than fifteen quarto pages, besides
a page about writings in Jewish-German; it enumerates substantially all the works of any consequence that might have
been registered in a catalogue of Rabbinica et Judaica at the
end of the seventeenth century, and the extracts in the two
volumes prove that the bibliography is not a parade. His quotations are given in Hebrew with a German translation and
exact references. Some of the chapters, especially in the second
volume, in which he undertakes to set forth the beliefs of the
Jews on such subjects as paradise, hell, angels, devils, the
Messiah, the duration of his reign and what comes after it, the
resurrection and judgment, though never losing sight·of the
polemic intent, are more constructive presentations of Jewish
teaching, and contain a vast mass of quotations from literature
of all ages. For reference on particular topics the volumes are
furnished with ample and excellent analytical indexes.

The author shared with the scholars of his age, Jewish and
Christian, the belief in the antiquity and authority of the
Cabala, and quotes it extensively, especially in the writings of
its later representatives, including not only Luria and Cor-
dovero but the Yalkut Rubeni of his own contemporary Reuben Hoshke (d. 1673). Eisenmenger is the notorious source of
almost every thing that has been written since his time in def-
amation of the Talmud or in derision of Jewish superstitions,
and abounds in accusation of all kinds of misdeeds perpetrated
against Christians, including the murder of children to use
their blood in unholy rites.[25] What modern writers retail about
the irreverence or childishness of the Jewish imagination of
God — for example, God as a Rabbi, studying and teaching
the law — comes ultimately from Eisenmenger, who fills sixty
pages with the like edifying matter. It is not so frequently

[25] Vol. ii, pp. 220 ff.

recognized how deeply his successors have been indebted to the less strident parts of his work; and, with all his prejudice, what he adduces from the rabbinical sources is much more trustworthy than the books on which recent scholars have chiefly depended.

The Reformation gave a motive of its own to rabbinical studies. Hitherto scholars had maintained the doctrines of the Catholic Church against the Jews, or tried to convert Jews to them, and in so doing strove to confirm the Christian interpretation and application of the Old Testament by arraying on their side the most highly reputed Jewish authorities against the modern Jews. Protestants, on the other hand, in rejecting the authority of the Church and its traditions, took upon themselves to build up the entire edifice of Christian doctrine upon a purely scriptural basis. They were thus under the necessity of treating constructively various topics which had long been issues in controversy with the Jews, and of correlating them to other parts of the system. A great deal of the old material that had come down through centuries of polemics was ready to their hand, but for the new use it had to be put together in a new way; and when it came to be thus put together gaps were disclosed which had to be filled up. There was, moreover, at many points a distinctively Protestant position to be maintained against the Catholic interpretation and dogma.

To meet this need a multitude of monographs were written which may be regarded as materials for Protestant dogmatics. Like the Catholic works of the same period they illustrate the progress that has been made since the close of the fifteenth century in biblical philology, and the authors of many of them, whether Lutheran or Reformed, were largely learned at first hand in Jewish literature, both rabbinical and cabalistic. Their use of this material is, from our point of view, uncritical, but the collections are in some cases almost exhaustive so far as the sources were at hand, and no one who today undertakes a study of the subjects they treated can afford to ignore them, or can employ them without mingling admiration with gratitude.

Nor should we do justice to the literature of that age if we failed to recognize in much of it, along with the dogmatic and polemic motive, the scholar's love of learning for its own sake, above all its uses. This is still more conspicuous in the works that deal not strictly with doctrine, but with religious and civil institutions in Bible times and later; with the temple, priesthood, cultus; the synagogue and its worship; with proselytes to Judaism; or with civil government, the laws, courts, and administration of justice; with marriage and divorce, education, and many subjects beside, in most of which Maimonides' Mishneh Torah with its commentaries served them admirably for an introduction. The same spirit is manifest in works on the topography of Palestine, on the zoölogy and botany of the Bible, on its chronology, and the like, in all of which fields the permanent monographs come from this period. A perennial monument of the learning of that age is Surenhusius' edition of the Mishna (1698–1703), in six folio volumes, with Latin translation of the text and the most approved Jewish commentaries, together with additional comments and notes by Christian scholars, and extensive indexes, enabling the student to acquaint himself directly with this primary legal authority. Translations were also made of numerous treatises of the Talmud, and of the ancient juristic Midrash. Many of these were published, together with reprints of most of the seventeenth century works on Jewish antiquities, in the enormous collection of Blaisio Ugolino, *Thesaurus Antiquitatum Sacrarum*, 34 volumes in folio, 1744–1769.

Rabbinical learning was put to a different use when it was employed to elucidate or illustrate the New Testament. This was often done sporadically in continuous commentaries, e.g. by Grotius, and by Drusius in his Praeterita. Subsequently works were composed which might be described as rabbinical glosses on the New Testament, in which, generally without any other commentary, single passages were annotated with pertinent quotations from rabbinical sources. One of the earliest of these was the *Mellificium Hebraicum* (1649) of Christopher Cartwright,[26] which glosses in this way not only the New Testa-

---

[26] Christopher Cartwright (1602–1658) is the author also of Electa Thargumico-Rabbinica, sive Annotationes in Exodum ex triplici Thargum seu Chaldaica paraphrasi, 1658. The Mellificium Hebraicum, seu Observationes Diversimodae ex Hebraeorum,

ment but the Old Testament and the Apocrypha, besides two books (iv and v) of more miscellaneous adversaria. The second and third books, on the New Testament, quote with especial frequency parallels from the exegetical and homiletic Midrashim, particularly the Rabboth.

To the compilers of such glosses, as indeed to all who worked in this field then or since, the elder Buxtorf's *Lexicon Chaldaicum Talmudicum et Rabbinicum*, published by his son in 1640, was of inestimable value. Based on the *Aruk* of R. Nathan ben Jehiel of Rome (died 1106), but with much additional matter, especially for the language of the Targums, in which he had a predecessor in Elias Levita (*Meturgeman*, 1541), and the Hebrew of mediaeval authors and commentators; the Zohar also is frequently cited. Some of the articles are virtual concordances; he quotes, for example, all the occurrences of the word 'Messiah' in the Targums. In view of the ingratitude of most of the learned to the dictionaries which supply them with so much of their learning, it enhances our respect for Cartwright that he so often gives credit to Buxtorf, even when he supplements the dictionary references or corrects them. The Mellificium, which seems to be quite unknown to modern writers, is a useful complement to Lightfoot and Schoettgen, because its parallels are so largely drawn from the Palestinian Midrashim in which the author had evidently read extensively. When it is added that it covers not only the Gospels, but the Acts, Epistles, and Revelation, sufficient reason has perhaps been given for reviving the memory of the learned Christopher Cartwright.

The best known work of this class is the *Horae Hebraicae et Talmudicae* of John Lightfoot. Only the parts on the Gospels and First Corinthians were published by the author; [27] Acts is posthumous, and Romans a fragment from Lightfoot's notes. To each of the Gospels is prefixed a discussion of regions and

praesertim antiquiorum, monumentis desumptae, unde plurima cum Veteris tum Novi Testamenti loca vel explicantur, vel illustrantur etc., was printed in the Critici Sacri, (London, 1660), ix, cols. 2943–3128.

[27] The parts of Lightfoot's Horae were published separately, Matthew 1658, Mark 1663, 1 Corinthians 1664, John 1671, Luke 1674, Acts and Romans, posthumously, 1678, by Richard Kidder.

places named in the Gospel, particularly in the light of descriptions or references in the Talmud, and these chorographic studies fill a considerable part of the volune — a partial precursor of the great work of Adrian Reland, *Palaestina ex monumentis veteribus illustrata* (1714). Unlike Cartwright, Lightfoot's chief sources are the two Talmuds, with which he frequently quotes Rashi and the Tosaphoth. Maimonides also is often cited, and the commentators on the Old Testament; his lexical authority is the Aruk. On points of especial interest the glossarial method gives place to an excursus, sometimes of considerable length, for example, on Jewish baptism, the sects, synagogues, Sanhedrin, the Passover ritual, and the like. Numerous obscurities in the Greek are cleared up by comparison with Hebrew or Aramaic idiom; a good example is the wholly unintelligible ὀψὲ δὲ σαββάτων, τῇ ἐπιφωσκούσῃ εἰς μίαν σαββάτων, ἦλθε Μαρία ἡ Μαγδαληνή, κ.τ.λ. (Matt. 28.1). Some modern commentators and critics might have made sense out of the verse and understood its relation to the parallels (Mark 16, 1; Luke 24, 1) if the horizon of their learning had been wide enough to take in the seventeenth and eighteenth centuries.[28]

The *Horae Hebraicae et Talmudicae in universum Novum Testamentum* of Christian Schoettgen (1733), is described on the title page and in the preface as a supplement to Lightfoot on the Gospels, and for the rest of the New Testament a continuation of that scholar's unfinished work. Appended to the volume are seven short dissertations on various topics, such as the Kingdom of Heaven,[29] the celestial Jerusalem in Jewish

---

[28] See Schmiedel, Encyclopaedia Biblica, iv, col. 4041 f., cf. 4072; and on the passage, Moore in the Journal of the American Oriental Society, xxvi (1906), 323–329.

[29] A slip of Schoettgen's in the first paragraph of the Dissertatio de Regno Coelorum (i, 1147) is probably the origin of a misstatement which runs through a whole procession of New Testament lexicons and commentaries, namely that ἡ βασιλεία τῶν οὐρανῶν in Matthew corresponds to מלכות השמים in rabbinical Hebrew. Schoettgen expressly says so; but if the scholars who took his word for it had looked at the examples he quotes in the following pages and elsewhere (on Matt. 11, 19, p. 115 f.), or at those collected by Lightfoot on Matt. 3, 2, they would have discovered that the rabbinical phrase is always מלכות שמים, which Lightfoot correctly explained as by metonymy for God. The solitary instance of השמים in Schoettgen (p. 116), 'Mechilta in Yalkut Rubeni fol. 176, 4,' is an error either in Yalkut Rubeni (1660) or more probably in Schoettgen himself; the Mekilta (Jethro, Par. 5, init. on Exod. 20, 2) has correctly שמים.

representation, and on Christ the greatest of Rabbis. One of them entitled 'De Exergasia Sacra,' observations on parallelism in Hebrew style, is an interesting anticipation of Lowth's theory of Hebrew poetry, published twenty years later. Schoettgen's reading, according to his preface and a Conspectus Autorum appended to it, was more extensive than Lightfoot's. He includes the Zohar (through Knorr von Rosenroth's *Kabbala Denudata*), and several cabalistic works, from Behai (Bahya ben Asher) down to the Yalkut Rubeni. In 1742 Schoettgen published a second volume, also under the title Horae Hebraicae et Talmudicae, but with the more specific description, 'in Theoiogiam Judaeorum dogmaticam antiquam et orthodoxam de Messia.' This portly monograph of more than 700 pages in quarto, with a pair of dissertations added, and an appendix on rabbinical literature and other things, bringing the whole up to a round thousand pages, is not, as the uninitiated reader would gather from the title page, and as the author doubtless in good faith believed, an exposition of the *locus de Messia* in the 'ancient and orthodox dogmatic theology of the Jews' — something that never existed — but an attempt to prove that the whole orthodox dogmatic Christology of the church was held by the Jews at the beginning of our era and taught in their ancient and authoritative books, exoteric as well as esoteric.

As in all similar demonstrations, the Cabala has to furnish the evidence; and Schoettgen is so fully convinced of the Christianity of the Zohar that he sets himself seriously to prove that its supposed author, R. Simeon ben Yohai, was himself a Christian (pp. 901–917). This thesis was controverted by Justus Glaesener (himself the author of a *Theologia Soharica*) in a Diatribe reprinted in Schoettgen (pp. 918–935), to which Schoettgen replies in defense his theory (*ibid.* pp. 935–949). What did more lasting mischief than all this cabalistic Christianity in Schoettgen and others was the fact that upon its presumptions the genuine rabbinical sources were interpreted by the Cabala, with which they were assumed to be in complete accord — only, as was natural in esoteric writings, intimating its sublime doctrines more obscurely, and in language the full meaning of which was comprehended only by those who had the cabalistic key. Since the middle of the last century the Cabala has ceased to be quoted as an exponent of Jewish teaching at the beginning of our era, but in more modern expositions of this teaching — on the nature and office of the so-called intermediaries in Jewish theology, for example — the rabbinical texts in Targums, Talmud, and Midrash are still interpreted in unconscious dependence on a cabalistic tradition.

One more volume, nearly contemporaneous with Schoettgen's Horae, demands a brief mention, namely, Joh. Gerhard Meuschen, *Novum Testamentum ex Talmude et antiquitatibus Hebraeorum illustratum* (1736). This is a collection of writings, partly *inedita*, by several authors, Meuschen's own contributions being only the preface and a diatribe on the Nasi, or Director of the great Sanhedrin. The first place in the volume (pp. 1–232) is taken by Balthasar Scheid, *Praeterita Praeteritorum*, illustrations of select passages in the New Testament, chiefly from the Babylonian Talmud, somewhat resembling Lightfoot, but with fewer mere glosses, and in general with fuller comment on the texts under consideration. At the beginning, Scheid collects and remarks briefly on the Talmudic passages in which there is mention of Jesus and his disciples, an anticipation of which recent writers on the subject seem not to be aware. Nearly 800 pages are occupied by dissertations, programmes, etc., by Johann Andreas Danz (died 1727). Danz was one of the foremost Hebraists of his age, and these writings, when occasion requires, show him widely read also in classical and patristic literature. Whatever subjects he takes up are discussed with exhaustive thoroughness, whether it be proselyte baptism in relation to the baptism of John, or the law of *talio*, or Jewish excommunication (to illustrate Matt. 18, 18), or the idea of redemption (1 Pet. 1, 18 f.). Particular attention may be called to the series of programmes on the Shekinah (on John 14, 23). Among the other contents of the volume may be noted the controversy between Rhenferd and Witsius on the phrase 'the World to Come' in the Jewish literature and the New Testament, the particular point at issue being whether עולם הבא is equivalent to the 'Days of the Messiah,' which Rhenferd disproves.

Wettstein, in his edition of the New Testament (1751, 1752, 2 vols. fol.), subjoined to the text and critical apparatus a *commentarius plenior*, illustrating *ex scriptoribus veteribus Hebraeis, Graecis et Latinis historiam et vim verborum*. For the illustrations from Greek and Latin authors, besides his own reading, Wettstein availed himself of the ample accumulations of such matter in commentators like Drusius, Grotius, and others; those from the Talmud and other rabbinical sources are derived chiefly from the works which have been described above, especially from those in glossarial form such as Lightfoot and Schoettgen. It was chiefly in Wettstein's convenient delectus, that these parallels and illustrations were used by subsequent commentators and theologians, and passed into a secondary tradition which in the course of repetition has forgotten its origins.

II. The Nineteenth Century to the Present Time

The seventeenth century was the great age of Hebrew learning among Christian scholars; it lasted on till toward the middle of the eighteenth and then abruptly ended. The works of that period embody the results of earlier researches in Jewish literature from Raymund Martini down, with large additions accumulated by the labors of later generations, both in rabbinic and cabalistic sources. To the apparatus then collected little has been added since. When, after a long interruption, a few scholars in the nineteenth century took up again the study of Judaism it was with a different end and with a correspondingly different method. These later authors would have described their aim as historical — to exhibit the beliefs and teachings of Judaism in New Testament times or in the early centuries of the Christian era. For this purpose they employed chiefly the material that came down from their predecessors, without giving sufficient consideration to the fact that it had been gathered for every conceivable motive except to serve as material for the historian.

The apologetic selections were confined to certain topics of Christian doctrine; a delectus of quotations made for a polemic purpose is the last kind of a source to which a historian would go to get a just notion of what a religion really was to its adherents. Moreover, apologetic and polemic are addressed to contemporaries, and draw their proofs indifferently from past and present; if they appeal to the past against the present, it is the authority of antiquity they seek, not the history of doctrine. It may be possible to order their selections from the sources chronologically, and then to assign them to their proper age, but not to supply from such collections those sides of the religion which they ignore. The more constructive works, particularly of the seventeenth century, are contributions to Christian — specifically Protestant — theology, to which the exposition of Jewish teaching is incidental. The rabbinical glosses to the New Testament, finally, were never intended to represent the Judaism of New Testament times, but to illustrate passages in the Gospels and other books by parallels from Jewish literature, in the same way in which Grotius and others illustrate the same books and often the same passages by a redundancy of quotations from Greek and Latin authors. Least of all did Cartwright or Lightfoot and the rest dream that their illustrations would be used by moderns to explain the *origin* of New Testament ideas. A striking example of such misuse of their collections is given by a whole succession of commentaries on 1 Cor. 15, 45, where it is said that the identification of the 'second Adam' with the Messiah was commonly made by the Rabbis in Paul's time, from whom he had doubtless learned it. This probably got into the exegetical tradition through Schoettgen, who gives (after Edzard) the reference 'Neve Schalom fol. 160 a.' The author of the book cited died in 1492, and no older reference has been adduced. It may be presumed that Schoettgen was aware of the age of the work; those who quote him seem to imagine that a book with a Hebrew title must be as old as Paul.[30]

The modern period in Christian studies of Judaism begins with August Friedrich Gfroerer,[31] *Geschichte des Urchristen-*

[30] See my note in Journal of Biblical Literature, xvi (1897), 158–161; Fr. Schiele, Zeitschrift für wissenschaftliche Theologie xlii (1899), 20 ff.

[31] August Friedrich Gfroerer (1803–1861) studied theology in Tübingen, 1821–1825, and was Repetent there in 1828. In 1830 he became librarian in Stuttgart, and from 1846 was professor of history in the university of Freiburg in Baden.

thums, the first part of which, under the title, *Philo und die alexandrinische Theosophie, oder vom Einflusse der jüdisch-ägyptischen Schule auf die Lehre des Neuen Testaments* (2 vols.), appeared in 1831. This was followed by *Das Jahrhundert des Heils* (2 vols. 1838); *Die heilige Sage* (on the Gospels of Matthew, Mark, and Luke, 2 vols); and *Das Heiligthum und die Wahrheit* (on the Gospel of John; all in 1838). The sub-title of his Philo propounds the thesis of the whole work. The first volume is an exposition of the philosophy and theology, or as Gfroerer prefers to call it, 'theosophy,' of Philo, which is of independent and permanent worth; in the second he undertakes to demonstrate, chiefly from the Apocrypha, that the principal features of Philo's theology are much older than his time and had long been current among the Alexandrian Jews, and to show how this theosophy was transplanted to Palestine through the Therapeutae, Essenes, and other sects. The two volumes of the *Jahrhundert des Heils* (together nearly 900 pages) might more descriptively be entitled The Theology of the Palestinian Jews at the Beginning of the Christian Era. As we have already seen, the author holds that this theology — or at least what, in distinction from popular notions, may be called the *higher* theology — was nothing else than the Alexandrian 'theosophy,' which, early introduced in Palestine, had taken firm root there and flourished greatly. The Cabala is a product of the mystical philosophy of the Palestinian schools; but Gfroerer was convinced that the same philosophy is represented in the Targums, and many passages in the Talmud and Midrash.

In the preface Gfroerer acknowledges his indebtedness to earlier scholars from Raymund Martini down, naming among others Surenhusius, Rhenferd, Voisin, and Eisenmenger, and for the Cabala, Knorr von Rosenroth. Where translations of Talmudic texts were accessible, he availed himself of them and often quotes them in Latin. In his own reading in the Talmud and Zohar he had the help of Jewish scholars, who served him also in the collection of passages. Thus, without any pretence of great rabbinical learning, Gfroerer was respectably equipped for the task he set himself.

In the first chapter he gives a sufficient account of the rabbinical sources, discussing the age of the Talmud, and for the dates of the rest following the then recent critical work of Zunz.[32] It should be remarked that, notwithstanding his prepossessions about the antiquity of the cabalistic theosophy, Gfroerer assigns the Zohar itself to the end of the thirteenth century. He believed, however, that the theosophy of the Zohar was far older than the book, which was only the literary precipitate of a secular tradition; and when he found the same ideas in Jewish writings from the first four centuries of our era, he felt warranted in quoting the Zohar as a representative of the ancient mystical doctrine of the Jews. It is a notable step in advance that Gfroerer includes among the sources for Palestinian Judaism in this period the writings collected by Fabricius in the *Codex Pseudepigraphus Veteris Testamenti* (1713), among which are the Testaments of the Twelve Patriarchs and the Psalms of Solomon, and gives especial attention to the Apocalypses, the Ethiopic Enoch and the Ascension of Isaiah, which had recently been brought to light,[33] and Fourth Esdras, the origin and age of all of which he submits to a critical discussion. In the heresies of Simon Magus and Elxai, and in the Clementine Homilies and Recognitions, which he calls a Greek Zohar, he finds further sources for the history of Jewish theology, and cites many passages from the Fathers in attestation.

One of the results of this widening of the scope of the inquiry is the discrimination of different types of Jewish doctrine concerning the Messiah and the last things. One of these, drawn from the Messianic prophecies of the Old Testament, he calls the common prophetic type; the second is the Danielic type — we should say the apocalyptic — the Messiah the Son of Man who comes from heaven; the third is named the Mosaic type, because the Messiah is conceived as the prophet like unto Moses

---

[32] Leopold Zunz, Die gottesdienstlichen Vorträge der Juden historisch entwickelt. 1832.

[33] The Ethiopic text of the Ascension was edited, with Latin and English translations, by Richard Laurence in 1819; the Latin translation was reprinted by Gfroerer in Prophetae veteres pseudepigraphi, 1840; Enoch in English translation by Laurence in 1821; the Ethiopic text in 1838.

of Deut. 18, 15; and finally, 'the mystical Mosaic type.' [34] The sharp distinction between the prophetic and apocalyptic forms of Messianic expectation, with the corresponding differences in the whole Jewish eschatology, put all these problems in a new light, and this chapter of Gfroerer's work had considerable influence on the further study of the subject.

Gfroerer had been a student at Tübingen under Ferdinand Christian Baur, to whom his Philo was dedicated. What he proposed was a history of primitive Christianity, and he addressed himself to the task with the spirit and method of a historian. The investigation of Alexandrian Judaism in the *Philo* and of Palestinian Judaism in the *Jahrhundert des Heils* was necessary, because only through a knowledge of contemporary Judaism can the beginnings of Christianity be historically understood. The author knew, however, that to have its full value for this ulterior purpose the investigation must be pursued without reference to it, and consequently *Das Jahrhundert des Heils* taken by itself is a history of Palestinian Judaism in New Testament times. It was the first time that the attempt had been made to portray Judaism as it was, from its own literature, without apologetic, polemic, or dogmatic prepossessions or intentions; and however greatly the Alexandrian influence in Palestinian theology is exaggerated, and whatever its shortcomings in other respects, this fact alone is enough to make the work memorable.

Gfroerer does not try to run Jewish teaching into the mould of any system of Christian theology, but adopts a disposition natural to the matter. After the chapter on the sources of which mention has already been made, and one on education and the learned class, he discusses the Jewish doctrine of revelation; the idea of God; the divine powers; the intermediaries between God and the world (Shekinah, Memra); angels and demons; creation, the world and its parts; man, the soul, immortality, freedom and destiny, sin, the fall; the means and ways by which man gains the favor of God or averts his wrath; God's purpose with the Jewish people, providence; this world and that to come; the time of the Messiah's advent; and

[34] *Das Jahrhundert des Heils*, ii, 289–444.

finally the chapter on the Messiah and the Last Things of which we have spoken above. The author's Alexandrinism — to label his theory thus — is particularly evident when he is dealing with the idea of God and the intermediaries, a subject to which we shall return presently. Elsewhere he gives in general a satisfactory account of Palestinian teaching, so far as his sources and his somewhat indiscriminate use of them permit.

Eminently good is the exposition of the ways by which the favor of God is gained, a chapter which comprehends in brief the whole of practical religion. The author is dealing here with matters on which Jewish teaching is abundant, clear, consistent, and always the same; but no one before him had undertaken to bring it together and set it forth for Christian readers; indeed the subject had been almost completely ignored by his predecessors — a striking example of the insufficiency for historical purposes not only of the polemic and dogmatic methods, but of the vast accumulation of material made in a polemic or dogmatic interest. For the question, What must men do to be well-pleasing to God? goes to the heart of the matter. The answer to it tells us more than anything else what a religion really is. Gfroerer not only recognized the significance of this question, but lets the Jews themselves answer it in their own way and mainly in their own words. The chapter has not merely the merit of a first exploration in a neglected field; it is to this day the most adequate presentation of the subject from the hand of a Christian scholar, and its excellence is the more conspicuous by comparison with the treatment of the matter by more recent writers, particularly Ferdinand Weber and those who get their notions of Judaism from him.

Gfroerer distinguishes among the Palestinian Jews two widely different ideas of God. The great majority, as in all religions and in all times, conceived of God after the analogy of human personality, only immeasurably greater and better, creator, sustainer, and moral governor of the world, as he is represented in the Scriptures. A smaller number embraced the Alexandrian speculations which allowed the name God in its proper sense only to the pure Being of its ontology (ὁ ὤν, τὸ ὄν), an Absolute, of which, as it is in itself, nothing can be known, no name given to it, no predicates applied, no attributes ascribed. Between this transcendent God and the world they posited an intermediary corresponding in nature and function to the Logos in Philo. The chief evidence that Gfroerer adduces to prove that a transcendent idea of God was entertained by influential Palestinian teachers is, in fact, the existence in the Targums [35] and Midrash of such figures as the Shekinah, Memra, Metatron, which he conceives to be explicable only as the intermediaries made necessary by a metaphysical idea of God that excludes him by definition from immediate transactions in nature or revelation. In this interpretation he was in accord with the long-standing traditions of Christian apologetics and dogmatics, proceeding from the same metaphysical idea of God.

Gfroerer is thus a precursor of the modern school which attributes to Palestinian Judaism as a fundamental dogma an idea of God which isolates him from the world in his infinite being and unapproachable holiness — the term transcendent is often used to define it. But he does not, like them, regard this as the general and dominant rabbinical conception; he confines it to the theosophic mystical circles who derived their theology from Alexandria and in which the Cabala was cultivated. And, so far from regarding it as something distinctively bad in Judaism by contrast with Christianity, he finds the same ideas in the Gospel of John, which he exalts above the others in a volume bearing the significant title, *Das Heiligthum und die Wahrheit*.[36] His theory of the origin and nature of the Shekinah and Memra is erroneous, and the inference from it invalid; but his discrimination saves him from the gross misrepresentation of the prevailing Jewish conception of God into which his successors fall. Gfroerer is now seldom quoted, in part perhaps because he did not provide his volumes with indexes to make it easy to quote without reading. Nor is the

---

[35] The Targums on the Pentateuch and the Historical Books, which (with the exception of the so-called Pseudo-Jonathan on the Pentateuch) he makes older than the destruction of Jerusalem, are among his chief witnesses to the early prevalence of Alexandrian mystical theology in Palestine.

[36] Recall also the subtitle of his Philo (above, p. 223), 'vom Einflusse der jüdisch-aegyptischen Schule auf die Lehre des Neuen Testaments.'

book, with its wilderness of quotations in Latin and German easy reading, but one who is willing to undergo the labor may still learn much from it.

The book that has for forty years been the chief resource of Christian writers who have dealt *ex professo* or incidentally with Judaism at the beginning of the Christian era is Ferdinand Weber's *System der altsynagogalen palästinischen Theologie* (1880).[37] For a just estimate of this work it is necessary to premise somewhat about its origin. The author grew up in a pietistic atmosphere; he studied at Erlangen, then one of the strongholds of the new-fashioned Lutheranism, under Johann Christian Hofmann and Franz Delitzsch, and is redolent of the 'heilsgeschichtliche Theologie.' There he imbibed the anticritical and unhistorical spirit of the school. His first publication was outlines of Introduction of the Old and New Testament, for teachers in higher schools and educated readers of the Bible (1863), of one of the later editions of which Heinrich Holtzmann said that the only thing it showed was how a man could write on these subjects without taking any note of what was going on about him. No less significant of his whole attitude was a series of articles in the Allgemeine evangelischlutherische Kirchenzeitung, entitled, *System des jüdischen Pharisäismus und des römischen Katholicismus* (1890).

Probably under Delitzsch's influence Weber conceived the idea of becoming a missionary to the Jews, and with this end in view began rabbinical studies under J. H. Biesenthal, a very competent scholar, himself a convert from Judaism and a missionary to the Jews, who like so many before him brought as a baptismal offering proofs of the Trinity and other Christian doctrines from the Cabala. Weber never succeeded in getting into the missionary calling, but the 'System' on which he spent the last years of his life was the outcome of studies undertaken to that end.

[37] Edited and published after the author's death by Franz Delitzsch and Georg Schnedermann; reissued with an extra title-page, 'Die Lehren des Talmuds' (1886), and in a second, 'improved' edition by Schnedermann under a third title, 'Jüdische Theologie auf Grund des Talmud und verwandte Schriften,' 1897. The improvements consist in an (incomplete) verification of the references by J. J. Kahan and occasional slight revision by the editor, not always for the better. (See, for example, the absurd Metatron-Crown Prince, 2d ed., p. 178.)

Now Jewish law, ritual, and observance, were ordered and codified in the Mishna and kindred works; but the Jews did nothing of the kind for the religious and moral teaching of the school and synagogue. No one even thought of extracting a theology from the utterances of the Rabbis in Midrash and Haggada, to say nothing of organizing the theology in a system; nor was the need of any connected presentation of Jewish doctrine felt until the controversies of the tenth century prompted Saadia to write the *Emunoth we-Deoth* after the example of Moslem Mutakallimin and upon the same philosophical principles. The fundamental criticism to be made of Weber's 'System' is precisely that it *is* a system of theology, and not an ancient Jewish system but a modern German system. This is far more than a mere matter of disposition, the ordering of the materials under certain heads taken from Christian dogmatics; the system brings its logic with it and imposes it upon the materials.

After the pattern of the 'material principle' and 'formal principle' of Lutheran dogmatics, Weber begins with *Das Materialprincip des Nomismus* and *Das Formalprincip des Nomismus*, each in several chapters. The 'material principle' is concisely formulated in the title of chapter 3: *Gesetzlichkeit das Wesen der Religion* — legalism is the sum and substance of religion, and is, in Jewish apprehension, the only form of religion for all ages. This 'nomism' is reflected in the idea of God (chap. 11): Where legalism is the essence of religion, religion is the right behavior of man before God, whereas 'we say,'[38] Religion is communion with God. God will admit man to his communion because he is not only holiness but love. In Judaism, on the contrary, where his holiness is exclusively emphasized, God remains absolutely exalted above the world and man, separated from them, abiding unchangeable in himself.

After a few sentences on the names of God, the remoteness of God in his supramundane exaltation becomes metaphysical:

---

[38] In the second edition Schnedermann transforms this opposition in the points of view ('wir sagen') into an antithesis in the proposition itself. The Jewish idea is that, 'Religion das rechte Verhalten des Menschen vor Gott ist, *nicht aber* Gemeinschaft des Menschen mit Gott.'

"From this fundamental conception of God as the Absolute, Jewish theology deduces two further (in reality antithetic) elements, which must be regarded as characteristic of the Jewish idea of God; namely, abstract monotheism and abstract transcendentism. The former was developed and fixed in opposition to the trinitarian unfolding (Erschliessung) of the one Godhead in three persons, the latter in opposition to the personal indwelling of God in the human race." [39] Subsequent writers who use Weber as evidence of the Jewish idea of God in New Testament times in order to contrast with it Jesus' conception have overlooked this most significant passage. It is necessary, therefore to emphasize his express assertion that the antithetic conceptions of 'abstract monotheism' (or 'monism'!) and the 'abstract transcendentism' in Jewish theology were 'developed and fixed' in opposition to the Trinitarianism and Christology of the church, and are therefore posterior to the development of those Christian doctrines.

It is equally important to remark that the 'fundamental conception' of an inaccessible God, whom, without perceiving the difference, he converts in the next breath into an Absolute God,[40] is derived from the principle that legalism is the essence of religion, from which, according to Weber, it follows by logical necessity. About this he deceives himself; the necessity is purely apologetic. The motive and method of the volume are in fact apologetic throughout; the author, like so many of his predecessors, sets himself to prove the superiority of Christianity to Judaism. In view of what is known of his life, it may perhaps without injustice be described more specifically as missionary apologetic: he would convince Jews how much better Christianity is than Judaism. This aim would explain the comparative absence of the polemic element which mingles so strongly with the ordinary apology.

A peculiar character is given to Weber's work also by his own religious and theological prepossessions. It is not catholic doctrine which is the explicit or implicit antithesis of Judaism,

[39] System, u. s. w., p. 145.
[40] As with equal obtuseness to the meaning of words he makes 'monism' equivalent to 'abstract monotheism.'

but Lutheranism of a peculiar modernized type of which Hofmann was the chief representative. The arbitrary contradiction created between the two conceptions of the essence of religion, conformity to the will of God and communion with God, with its consequences for the idea of God, and the singular theory of the Trinity to which we have already adverted are of this origin. A conspicuous example is to be found also in the treatment of 'Die Gerechtigkeit vor Gott und das Verdienst' (chap. 19), in which antipathy to the Roman Catholic doctrine of good works and merit transfers itself to Judaism.

In an introduction of thirty-four pages the rabbinical sources are described after Zunz and other Jewish authors, and in general with Zunz's dates, and the editions from which the author ordinarily quotes are specified — an unusual thoughtfulness for which those who verify their quotations would be more grateful if he had applied it to his references to the Rabboth. The Cabala and the Pseudepigrapha are excluded; Hellenistic Judaism is outside the author's plan. The omission of the liturgy of the synagogue and forms of private prayer in the survey of the sources is, however, an error of grave consequence. Incidentally it shows with how little independence Weber planned and performed his task — his predecessors had not concerned themselves with this material. The principles on which the sources are to be employed are briefly stated; they are sounder than his application of them in practice. Finally, there is a survey of the older literature down to Wagenseil and Bodenschatz, on which somewhat sweeping unfavorable judgment is passed. No mention is any where made of Gfroerer, and the omission is hardly accidental; a pupil of Baur and a convert to Catholicism was anathema in Weber's circle on both counts.

No intimation is given of the nature and extent of Weber's indebtedness to the predecessors who in the course of centuries had collected for one purpose or another a vast mass of quotations and references. Perhaps if he had lived to publish the volume himself, he might have acknowledged his obligations in a preface, though the Introduction would have been the natural place for them. As it is one might get the impression that Weber meant to give the appearance of having gone at the Targum, Talmuds, and Midrashim as though nobody had been there before him, and collected all his materials for himself; and in fact Christian scholars unfamiliar with the older literature have generally taken him at this estimate and attributed to him a measure of learning much beyond the reality.[41] There is no question that he had read industriously and had the assistance of converted Jews; but that he built on other men's foundations and largely with their materials is easily demonstrable. Most of his quotations come out of the common stock which had been accumulated by the labors of many generations, not all of them even verified. Confiding successors have appropriated these errors, and not always given Weber the credit of them.

The passages which Weber adduces from the sources (in German translation) are copious and in general relevant to his proposition. It must be emphasized, however, that in detaching them from their original associations and using them as *dicta probantia* for the *loci* of a systematic theology whose 'system' is the antithesis of Judaism to Christianity, they are methodically misused. To much of this material — to the exegetical ingenuities and homiletical conceits of the Midrash and the playful imaginations of the Haggada, for example — the Jews attached no theological character or authority. Weber on 'Die Judaisirung des Gottesbegriffes' (pp. 153–157) is a salient instance of such misuse of the sources. Incidentally also of his use of his predecessors. If any one will take the trouble to compare this section with Eisenmenger's chapter, 'Was vor ungeziemende und theils lästerliche Dinge die verstockten Juden von Gott dem Vater lehren und schreiben'

---

[41] It does not inspire confidence in the author's rabbinical erudition to read (p. xx) that according to Sanhedrin 86a the anonymous utterances in Sifra are to be taken as sayings of R. Judah the Holy, 'from which it follows that the Talmud regards R. Judah the Holy as the author of Sifra.' The Talmud says R. Judah, by which name not 'Judah the Holy,' but Judah ben Ilai (in the preceding generation) is regularly designated. In the second edition 'the Holy' disappears; but with the consequence that in the sequel Rab is said to have been a disciple in the school of Judah, which would seem to give Rab an extraordinarily long life.

(i, 1 ff., esp. pp. 1–54), will find Weber's references sometimes for a page together in the same order. It is curious that he should have made such use of a work of which, with others of the kind, he says that they are "weit mehr Sammlungen aller möglichen Absurditäten und Frivolitäten, als religionsgeschichtliche Darstellungen," and of a chapter in which Eisenmenger outdoes himself in that vein. Eisenmenger, however, got together this material (and much more) only to hold up the Jews to derision and contempt; Weber seriously derives from it a 'Judaized' idea of God, and has a serious theory to explain how an idea so incongruous with their 'transcendentism' ever came to be entertained—it was the growing dominance of 'the principle of nomocracy' which transformed God into 'a God of the Torah.'

Weber's original contribution to the misunderstanding of Judaism was what he calls 'transcendentism,' the inaccessibility of God, wherein he finds the characteristic difference of the Jewish idea of God, and its immense inferiority to the Christian idea. That this was the Jewish idea, is proved for him, as has been already noted, by the intermediaries which, according to him, Judaism interposed between God and the world: if God himself were not transcendent, there would be no use for them. The older apologetic, better instructed in Christian theology, had consistently labored to prove that these intermediaries corresponded exactly to their own Logos, the Son, Christ, discovering in them no difference between the Jewish idea of God and the Christian — the identity is, indeed, always assumed. The Christology of the church and its Trinitarian dogma are in fact based upon a metaphysical doctrine of the Absolute; and from their first acquaintance with it Christian scholars recognized their own philosophy of religion in the transcendental Neoplatonism of the speculative Cabala, which they regarded as the ancient esoteric doctrine of Judaism. Weber's antithesis between the transcendent God of Jewish theology and the contrary in Christian theology [42] shows how little he knew about either the history or the content of Christian dogma. What

---

[42] The contrary of a transcendent God, is not, as historically and logically it should be, an *immanent* God, but what may be called a sociable God.

has led recent scholars of other schools and of greatly superior theological learning to adopt Weber's interpretation and judgment of Judaism and to put the Jewish idea of God in a new antithesis to Christianity is a question to which we shall revert later.

Besides the causes of misunderstanding that have been remarked above, particular misinterpretations are not infrequent, and are sometimes of far-reaching consequence. A striking instance of this kind may be found on page 174 f., where Weber discovers in the *dibbūr* of *Shir ha-Shirim Rabbah* fol. 3 a (Sulzbach; ed. Wilna, 1884, fol. 4 b) 'the basis for the understanding of the Memra of Jehovah in the Targums,' "des aus dem Munde Gottes hervorgegangenen Wortes, welches als göttliche Potenz innerhalb der Heilsgeschichte wirkend sich in der Anschauung des Judentums zur Person verdichtet hat und als mittlerische Hypostase zwischen Gott und seinem Volke steht." As Weber paraphrases: "At the proclamation of the Ten Commandments, the *dibbūr* proceeded out of the mouth of God, and then went to each Israelite in the camp and asked him whether he would accept it, setting before him at the same time all the obligations as well as the reward involved in the acceptance. As soon as an Israelite had answered in the affirmative and accepted the Word, the Dibbur kissed him on the mouth."

The passage on which such large dogmatic conclusions are based is a peculiarly far-fetched homiletic conceit on Cant. 1, 2, 'Let him kiss me with the kisses of his mouth.' R. Johanan said that at the lawgiving at Sinai, "An angel brought out the word (*dibbūr*) from the presence of God, each word separately,[43] and took it around to every individual Israelite, saying to him, Do you take upon you this word?" He explained all that was implied in the commandment as well as what was explicitly required, the penalties of transgression, and the reward of obedience. "If the Israelite said, Yes, the angel further asked, Do you take upon you the Godhead of the

---

[43] *Dibbūr* is 'speech, utterance'; specifically one of the Ten Utterances (*debarim*, rabbinical, *debaroth*), which the Greek version (Exod. 34, 28) and Philo call δέκα λόγοι, and we after them the Decalogue.

Holy One? If he answered, Yes, Yes, the angel kissed him on the mouth — this is what is said (in Deut. 4, 35): 'Thou wast made to see, to know' (by the hand of a messenger)." [44] The majority, however, gave a slightly different turn to the conceit — and here we come to Weber's quotation: The several commandments were not carried about one by one by an angel, but each *dibbūr* ('commandment') itself went about on the same errand, made the same explanations, and, being accepted, kissed the man on his mouth, etc.

The difference between R. Johanan and the majority is not over the impersonality or personality of the word: a more plausible suggestion is offered by a commentator steeped in the mind of the Midrash, that it has its origin in a different interpretation of 'the great host' in Psalm 68, 12, one taking it of the angels, the others of the Israelites. But whatever remoter conceits may have been in the homilists imaginations, Weber's partial quotation needs only to be completed from its context to prove his interpretation and application false. And, even if not misinterpreted and misapplied, what kind of a basis for the 'hypostatic Word of God' are such curiosities of ingenuity as are displayed in asking and answering the question who is the kisser and who the kissed in Cant. 1, 2, and when, and where, and what for? I have dwelt on this case at some length, as a warning against that implicit confidence in Weber which prevails among those who are not able to bring him to book. Before I leave the subject I am going to give one illustration of how Weber at second-hand is worse than himself. Oesterley and Box, with the remark that it 'illustrates the underlying conception of the *Memra*,' reproduce as follows the passage from Weber quoted above: "The passage is dealing with the account of the giving of the Law on Mount Sinai, and it is explained that the 'Word' (*Memra*) came forth from the mouth of God when the Ten Commandments were pronounced, and went forth to each Israelite, asking each if he would accept these commandments," etc. "As soon as an Israelite signified

[44] The quotation of these catch-words must be understood to call to mind the sequel, 'that the Lord, he is God; there is none beside him. Out of heaven he made thee to hear his voice that he might instruct thee,' etc.

his willingness to become obedient to the Law, the 'Word' kissed him on his lips." [45]

Numerous equally striking examples of Weber at second hand may be found by those who are in search of such entertainment in the article 'Shekinah' in Hastings' Dictionary of the Bible, by J. T. Marshall. I can make room here for only one of them. In a paragraph on the activity of the Shekinah not only on earth but in Sheol (p. 489 A) we read: "But in Bereshith Rabba to Gn. 44, 8 the Shekinah is the deliverer. It affirms that the wicked Jews now 'bound in Gehinnom' will ascend out of hell, *with the Shekinah at their head.*" For this, reference is made with a certain superfluity to both editions of Weber. In abridging Weber, Marshall has eliminated the association with Micah 2, 13 ('and their King shall pass over before them and the Lord at their head') which alone makes the Midrash intelligible. This by the way. The point of the story is in the reference to 'Bereshith Rabba to Gn. 44, 8.' A reader whose skepticism was properly aroused by this altogether unusual method of citing the Midrash, and who undertook to find the place, would find nothing but a justification of his skepticism. The quotation, in fact, is not from the Midrash Bereshith Rabbah at all. It is derived from the Pugio Fidei (p. 685), where it is attributed to the Bereshith Rabba *of Rabbi Moses ha-Darshan,* that is to say to a lost work by a French Rabbi at the close of the eleventh century. But the end is not yet. In Carpzov's edition of the Pugio which Weber used the reference 'Gen. 44. v. 8' is a misprint, as the first words of the quotation ויגש אליו יהודה — the *incipit* of the Parasha ויגש, Gen. 44, 18 — would betray at a glance to any reader who paid attention to what he was about. The case incidentally demonstrates that neither Weber nor Marshall had ever tried to verify the reference. In the second edition of Weber, Kahan has put a (?) after the reference, showing that he had looked for it but not been able to find it in Bereshith Rabbah, which might at least have served as a danger signal to Marshall.

[44] Religion and Worship of the Synagogue, p. 182 f.

Finally, it is to be observed that in treating of the intermediaries (Shekinah, Memra, Metatron), although Weber abjures the testimony of the Cabala, he takes over the conceptions and associations which his predecessors had derived from the Cabala, and interprets in accordance with them the testimony of the Targums and Midrash — a fallacy of method in which he has many fellows. A bad example of such contamination occurs in the section on the Metatron (p. 174), where, having by way of the mediaeval Gematria, מטטרון = 314 = שדי, discovered that Metatron is a 'representative of the Almighty,' he continues: "In this sense he bears in Hullin 69 a and Yebamoth 16 b the name שר העולם, Prince of the World; he represents God's sovereignty (*Herrscherstellung*) in the world." The Talmud neither in the places cited nor anywhere else calls Metatron *sar ha-'ōlam*. To judge from a comparison of the contexts, Weber had his references from Levy (*Chaldäisches Wörterbuch*, II, 31), where, however, the identification is not attributed to the Talmud, but (incorrectly) to the Tosaphoth, or supplementary glosses (supplementary, that is, to Rashi), chiefly from the French schools of the thirteenth century. In the Tosaphoth themselves the identity is discussed, a propos of the apparently conflicting use of the title in certain mediaeval hymns, but is *not* affirmed. Eisenmenger (II, 397), and so far as I know every one who touched the subject before Weber, stated the matter correctly.

Six years before Weber, appeared another work which was destined more than any other in its time to influence Christian notions of Judaism, namely, Emil Schürer, *Lehrbuch der Neutestamentlichen Zeitgeschichte* (1874). The name, which came into vogue in the sixth and seventh decades of the last century, did not mean a history of New Testament times, but designated a part of what in earlier days would have been comprehended under Introduction to the New Testament. Its practical purpose was to put the student in the way of acquiring a variety of knowledges which are necessary to the understanding of the New Testament and the beginnings of Christianity. Schneckenburger (1862) had included the Gentile world of the time, but Schürer limits the scope of his Lehrbuch to the Jewish side. After an introduction on the sources he devotes half the volume to the political history of Palestine from 175 B.C. to 70 A.D. The second part has the subtitle, 'Das innere Leben des jüdischen Volkes im Zeitalter Christi,' and deals with the country and its populations, Jewish institutions, the sects, the scribes and their learning, schools and synagogues, life under the Law; then (on a much larger scale), the apocalyptic literature, and the Messianic expectation. The volume concludes with chapters on Judaism in the dispersion, and on Philo.

Subsequent editions, greatly enlarged, appeared under the title, *Geschichte des jüdischen Volkes im Zeitalter Jesu Christi*, but without any considerable change in the character or plan of the work. Schürer's volumes are an indispensable repértory for all sorts of things about the Jews — history, archaeology, geography, chronology, institutions, cultus, sects and parties, literature, etc. — treated as distinct subjects of investigation and presentation. The work has an external unity in serviceability for a practical purpose, but lacks the historical bond which alone could give it an inner unity. This observation is not an adverse criticism on the work; Schürer did what he set out to do, and made an immeasurably useful handbook. But the reader must take it and use it for what it is, not for what its author, notwithstanding the title, never intended it to be — history. Least of all did he propose to write a history of the Jewish religion in the period he covers, or a description of it as it was at the beginning of our era. He treats at large the Messianic expectation—under which he included the whole eschatology — twice, first in its development and then again systematically. The only other subject in the sphere of religion which is given a place of its own is 'Life under the Law.' The selection of these two subjects and no others is explained by their signal importance for the understanding of the beginnings of Christianity — the different forms of Messianic expectation among the Jews in relation to correspondingly varied forms of belief among Christians about Jesus the Messiah, and Life under the Law as explaining and justifying Jesus' criticism of the Scribes and Pharisees.

The consequence of the isolation of these subjects from their place in Jewish religion as a whole is to give the erroneous impression that the Law and the Messianic expectation are not only, as Schürer puts it, the two poles of Judaism, but that they are the sum and substance of it. This impression is greatly strengthened by the contents of the section on Life under the Law. To Schürer, notwithstanding his very different theological standpoint, as much as to Weber, Judaism was synonymous with 'legalism,' and 'legalism' was his most cherished religious antipathy. The motive of the legalized religiousness of the Jews was retribution, reward and punishment here and hereafter, in the exact measure of the merit or demerit of particular acts of transgression or omission — retribution for the individual and the people. As this motive is essentially external, the result was an incredible externalizing of the religious and moral life, the whole of which is drawn down into the 'juristic' sphere. The evil consequences that necessarily follow are developed at large; the upshot of it is that life becomes a service of the letter for the letter's sake. The outward correctness of the action is the thing, not the inward end and motive. "And all this trivial and perverted zeal professes to be the true and right religion. The more pains men took, the more they believed that they gained the favor of God." [46]

Schürer goes on to illustrate the errors into which this 'zeal for God not according to knowledge' (Rom. 10, 2) led, and the heavy burdens it laid on the Israelite, by describing in detail, chiefly after the Mishna, the regulations for Sabbath observance, the rules of clean and unclean, the prescriptions about the wearing of fringes, phylacteries, prayer-shawls; the formalizing of prayer, fasting, and the like. Even the occasional fine sayings of individual Rabbis are for him only streaks of light which make blacker the shadows they can not illumine. In conclusion, Schürer pronounces judgment on the Jewish religion in terms of solemn condemnation. It is significant that, while almost everything else in the work was revised and rewritten in the successive editions, this chapter remains nearly

---

[46] Neutestamentliche Zeitgeschichte, § 27; especially pp. 483 f., 510 f.; Geschichte des jüdischen Volkes, u. s. w., § 28; 3d edit. ii, 464 ff., 469, 495, etc.

verbatim to the last; even the original vehemence of expression is unsoftened by years.

It is to be taken into account in estimating his depreciatory judgment that Schürer was never widely read in the literature of the school and the synagogue, and that he paid the least attention to precisely those parts of it from which most may be learned about religious feeling and the inwardness of Jewish piety. It may be added that Schürer himself was temperamentally lacking in the sympathetic imagination which re-creates other times, other men, other manners, alien ways of thinking and feeling, philosophies and religions remote from our own, in the endeavor to realize what they meant in their own time and place. But after all allowance is made the final word must be that 'Life under the Law' was conceived, not as a chapter of the history of Judaism but as a topic of Christian apologetic; it was written to prove by the highest Jewish authority that the strictures on Judaism in the Gospels and the Pauline Epistles are fully justified. It is greatly to be regretted that Schürer's eminent merits in everything external should have led New Testament scholars generally to attach equal authority to his representation and judgment of the Jewish religion.

In another respect Schürer's work marks a change in the point of view. His predecessors, generally speaking, compare and contrast Judaism and Christianity as wholes, and from the point of view of their own time; Weber compares the Palestinian Judaism of the first five centuries of our era with his own variety of nineteenth century Protestantism, unhistorically imagined to be Christianity itself. Schürer's purpose to furnish the necessary knowledge for the understanding of the beginnings of Christianity confines the comparison to narrower limits. The Messianic expectations of the contemporary Jews are reflected in Christian conceptions; the opposition to legalism is a primitive factor in the gospel. The problem of the origin of Christianity historically conceived demands, however, an investigation of every other phase of Judaism at the beginning of our era, and the endeavor to define what Christianity took over from Judaism as well as what was new in it. For such

a purpose a critical history of Judaism in that age, say from the
beginning of the second century B.C. to the end of the second
century A.D., both Palestinian and Hellenistic, became indispensable.

This is what the title of Bousset's *Die Religion des Judentums
im neutestamentlichen Zeitalter* (1903; 2d ed. 1906) promises.
The author is conscious that in undertaking a comprehensive
presentation of what he strangely calls 'die Religion des Spät-
judentums' he is assuming a task which no one since Gfroerer
had set his hand to, and, while pointing out the limitations of
Gfroerer's work, he has a juster appreciation of its merits than
those of his predecessors who have anything to say about it:
"Der ganze Wurf ist gross und kühn gedacht. Man wird von
him immer aufs neue lernen müssen."

Bousset was, like Schürer, a New Testament scholar, and his
interest in Judaism also was not for its own sake, but for the
light it might throw on the beginnings of Christianity. One
of his first published writings was, *Jesu Predigt in ihrem Gegensatz zum Judentum. Ein religionsgeschichtlicher Vergleich*
(1892). In it the author seeks to prove that the character and
teaching of Jesus can be explained, not as having their roots in
Judaism, but only as the antithesis to Judaism in every essential point. The book is closely associated with Baldensperger,
*Das Selbstbewusstsein Jesu im Lichte der messianischen Hoffnung-
en seiner Zeit* (1888), and Johann Weiss, *Die Predigt Jesu vom
Reiche Gottes* (1890),[47] and like them endeavors to solve its
problems by bringing the teaching of Jesus into connection
with the religion in which he had been brought up. The idea
was not as new as some of the advertisements of the 'religionsgeschichtliche Methode' might lead one to think — no philolo-
gist would ever have admitted that there was any other method
— but it was at least potentially more fruitful than a prosecu-
tion *in infinitum* of the internal criticism and exegesis of the

[47] It is not without significance that all these authors — Schürer, Baldensperger,
Weiss, Bousset — were New Testament scholars, the oldest of them scarcely past
thirty years old. Schürer was the only one who thought it necessary to know anything
about the rabbinical sources, and he found in Surenhusius' Mishna just the right material for the demonstration of 'legalism.' Beyond this he never went; the others did
not go so far.

Gospels. Whether it should bear good fruit or evil depended, however, on the knowledge of Judaism the investigators brought to bear on their subject. In Bousset's case, as with Baldensperger and Weiss, this knowledge was a negligible quantity. It could not have been otherwise: a Privatdozent of twenty-seven, only getting fairly started with his courses on the New Testament, would be a prodigy if he had, of his own, anything properly to be called knowledge in so diverse and difficult a field. What Bousset lacked in knowledge, he made up, however, in the positiveness and confidence of his opinions, and for the failure to present evidence, by an effective use of what psychologists call suggestion — unsupported assertion coming by force of sheer reiteration to appear to the reader self-evident or something he had always known.

The fundamental contrast between Jesus and Judaism as Bousset asserts it, is in the idea of God and the feeling toward him. The God of Judaism in that age was withdrawn from the world, supramundane, extramundane, transcendent. "The prophetic preaching of the exaltation and uniqueness of Jehovah became the dogma of an abstract, transcendent monotheism." So it is reiterated page after page. "God is no more in the world, the world no more in God." For the evidence, the reader is habitually referred to Baldensperger, and by Baldensperger chiefly to the apocalyptic literature. In contrast to this, "What is most completely original and truly creative in the preaching of Jesus comes out most strongly and purely when he proclaims God the heavenly Father." "The later Judaism (i.e. that of Jesus' time) had neither in name nor in fact the faith of the Father-God; it could not possibly rise to it." And as the whole 'Gesetzesfrömmigkeit' of Judaism is based upon its increasingly transcendent conception of God, so the new conception introduced by Jesus is the ground of a wholly new type of piety.

The symptomatic thing in this book is the implication that the specific difference between Christianity and Judaism is to be sought in the teaching of Jesus. Christian theology had always found it in the doctrine of the person and work of Christ, and, so far as the teaching of Jesus was concerned, in what he said about his personal relation to God and his mission in the world, not in what he thought and taught about God nor in the form of his personal piety and its supposed perpetuation in Christianity. The historian can only characterize the notion that the fatherhood of God is the cardinal doctrine of Christianity and its cardinal difference from Judaism as a misrepresentation of historical Christianity no less than of Judaism. I have given more space to this little volume than its intrinsic importance would warrant because it exhibits the presumptions which underlie Bousset's later and larger work in which he sets himself to portray the Judaism of that age as a whole.

The censure which Jewish scholars have unanimously passed on *Die Religion des Judentums* is that the author uses as his primary sources almost exclusively the writings commonly called Apocrypha and Pseudepigrapha, with an especial penchant for the apocalypses; and only secondarily, and almost casually, the writings which represent the acknowledged and authoritative teachings of the school and the more popular instruction of the synagogue. This is much as if one should describe early Christianity using indiscriminately for his principal sources the Apocryphal Gospels and Acts, the Apocalypses of John and Peter, and the Clementine literature.[48] Bousset defends his procedure on two grounds; *First*, he thus methodically confines himself to the evidence of writings which were approximately contemporaneous with the New Testament, whereas the oldest of the books in which the rabbinical teaching is preserved date from the close of the second century of our era, being separated from the time of Christ not only by several generations but by two great crises in Judaism, the destruction of Jerusalem and the war under Hadrian, while the bulk of the literature consists of compilations made some centuries later. The only criterion by which it can be determined what of all their voluminous contents was really taught

[48] This parallel must often have occurred to critics. Perles (Boussets Religion des Judentums, p. 23) quotes Chwolson, Das letzte Passamahl Christi (1892), p. 71: So wenig man das Wesen des Christenthums aus der Apokalypse Johannis oder aus apokryphischen Evangelien kennen lernen kann, ebensowenig kann man das Judenthum zur Zeit Christi aus dem Buche Enoch, dem Buche der Jubiläen und ähnlichen Schriften erforschen.

in the time of Christ is the New Testament itself and the Jewish apocryphal writings to which he gives the preference. *Second*, his aim is not to present what the scribes taught in the schools (*Schriftgelehrtentum*) but the religious conceptions and sentiments of the people (*Volksfrömmigkeit*), and this he assumes to be expressed in the popular literature, particularly in the apocalypses.

This is not the place to discuss the propriety of these limitations from the point of view of historical method, or the validity of the contrast drawn between the teaching of the Rabbis and the piety of the people; but it is clear that the author ought not to have called his book *Die Religion des Judentums*, for the sources from which his representation is drawn are those to which, so far as we know, Judaism never conceded any authority, while he discredits and largely ignores those which it has always regarded as normative. That the critical use of the latter is difficult is indisputable, though Bousset exaggerates the difficulty into an impossibility; but the critical problems which the former present, while of a different kind, are no less difficult, though Bousset blinks the most serious of them. How wide, for example, was the currency of these writings? Do they represent a certain common type of 'Volksfrömmigkeit,' or did they circulate in circles with peculiar notions and tendencies of their own? How far do they come from sects regarded by the mass of their countrymen as heretical? So far as concerns the influence of the ideas found in such sources on the Messianic conceptions and beliefs of the disciples of Jesus or of Jesus himself, these questions are of comparatively little consequence; the connection itself is the thing to be established. They become of the highest consequence, however, when it comes to using this literature as a principal source for the history of Judaism, and especially to giving it precedence over the teaching of the school and synagogue represented in the rabbinical sources.

The relative age of the writings is of much less importance than their relation to the main line of development which can be followed from the canonical Scriptures through many of the postcanonic writings, including the Synoptic Gospels and the liturgy of the synagogue, to the Midrash and Halakah of the second century. No account of Judaism would be complete which ignored the apocalypses and the kindred literature, but such incompleteness would not fundamentally misrepresent its subject as does an account based chiefly on them. The criterion is exactly the same which the historian applies to the history of Christianity, say in the first two centuries. Anonymous writings like the recently discovered Epistola Apostolorum, which fall into the line of development that we reconstruct or postulate between the New Testament and Irenaeus, Tertullian, Clement of Alexandria, Hippolytus, belong to the history of catholic Christianity, and may be important additions to our sources for it. Writings that lie, on the whole, to one side or the other of this line, may contain much that by this criterion is the common Christianity of the age, and so far these also may be used, with proper caution, as adjunct sources. On the other hand, what in them, individually or as classes, is not thus verified by the common tradition, whatever currency it may have had at the time in certain circles or sects, is a source only for variations of Christianity which it eventually repudiated. To ignore, or deliberately reject, this self-evident principle of historical criticism in dealing with Judaism is to disqualify oneself at the outset.

In truth, Bousset never conceived his task as a historian; it was not Judaism as a religion, but Judaism as the background, environment, source, and foil of nascent Christianity that he had in mind, with a strong secondary interest in the 'das religionsgeschichtliche Problem,' the relation of Judaism to the Babylonian religion, and especially to Zoroastrianism. Since for both purposes he found the most convenient material in the Apocrypha and Pseudepigrapha, particularly the apocalyptic literature, he made them his chief authorities. There was another reason for his neglect of the rabbinical sources: he had only second-hand acquaintance with them, and that of the most superficial character. It is only necessary to read the half-dozen pages he devotes to 'Die spätere Litteratur' in his chapter, 'Die Quellen,' to recognize that even what he knew *about* them was negligently and unintelligently compiled from

bibliographical descriptions. The single foot-note (2) on page
43 (repeated in the second edition, p. 47 f., with the correction
of a minor error which had been signalized by Perles), is a
testimonial of incompetence in this field, the more significant
because he had Schürer in his hands. It is not surprising that
Jewish scholars criticized the work harshly. They found it
easy to convict the author of portentous blunders in his incidental adventures into Hebrew; as when (following Schlatter —
the blind leading the blind into the ditch — see Perles, 'Boussets
Religion des Judentums,' p. 15) he renders נאמן ('trustworthy,'
in matters of tithes and the like, M. Demai, ii, 2) by 'gläubig,'
('believing'), and introduces it into a discussion of Faith; nor
is it strange that Perles and others made themselves disagree-
able over Bousset's rabbinical erudition.[49] The temper of
Bousset's *oratio pro domo sua* is not more urbane, and, as often
happens with apologias, he only made a bad case worse by
arguing it.

Bousset, nevertheless, frequently cites the utterances of the
Rabbis, especially when they coincide with his primary sources,
supplementing the inevitable Weber from Bacher's *Agada der
Tannaiten* and from Wünsche's translations, and, within a
limited range, from Dalman's *Worte Jesu*. In not a few instances the interpretation he gives to them and the use he
makes of them show how perilous the quotation of quotations
is, and emphasize the observation that the ways of the Midrash
are not to be understood by any one who has not habituated
himself to them by voluminous reading of the original texts
in their continuity and acquiring something of a midrashic
mind. The whole point, meaning, and reason of its interpretations are often impossible to reproduce in translation, or to
explain to the uninitiated in notes, which give the appearance
of absurdity to what in the Midrashic exegesis is self-evident.

Of Bousset's general attitude toward Judaism and his judgment of it enough has already been said; it is only necessary

---

[49] He thinks, for example, that the language of the Talmuds is Aramaic. Even in
Biblical Hebrew he was ill-grounded, as is convincingly shown by the remark: 'Die
alttestamentliche Sprache hat noch kein Wort fur Schöpfer, und muss den Mangel
durch Partizipialkonstruktionen ersetzen' (p. 412).

to add that in the later and larger book, they remain essentially unchanged, still dominated by the antithesis to the teaching of Jesus. The second edition (1906) is in many ways an improvement on the first. The original plan, which put in the forefront 'Die Entwickelung der jüdischen Frömmigkeit zur Kirche,' evoked protest from Christians, to whom this seemed to make the development into a church a retrogression from the religion of the Old Testament; and though the author maintained the correctness of his point of view, he abandoned this highly artificial disposition because he found that he could not bring under this head all that he wanted to put in this part of the volume. There are other changes for the better in the arrangement of the book, and some important additions, notably a chapter on prayer, the absence of which in the first edition was eloquent. Corrections in detail are also numerous, though far from numerous enough. One instructive example may be noted. In his earlier work he asserted that the later Judaism had neither the name nor the faith of the Father-God; it could not rise to it. In the first edition of Die Religion des Judentums, he wrote: "Sehr charakeristisch ist es, wie selten . . . die Bezeichnung Gottes als des Vaters im Spätjudentum vorkommt." In the second edition this is replaced by, "Hervorzuheben ist . . . dass auch die Bezeichnung Gottes als des Vaters der Einzelnen Frommen im späteren Judentum entschieden häufiger ist." [50] But even then he makes all possible subtraction from the significance of the concession. The chapter on monotheism, with the following on angelology, demonology, and 'die Hypostasen-Spekulation,' repeat the familiar theses which need not again be recited.

One remark, however, may properly be made: Whoever derives the Jewish idea of God chiefly from apocalypses will get the picture of a God enthroned in the highest heaven, remote from the world, a mighty monarch surrounded by a celestial court, with ministers of various ranks, of whom only the highest have immediate access to the presence of the sovereign, unapproachable even by angels of less exalted station, to say

---

[50] Bousset, Jesu Predigt in ihrem Gegensatz zum Judentum (1892), p. 43; Religion des Judentums (1903), p. 355; 2d edition (1906), pp. 432 f.

nothing of mere mortals; and this not because theological reflection has elevated him to transcendence, but because the entire imaginative representation is conditioned by the visionary form. If the prophet has a vision of the throne-room of God's palace, as in Isaiah 6, or the seer is conducted by an angel through one heaven after another to the very threshold of the adytum, what other kind of representation is possible? To extract a dogma from such visions is to misunderstand the origin and nature of the whole apocalyptic literature. It is the same thing with the so-called 'pre-existent Messiah' in these writings: when once vision takes the place of prediction, the Messiah has to be there in order to be seen; it is not a doctrine, but a simple condition of visionary representation. The creation of the *name* of the Messiah before the world in rabbinic sources is something totally different.

If Bousset's book be taken for what it is, it is a serviceable hand-book. The accumulation of references to terms and phrases in the Apocrypha and Pseudepigrapha upon the several topics is often almost exhaustive, but they have not always been made from the original texts. Aristeas § 37 appears (ed. 2, p. 257) among the places where ὕψιστος occurs, because the translator in Kautzsch's Pseudepigrapha happened to render τῷ μεγίστῳ θεῷ by 'dem Höchsten.' German idiom has played the author other tricks. On the preceding page, speaking of עליון as a surrogate or circumlocution for God, he writes: 'Die Prädikate der höchste Gott, der Höchste, versetzen uns ja eigentlich auf den Boden polytheistischen Empfindens. Vom höchsten Gott kann streng genommen nur da die Rede sein, wo es mehrere Götter für den Glauben gibt.' It is quite true that the German superlative 'der Höchste,' may imply that there are others not so high; but it is also true that the superlative and its implications are not in the Hebrew.

A word may be said in conclusion about a recent popular book in English, Oesterley and Box, *The Religion and Worship of the Synagogue. An Introduction to the Study of Judaism from the New Testament Period* (1907). The part with which alone we are here concerned, 'Dogmatic Judaism,' is based entirely on modern authors — among whom Jewish scholars are more frequently allowed the word than in most similar books — not at all on immediate knowledge of the sources. The latter are, indeed, abundantly cited in a way that makes it look as if they had been consulted, but it is evident in many cases that the authors did not even verify their references. The chapter on 'Intermediate Agencies between God and Man' is one long proof of this. One or two striking examples have been incidentally mentioned above.[51] Here I will name but one or two at random: "In *Bemidbar rabbah*, c. 12, the term 'Mediator' is directly applied to *Metatron*, and, what is still more significant, he is represented as the reconciler between God and the Chosen People" (p. 175). To begin with, this part of Bemidbar Rabbah is mediaeval (perhaps 12th century), dependent on late Midrashim and cabalistic sources; its testimony would be worthless if it gave any. In the second place, there is no word in the text or context that remotely suggests 'Mediator,' to say nothing of being directly applied to Metatron; in the third place, what is said about Metatron is that he offers (on the heavenly altar) 'the souls of the righteous to atone for Israel in the days of their exile,' an office elsewhere performed by Michael. Again: "In a number of passages in the *Old Testament* the expression the 'Word,' in reference to Jehovah, is used in a way which, one can easily understand, appeared to Jewish thinkers of a later age to indicate that the 'Word' meant something more than a mere abstraction" (p. 179). Among other passages of this kind they quote Deut. 5, 5: "I stood between the Lord and you at that time to show you the word of the Lord." That is the Authorized English version; the Hebrew has "to report to you (להגיד לכם) the word of the Lord, because ye were afraid of the fire," etc. The authors apparently took the English 'show' in the sense of 'exhibit.' In this whole string of passages the English version is the beginning and end of knowledge. Thus, in Wisdom 9, 1: "O God of my fathers, and Lord of mercy, Who hast made all things with thy word," they understand *with* as 'in association with, with the assistance of.' The Greek is ἐν ('by') not σύν. One of the most amusing is the quotation of 2 (4) Esdras 6, 38 for

which they give: "Thy word was (i.e., *made*) a perfect work."
This is the Authorized Version from the corrupt text in the appendix to the standard Latin Bible: In the beginning of the
creation God said, 'Fiat caelum et terra, et tuum verbum opus
perfectum.' The true reading, as has been established for a
half-century, is *opus perfecit*, 'Thy word brought the work to
pass.' Mr. Box himself has since reprinted the Latin text of
4 Esdras from Fritzsche (1871), where the correct reading
might have been found in 1907 as easily as in 1912, not to
mention Hilgenfeld (1869) or Bensly-James (1895). If this
reading, instead of being that of the manuscripts, were unsupported by a single codex, it would infallibly be restored by
conjecture. To create doctrine for the Jews at the beginning
of our era out of a misunderstanding of the authorized English
version of 1611, or from the translation in the same version of
a nonsensical reading in a Latin Apocryphon, is, to say the
least, not in accordance with the best practice among scholars.

It may not be unprofitable, here in conclusion, to review
briefly the course of this long history. Beginning with an early
Christian apologetic, in which the controversial points were
the interpretation and application of passages in the Old Testament, the fulfilment of prophecies of the Messiah in the nativity of Jesus, his life and death, resurrection, and ascension, the
identification of Christ with the manifest God, or Angel of the
Lord, in the Old Testament, the discussion in the Middle Ages
took a wider range and assumed a more learned character in
the endeavor to demonstrate that Christian doctrines were supported by the authentic Jewish tradition — Targum, Talmud,
Midrash — or by the most highly reputed Jewish interpreters.
In the progress of the controversy polemic prevailed over apologetic on both sides, the champions of each seeking out for attack
the most vulnerable points in the cause of their opponents. The
direct outcome of this conflict was the war waged upon the
Talmud itself and the effort to procure the destruction of obnoxious Jewish literature as a whole.

The Christian scholars who resisted this obscurantist programme in the sixteenth century argued on the other hand that

these books should be preserved because from them, above all from the Cabala, all the doctrines of Christianity — the Trinity, the Deity of Christ and the rest — could be proved to be the ancient esoteric theology of the Jews themselves.

The Reformation put upon Protestants the task of building up upon the Scriptures alone a complete system of doctrine, and they endeavored not only to show that the ancient Jewish doctrine was in essential accord with the common Christian dogma, but that on the issues in debate between Protestants and Catholics the Jews were on the Protestant side. Thus a strong dogmatic interest took its place beside the older apologetic and polemic. A broader interest in learning for its own sake as well as its uses prevailed largely in the seventeenth and early eighteenth centuries, and led, as has been sufficiently remarked, to the creation of a great body of learned literature in every branch of Hebrew antiquities.

The early Protestant exegesis of the Old Testament was almost wholly dependent on Jewish commentaries and apparatus, and the illustration of many passages in the Old Testament from later Jewish law and custom also began early. The same thing was done for the New Testament, particularly the Gospels, not only in commentaries but in a succession of notably learned works specifically devoted to his end, the *Horae Hebraicae* and whatever else they may be called; and, directly or through Wettstein, these illustrations from Talmud and Midrash became part of the perpetual tradition of New Testament commentaries.

In all this time no attempt had been made by Christian scholars to present Judaism in the age which concerned them most — say from the time of Alexander to that of the Antonines — as a whole and as it was in and for itself. Nor did those who came after them address themselves to this neglected task. When in the nineteenth century the study of Judaism was in some measure revived, the actuating motive was to find in it the milieu of early Christianity. Gfroerer conceived this problem historically, and, as we have seen, actually included his description of the Judaism of that period in his Critical History of Primitive Christianity. Weber set himself to ex-

hibit the system of Palestinian Jewish theology in the first
three or four centuries of our era as the antithesis of Christian
theology and religion as they were taught in certain contemporary German schools. Since Weber the subject has been dealt
with only by New Testament scholars, either with reference to
certain special problems or to a more general understanding of
nascent Christianity. Bousset's Religion des Judentums, which
by its title and scope (including some four centuries), gives
promise of a historical treatment, is in fact — and in the author's intention — a piece of apparatus for the student of the
New Testament.

The characterization of Judaism in Weber and his followers
is strikingly different from the older apologetic and polemic.
None of the learned adversaries of Judaism in the seventeenth
and eighteenth centuries, though they knew the literature immeasurably better than their modern successors, ever suspected
that the Rabbis entertained an 'abstract monotheism' —
whatever that may be — or a 'transcendent' idea of God as
the Absolute, or, to use the language of men, that in the ex-
travagance of their 'fear of the Lord' they had magnified and
exalted him out of his world, which, like an absentee proprietor,
he administered henceforth by agents. Eisenmenger, who collected with inordinate zeal what he called the foolish and blas-
phemous things that the Jews said about God, never laid this
to their charge. Nowhere, so far as I know, is a suggestion made
that in this respect the Jewish idea of God differed from the
Christian. So it is also with the 'legalism' which for the last
fifty years has become the very definition and the all-sufficient
condemnation of Judaism. It is not a topic of the older polemic;
indeed, I do not recall a place where it is even mentioned.
Concretely, Jewish observances are censured or ridiculed, but
'legalism' as a system of religion, not to say as the essence of
Judaism, no one seems to have discovered. This is the more
remarkable because this line of attack might seem to have been
indicated by Paul, and because the earlier Protestant, and
particularly Lutheran controversialists, were peculiarly keen
on the point by reason of their conflict with the Catholic
Church over works and merit.

What then brought legalism to the front in the new apologetic? Not a fresh and more thorough study of Judaism at the beginning of our era, but a new apologetic motive, consequent on a different apprehension of Christianity on the part of the New Testament theologians who now took up the task. The 'essence' of Christianity, and therefore its specific difference from Judaism, was for the first time sought in the religion of Jesus — his teaching and his personal piety. The title of Bousset's first work, *Jesu Predigt in ihrem Gegensatz zum Judentum*, is the programme of the younger school. Jesus' conflict with the Scribes and Pharisees prescribed for this apologetic the issue of legalism; the 'Father in heaven,' the piety assumed to be distinctive of Jesus and of his teaching, demanded an antithesis in Judaism, an inaccessible God, which Weber from his different starting point was supposed to have demonstrated.

In conclusion there is one thing more to be said: Where the subject of investigation is the relation of primitive Christianity to its contemporary Judaism, whether the motive be a historical understanding of nascent Christianity or an apologetic exhibition of the superiority of the religion of Jesus to that of the Scribes and Pharisees, the critical ordering and evaluation of the Jewish sources is of much greater importance than when a general comparison of Judaism and Christianity is proposed, or even when, as in Weber, the comparison is restricted to the Palestinian Judaism of three or four centuries following the Christian era. Upon this critical task, Jewish scholars, with exhaustive knowledge of the material and through philological and historical training, have in the last thirty or forty years done fundamental work. The investigation of the composition and sources of the Tannaite Midrash, for example, which is here of primary importance, has a significance comparable to the criticism of the Synoptic Gospels; and, it may perhaps be added, its results are established on a more secure basis, external and internal evidence corroborating each other. For recent Christian writers, however, all this criticism is nonexistent. Even the writings themselves are known only by name. Bousset writes: "Die ältesten wesentlich halachischen

Midrasche sind Mechilta (Exodus), Siphra (Levit.), Siphre (Numeri, Deuteron.) lat. Ubersetzung bei Ugolini, Thesaurus XIV–XV). Auf diese folgen die vorwiegend haggadischen, daher für uns wertvolleren Rabboth." Although Perles had made sarcastic comment on it as it stood in the first edition, this note remains unchanged in the second, perhaps because Bousset did not see the point of the sarcasm.

After so much criticism it is a welcome change to close this article with commendation of a book which, proposing only to explain and illustrate the most important conceptions and phrases in the Gospels, gives more than it promises, and shows how much light may be thrown upon the subject from Rabbinical sources by a competent scholar, I mean Gustav Dalman's *Die Worte Jesu, mit Berücksichtigung des nachkanonischen jüdischen Schrifttums und der aramäischen Sprache* (1898).

APPENDIX

Inasmuch as some of these books are rare, the titles may be given here in full:

Porchetus:

The full title in Giustiniani's edition is: Victoria Porcheti adversus impios Hebraeos, in qua tum ex sacris libris tum ex dictis Talmud ac Caballistarum et aliorum omnium quos Hebraei recipiunt monstratur veritas catholicae fidei. Ex recensione R. P. Aug. Iustiniani ordinis Praedicatorii, episcopi Nebiensis. François Regnault. Paris 1520. It is a folio volume of f. xciiii (188 pp.). The author begins (f. ii A): In nomine domini. Amen. Incipit liber Victoriae a Porcheto de Saluaticis Genuensi divina fauente gratia compilatus ad Judaicam perfidiam subvertendam et ut praestantius veritas fulgeat fidei christianae. The work is now very rare. I used a copy in Munich some years ago; one has recently been acquired by the library of the Jewish Theological Seminary of America, in New York.

Galatinus:

Opus toti christianae Reipublicae maxime utile, de arcanis catholicae veritatis, contra obstinatissimam Iudaeorum nostrae tempestatis perfidiam: ex Talmud, aliisque hebraicis libris nuper excerptum et quadriplici linguarum eleganter congestum. The title page bears no date, but at the end (f. cccx A) we read: Impressum vero Orthonae maris, summa cum diligentia per Hieronymum Suncinum: Anno christianae natiuitatis M.D.XVIII. quintodecimo kalendas martias. On an imaginary edition of Bari 1516 see the article cited in note 8.

Raimundus Martini:

Pugio Fidei Raimundi Martini Ordinis Praedicatorum adversus Mauros et Judaeos; nunc primum in lucem editus. . . . Ope et Opera Illustrissimi ac Reverendissimi D. Episcopi Lovensis [Franciscus Bosquet], Illustrissimi Praesidis D. de Maussac Comitis Consistoriani. Cum observationibus Domini Josepho de Voisin Presbyteri, ex-Senatoris Burdegalensis. Paris, 1651.

THE LAW AND RECENT CRITICISM

A Discourse on C. H. Toy's
Judaism and Christianity

by
S[OLOMON] SCHECHTER

THE LAW AND RECENT CRITICISM.[1]

PROFESSOR TOY'S new work, *Judaism and Christianity*, gives an admirable conspectus of the results of the modern critical school on the genesis of Christianity. The author takes various important doctrines of Christianity, traces them back to their origin in Israelitism, pursues their course through their various phases in Judaism, until they reach their final development in the teaching of Jesus and his disciples, which, in the author's judgment, is the consummation of that which the prophets and their successors had to give to the world. Laying so much stress as Professor Toy does on the saying, "By their fruits shall ye know them," he ought also, perhaps, to have told us what, in the course of time, has become of these several doctrines. For when, for instance, with regard to the doctrine of original sin, he remarks that "in certain systems of Christian theology the human race is involved in the condemnation of the first man" (p. 185, *n.* 1); or that, in the New Testament, "the demand for a mediating power between God and humanity is pushed to the farthest point which thought can occupy consistently with the maintenance of the absoluteness of the one Supreme Deity" (p. 121), he is rather evading a difficulty than answering it. Such elaboration would, however, have been outside the scope of Professor Toy's book, which claims only to be a sketch of the progress of thought from the Old Testament to the New. For his own solution of the indicated difficulty, Toy, to judge from his liberal standpoint, would probably refer us to Dr. Hatch's Hibbert lectures ; the issue of such an appeal must, I imagine, remain for long doubtful and disputed.

---

[1] *Judaism and Christianity, a sketch of the progress of thought from Old Testament to New Testament*, by C. H. Toy. Professor in Harvard University. London, 1890.

A delightful characteristic of Toy's book is its transparent clearness and sobriety, which will make it interesting reading, even to those who are acquainted with the writer's authorities in their original sources. Almost entirely new, as well as most suggestive, is the justice which Toy does to the law in recognising it as a factor for good in the history of religion. In this point Toy is not only up to his date, but beyond it. It is true that even the Pharisees have made some advance in the estimation of the liberal school. They are no longer condemned *en masse* as so many hypocrites. It is even admitted that there were a few honest men among them, such as Rabban Gamliel, the teacher of Paul, or R. Akiba, the patriot of Bethar. We are now too polite to be personal. But with regard to the law, on the other hand, there is at present a markedly opposite tendency. The general idea seems to be that, as the doctrine of the resurrection of Christ must be loosely interpreted in a spiritual sense, it must logically have been preceded by a universal spiritual death, and the germs of the disease which brought this death about are to be sought for in the law. Hence the strained efforts to discover in the law the source of all religious evil, —cant, hypocrisy, formalism, externalism, transcendentalism, and as many "isms" more of bad reputation.

It was probably with a view to this current representation of the law that Toy, when speaking of the Levitical legislation, and of its fixing "men's minds on ceremonial details which, in some cases, it put into the same category and on the same level with moral duties," asks the question: "Would there not thence result a dimming of the moral sense and a confusion of moral distinctions? The ethical attitude of a man who could regard a failure in the routine of sacrifice as not less blameworthy than an act of theft cannot be called a lofty one " (p. 186). The answer which he gives is more favourable than such a leading question would induce us to expect. He tells us that, " in point of fact, the result was different (*ibid.*). The Levitical law is not to be looked on as a mere extension and organisation of the ritual. . . . Its ritual was, in great part, the organised expression of the consciousness of sin " (p. 226). Of the law in general Toy says that it had "larger consequences than its mere details would suggest," for it "cultivated the moral sense of the people into results above its mechanical pre-scriptions," and "it developed the sense of sin, as Paul points out (Gal. iii. 19), and therewith a freer feeling, which brought the soul into more immediate contact with God" (p. 227) ; whilst in another place he reminds us "that much of the law is moral, and that no one could fail to feel a spiritual significance beneath its letter" (p. 245), and he even admits that "the great legal schools which grew up in the second century, if we may judge by the sayings of the teachers which have come down to us, did not fail to discriminate between the outward and the inward, the ceremonial and the moral" (p. 186).

These and similar passages will suffice to show that Toy's estimate of the law is a very different one from that of Smend and his school. However, it must not be supposed that he is not on the look-out for the germs of the disease. He must find these germs somewhere, or else the progress, which his book is intended to illustrate, would be difficult to detect. And thus he repeats the old accusations, though not without modification.

Professor Toy's objections may, perhaps, be summed up in the passage in which he represents the Jewish law as "an attempt to define all the beliefs and acts of life" (p. 239), or as "the embodiment of devotion to a fixed rule of belief and conduct" (p. 237). Toy does not entirely condemn this system, and even speaks of it as a "lofty attempt" (p. 239) ; but, on the whole, he considers that it must have resulted in bad theology, as well as in doubtful conduct. Without following Professor Toy over the whole area of his investigations, which would require a volume for itself, I will only take the opportunity of making a few general remarks upon the nature and character of this legal system, which seems to hold the key to the spiritual history of Judaism.

First, as to its theology, Toy's description of the law as an attempt to define all the *beliefs* of life—an assertion which is also made by Schürer—is not wholly accurate. For such an attempt was never made by Judaism. The few dogmas which Judaism possesses, such as the Existence of God, Providence, Punishment and Reward—without which no revealed religion is conceivable – can hardly be called a creed in the modern sense of the term, which implies something external and strange to man's own knowledge, and only acceptable through the weight of authority. To the Jew of the Christian era, these simpler dogmas were so self-evident that it would have cost him the greatest effort *not* to believe them. Hence the fact that, whilst there have come down to us so many controverted points between the Sadducees and Pharisees with regard to certain juristic and ritual questions, we know of only one of an essentially dogmatic character, viz., the dispute concerning the Resurrection.

It is thus difficult to imagine to what Professor Toy can be alluding when he speaks of the "interest they (the Jews) threw into the discussion and determination of minutiæ of faith" (p. 241). Discussions upon *minutiæ* of faith are only to be read in the works of the later schoolmen (as Saadiah, Maimonides and their followers), in which such subtle problems as *creatio ex nihilo*, the origin of evil, predestination, free will and similar subjects are examined ; but this period is very distant from that with which Toy is concerned. The older schools and the so-called houses of Shammai and Hillel, most of whose members were the contemporaries of the Apostles, show very little predilection for such *minutiæ*. Their discussions and differences of opinion about ritual matters are very numerous, scattered as they are over the whole of the ancient rabbinic literature, but I can only remember two of a metaphysical character, or touching upon the *minutiæ* of faith. The one dealing with the efficacy of certain sacrifices discusses whether it only extends to the suppression of the pending punishment for sins, or also includes their purification and washing away (see *Pessikta*, ed. Buber, 61*b*, and parallels) ; the other considers the question whether it would not have been better for man not to have been created (*Erubin*, 13*b*). But this latter controversy, which is said to have lasted for two years and a-half, by no means led to any big metaphysical or theological system, but only to the practical advice that, as we have been created, we ought to be watchful over our conduct. It is, indeed, a noteworthy feature of Judaism that theological speculations have never resulted in the formulation of any imposing or universal doctrine, but usually in divers ceremonial practices. To give one illustration : according to Prof. Toy (p. 210) the conclusion which the author of 1 Tim. ii. 11-14 draws from the fact that woman was the immediate agent of the introduction of sin was the subordination of her sex. The Rabbis also noticed the same fact, and in their less abstract language speak of woman as having brought death and grief into the world, but the conclusion which they drew was that since woman had extinguished the " light of the world," she ought to atone for it by lighting the candles for the Sabbath (Jerushalmi, *Sabbath*, 5*b*). Nor is Toy quite correct when he maintains that the conception of the Memra as Creator and Lord, etc., and as "representative of the immediate divine activity," did not keep its hold on Jewish thought, having been discarded in the later literature (p. 104). For the Shechinah of the Talmud, the *Metatron* of the Geonaic-mystical literature, the Active Intelligence of the philosophical schools, as well as the Ten Sephiroth (Emanations) of the Cabbalists, all owe their existence to the same theosophic scruples and subtleties in which the Logos of Philo and the Memra of the Targumim originated. Thus, they always kept—though under various forms—their hold on the Jewish mind. Judaism was always broad enough to accommodate itself to these formulæ, which for the one may mean the most holy mysteries, and for the other empty and meaningless catchwords. The objection—in fact, the active opposition—of the synagogue began when these possible or impossible explanations of the universe tended to transgress the bounds of abstract speculation, and passing over into real concrete beings, to be worshipped as such. An instance from comparatively modern times might be found in one of the vagaries of the followers of the Pseudo-Messiah, Sabbathai Zebi. For many generations the controversy had raged among the Cabbalists, whether the first of the above-mentioned Ten Emanations (called by some *Adam Kadmon*, by

others, *Kether*) is to be considered as a part of Dthe eity or
as something separate, and so to speak, having a reality in
itself. The danger of establishing a Being near the Deity
having an existence of its own and invested with divine
attributes could not have escaped the thoughtful, and there
are indeed some indications to this effect. The Synagogue
as such, however, remained during the whole controversy
strictly neutral, and allowed these theosophists to fight in the
air as much as they liked. But the moment that the sect
of Sabbathai Zebi identified the incarnate Adam Kadmon
with their leader, and worshipped him as a sort of God-
Messiah, the Synagogue at once took up a hostile attitude
against those who separated God from his world, and de-
claring Sabbathai Zebi and his followers to be apostates,
excluded them from Judaism for ever.

Nor can it be proved that legalism or nomism has ever
tended to suppress the spiritual side of religion, either in
respect of consciousness of sin, or of individual love and
devotion. With an equal logic quite the opposite might be
argued. Professor Toy tells us himself that it is no " accident that along with this more definite expression of ethical-
religious law we find the first traces of a more spiritual conception of righteousness in the 'new heart' of Jeremiah and
Ezekiel " (p. 235), whilst in another passage we read that " a
turning point is marked by the Deuteronomist Jeremiah and
Ezekiel, who announce the principles of individual responsibility and inwardness of obedience" (p. 184). Now, two
things are certain ; first, that Ezekiel urges the necessity of the
new heart as well as of individual responsibility more keenly
than any of his predecessors ; secondly, that in Ezekiel the
legalistic tendency is more evident than in Deuteronomy and
Jeremiah. The logical conclusion would thus be that the
higher ideals of religion are not only not inconsistent with
legalism, but are the very outcome of it, and the so-called
Priestly Code, by the very fact of its markedly legalistic tendency, should be considered as a step in the right direction.
The latter assertion sounds like a paradox, but it will seem
less so when the prevailing characteristic of this portion
of the Pentateuch, as given even by Kuenen, who is by

no means a champion of the Law, is borne in mind. " The centre of gravity," according to the great Dutch critic, " lies for the priestly author elsewhere than for the prophet ; it lies in man's attitude not towards his fellow-men, but towards God ; not in his social, but in his personal life " (Hibbert Lectures, p. 161.) It is here that we seem to strike the keynote of the *Weltanschauung* of the Priestly Legislation. In it man is more than a social being. He has also an individual life of his own, his joys and sorrows, his historical claims, his traditions of the past, and his hopes for the future—and all these have to be brought under the influence of religion, and to become sanctified through their relation to God. Hence, the work of the Priestly narrator and legislator opens with a cosmogony of his own, in which we find the grand theological idea of man being created in the Divine image ; hence, too, his religious conception of the history of the nation and his claimed control over all the details of human life, which became with him so many opportunities for the worship of God. To him, God is not a mere figurehead ; he not only reigns, but governs. Everywhere, in the temple, in the judge's seat, in the family, in the farm, and in the market-place, his presence is felt in exacting the laws bearing his *imprimatur*, " I am the Lord thy God." By this diffusion of religion over the whole domain of human life— not confining it to the social institutions which are represented only by a few personages, such as the king, the princes, the priests, the judges or elders—it became the common good of the whole people, and the feeling of personal responsibility for this good became much deeper than before. Thus it came to pass that whilst, during the first temple, the apostasy of kings and aristocracy involved the entire people, so that the words " And he (the king) did evil in the sight of the Lord " embrace the whole nation, during the second temple it was no longer of much conse- quence which side the political leaders took. And both during the Hellenistic persecutions, as well as afterwards in the struggles of some Maccabæan kings with the Pharisees, the bulk of the people showed that they considered religion as their own personal affair, not to be regulated by the conscience of either priest or prince. It is true that this success may largely be ascribed to such contemporary religious factors as the Synagogue with its minimum of form, to the Scribes with their activity as teachers, and to the Psalmists with their divine enthusiasm, but the very circumstance that these factors arose and flourished under the influence of the Priestly Code would suffice to prove that its tendency was not so sacerdotal as some writers would have us believe. Jewish tradition indeed attributes the composition of the daily public prayers, as well as of others for private worship, to the very men whom biblical criticism holds responsible for the introduction of the Priestly Code. Now this fact may perhaps be disputed, but there is little doubt that the age in which these prayers were composed was one of flourishing legalism. Nor is there any proof that the synagogues and their ritual were in opposition to the temple. From the few documents belonging to this period, it is clear that there was no opposition to the legalistic spirit by which the Priestly Code was actuated. This would prove that legalism meant something more than tithes and sacrifices for the benefit of the priests.

Nor is it true that the legal tendency aimed at narrowing the mind of the nation, turning all its thoughts into the one direction of the law. Apart from the fact that the Torah contained other elements besides its legalism, the prophets were not forgotten, but were read and interpreted from a very early age. It was under the predominance of the law that the Wisdom literature was composed, which is by no means narrow or one-sided, but is even supposed by some to contain many foreign elements. In the book of Job, the great problems of man's existence are treated with a depth and grandeur never equalled before or since. This book alone ought partly to compensate the modern school for the disappearance of prophecy, which is usually brought as a charge against the Law. Then, too, the Psalms, placed by the same school in the post-exilic period, are nothing but another aspect of prophecy, with this difference, perhaps, that in the Prophets God speaks to man, while in the Psalms it is man who establishes the same communion by

speaking to God. There is no reason why the critical
school, with its broad conception of inspiration, and insisting, as it does, that prophecy does *not* mean prediction,
should so strongly emphasise this difference. If "it is no
longer as in the days of Amos, when the Lord Yahveh did
nothing without revealing his counsel to his servants the
prophets," there is in the days of the Psalmists nothing in
man's heart, no element in his longings and meditations
and aspirations, which was not revealed to God. Nay, it
would seem that at times the Psalmist hardly ever desires
the revelation of God's secrets. Let future events be what
they may, he is content, for he is with God. After all his
trials, he exclaims, "And yet I am continually with thee ;
thou hast taken hold of my right hand. According to thy
purpose wilt thou lead me, and afterwards receive me with
glory. Whom have I (to care for) in heaven ? and possessing thee, I have pleasure in nothing upon earth. Though
my flesh and my heart should have wasted away, God
would for ever be the rock of my heart and my portion"
(Ps. lxxiii. 23—26). How an age producing a literature
containing passages like these—of which Wellhausen in his
Abriss (p. 95) justly remarks, that we are not worthy even
to repeat them—can be considered by the modern school as
wanting in intimate relation to God and inferior to that of
the prophets is indeed a puzzle.

Now a few words as to the actual life under the Law.
Here, again, there is a fresh puzzle. On the one side, we
hear the opinions of so many learned Professors, proclaiming
ex cathedrâ, that the Law was a most terrible burden, and
the life under it the most unbearable slavery, deadening body
and soul. On the other side we have the testimony of a literature extending over about twenty-five centuries, and including all sorts and conditions of men, scholars, poets, mystics,
lawyers, casuists, schoolmen, tradesmen, workmen, women,
simpletons, who all, from the author of the 119th Psalm to
the last pre-Mendelssohnian writer—with a small exception
which does not even deserve the name of a vanishing
minority—give unanimous evidence in favour of this Law,
and of the bliss and happiness of living and dying under it,

—and this, the testimony of people who were actually living under the Law, not merely theorising upon it, and who experienced it in all its difficulties and inconveniences. The Sabbath will give a fair example. This day is described by almost every modern writer in the most gloomy colours, and long lists are given of the minute observances connected with it, easily to be transgressed, which would necessarily make of the Sabbath, instead of a day of rest, a day of sorrow and anxiety, almost worse than the Scotch Sunday as depicted by continental writers. But, on the other hand, the Sabbath is celebrated by the very people who did observe it, in hundreds of hymns, which would fill volumes, as a day of rest and joy, of pleasure and delight, a day in which man enjoys some presentiment of the pure bliss and happiness which are stored up for the righteous in the world to come, and to which such tender names were applied as the " Queen Sabbath," the " Bride Sabbath," and the " Holy, dear, beloved Sabbath." Somebody, either the learned Professors, or the millions of the Jewish people, must be under an illusion. Which it is I leave to the reader to decide.

It is also an illusion to speak of the burden which a scrupulous care to observe 613 commandments must have laid upon the Jew. Even a superficial analysis will discover that in the time of Christ many of these commandments were already obsolete (as for instance those relating to the tabernacle and to the conquest of Palestine), while others concerned only certain classes, as the priests, the judges, the soldiers, the Nazirites, or the representatives of the community, or even only one or two individuals among the whole population, as the King and the High-Priest. Others again, provided for contingencies which could occur only to a few, as for instance the laws concerning divorce or levirate marriages, whilst many—such as those concerning idolatry, and incest, and the sacrifice of children to Moloch—could scarcely have been considered as a practical prohibition by the pre-Christian Jew ; just as little as we can speak of Englishmen under the burden of a law preventing them from burning widows or marrying their grandmothers, though such acts would certainly be considered as crimes.

Thus it will be found by a careful enumeration that barely a hundred laws remain which really concerned the life of the bulk of the people. If we remember that even these include such laws as belief in the unity of God, the necessity of loving and fearing him, and of sanctifying his name, of loving one's neighbour and the stranger, of providing for the poor, exhorting the sinner, honouring one's parents and many more of a similar character, it will hardly be said that the ceremonial side of the people's religion was not well balanced by a fair amount of spiritual and social elements. Besides, it would seem that the line between the ceremonial and the spiritual is too often only arbitrarily drawn. With many commandments it is rather a matter of opinion whether they should be relegated to the one category or the other.

Thus, the wearing of Tephilin or phylacteries has, on the one hand, been continually condemned as a meaningless superstition, and a pretext for formalism and hypocrisy. But, on the other hand, Maimonides, who can in no way be suspected of superstition or mysticism, described their importance in the following words : " Great is the holiness of the Tephilin ; for as long as they are on the arm and head of man he is humble and God-fearing, and feels no attraction for frivolity or idle things, nor has he any evil thoughts, but will turn his heart to the words of truth and righteousness." The view which R. Jochanan, a Palestinian teacher of the third century, took of the fulfilment of the Law, will probably be found more rational than that of many a rationalist of to-day. Upon the basis of the last verse in Hosea, " The ways of the Lord are right, and the just shall walk in them, but the transgressors shall stumble therein," he explains that while one man, for instance, eats his paschal lamb for the sake of the *Mizvah* (that is, to do God's will who commanded it), and thereby commits an act of righteousness, another thinks only of satisfying his appetite by the lamb, so that his eating it (by the very fact that he professes at the same time to perform a religious rite) becomes a stumbling-block for him (*Nazir* 23 *b.*). Thus all the laws by virtue of their divine authority—and in this there was in the first century no difference of opinion between Jews and Christians—have their spiritual side, and to neglect them implies, at least from the individual's own point of view, a moral offence.

The legalistic attitude may be summarily described as an attempt to live in accordance with the will of God. But, nevertheless, on the whole this life never degenerated into religious formalism. Apart from the fact that during the second temple there grew up laws and even beliefs, which show a decided tendency towards progress and development, there were also ceremonies which were popular with the people, and others which were neglected. Men were not, therefore, the mere soulless slaves of the Law ; personal sympathies and dislikes also played a due part in their religion. Nor were all the laws actually put upon the same level. With a happy inconsistency men always spoke of heavier and slighter sins, and by the latter—excepting, perhaps, the profanation of the Sabbath—they mostly understood ceremonial transgressions. The statement made by Professor Toy (p. 243), on the authority of James (ii. 10), that "the principle was established that he who offended in one point was guilty of all," is hardly correct ; for the passage seems rather to be laying down a principle, or arguing that logically the law ought to be looked upon as a whole, than stating a fact. The fact was that people did not consider the whole law as of equal importance, but made a difference between laws and laws, and even spoke of certain commandments, such as those of charity and kindness, as outweighing all the rest of the Torah. It was in conformity with this spirit that in times of great persecution the leaders of the people had no compunction in reducing the whole Law to the three prohibitions of idolatry, of incest, and of bloodshed. Only these three were considered of sufficient importance that men should rather become martyrs than transgress them.

These, then, are some of the illusions and misrepresentations which exist with regard to the Law. There are many others, of which the complete exposure would require a book by itself. Meanwhile, in the absence of such a book to

3 B 2

balance and correct the innumerable volumes upon the other side, Professor Toy has done the best he could with existing materials, and produced a meritorious work deserving of wide recognition and approval.

S. Schechter

SOME RABBINIC PARALLELS
TO THE NEW TESTAMENT

by
S[OLOMON] SCHECHTER

SOME RABBINIC PARALLELS TO THE NEW TESTAMENT[1].

IT is now more than half a century since Renan put the question, "Has Jewish tradition anything to teach us concerning Jesus?" This question must be answered in the negative. As far as the contemporaneous Jewish literature goes, it does not contain a single reference to the founder of Christianity. All the so-called Anti-Christiana collected by mediaeval fanatics, and freshened up again by modern ignoramuses, belong to the later centuries, when history and biography had already given way to myth and speculation. Almost every Christian sect, every Christian community, created a Christ after its own image or dogma. The Jewish legend—a growth of these later centuries— gave him an aspect of its own, purely apocryphal in its character, neither meant nor ever taken by the Jews as real history.

But if the Rabbis have nothing to tell us about the personality of Jesus, Rabbinic literature has a good deal to teach us about the times in which he lived and laboured. And what is more important is that a thorough study of this literature might, with due discretion, help us towards a better understanding of the writings attributed to Jesus and his disciples. To prove this by a few instances will be the aim of my present lecture. It is intended as an invitation to fellow students to devote more attention to

[1] Paper read before the Hebrew class at University College, London, on October 19, 1899. The references to the authorities in the following notes are confined to a minimum.

a branch of literature, from the study of which the Christian divine might derive as much profit as the Jewish Rabbi.

In justice to bygone times, it should be pointed out that this fact had by no means escaped the searching eyes of Christian scholars of previous generations.   They both recognized the importance of the Talmud for a better knowledge of the two Testaments, and applied themselves to an honest study of its contents.   As the fruits of these studies, it is sufficient to mention here the *Porta Mosis* of Pocock, the *De Synedriis* of Selden, the *Horae Rabbinicae* of Lightfoot.   The Cambridge Platonists also deserve honourable mention in this connexion.   These great and hospitable minds extended the range of their literary acquaintances also to the Rabbis, and the *Select Discourses* of John Smith, and the *Discourse on the Lord's Supper* by Cudworth[1], show that this acquaintance was by no means a passing one.

All the names just given belong to this island, but the continent in no way remained behind England.   The names of the continental students of Rabbinism are duly recorded in Zunz's *Zur Literatur und Geschichte* and in other bibliographical works.   It is sufficient to mention in this place the name of Reuchlin, who saved the Talmud from the torch which a converted Jew was about to apply to it; the two Buxdorfs, whose works bearing on Rabbinic literature fill pages in the catalogues of the British Museum; and Vitringa, whose books on Rabbinic topics are considered by the best scholars as classical pieces of work.

However, these good things are (as already indicated) a matter of the past.   The present shows a decided deterioration.   Not only has the number of students devoting

---

[1] In connexion with this work I should like to call the attention of students to the *Das letzte Passahmahl Christi und der Tag seines Todes*, by Professor D. Chwolson (St. Petersburg, 1892), a work which, for the depth of its Rabbinic learning and the critical acumen displayed in it, has hardly its equal.   It is indeed, as far as I know, the first attempt to treat what one may call the *Halachic* part of the New Testament with the thoroughness and devotion usually bestowed only on doctrinal points.

themselves to Rabbinic literature shrunk to a miserable minimum, but the quality of the work produced by these latter-day students is such as to show a distinct decay, among the very few praiseworthy exceptions being, for instance, the theological works of Dr. C. Taylor. No student who is interested in the constitution of the ancient Synagogue dare neglect Vitringa's *De Synagoga Vetere*, which appeared in the year 1696; but he would certainly lose nothing by omitting to read most of the productions of our own century on the same subject.

The causes of this decay are not to be sought for far off. There was first the influence of Schleiermacher, whose interpretation of Christianity formed, as far as its negative side was concerned, one long strained effort to divorce it from Judaism. "I hate historic relations of this sort," he exclaims in one place; and proceeds to say, "every religion is conditioned by itself, and forms an eternal necessity." Schleiermacher's theory of the origin of Christianity was, as is well known, mainly based on the Johannine Gospel to the disparagement of the Synoptics. The German Marcion had thus every reason to hate history. But as the Talmud still reminded the world of these historical relations, Schleiermacher and his school adopted the course of vulgar parvenus, and cut the Rabbis and their literary remains. The second cause of this decay is the suspicion thrown on all Jewish tradition by the higher criticism. Anybody who has ever read any modern Introductions to the Old Testament will remember that as a rule they open with a reference to the Rabbinic account of the rise of the canon, to be followed by a lengthy exposition showing its utter untrustworthiness. To make matters more complete, efforts were made to disqualify the Rabbis from bearing witness even to events which took place when the Synagogue was already a fully-established institution, administered by the ancestors of the Rabbis in their capacity as scribes and saints or Chassidim. I am referring to the controversy as to the existence of the so-called Great Synagogue, commencing, according to tradition, with Ezra the scribe, and succeeded by a permanent court consisting of seventy-one members called Synhedrin; which court again was, according to tradition, presided over by two eligible members, the one called Nasi or Prince-President, whilst the other bore the title of Ab-Beth-Din, Father of the Court of Justice or Vice-President, both of whom were recruited for the most part from Pharisaic circles. Modern criticism, mainly on the strength of certain passages in Josephus and in the New Testament, maintains a negative attitude towards these accounts. The questions involved are too important and too complicated to be entered upon in a casual way. We need only notice the following fact. This is, that the doubts regarding the traditional account of the constitution of the Synhedrin were first raised in this century by Krochmal in the forties, taken up again by Kuenen in the sixties, to be followed by Wellhausen in the eighties. But when reading their works you will observe that, whilst Krochmal respectfully questions tradition, and Kuenen enters into elaborate examination of the documents, Wellhausen summarily dismisses them. Matters have now indeed come to such a pass that the principle has been laid down that it is not necessary to have a thorough knowledge of Rabbinic literature in order to express an opinion about its merits or demerits. It is probably thought that we may condemn it by mere intuition. It is impossible to argue with transcendental ignorance.

Trusting that none of those present have any reason to hate history, or to believe in the superior virtue of ignorance, I will now proceed to the subject of my lecture.

Let me first state the fact that the impression conveyed to the Rabbinic student by the perusal of the New Testament is in many parts like that gained by reading an old Rabbinic homily. On the very threshold of the New Testament he is confronted by a genealogical table[1], a feature

---

[1] Cf. *Moreh Neboche Hazzeman*, p. 45, השרות.

not uncommon in the later Rabbinic versions of the Old Testament, which are rather fond of providing Biblical heroes with long pedigrees. They are not always accurate, but have as a rule some edifying purpose in view. The Rabbis even declare that the Book of Chronicles, with its long series of names, has no other purpose than that of being interpreted[1], that is to say, of enabling us to derive some lesson from them. In the fifth chapter of the sayings of the Jewish Fathers, dealing mostly with round numbers, we read : " There were ten generations from Noah to Abraham to make known how long-suffering God is."

In the second chapter of Matthew the Rabbinic student meets with many features known to him from the Rabbinic narratives about the birth of Abraham ; the story of the Magi in particular impresses him as a homiletical illustration of Num. xxiv. 17, " There shall come a star out of Jacob," which star the interpretation of the Synagogue referred to the star of the Messiah[2]. This impression grows stronger, the more we advance with the reading of the Apostles' writings. Take, for instance, Matt. iii. 9 : " Bring forth fruit worthy of repentance." This verse, like so many others in the New Testament in which fruits or harvest are used as metaphors or similes in parables, gains both in intensity and in freshness when studied in connexion with so many allegorical interpretations of the Rabbis, in which the produce of the field and the vineyard play a similar part. One or two instances will not be uninteresting. Thus, with reference to Song of Songs, ii. 2, " As the lily among the thorns, so is my love among the daughters," a famous Rabbi says: There was a king who had a paradise (or garden), which he had laid out with rows of fig-trees, rows of vine, and rows of pomegranates. He put the paradise in the hands of a tenant, and left. In after days the king came to see what his tenant had accomplished. He found the garden neglected, and full of thorns and thistles. He then brought wood-cutters to

[1] *Lev. Rabbah*, I. [2] See especially the Midrash, *Lekach Tob.*, ad loc.

cut it down. Suddenly he perceived a lily. The king plucked it, and smelled it, and his soul returned upon him. He turned and said, "For the sake of the lily the garden shall be saved." The lily is the congregation of Israel; intent on the strength of its devotion to the Torah, it saved the world from the destruction to which the generation of the deluge condemned it by their wicked deeds[1].

In another place, however, it is the individual who is compared to the lily. Thus, Song of Songs, vi. 2, "My beloved went down to his garden to gather the lilies," is applied to the death of the righteous, whose departure from this world is a gathering of flowers undertaken by God himself, who is the beloved one[2].

In this connexion we may mention here another Rabbinic parable, in which the wheat takes the place of the lily. It is given as an illustration of Song of Songs, vii. 3, and Psalm ii. 12. The scriptural words in the latter place are נשקו בר, which the Rabbis explain to mean "Kiss the wheat," illustrating it by the following parable:—The straw and the chaff are arguing together. The straw maintained, that it is for its sake that the field was sown and ploughed, whilst the stem claimed that it was on its account that the work was undertaken. Thereupon the wheat said, "Wait until the harvest comes, and we shall know with what purpose the field was sown." When the harvest came and the work of threshing began, the chaff was scattered to the wind, the stem was given to the flames, whilst the wheat was carefully gathered on the floor. In a similar way the heathens say, "It is for our sake that the world was created," whilst Israel makes the same claim for itself. But wait for the Day of Judgment, when the chaff will be eliminated, and the wheat will be kissed. I need hardly remind you of the parable in Matt. xiii[3].

---

[1] *Cant. Rabbah*, ad loc.   [2] Ibid.

[3] *Pesikta Rabbathi* (ed. Friedmann), p. 36, text and notes.

To return to chapter iii. I will quote verse 11 in which
the Baptist in his testimony to Jesus says, "I indeed
baptized you with water unto repentance, but he that
cometh after me is mightier than I, whose shoes I am not
worthy to bear; he shall baptize you with the Holy Ghost
and with fire." The baptism of course represents the טבילה
or immersion of the Bible, enforced by the Rabbis in the
case of proselytes. According to some authorities it was
also customary with people entering on a course of repentance[1]. The expression "whose shoes I am not worthy to
bear," reminds one of the similar Talmudic phrase, running
"He who will explain to me a certain word, I will carry
his cloth after him to the bath[2]." That is to say, that
he will show submission to his authority by performing
for him menial work. As to the term "baptism with the
Holy Ghost and fire," the latter has a parallel in the
Talmudic dictum, that the main טבילה immersion, as a
means of purification, is by fire[3]. The former term,
"baptism by the Holy Ghost," is certainly obscure, and
has given a good deal of trouble to the commentators;
but it must have been readily understood by the Jews,
who even spoke of drawing the Holy Spirit שואבין רוח
הקודש, a term only applied to liquids[4]. Note also the
following passage from a sermon by R. Akiba: "Blessed
are ye Israelites. Before whom are ye purified, and who
is he who purifies you? Ye are purified before your Father
in Heaven, and it is he who purifies you," as it is said,
"The Lord is the *Mikveh* of Israel[5]." The word מקוה is
taken in the sense in which it occurs several times in the
Pentateuch, meaning "a gathering of waters," or a ritual
bath taken after various kinds of uncleanliness. The Rabbi
then derives from the words of Jeremiah xvii. 13 the lesson
that as the *Mikveh* is the means of purification for defile-

---

[1] *Shibbole Hakket*, 145 a.
[2] B. T. *Baba Mezia*, 45 a, and parallel passages.
[3] B. T. *Sanhedrin*, 39 a.   [4] Jer. T. *Sukkah*, 55 a.
[5] Mishneh, *Yoma*, VIII, 9.

ment (in the sense of the Levitical legislation), so God
is the source of purity for Israel. It should be borne
in mind, that according to the Rabbinic interpretation,
the term טומאה, "defilement," applies to all sorts of sins,
especially those of an immoral nature, whilst the process
of purifying mostly concerns the heart. "Purify our
hearts, that we serve thee in truth," is the constant prayer
of the Synagogue.

טָהֳרָה, or "purification," is, according to the mystic,
R. Pinchas b. Yair, of the second century, one of the higher
rungs in the ladder leading to the obtainment of the holy
spirit[1]. I do not know how far this conception may be
connected with the gospel narrative, according to which
the baptism of Jesus (or the Taahara of Jesus) was followed
by the descent of the holy spirit. If R. Pinchas b. Yair
could be taken, as some maintain, as one of the last representatives of the Essenes, there would indeed be no
objection to see in the synoptic account an illustration
of the principle laid down by these mystics. At any rate
it may serve as a transition to the verses I am about to
quote from Matt. iii. 16, 17, running thus: "And Jesus,
when he was baptized, went up straightway from the
water: and lo, the heavens were opened unto him, and
he saw the Spirit of God descending as a dove, and coming
upon him: and lo, a voice out of the heavens saying, This
is my beloved son, in whom I am well pleased." The
symbolism of the Holy Ghost by a dove is a common
notion in Rabbinic literature. The dove is considered as
the most chaste among the birds, never forsaking her mate.
The congregation of Israel, which never betrays its God,
is therefore compared to the dove[2]. "Once upon a time,"
so runs a Rabbinic legend, which I give here in substance,
"King David went out for a hawking expedition. Whereupon Satan came and turned himself into a deer, which
David tried to hit, but could not reach. Constantly pur-
suing the animal, David was thus carried from his suite,

[1] *Cant. Rabbah*, I, and parallel passages.   [2] Ibid.

owing to the machinations of Satan, into the land of the Philistines, where he was suddenly confronted by the relatives of Goliath, who were all thirsting for his blood. Thereupon a dove descended before Abishai, who had remained behind in the king's camp, and began to emit wailing tones. Abishai at once understood its meaning, saying, 'The congregation of Israel is compared to a dove, as it is said, Wings of a dove covered with silver' (Ps. lxviii. 14), and thus interpreted the appearance of the dove as a sign that King David, the hope of Israel, was in danger of his life, and he set out to his rescue[1]."

A closer parallel, however, is the following passage attributed to the well-known mystic, B. Soma, a younger contemporary of the Apostles. The passage runs thus :— R. Joshua b. Chananyah was standing upon the terrace of the temple-mountain. B. Soma saw him, but did not rise up before him (as he ought to have done, seeing that R. Joshua was his master). R. Joshua asked him "Whence and whither, Ben Soma ?" The answer B. Soma gave him was, "I was looking at (or rather meditating upon) the upper waters (above the firmament) and the under waters (under the firmament). The space between the two waters is not broader than three fingers ; as it is said, 'the Spirit of God was brooding upon the face of the waters,' like a dove brooding over her young, partly touching them and partly not touching them[2]."

I need hardly say that we have here to deal with a fragment of a Jewish Gnosis, and I must refer you to the works of Joel, Graetz, and Freudenthal, for more information upon this point, but it must be noted that some parallel passages read "eagle" instead of "dove." Deut. xxxii. 11 lends some countenance to this reading, but the parallels just quoted from the New Testament as well as the famous vision of R. Jose, in which the daughter-voice is complaining in a tender voice like a dove, saying "Woe unto the

[1] B. T. *Sanhedrin*, 95 a.
[2] B. T. *Chaggigah*, 15 a, and parallel passages.

father, whose children were expelled from his table[1]," speak
for the reading given first.

After the appearance of the Holy Ghost, Jesus is greeted,
as we have seen, by a voice from the heavens, saying, "This
is my beloved son, in whom I am well pleased." These
words represent, as rightly remarked by the commentators,
a combined paraphrase of Ps. ii. 7 and Isa. xli. 1. The
voice from heaven, as is well known, corresponds with the
Rabbinic "Daughter of a voice" (בּתקוֹל) or daughter-voice,
occupying the third place in the scale of revelation. I
cannot enter here into the various aspects and functions of
the daughter-voice, about which a good deal has been
written, but I should like to note its following two peculiar
features[2].

The first is, that in many cases the daughter-voice, when
employed as a means of revelation, finds its expression
not in a fresh message but in reproducing some verse or
sentence from the Hebrew Bible. Thus it is recorded
by the Rabbis that when they (the authorities) intended
to include King Solomon in the number of those who
forfeited their salvation, the daughter-voice put in the protest of heaven, in the words of Job xxxiv. 33, "Shall his
recompense be as thou wilt, that thou refusest it?[3]" The
great reconciliation again of God with the house of
David, as represented by the exile king Jeconiah, when
the Babylonian captivity was nearing its end, was announced by the daughter-voice in the words of Jeremiah,
"Return, ye backsliding children, and I will heal your
backslidings. Behold, we come unto thee: for thou art
the Lord our God" (iii. 22)[4]. It should be noted, however,
that the daughter-voice is not confined in its quotations
to the canonical scriptures. Sometimes the daughter-
voice even quotes sentences from the Apocrypha. This

---

[1] B. T. *Berachoth*, 3 a.

[2] See Löw, *Gesammelte Schriften*, II, p. 58, n. 1. A good essay on the
subject is still a desideratum.

[3] *Num. Rabbah*, XIV, and parallel passages.   [4] *Lev. Rabbah*, XXI.

was the case in Jabneh, where the Synhedrin met after
the destruction of the Temple. There a voice from heaven
was heard reproducing a verse from the Wisdom of Ben
Sira (iii. 22), "Ye have no need of the things that are
secret[1]." It is true that Ben Sira has "thou hast no need"
(in the singular), but it would seem as if the voice from
heaven is not always very exact in its quotations, adapting
them in its own way to the message to be announced.
Thus, for instance, on the occasion of Saul disobeying the
commandment of God regarding the extermination of the
Amalekites, there came the daughter-voice and said unto
him, "Be not more righteous than thy Maker" אל תצדק יתר
מקונך[2]. You will easily recognize in this warning the words
of Ecclesiastes (vii. 16), "Be not righteous over much" אל
תצדק הרבה, only that הרבה was altered into יתר, required by
the prefix of מקונך, which word was apparently added
by the voice from heaven.

Another important feature of the daughter-voice is, that
in some cases it is only audible to those who are prepared
to hear it. "Every day," says the rather mystically inclined R. Joshua b. Levi, "goes forth a voice from Mount
Sinai, and makes proclamation and says, "Woe to the
creatures for their contempt of the Torah." As rightly
pointed out by the commentators, this voice is only heard
by fine, sensitive natures, that are receptive of divine messages even after the discontinuance of prophecy[3]. In this
case the daughter-voice becomes something quite subjective, and loses a great deal of its authoritative character.
The renegade Elisha ben Abuyah, or as he is commonly
called אחר, the "other one," in his despair of doing repentance, heard a voice coming straight from behind the
throne of God, saying unto him, "Come back, ye backsliding
children, except thou 'other one,'" and thus he abandoned
himself to an immoral life[4]. Contrast this story with that

[1] Jer. T. *Sotah*, 22 a.

[2] *Chapters of R. Eliezer*, XLIV, but see also B. T. *Yoma*, 22 b.

[3] See *Perek R. Meir*.   [4] B. T. *Chaggigah*, 15 a.

of Manasseh, the worst sinner among the kings of Judah.
It is to this effect. When the captains of the king of
Assyria defeated Manasseh and put him among thorns,
and inflicted upon him the most cruel tortures, he invoked
all the strange gods he was in the habit of worshipping,
but no relief came. Suddenly he said, " I remember my
father once made me read the following verses (from Deut.
iv. 30, 31), 'When thou art in tribulation, and all these
things are come upon thee, . . . return thou to the Lord
thy God. For the Lord thy God is a merciful God ; he
will not forsake thee nor destroy thee.'" He then began
to address his prayers to God. The angels—in a most
unangelic way, I am sorry to say—shut up the gates of
heaven against his prayer, but the Holy One, blessed be
he, said, " If I do not receive him I shut the gate in the face
of repentance." And thus " he was entreated of him and
heard his supplication[1]." The moral of the two stories is,
that the "other one" trusted to fresh messages, and went to
perdition, while Manasseh fell back upon the family Bible
and was saved. It is probable that it was such moral
catastrophes as recorded in the case of the "other one" which
brought the voice of heaven into disrepute. The verdict
of the Rabbis in the second century was, that no attention
is to be paid to it when arrogating to decide against the
moral conviction of the majority. The Torah is not in
heaven[2]. Its interpretation is left to the conscience of
catholic Israel.

Now it is this conscience of Israel which is not satisfied
with the lesson to be derived from the Scriptures at the
first glance, or rather the first hearing, but insists upon its
expansion. Thus when interpreting Lev. xix. 36, the
Rabbis somehow managed to derive from it the law of
"let your speech be yea, yea ; nay, nay[3]." Again, when
commenting upon the seventh commandment, they interpreted it in such a way as to include the prohibition

---

[1] *Pesikta* (ed. Buber), p. 162 sq.　　　[2] B. T. *Baba Mezia*, 59 a.

[3] *Torath Kohanim* (ed. Weiss), 91 b.

of even an unchaste look or immoral thought[1]. The rules
of interpretation by which such maxims were derived
from the Scriptures would perhaps not satisfy the modern
philologian. They indeed belong to the " second sense " of
the Scriptures, the sense which is the heart and soul of all
history and development. " God hath spoken once, twice
I have heard this " (Ps. lxii. 12), which verse is interpreted
by the Rabbis to mean that Scripture is capable of
many interpretations or hearings[2]. But it is interesting
to find that these interpretations of the Scriptures tending
to improve upon the " first sense " are sometimes introduced by the formula: " I might hear so-and-so, therefore
there is a teaching to say that," &c. שומע אני ... תלמוד לומר[3].
Put into modern language the formula means this: The
words of the Scriptures might be at the first glance (or
first hearing) conceived to have this or that meaning, but
if we consider the context or the way in which the
sentences are worded, we must arrive at a different conclusion. This parallel may perhaps throw some light on
the expression ἠκούσατε, " you have heard that it was said ...
but I say unto you," a phrase frequent in the Sermon on
the Mount. After the declaration made by Jesus of his
attachment to the Torah, it is not likely that he would
quote passages from it showing its inferiority. The only
way to get over the difficulty is to assume that Jesus used
some such phrase as the one just quoted, שומע אני, " I might
hear," or " one might hear," that is to say, " one might be
mistaken in pressing the literal sense of the verses in
question too closely." Against such a narrow way of
dealing with Scripture he warned his disciples by some
formula, as תלמוד לומר, " there is a teaching to say that
the words must not be taken in such a sense." But the
formula being a strictly Rabbinic idiom, it was not rendered
quite accurately by the Greek translator. Hence the
apparent contradiction between Matt. iii. 17, 20, and the

---

[1] See *Pesikta Rabbathi*, p. 124 b.   [2] B. T. *Sanhedrin*, 34 a.
[3] *Mechilta*, 3 a, 6 a, &c.

matter following upon these verses. I only wish to add
that in Rabbinic literature, it is sometimes God himself
who undertakes such rectifications. Thus we read in an
ancient Midrash with reference to Jer. iv. 2, "And thou
shalt swear as the Lord liveth, in truth and in judgment": "The Holy One, blessed be he, said unto
Israel, 'Think not that you may swear by my name, even
in truth.' You may not do so unless you have obtained
that high degree of sanctity by which Abraham, Joseph,
and Job were distinguished, who were called God-fearing
men," יראי אלהים. This limitation of swearing, even in
truth, is indicated according to the Rabbis in Deut. xx. 10,
which verse is interpreted to mean, "If thou fear thy God,
and art exclusively in his service, thou mayst swear by
his name," not otherwise[1].

Having mentioned the name of the patriarch, I may
perhaps state the fact that, besides the epithets "the God-
fearing" Abraham, or Abraham "the friend of God,"
Abraham also bears in Rabbinic literature the title of
Rock. The wording of the Rabbinical passage and the terms
used in it will not be uninteresting to the student of the
New Testament. In Matt. xvi. 18 we read: "And I also
say unto thee, that thou art *Petros*, and upon this *petra*
I will build my church." The Rabbinic passage forms an
illustration of Num. xxiii. 9, "For from the top of the rocks
I see him," and runs thus: There was a king who desired
to build, and to lay foundations he dug constantly deeper,
but found only a swamp. At last he dug and found a *petra*
(this is the very word the Rabbi uses). He said, "On this
spot I shall build and lay the foundations." So the Holy
One, blessed be he, desired to create the world, but
meditating upon the generations of Enoch and the deluge,
he said, "How shall I create the world whilst those wicked
men will only provoke me?" But as soon as God perceived
that there would rise an Abraham, he said, "Behold, I have
found the *petra* upon which to build and to lay foundations."

---

[1] *Tanchuma,* מטה.

Therefore he called Abraham Rock, as it is said, " Look
unto the rock whence ye are hewn. Look unto Abraham,
your father" (Is. li. 1, 2)[1].

The parallels given so far have been more according to
the letter. I will now give one or two parallels according
to the spirit.

I have already referred to the attempts made by various
authors to describe the life and times of Jesus Christ. The
best book of this class is undoubtedly Schürer's *History
of the Jewish People in the Age of Jesus Christ*. It is
a very learned work, particularly as far as the Greek and
Roman documents are concerned. Its treatment of such
topics as the geography of Palestine, the topography of
Jerusalem, the plan of the Temple, and kindred subjects
is almost perfect. A most excellent feature in it is the
completeness of its bibliography, there being hardly any
dissertation or article in any of the learned periodicals,
which is not duly registered by the author. But all these
fine things are, to use a quaint Rabbinic phrase, only "after-
courses of wisdom." Bibliography in particular is not even
an after-course. It partakes more of the nature of the
menu served sometimes by very ignorant waiters, possessing
neither judgment nor discretion. The general vice attaching to this whole class of works is, that no attempt is made
in them to gain acquaintance with the inner life of the
Jewish nation at the period about which they write. Take
for instance, the subject of prayer. Considering that pre-
Christian Judaism gave to the world the Psalms, and that
post-Christian Judaism produced one of the richest liturgies ;
considering again that among the various prayers which
have come down to us through the medium of the Talmud,
there is also one that forms a close parallel to the Lord's
Prayer ;—considering all this one might expect that also in
the times of Jesus the Jews were able to pray, and in fact
did pray. The contents of their prayers might be of the

---

[1] *Yalkut*, I, § 766. See Dr. Taylor's *Sayings of the Jewish Fathers*, ed. 2,
p. 160.

greatest importance for the student, expressing as they
probably did the religious sentiments of the age and the
ideal aspirations of the nation. But what our theological
waiters dish up is a minimum of prayer dressed up in
a quantity of rubrics in such a fashion as to stigmatize
their authors as miserable pedants. And no attempt is
made to enter into the spirit of even this minimum. No
explanation is given, for instance, of the meaning of the
terms "the kingdom of heaven," the yoke of which the
Rabbi was supposed to receive upon himself, the "Hear,
O Israel," &c. The terms "sanctification of the name of
God," "Father in heaven," and "renewed world" are also
frequent in Jewish literature and in the Jewish Prayer-
book, but no sufficient attention is given to them. To
my knowledge Dalman is the only modern scholar who
recognizes the importance of these terms, and similar ones,
in their bearing upon a clearer understanding of the New
Testament, and has at least made an attempt at their
analysis in his book *Die Worte Jesu.*

Another important point, which has never been properly
examined, is the unique position which the Kenesseth
Israel the congregation of Israel, or ideal Israel, occupies
in Rabbinic theology. Yet it forms a striking parallel to
that held by Jesus in Christian theology. The Kenesseth
Israel was, like the Spirit of the Messiah, created before the
world was called into existence. "She is the beloved of
God, in whom he rejoices"; and there is no endearing
epithet in the language, such as son, daughter, brother,
sister, bride, mother, lamb, or eye, which is not, according
to the Rabbis, applied by the Scriptures to express the
intimate relation between God and the Kenesseth Israel.
Not even the title of "god," of which God is otherwise so
jealous, is denied to Israel, as it is written, "I have said ye
are gods." Nay, God even says to Moses, "Exalt Israel
as much as thou canst, for it is as if thou wert exalting
me"; whilst he who denies Israel or rises against Israel is
denying God. In fact, it is only through the witness of

Israel that God is God, and he would cease to be so were
Israel to disappear, as it is written, "Ye are my witnesses,
... and I am God[1]." But there is no fear of such a
calamity. Israel is older than the universe and forms the
rock on which the world was built. As a rock towering
up in the sea, so the Kenesseth Israel stands out in history,
defying all tempests and temptations ; for " many waters
cannot quench the love" between God and the Kenesseth Israel[2]. She is indeed approached by the nations
of the world with the seducing words, "What is thy
beloved more than another? Beautiful and lovely thou
art, if thou wilt mingle among us. Why dost thou permit
thyself to go through fire for his sake, to be crucified for
his name ? Come unto us, where all the dignities in our
power are awaiting thee." But Israel resists all temptations ;
they point to their connexion with God throughout their
history, to his love unto them, shown by conferring upon
them the gift of holiness, which even a Balaam envied, and
to the promise held out to them of the Messianic times,
when suffering will cease and Israel will revel in the glory
of God[3]." These few quotations suffice to show what an
interesting chapter might be added to our knowledge of
comparative theology.

Again, our knowledge of the spiritual history of the Jews
during the first centuries of our era might be enriched by
a chapter on miracles. Starting from the principle that
miracles can only be explained by more miracles, an
attempt was made some years ago by a student to draw
up a list of the wonder-workings of the Rabbis recorded in
the Talmud and the Midrashim. He applied himself to the
reading of these works, but his reading was only cursory.
The list therefore is not complete. Still it yielded a harvest
of not less than two hundred and fifty miracles. They

[1] See JEWISH QUARTERLY REVIEW, VI, pp. 419 and 634, for references.

[2] *Yalkut*, ibid.; *Genesis Rabbah*, I, and *Cant. Rabbah*,VIII.

[3] *Cant. Rabbah*, VII ; *Num. Rabbah*, II ; *Siphré* (ed. Friedmann), p. 143 a ;
and Rashi's *Commentary* to Cant. V, 9.

cover all classes of supernatural workings recorded in the
Bible, but occur with much greater frequency.

A repetition of these miracles would be tiresome. I will
content myself with reproducing a story from Tractate
Chagigah, which will illustrate to you how much even the
individual Jew shared in the glories conferred upon the
Kenesseth Israel. I am speaking of course of that individual
who is described by the Rabbis as one "who labours in the
Torah for its own sake, who is called a lover of God and
a lover of humanity. Unto him kingdom and authority are
given. Unto him the secrets of the Torah are revealed." The
term "authority," by the way, is given with the word ממשלה,
suggested probably by Ben Sira xlv. 17, וימשילהו בחוק ומשפט,
"and he made him have authority over statute and judgment"; whilst Matt. vii. 29, "and he taught them as one
having authority," was probably suggested by Ben Sira
iii. 10, ומושל בה ילמדנה, "and he who has authority over it
shall teach it." As a man of such authority we may
consider R. Jochanan b. Zakkai, the hero of the story I am
about to relate. He was the younger member of the
"Eighty Club" of the school of Hillel, and thus a contemporary of the Apostles, though he survived them. He
was an eye-witness of the terrible catastrophe of the
destruction of the Temple by the Romans, an event which
he prophesied forty years before it took place. He is best
known by the school he established in Jabneh, where the
Synhedrin, and with them the divine presence presiding
over this assembly, emigrated after the fall of Jerusalem.
There (in Jabneh) he died about 108 A.C.

It is related that Rabbi Jochanan b. Zakkai was riding
upon his ass on the road, while his pupil, R. Eleazar b.
Arach, was walking behind him. Said R. Eleazar to him,
"Master, teach me a chapter about the matter relating to
the chariot, that is, the vision in the first chapter of Ezekiel."
The master declined, preferring to hear the pupil.
R. Eleazar said again, "Wilt thou permit me to repeat in
thy presence one thing which thou hast taught me?" to

which he gave his assent. R. Jochanan then dismounted from his ass, and wrapped himself up in his gown and seated himself upon a stone under an olive-tree. He said it was disrespectful that he should be riding on his beast whilst his pupil was lecturing on such awful mysteries and the Shechinah (the divine presence) and the Malache Hashareth (the angels-in-waiting) were accompanying them. Immediately R. Eleazar began his exposition. And there came down a fire from heaven and encircled them and the whole field. And the angels assembled and came to hearken, as the sons of men assemble and come to look on at the festivities of bride and bridegroom. And the trees in the field opened their mouths and uttered a song, "Praise the Lord from the earth, ye dragons and all deeps. . . . Fruitful trees and all cedars, . . . praise ye the Lord." And an angel answered from the fire and said, "This is the matter of the chariot." When he had finished, R. Jochanan b. Zakkai stood up and kissed him on his head, saying, "Praised be the God of Abraham, Isaac, and Jacob, who has given our father Abraham a wise son, who knows to discourse on the glory of our Father in heaven." So much for the story. I need hardly recall to your mind the parallels in the Book of Enoch and in the New Testament[1].

My lecture is at an end, not so the subject it treats. To accomplish the latter in a proper critical and scientific manner the aid of fellow workers is necessary. I have often heard the wish expressed that a Jew should write a history of the rise of Christianity, who could bring all his Rabbinic learning to bear upon the subject. I do not think that the time is as yet ripe for such an experiment. The best thing to be done at present is, that Christians should devote themselves to the study of Rabbinic litera-ture. The history which would be written after such a study would certainly be more scientific and more critical.

S. SCHECHTER.

[1] B. T. *Chaggigah*, II, and the Jerusalem Talmud, ibid.

HOW THE JEWS WILL RECLAIM JESUS

by
HARRY A. WOLFSON

How the Jews Will Reclaim Jesus

By Harry A. Wolfson

HROUGHOUT the history of religious controversies between Christians and Jews in the Middle Ages, Christianity was on the defensive. The Christians considered themselves called upon to prove the claims they made on behalf of Jesus by endeavoring to show that the vague prophetic promises were all fulfilled in Christ. The Jews had no counterclaims to make; they simply refused to be impressed. As the historical custodians of the Bible text as well as of its manifold interpretations, the Jews were rather amazed and at times even amused by the confidence with which the erstwhile heathen interpreted at their own pleasure the mistaken Scriptures quoted from the Vulgate. This attitude of aloofness and incredulity was sufficient to enrage even saints among Christians, for it gave them an uneasiness of feeling, deepening into fear and doubt and a general sense of discomfort, which explains much of the Christian intolerance of the Jews. The great victories achieved by Christianity, its conquest of many youthful barbarian races and its destruction of many effete civilizations—all this did not compensate its adherents for their failure to win over the handful of survivors of the race that had witnessed the birth of Christianity. And so the Jews were dragged to churches and to royal courts to listen to sermons and to partake in disputations in order to be impressed and become convinced.

Today many of us Jews have taken the burden of proof upon ourselves. A century of infiltration of Christian ideas into our life through all the agencies of education has robbed many of us of our essential Jewish character, of our distinctive Jewish philosophy of life, and has left us Jews only in appearance, in occupation, and in the semblance of an external social coherence. In everything that guides our life and determines our view thereof, we have become Christianized, for we have somehow accepted Christ if not in the theological sense of a savior at least in the historical sense of a civilizer. We have fallen in with the prevalent view that Christianity is essential to the progress of human civilization, which is, after all, another version of the Christian belief that Christ is necessary for the salvation of one's soul. If indeed we do not openly acknowledge that Christ has fulfilled the promises of the prophets, we proceed on the assumption that modern civilization is the fulfillment of the promises of Christ. And everything we have of late learned to read into the utterances of Christ we assume to have been contained in them from the beginning and to have been obvious to everyone who stood by and listened. We thus wonder at the blindness of our forefathers, the eyewitnesses of Christ, for not seeing all this. We ask ourselves, why did they not accept Jesus?

From this question it is only another step to the greater question, why should we not accept Jesus? There are many among us who, while not quite convinced that civilization has already fulfilled the promises of Christ—for occasionally facts stare us in the face and awaken us from the spell of words—still believe in the potency of Christ's sayings, a potency almost magical, by which the world is yet to be saved. We seem to think with the sentimental part of Christendom that evil can be cured not by removing its causes but by exhortation and by calling to repentance and by a closer study of the sayings of Jesus. If we are sometimes reminded that as Jews we are already supplied with a complete assortment of similar sayings by the rabbis, Claude Montefiore answers for us, in effect, that it is easier for the modern Jew to learn New Testament Greek than rabbinic Hebrew.

W E thus have two questions: Why did not the Jews accept Jesus? Why should not the Jews accept Jesus?

Of the historical question there are many attempts at a solution. All the attempted solutions, however, proceed upon the assumption that there were certain elements in the teachings of Jesus which made them unacceptable, if not repugnant, to the Jews of his time. It is sometimes said that it was due to the fact that Jesus was too willing to render unto Caesar the things which were Caesar's, as if the Jews of that time, and immediately after, were at one in their open defiance of the powers that be. More often it is said that the boldness of his legal decisions offended the sensibilities of the Law-abiding Jews, as if the Law were already rigid and fixed by that time and as if the Pharisees themselves were not torn by internal dissensions which had almost divided the Law into two Laws. Occasionally fine-spun speculations are expended upon subtle distinctions between the ethical teachings of Jesus and those of the leading contemporary Pharisees, distinctions in which one finds no greater difference than that between the negative form of the Golden Rule as given by Hillel and its positive form as given by Jesus. One would not like to become irreverent and dismiss the entire question by repeating with Pontius Pilate in Anatole France's *Le Procurateur de Judée*: "*Jesus le Nazaréen? Je ne me rappelle pas.*"

But what we should really like to know is what exactly is meant by the question of the Jewish acceptance of Jesus. The person of Jesus as conceived in the manner of the various forms of christology could never find a place in Judaism, for it is altogether foreign to its fundamental principles and is a later importation from without. As the promised Messiah, he simply did not meet the conditions which in the conception of the people of that time had to attend the coming of the promised Messiah. As a leading authority on questions of the Law, the contemporaries of Jesus could not be expected to accept Jesus more than they did Shammai or Hillel. As a moral and religious teacher, it seems that he succeeded quite well in attracting a goodly number of Jews of the lowlier station of life and culture among whom he appeared and to whom he delighted to deliver his messages. What really requires an explanation is not the paucity of Jewish followers but rather the great number of Gentiles that were soon to follow him or, rather, his idealized name.

The only intelligent meaning that a Jew may attach to the problem of the acceptance of Jesus is of a literary nature, namely, why were not the teachings of Jesus incorporated in Jewish literature together with those of other great teachers? One naturally would not expect them to be formed into a new book of the Bible. Only those who are unacquainted with literary conditions in Palestine at that time and are accustomed to think of the New Testament as a continuation of the Old could ever dream of such a possibility. Jesus is not a rejected prophet; at best he is a rejected sage. Prophecy in the sense of that which inspired the authors of the books of the Bible was believed to have come to an end long before Jesus made his appearance. The Jews did not put a limit to the books of the Bible in order to keep Jesus out; Jesus simply happened to come at a time when that body of literature, in the opinion of the authorities of the time, was practically closed. The question is merely, why were not the teachings of Jesus included in the Tannaitic collection of a subsequent generation which includes the teachings of men who lived at about the time of Jesus? To put it more concretely, why is the Sermon on the Mount not included in the collection of sayings of the post-Biblical sages known as the *Sayings of the Fathers?* That Jesus had fallen from grace could not account for that omission, for Elisha ben Abuyah, too, fell from grace, and still he is quoted in that collection of traditional wisdom.

THE answer seems to lie in the nature of the records which entered into the making up of the Tannaitic collection of ancient traditions.

The Tannaitic literary collections contain the teachings recorded in the name of individual authors from the time of Simeon the Just, about three centuries before the Christian era, to the early part of the third century after the Christian era. There is, however, a marked difference between the earlier records and those of the period following the establishment of the school of Jabneh, after the fall of Jerusalem. In the earlier period only those who were officially at the head of the schools are quoted by name; otherwise scholars are grouped together and referred to as collective bodies. To this generalization there are only a few exceptions, for which there is always an obvious explanation. In the later period, individual scholars in great numbers, whether official dignitaries in the schools or not, are quoted by name. There is no doubt that in the period from which the Tannaitic collections contain only the common decisions of the schools transmitted in the names of Bet Shammai and Bet Hillel (House of Shammai, House of Hillel) but no teachings in the name of individual scholars, there must have been many individuals who in their private capacity, unaffiliated with these two great schools, taught and preached in the synagogues, but whose teachings, for lack of any agency for their collection and preservation, were lost to the world. Jesus was one of these unaffiliated teachers who taught and preached during the period of the Bet Shammai and Bet Hillel. If the teachings of Jesus were not similarly consigned to oblivion, it is due to the fact that his followers banded themselves, not into a sect, as it is usually supposed, but into a "House," a Bet Jeshua, corresponding to the Bet Shammai and Bet Hillel, and this "House" it was that collected and preserved the teachings of Jesus just as the other "Houses" collected and preserved the teachings of their respective founders.

Accordingly, once the teachings of Jesus were collected and written down and were issued for public circulation, which took place some time before any official collection of the Tannaim was allowed to be publicly circulated in writing, they were declared by the leaders of the Tannaitic schools to be unauthorized writings. It is thus not as an individual that Jesus was excluded from the Tannaitic literary collections but rather as an unaffiliated teacher, of no official position in any of the Tannaitic schools, who lived at a time when, as a result of a general practice, the teachings of that class of men were not included in the official records of the schools which later made up the Tannaitic collections.

By the same token the present-day problem of the Jewish acceptance of Jesus should be treated as a problem of the reclamation of a lost literature rather than that of the recognition of a new moral philosophy which is needed for our salvation. Good souls always rush to gnomic sayings for guidance. Epictetus and Marcus Aurelius, Confucius and the Buddha, the rabbis and the folk sayings of every nation are drawn upon for that purpose; though these differ from the Sermon on the Mount in that we are not expected to make them into a creed. But gnomic sayings and parables and homely examples hardly guide our lives. All this kind of homespun wisdom was produced in the infancy of mankind, in the simplicity of life, and has been with us for centuries, and in spite of it all we have built up our atrocious civilization. If from the complexity of our life we occasionally seek refuge in the simple utterances with which the sages of the past attempted to solve the difficulties of their time, it is only to realize painfully how inadequate they are to solve the problems of today.

No social reformer, for instance, would take the exaltation of poverty and damnation of riches by Jesus as a program for a reconstructed society; or the examples of the fowls of the air and the lilies of the field as a remedy for unemployment; or the miracles of the feeding of the five and the four thousand as a way to alleviate the blight of famine; nor would any medical man take the stories of the miraculous healings as a guide to the cure of disease. More than one leader of liberal Christian thought has called upon Christians to give up the pretense that they seriously believe all the teachings of Jesus to be adequate as a practical guide to life. Gnomic sayings, whether rabbinic or evangelical, are sufficient neither to change the human heart nor to alter conditions. At best they can be used only to adorn an economic report or to illustrate a sociological survey.

THE Jewish reclamation of Jesus will not be brought about by efforts of evangelical piety on the part of some Jews, or by a sentimental yearning for what we haven't got, or by a servile imitation of the most powerful element in our environment. It will come about as a result of a wider and more comprehensive conception of the scope of Jewish learning and Jewish literature and of a general restoration of our lost literary treasures. When the works of Josephus, and the Apocrypha, and the Hellenistic writings have all been restored by us and given a place beside the hallowed literature of our tradition, then the works of Jesus also will find a place among them. It is not as a returning hero that Jesus will be restored, and not as a beatified saint—we shall not regret the past nor shall we apologize for our forefathers. But when with the revival of Jewish culture and Jewish learning under free and unhampered conditions in a Jewish environment, painstaking Jewish scholars, in an effort to reorganize and reclassify our literary treasures, will come to compile anthologies of the wise sayings and inspiring teaching of our ancients, they will include among them the sermons and parables of Jesus the Nazarene, the Galilean rabbi who, like Philo and Josephus, has by force of historical circumstances been for centuries better known among non-Jews than among Jews. The readers of those anthologies will pass on from Talmudic and Midrashic selections to those of the Gospels without being conscious of any difference, except of such individual differences as mark the sayings of men. The sayings of Jesus together with the sayings of other rabbis will win their way into the speech of the people, will become blended and interwoven, and misquoted, after the manner of such things—for they all breathe the same spirit. His sayings will be considered as part of the maxims of the anonymous body of the wise, of blessed memory, who express the national genius of the people, not as those of an inspired individual to be worshiped and exalted above all others.

And perhaps at that time our people will resume their creative activity at the point it was nipped off, in the time of the Mishnah and Midrash. If prophecy will not return, the spirit of the Haggadah will again rest upon our sages. Tired of the fettered forms of verse and the diffuse forms of prose, we shall return to our native original forms of expression. We shall write textbooks of science in the style of the Mishnah, we shall compose works of erudition in the style of the Midrash, and we shall once more give expression to the great truths of life in the form of the Haggadah.

Then in a cloistered synagogue in a re-Judaized Galilee a sage, continuing the traditions of an ancient rabbi, will con over a new tome, modeled after an old tome. It will be a new and complete collection of sayings of the Fathers, recording the wisdom of the ages from the Men of the Great Synagogue to the men of the littlest of the synagogues, and among these will be included the sayings of the Alexandrian Philo and the Palestinian Jesus. Our sage will read the utterances recorded in the name of Jesus the Galilean about the Pharisees and will say to himself: "O Rabbi Jesus, dost thou condemn the many for the sins of the few? Where is the quality of justice, not to speak of mercy?" But with characteristic Jewish charity he will quote from an ancient rabbi: "No man is taken to account for what he speaks in his distress." He will read his sayings about divorce and mutter: "O Rabbi Jesus, verily thou art a Shammaite; but we have long decided to follow the more lenient views of Hillel. We are not bound by thee." He will read his views about the Sabbath, and say: "Verily this is a precious sentiment of the rabbis, but where is the line to be drawn between the conflicting rights and the mutual obligations of institutions and individuals?" And thus he will go on commenting in the spirit of an ancient rabbi. Then he will weave in a story in the fashion of a Haggadah: "Come and see, how great is the power of Israel. Once there was a child in Galilee. He was taken captive and carried off into the great city of Rome. There they made a God of him; but some say they made of him only a son of God, and others say only a prophet of God. They built temples and churches to his name in every land, and each nation worshiped him according to its tongue, according to its manner, and according to its custom. But the mind of the child was not at rest until he returned to Galilee and saw his name inscribed in an ancient tome among the names of his castigated Pharisees. It is this which Scripture says:—and here an apt or an inapt quotation from the Scripture will follow.

This is how the Jews will reclaim Jesus.

THE JEWISH PEOPLE

HISTORY • RELIGION • LITERATURE

AN ARNO PRESS COLLECTION

Agus, Jacob B. **The Evolution of Jewish Thought:** From Biblical Times to the Opening of the Modern Era. 1959

Ber of Bolechow. **The Memoirs of Ber of Bolechow (1723-1805).** Translated from the Original Hebrew MS. with an Introduction, Notes and a Map by M[ark] Vishnitzer. 1922

Berachya. **The Ethical Treatises of Berachya, Son of Rabbi Natronai Ha-Nakdan:** Being the Compendium and the Masref. Now edited for the First Time from MSS. at Parma and Munich with an English Translation, Introduction, Notes, etc. by Hermann Gollancz. 1902

Bloch, Joseph S. **My Reminiscences.** 1923

Bokser, Ben Zion, **Pharisaic Judaism in Transition:** R. Eliezer the Great and Jewish Reconstruction After the War with Rome. 1935

Dalman, Gustaf. **Jesus Christ in the Talmud, Midrash, Zohar, and the Liturgy of the Synagogue.** Together with an Introductory Essay by Heinrich Laible. Translated and Edited by A. W. Streane. 1893

Daube, David. **The New Testament and Rabbinic Judaism.** 1956

Davies, W. D. **Christian Origins and Judaism.** 1962

Engelman, Uriah Zevi. **The Rise of the Jew in the Western World:** A Social and Economic History of the Jewish People of Europe. Foreword by Niles Carpenter. 1944

Epstein, Louis M. **The Jewish Marriage Contract:** A Study in the Status of the Woman in Jewish Law. 1927

Facets of Medieval Judaism. 1973. New Introduction by Seymour Siegel

The Foundations of Jewish Life: Three Studies. 1973

Franck, Adolph. **The Kabbalah, or, The Religious Philosophy of the Hebrews.** Revised and Enlarged Translation [from the French] by Dr. I. Sossnitz. 1926

Goldman, Solomon. **The Jew and The Universe.** 1936

Gordon, A. D. **Selected Essays.** Translated by Frances Burnce from the Hebrew Edition by N. Teradyon and A. Shohat, with a Biographical Sketch by E. Silberschlag. 1938

Ha-Am, Achad (Asher Ginzberg). **Ten Essays on Zionism and Judaism.** Translated from the Hebrew by Leon Simon. 1922. New Introduction by Louis Jacobs

Halevi, Jehudah. **Selected Poems of Jehudah Halevi.** Translated into English by Nina Salaman, Chiefly from the Critical Text Edited by Heinrich Brody. 1924

Heine, Heinrich. **Heinrich Heine's Memoir:** From His Works, Letters, and Conversations. Edited by Gustav Karpeles; English Translation by Gilbert Cannan. 1910. Two volumes in one

Heine, Heinrich. **The Prose Writings of Heinrich Heine.** Edited, with an Introduction, by Havelock Ellis. 1887

Hirsch, Emil G[ustav]. **My Religion.** Compilation and Biographical Introduction by Gerson B. Levi. **Including The Crucifixion Viewed from a Jewish Standpoint:** A Lecture Delivered by Invitation Before the "Chicago Institute for Morals, Religion and Letters." 1925/1908

Hirsch, W. **Rabbinic Psychology:** Beliefs about the Soul in Rabbinic Literature of the Talmudic Period. 1947

Historical Views of Judaism: Four Selections. 1973

Ibn Gabirol, Solomon. **Selected Religious Poems of Solomon Ibn Gabirol.** Translated into English Verse by Israel Zangwill from a Critical Text Edited by Israel Davidson. 1923

Jacobs, Joseph. **Jesus as Others Saw Him:** A Retrospect A. D. 54. Preface by Israel Abrahams; Introductory Essay by Harry A. Wolfson. 1925

Judaism and Christianity: Selected Accounts, 1892-1962. 1973. New Preface and Introduction by Jacob B. Agus

Kohler, Kaufmann. **The Origins of the Synagogue and The Church.** Edited, with a Biographical Essay by H. G. Enelow. 1929

Maimonides Octocentennial Series, Numbers I-IV. 1935

Mann, Jacob. **The Responsa of the Babylonian Geonim as a Source of Jewish History.** 1917-1921

Maritain, Jacques. **A Christian Looks at the Jewish Question.** 1939

Marx, Alexander. **Essays in Jewish Biography.** 1947

Mendelssohn, Moses. **Phaedon; or, The Death of Socrates.** Translated from the German [by Charles Cullen]. 1789

Modern Jewish Thought: Selected Issues, 1889-1966. 1973. New Introduction by Louis Jacobs

Montefiore, C[laude] G. **Judaism and St. Paul:** Two Essays. 1914

Montefiore, C[laude] G. **Some Elements of the Religious Teaching of Jesus According to the Synoptic Gospels.** Being the Jowett Lectures for 1910. 1910

Radin, Max. **The Jews Amongs the Greeks and Romans.** 1915

Ruppin, Arthur. **The Jews in the Modern World.** With an Introduction by L. B. Namier. 1934

Smith, Henry Preserved. **The Bible and Islam; or, The Influence of the Old and New Testaments on the Religion of Mohammed.** Being the Ely Lectures for 1897. 1897

Stern, Nathan. **The Jewish Historico-Critical School of the Nineteenth Century.** 1901

Walker, Thomas [T.] **Jewish Views of Jesus:** An Introduction and an Appreciation. 1931. New Introduction by Seymour Siegel

Walter, H. **Moses Mendelssohn:** Critic and Philosopher. 1930

Wiener, Leo. **The History of Yiddish Literature in the Nineteenth Century.** 1899

Wise, Isaac M. **Reminiscences.** Translated from the German and Edited, with an Introduction by David Philipson. 1901